Discourse in Context

CONTEMPORARY APPLIED LINGUISTICS

Series Editor: Li Wei, Birkbeck College, London, UK

Contemporary Applied Linguistics Volume 1: Language Teaching and Learning,
edited by Vivian Cook and Li Wei

Contemporary Applied Linguistics Volume 2: Linguistics for the Real World,
edited by Vivian Cook and Li Wei

Discourse in Context

Contemporary Applied Linguistics Volume 3

EDITED BY

JOHN FLOWERDEW

BLOOMSBURY
LONDON · NEW DELHI · NEW YORK · SYDNEY

Bloomsbury Academic

An imprint of Bloomsbury Publishing Plc

50 Bedford Square	1385 Broadway
London	New York
WC1B 3DP	NY 10018
UK	USA

www.bloomsbury.com

Bloomsbury is a registered trade mark of Bloomsbury Publishing Plc

First published 2014

© John Flowerdew and Contributors, 2014

British Library Cataloguing-in-Publication Data
A catalogue record for this book is available from the British Library.

ISBN: HB: 978-1-6235-6305-9
ePub: 978-1-6235-6235-9
ePDF: 978-1-6235-6301-1

Library of Congress Cataloging-in-Publication Data
A catalog record for this book is available from the Library of Congress.

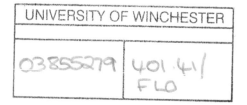
Typeset by Deanta Global Publishing Services, Chennai, India
Printed and bound in Great Britain

Table of Contents

List of Contributors

Paul Baker, University of Lancaster, UK

Monika Bednarek, University of Sydney, Australia

Katherine Carroll, University of Technology, Sydney, Australia

Janet Cotterill, Cardiff University, UK

Marissa K. L. E, National University of Singapore, Singapore

Britt-Louise Gunnarson, Uppsala University, Sweden

Michael Handford, University of Tokyo, Japan

Roxy Harris, Kings College, University of London, UK

Christopher Hart, University of Northampton, UK

Rick Iedema, University of Technology, Sydney, Australia

Jackie Jia Lou, City University of Hong Kong, Hong Kong

James Martin, University of Sydney, Australia

Anna Mauranen, University of Helsinki, Finland

Kay O'Halloran, Curtin University, Australia

Ben Rampton, Kings College, University of London, UK

David Rose, University of Sydney, Australia

Sabine Tan, National University of Singapore, Singapore

Hansun Zhang Waring, Teachers College, Columbia University, USA

Ruth Wodak, University of Lancaster, UK

Acknowledgements

I should like to thank Li Wei and Gurdeep Mattu for commissioning this volume and for their support throughout the publication process.

Each of the chapters in this volume was externally reviewed. The reviewers who kindly helped me in this task include the following people:

Mariana Achugar; John Bateman; Stephen Bremner; Jonathan Charteris-Black; Emilia Dojonov; Gibson Ferguson; Giuliana Garzone; Christoph Hafner; Linda Harklau; Juliane House; Christopher Hutton; Adam Jaworski; Brian King; Veronika Koller; Kenneth Kong; Irene Koshik; Ryuko Kubota; Nuria Lorenzo-Dus; Gerlinde Mautner; John Morley; Gina Poncini; Kay Richardson; Ingrid de Saint-Georges; Tony Berber Sardinha; Stef Slembrouck; Peter Chin Soon Teo; Richard Young

An earlier version of the chapter by Harris and Rampton appeared in M. Wetherell (ed.) 2009, *Identity in the twenty-first Century: New Trends in Changing Times* (Palgrave), a volume containing papers from the 2005 to the 2008 ESRC Identities and Social Action Programme. The revised version is reproduced here with permission.

Some of the data and some explanations in the chapter by Iedema and Carroll have been drawn (with permission) from their previous article: Iedema, R. and Carroll, K. (2010), Discourse research that intervenes in the quality and safety of care practices. *Discourse & Communication*, 4(1): 68–86.

1

Introduction:
Discourse in context

John Flowerdew

This volume presents a collection of analyses of spoken, written and multimodal discourses in a range of situations and contextual domains. In using the term 'discourse', I have in mind, on the one hand, the notion of what Gee (1999) calls 'little d' discourse – the non-count usage of the term – as language in the contexts of its use and above the level of the sentence, and, on the other hand, what Gee calls 'big D' discourse(s) – the count usage of the term – as systems of knowledge and beliefs, social practices and socially recognizable identities. The chapters in this volume focus on both of these approaches. In using the term 'context', I have in mind, on the one hand, different situations and domains in which discourse is produced and, on the other, how analysts construe context in their work. The volume is thus concerned, in general terms, with language in its context of use (little d discourse), but at the same time, more specifically, in individual chapters, with particular discourses (big D discourses) as they are manifested in particular contexts.

The volume brings together researchers from different approaches, but all with a commitment to the study of language in context. The studies situate their chosen target situation or domain within their particular model of context. Context is construed differently by the various authors; it may be historical, social, local, (socio)-cognitive or some combination thereof. Similarly, the authors represent different approaches and methods in their analyses, including (in alphabetical order) conversation analysis, corpus linguistics, critical discourse analysis, ethnographic discourse analysis, mediated discourse analysis, multimodal discourse analysis and systemic functional linguistics. In juxtaposing the chapters in this way, readers are invited to compare and contrast these different contexts and approaches and the application of their particular models of context.

There have been a number of volumes devoted to context in recent decades (Auer and Di Luzio 1992; Fetzer 2004; Duranti and Goodwin 1992), but while certainly relevant to discourse analysis, these collections have been written from the perspective of anthropological linguistics, interactional sociolinguistics or pragmatics, rather than being overtly discourse analytic. The present collection is thus, to my knowledge, the first published collection of papers to focus on context from a specifically discourse analytic perspective.

Discourse analysis is concerned with the interpretation of texts and an important part of this analysis is how texts are related to the contexts in which they are produced and received. An understanding of context is thus an essential feature of the analysis. However, while, in its relatively short history, discourse analysis has spent a lot of time identifying the structure and functions of the various features which make up text and talk, with notable exceptions, there has been relatively less emphasis on defining just what is meant by context; it has tended to be taken as a 'given'. This may be because, as Goodwin and Duranti (1992: 2) state, context is 'notoriously hard to define'.

In spite of the difficulty of pinning down the meaning of the term *context*, fairly general definitions are to be found. Blommaert (2005: 251), for example, defines context as 'the totality of conditions under which discourse is being produced, circulated and interpreted'. In the present volume, Iedema and Carroll describe context as 'the domain of the "taken-as-given"', and Baker defines it as 'the constraints on a communicative situation that influence language use', while Mauranen breaks it down into component parts:

> Context at a general level is understood to be the environment that an object is embedded in or part of; in the case of language use, the two most relevant contexts are the social environment and the linguistic environment, although the comparative neglect of visual, physical and perhaps technological contexts may not be based on very good reasons.

Wodak (this volume) also differentiates different features of context, as follows:

i   the immediate text of the communicative event in question;

ii the intertextual and interdiscursive relationship between utterances, texts, genres and discourses;

iii the extralinguistic social, environmental variables and institutional frames of a specific 'context of situation';

iv and the broader sociopolitical and historical context which discursive practices are embedded in and related to.

Taking a different tack, Bednarek (this volume) defines context in terms of a set of questions:

●   How was this text produced, by whom and with what purpose?

●   Who does this text address? Who is its target audience?

●   How does the text mediate between its producers and its audience?

- What is the relationship between texts and ideologies (of producer/audience/ industry cultures), commercial realities, generic conventions, industry/ professional conventions, practical/technical codes, etc?

Finally, van Dijk (2005: 237) brings in a cognitive element, defining context as 'the cognitive, social, political, cultural and historical *environments* of discourse' (original emphasis).

In spite of the difficulty in defining what we mean exactly by *context*, speakers and writers are remarkably adept at knowing which features of context to rely on to make their utterances meaningful and listeners and readers are equally adept at contextualizing what they read or hear in order to understand it. As Blommaert tells us again, people have *contextualization universes*, that is to say, 'complexes of linguistic, cognitive, social, cultural, institutional etc. skills and knowledge which they use for contextualising statements (Ibid.)', or as Harris and Rampton (this volume) put it, 'people are extraordinarily adept at using very small pieces of linguistic/semiotic form to guide or challenge the understandings of the world emerging in the talk'.

Some notions in the analysis of context

One approach to the notion of context is that of *figure* and *ground*, where the figure is the focal point of the analysis and the ground is the background context. Thus, Goodwin and Duranti (1992: 9) describe this distinction as follows:

> One key way in which context and focal event differ is in their perceptual salience. Generally the focal event is regarded as the official focus of the participants' attention, while features of the context are not highlighted in this way, but instead treated as background phenomena. The focal event is placed on center stage, while context constitutes the stage itself. . . . Focal event and context thus seem to stand in a fundamental figure-ground relationship to each other . . .[1]

Another metaphor for the text/context relationship is that of *frame* (Bateson 1955; Goffman 1974; Tannen 1993). According to this conceptualization, context is the frame which surrounds the focal event, to use Goodwin and Duranti's term. It is the frame which allows for the interpretation of the focal event. According to Bateson (1954), who introduced the term *frame*, a message can only be interpreted if it carries with it a meta-message about what is going on, that is to say a frame of reference which can be used to understand how to interpret the message. This idea of Bateson's was taken up by Goffman (1974). According to Goffman (1974: 10–11), frames are basic cognitive constructs which guide our perception of reality:

> I assume that definitions of a situation are built up in accordance with principles of organization which govern events . . . and our subjective involvement in them; frame is the word I use to refer to such of these basic elements as I am able to identify.

Frames guide us in deciding what to pay attention to and what to put into the background; *framing* is the process by which we select certain features of the situation and make them more salient. To put it another way, the frame is the context which allows for the interpretation of a particular feature of the situation. Goffman's concept of frame implies a model of frames within frames, of one frame framing another in a recursive patterning. This *lamination* is necessary because it is possible to have more than one context of understanding and interpretation present in a given situation.

If, in the analysis of language, we can distinguish different levels, such as morpheme, word, group, clause, sentence, etc., the question arises as to what units of analysis might be appropriate for context. There is a traditional distinction between *context* and *co-text*, where context is the social situation in which an utterance is made and co-text is the text surrounding a given utterance (e.g. Halliday and Hasan 1985). van Dijk (2008a: 242–3) distinguishes two rather different levels of context: the micro and the macro. The micro is the face-to-face situation of interaction and the macro is relevant elements of the social structure within which the discourse occurs. Blommaert (2005: 40) tells us that context comes in various shapes and that it operates at various levels, 'from the infinitely small to the infinitely big'. As Giddens (1984: 119) puts it, '[c]ontext . . . connects the most intimated and detailed components of interaction to much broader properties of the institutionalization of social life.' Harris and Rampton (this volume) emphasize the importance of the small features of context when they write that 'the choice of one word rather than another can introduce a different issue, a particular pronunciation can reframe the significance of what's going on, a shift in facial expression can convey a specific stance or attitude'. A (very) big feature of context, on the other hand – the whole phenomenon of globalization – time-space distanciation, disembedding of social systems and reflexivity and continual evaluation of social practice (Giddens 1990) – is fundamental in Gunnarsson's analysis (this volume) of online postings by multinational corporations. Drawing on Bhatia, Handford (this volume) distinguishes four levels of context: starting with discursive practice, moving to professional practice, then to social practice and finally to discourse itself. Harris and Rampton (this volume) suggest an interplay of different levels of context, talking of

> 'the shifts and layering of contexts currently in play – the institutional and social network relations among the participants and their histories of interaction together, the types of activity they're engaged in, their positioning in and around institutional discourses and circumambient ideologies, and what's just been said and done'.

Other discourse analysts (including in this volume) have employed various other levels of analysis in their consideration of context. There is no particular model which has been universally accepted.

The model adopted very much depends on the analyst, the particular goals of the analysis and the context of the study (see below on the role of the analyst). Recently, sociolinguists and discourse analysis have begun to consider how discursive processes operate across time and space, by appealing to the notion of sociolinguistic *scales*

(Blommaert 2007, 2010) and how higher- and lower-level scales (times or spaces) can interact, sometimes leading to conflicting contexts, when, as a result of globalization, for example, traditional contextual features are merged with more contemporary ones. Shifts and layering of contexts are a particular feature of Harris and Rampton's chapter in this volume.

Goodwin and Duranti (1992: 31) tell us that context and discourse (they use the term *talk*) are 'mutually reflexive', with discourse shaping context as much as context shapes discourse. van Dijk (2008a: 241) describes this mutually constitutive relationship as follows:

> [t]here is ongoing, dynamic mutual influence between talk or text and its production or comprehension on the one hand, and the way the participants see, interpret and construe the other "environmental" aspects of such discourse, such as the setting, the participants, the ongoing action, as well as the goals and knowledge of the participants.

This mutual reflexivity notwithstanding, there is a tendency in many examples of analysis to view context as shaping discourse rather than vice versa. A more appropriate view, however, is of a continual shunting between text and context (Fairclough, Mulderrig and Wodak 2011).

The dynamic nature of context

While there is a danger with some models of context of viewing it as a static phenomenon, as something which is 'out there', other models see it as a dynamic construct. According to this view, context develops in an ongoing fashion, as the discourse progresses (Goodwin and Duranti 1992; O'Halloran et al., this volume). Interactants are able to change the context with each utterance that they produce. In such models, context is both product and process. This view is prevalent in conversation analysis (CA), where each utterance is interpreted in the light of the immediately prior and the immediately following utterance (Schegloff 1987). As Waring (this volume) puts it: 'Every current action is shaped by the context set up by the preceding action, and every current action renews the context for its next action.' At the same time, some contexts are more predictable than others. The context of everyday conversation may be relatively unpredictable, with interlocutors free to switch topic at will, but the context of a marriage ceremony or a coronation is much more fixed, and, as a result, the language produced is matched up closely with everyone's expectations, that is to say, the interrelation between text and context is rigid and predictable.

At the same time, context may be misunderstood, leading to pragmatic failure or, in intercultural situations, *cross-cultural pragmatic failure* (Thomas 1983: 188), referred to, within another framework, that of Gumperz (1992: 239), as 'culturally based differences in contextualization conventions'. While the contributions to this volume do not focus on this issue, Mauranen's study of *English as a lingua franca* (ELF) discourse highlights how, in such communication, interlocutors go out of their way to avoid misunderstanding. As Mauranen writes:

> One reason for engaging in collaborative behaviour, which largely accounts for the relative absence of miscommunication in ELF, is speakers' reliance on the commonsense assumption that speaking a language that is not participants' mother tongue must be particularly prone to misunderstanding, and therefore calls for cooperation from everyone to succeed.

Furthermore, context may be contested; what one interactant considers to be the appropriate context for, and hence way of interpreting, an utterance, may not be the same as that of his or her interlocutor. I demonstrated, in an earlier publication (Flowerdew 2013), how this happened in the case of the return of sovereignty over Hong Kong from Britain to China. The British had one understanding of the context of this process, as an honourable withdrawal from 150 years of (benign) imperial rule, while the Chinese understood the context of the event as that of just retribution for 150 years of national humiliation and shame.

A number of contributors to this volume (e.g. Baker, Handford, Iedema, Mauranen) emphasize how the analyst's selection of what is relevant in the context in order to interpret a text is crucial. Handford adopts a model of context with four levels, or approaches, as described above. He writes about his approach as follows:

> While the combination of these approaches illuminates more parts of the elephant than a single approach would permit, the data could also be analysed from various other perspectives to let us see more, such as intercultural communication, gender studies, management studies and social network theory.

Similarly, Baker writes that 'some contexts are more relevant than others, and so researchers need to make judicious decisions about what to include and how far to go'. Baker, in fact, goes further than this, seeing researchers themselves as part of the context and recognizing that they may influence the outcome of the research, in a process he refers to as 'researcher reflexivity'. Others have gone a stage even further in researcher reflexivity, with researchers handing over control of data collection to their participants and the goals of the research being negotiated with participants, who also become collaborators and consultants (Holmes et al. 2011). Although there is no contribution in the present volume applying this approach, . . . in a number of the chapters, discourse analysts are involved with other professionals in making sense of professional practice, with a view to bringing about change; these are the chapter by Rose and Martin and by Waring, in the context of the school, Handford, in the context of a bridge design situation, and that of Iedema and Carroll, in the context of health care.

As regards how to consider context, as I have already noted earlier, different analysts have different approaches. In this volume, contributions go from a minute analysis of preceding turns (Waring) (although the institutional context is also considered[2]) to ethnographic analysis (Wodak). This contrast further emphasizes the point that context very much depends upon the analyst, as already mentioned.

Processes of contextualization

Throughout this discussion, I have been working according to the assumption that discourse analysis consists in a bringing together of text and context. This process of the relating of text to context and vice versa can be referred to as *contextualization* (although there are a variety of understandings of this term). Auer (1992: 4) defines contextualization as follows:

> In most general terms, *contextualization therefore comprises all activities by participants which make relevant, maintain, revise, cancel . . . any aspect of context which, in turn, is responsible for the interpretation of an utterance in its particular locus of occurrence* (*original emphasis*).

The phenomenon by which contextualization comes about is referred to as *indexicality*, using the term in its broadest sense as referring to all linguistic and paralinguistic features which refer directly to the context. Every linguistic sign carries with it social meanings which tell us something about its speaker, the relation between the speaker and hearer, and the social context in which the utterance is made (Ochs 1992). Deictic markers such as 'I', 'here', 'now', 'today', 'he', 'she' and 'that' are obvious indexicals. If I say 'I am working here', first in my study at home and later in my office at work, there are obviously two different (indexical) meanings in these examples. But other linguistic features can function as indexicals. Gumperz highlighted the indexical nature of language with his notion of *contextualization cues*, which he defined as follows:

> speakers' and listeners' use of verbal and nonverbal signs to relate what is said at any one time and in any one place to knowledge acquired through past experience, in order to retrieve the presuppositions they must rely on to maintain conversational involvement and assess what is intended. (Gumperz 1992: 230)

Gumperz (1992: 231) claimed that contextualization relies on cues which operate primarily at four levels: prosody, paralinguistics, code choice and choice of lexical forms or formulaic expression. Contextualization cues work as follows (Ibid.:232):

> They serve to highlight, foreground or make salient certain phonological or lexical strings vis-a-vis other similar units, that is, they function relationally and cannot be assigned context-independent, stable, core lexical meanings. Foregrounding processes, moreover, do not rest on any one single cue. Rather assessments depend on co-occurrence judgments . . . that simultaneously evaluate a variety of different cues.

Furthermore, Gumperz claimed, '[s]ituated interpretations are intrinsically context-bound and cannot be analysed apart from the verbal sequences in which they are embedded (Ibid.)'.

A particular type of contextualization is intertextuality (Bakhtin 1981; Kristeva 1980), referred to in Baker, Lou and Wodak (this volume) and defined by Wodak (this volume) as 'the linkage of all texts to other texts, both in the past and in the present'. As Wodak points out (Ibid.) 'such links can be established in different ways: through continued reference to a topic or to its main actors; through reference to the same events as the other texts; or through the reappearance of a text's main arguments in another text.' Related to intertextuality is *recontextualization*, referred to in O'Halloran et al., Rose and Martin and Wodak (this volume), and defined by Wodak (this volume) as 'taking an argument, a topic, a genre, or a discursive practice out of context and restating/realizing it in a new context'. As Wodak notes, in this process, the feature is first taken out of one context – *decontextualized* – and then, when inserted in a new context, *recontextualized*, thereby acquiring a new meaning. Fairclough (1992) introduced the term *interdiscursivity* (see Wodak, this volume) to extend the idea of intertextuality to include the phenomenon of how whole (big D) discourses may be invoked inside other ones. Iedema (2001) uses the term *resemiotization*, to refer to how one semiotic system is mobilized into another semiotic system (also Lou, this volume).

A further type of contextualization cue is that of *metadiscourse* or *metalanguage* (referred to by Handford and Mauranen in this volume). Metadiscourse (Hyland 2005) is a means by which speakers/writers frame a desired context, how they want listeners/readers to contextualize/interpret the text.[3] Hyland (2005: 37) gives the following definition:

> Metadiscourse is a cover term for the self-reflexive expressions used to negotiate interactional meanings in a text, assisting the writer or speaker to express a viewpoint and engage with readers as members of a particular community.

All language use is indexical in the sense that the meaning of any word or utterance can only be determined by reference to its context. However, the examples I have given above are particularly important in discourse analysis and feature in many of the contributions in this volume.

Approaches to context

The code model of communication

Traditional models of communication did not take context into account at all. The best known of these models, the so-called code, or conduit, model construes the communication of a message as a simple process, whereby the sender encodes the message, which passes along the communication channel in the form of a signal, which is then decoded by the receiver. Provided that there is no deficiency in the channel and that both the sender and the receiver are using the same code, successful communication is guaranteed (Shannon and Weaver 1949). According to this model, therefore, there is no role in the interpretative process for contextual factors such as the identity of the speaker and hearer or any other features of the context which might affect the meaning of the message.

Pragmatics

Pragmatics, the study of language in context, according to many definitions (e.g. Levinson 1983; Leech 1983), and Gricean pragmatics (Grice 1989 [1967]; Sperber and Wilson 2005), in particular, take a radically different view to the code model, assigning an essential role in communication to context. According to this approach, the interpretation of utterances is an inferential process, based on rational thought and context. Utterances may have a (decontextualized) literal meaning, but their meaning in actual use will depend upon the context within which they are made. This role of context is clear in Grice's *cooperative principle*:

> Make your conversational contribution such as is required, at the stage at which it occurs, by the accepted purpose or direction of the talk exchange in which you are engaged (1989 [1967]: 26).

This principle is broken down into the four well-known sub-maxims of *quality*, *quantity*, *relation* (relevance) and *manner*. The cooperative principle and associated maxims are thus guidelines used by speakers to match their utterances to context.

The inferential process, which is referred to by Grice as *implicature*, depends upon the following factors:

1   The conventional meaning of the words used, together with the identity of any references that may be involved.

2   The cooperative principle and its maxims.

3   The context, linguistic or otherwise.

4   Other items of background knowledge.

5   Mutual awareness of 1–4.

So, to reiterate, the maxims, as sub-components of the overall principle, act as a default against which hearers interpret utterances. To take an example, if someone is asked if they prefer tea or coffee and they reply that they do not like coffee, although this might not appear to be a reply to the question (that is, it does not comply with the maxim of relevance), it will nevertheless be interpreted as relevant and therefore set up the implicature that the hearer prefers tea. While pragmatics has traditionally been focussed on introspectively generated examples, the study of implicature, the working out of what is meant from what is said, plays a fundamental role in discourse analysis.[4]

Langue *and* parole, *and competence and performance*

Mainstream linguistics has a history of denying a role for context, as context is seen as somehow muddying the water and blurring our focus on the decontextualized sentence, which should be the focus of attention. This goes back at least to de Saussure (1916) and his distinction between *langue*, the underlying system of a language, and *parole*, the actual speech produced by individuals. The purpose of the distinction was to be able to isolate the object of linguistic investigation, which was *langue*, the idealized structures of the system, and to reject parole which was not considered to be the object of study.

Later, Chomsky and his followers, while similarly aware of the role of context, again explicitly excluded it from their model of language, describing language in meaningful context as *performance* and preferring to focus on individual sentences in isolation, as *competence*. Performance, as actual language use, was viewed as 'fairly degenerate in quality' (Chomsky 1965: 31), because it does not correspond to the idealized model of perfectly formed grammatical sentences which make up competence.

Hymes's SPEAKING mnemonic

Since the Chomskyan revolution in linguistics, much work in various branches of linguistics incorporating context can be seen as a reaction to this model. Thus, Hymes introduced the notion of *communicative competence* as a counterpart to Chomsky's *linguistic competence*, communicative competence being knowledge of not only grammar, but also social knowledge, knowledge about how, when, where and why to use language appropriately in a given context. As Hymes (1971: 278) famously stated, 'there are rules of use without which the rules of grammar would be useless'. Hymes proposed an 'ethnography of speaking' to study how language is used in specific communicative settings. He proposed a mnemonic – SPEAKING – to remember the features he considered to be important in any analysis of the communicative situation or context (Table 1.1).

Hymes describes how this framework can be used in the interpretation of utterances as follows:

> The use of a linguistic form identifies a range of meanings. A context can support a range of meanings. When a form is used in a context, it eliminates the meanings

Table 1.1 Hymes' speaking mnemonic

Setting	Physical or abstract setting (e.g. office or church service)
Participants	Speaker, hearer, overhearer
Ends	Purposes, goals and outcomes
Act Sequence	Form the event takes, ordering of speech acts
Key	Tone, manner, spirit of the speech acts
Instrumentalities	Channel or mode (e.g. telephone, spoken or written)
Norms	Norms of interaction and interpretation
Genre	Type of speech event (e.g. story, joke, lecture)

possible to that context other than those the form can signal: the context eliminates from consideration the meanings possible to the form other than those the context can support. (Hymes 1962: 14)

Clearly, the different features of the model cannot be considered in isolation from the others. As well as considering the different features, the analyst also needs to think about how they interact, how certain participants are associated with particular genres, for example, or how certain settings are associated with particular act sequences, as another example. Thomas (1995) notes that, as a sociolinguist, Hymes sees context as constraining language and that a pragmatist would take the opposite tack and see the individual as changing the situation they find themselves in. I might argue that a discourse analyst should look in both directions.

Malinowski, Firth, Sapir and Whorf

Earlier, based on fieldwork in the Pacific Islands, the London University anthropologist Malinowski, who, incidentally, was an influence on Hymes (1962), had argued for the importance of considering context in the interpretation of utterances:

A word without linguistic context is a mere figment and stands for nothing by itself, so in the reality of a spoken living tongue, the utterance has no meaning except in the context of situation (1923: 307).

Malinowski argued for a consideration of not only the here and now of the utterance – the context of situation-, but also the cultural background or the *context of culture*. Jumping ahead a little, this distinction between context of situation and context of culture was later taken up by Halliday (1988: 7) who wrote as follows: '[t]he context for the particular instances – for language as processes of text – is the context of situation. And just as a piece of text is an instance of language, so a situation is an instance of culture'.

Building on the work of Malinowski, Firth, also at London University, developed his own contextually based linguistic theory. Asserting that 'meaning . . . is to be regarded as a complex of contextual relations, and phonetics, grammar, lexicology and semantics each handles its own components of the complex in its appropriate context' (Firth 1957: 19), Firth (1950: 43–4) developed his own theory of *context of situation*, which he summarized as follows:

A   The relevant features of the participants: persons, personalities.

    (i)   The verbal action of the participants.

    (ii)   The non-verbal action of the participants.

B   The relevant objects.

C   The effects of the verbal action.

During roughly the same period when Malinowski and Firth were writing, across the Atlantic in the United States, Sapir and Whorf, although not using the term *context of culture*, nevertheless expressed the idea of a language as representing the mental life, or culture, of its speakers. The so-called Sapir-Whorf hypothesis states that because different languages represent reality differently, speakers of different languages will perceive reality differently. Thus, the culture underlying a language provides the context within which language is interpreted. This mental, or cognitive, view represents a fundamental distinction in theories of context, setting apart the social view (as in Hymes) and the cognitive view (as in Sapir-Whorf).

Systemic functional linguistics

Firth's ideas were developed further by his student Halliday and his followers. In Halliday, McIntosh and Strevens (1964), already, the authors conceptualized *context of situation* into three dimensions: *mode of discourse*, *field of discourse* and *style of discourse* (later relabelled *tenor of discourse*), which can be explicated as follows:

FIELD OF DISCOURSE: what is happening, the nature of the social action that is taking place.

TENOR OF DISCOURSE: who is taking part, the nature of the participants, their statuses and roles.

MODE OF DISCOURSE: what part the language is playing, what is it that the participants are expecting the language to do for them in the given situation.

These three parameters together contribute to varieties of language which Halliday, McIntosh and Strevens referred to as *registers*. An example of how this system operates (with adaptations) is to be found in Rose and Martin's chapter in this volume, where a pedagogic register is characterized as sequences of learning activities (field), pedagogic relations between learners and teachers (tenor), and modalities of learning – spoken, written, visual and manual (mode).

Halliday's model has subsequently formed the basis of the contextual model of language which has come to be called systemic functional linguistics (SFL). The assumption underlying this model has been articulated by Hasan (2009: 170), as follows:

> To explain why anyone says anything one must appeal to the context which exerts pressure on the speaker's choice of meaning; and to explain why these patterns of wordings appear rather than any other, one must appeal to the meanings which, being relevant to the context, activated those wordings.

One of the strengths of the SFL approach to context is in its power to identify form–function links, to relate language form to context. The three contextual parameters of field, tenor and mode can be mapped onto corresponding metafunctions – ideational, interpersonal and textual, respectively – which in turn can be identified with particular lexicogrammatical systems. Thus, the ideational function (field) is expressed typically through choice of lexis and transitivity systems; the interpersonal function (tenor) is expressed typically through the systems of mood, modality and person; and the textual function (mode) is expressed typically through cohesion, given/new and information structure.[5] This is a powerful tool in textual analysis.

As Hasan (2009: 179) herself has acknowledged, however, descriptions of context in SFL have not been developed in the same detailed way as the grammar has. To illustrate this rather ad hoc, common sense approach typical in SFL, Hasan (Ibid.) provides a table of the variables that might be specified in a typical SFL analysis of context (Table 1.2):

Table 1.2 A partial account of an imaginary contextual configuration (based on Hasan 2009: 180)

Variables	Values of the variables
Field	Professional consultation: medical; application for appointment . . .
Tenor	Client: patient-as-applicant and agent for consultant: receptionist; maxim social distance . . .
Mode	Aural channel: minus visual contact; telephone conversation; spoken medium

Critical discourse analysis

Influenced by SFL, critical discourse analysis (CDA) is an approach which is equally contextually based, although it tends to pay more attention to the macro-context (social structure) than SFL typically does. Fairclough, for example, sees text as embedded in the context of its production, distribution and reception in the social, economic and cultural world. Discourse analysis, according to this view, involves:

> analysing the relationship between texts, processes, and social conditions, both the immediate conditions of the situational context and the more remote conditions of institutions and social structures. (Fairclough 1989: 26)

Fairclough identifies three integrated levels of discourse in analysis, involving analysis of text, analysis of discourse practices and analysis of social practices (1992: 73). This can be represented in an often-reproduced diagram (Figure 1.1).

From this, we can see that the micro-level of the *text* is constrained by the meso level of *discourse practice*, which is in turn constrained by the macro level of *social practice*, or social conditions. This latter level involves relations of power. In the role of power as a contextual factor, Fairclough, as do other CDA practitioners, draws on Foucault (e.g. 1982) and his ideas on the ubiquity of power in society and on Gramsci's (1977) theory of hegemony, the process by which the powerful maintain their authority. This contextual parameter of power is very clearly exemplified in Cotterill's study

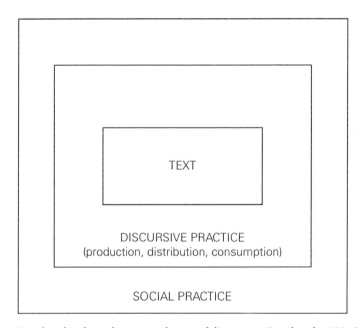

TEXT

DISCURSIVE PRACTICE
(production, distribution, consumption)

SOCIAL PRACTICE

FIGURE 1.1 *Fairclough's three-dimensional view of discourse. (Fairclough 1989: 25, adapted)*

(this volume) of how power constrains the discourse of the courtroom. As Cotterill writes, citing Eades (2010: 106), 'not only do lawyers have the power to control witnesses' stories, but lawyers and judges have enormous power to control witnesses in other ways – whether they stand or sit, when they can talk, what they can talk about and when they have to remain silent'. While the diagram of Figure 1.1 might suggest a reified model, Fairclough's approach is to be viewed as an interactive one, involving a continual shunting between the micro-analysis of texts and the macro-analysis of social structures and formations and power relations.

While Fairclough allows for an ethnographic dimension to analysis, this is not part of his practice. For Wodak, on the other hand, an ethnographic perspective is essential to her method, ethnographic methods allowing for a more detailed analysis of contextual factors. Wodak's approach (1996, this volume) is referred to as the discourse-historical approach (DHA), because it emphasizes how discourse is always linked to its historical context (Wodak 2002). The DHA involves four levels of contextual analysis (Wodak 2002, this volume):

- the immediate co-text;
- the other texts and discourses that the text draws upon;
- the conditions of text production, distribution and reception;
- the wider sociopolitical formation.

A third proponent of the CDA approach to discourse analysis, who has a rather different approach to context as compared to Fairclough and Wodak and other practitioners, is van Dijk (2008b, 2009), who has a socio-cognitive view of context, social cognition being concerned with the mental processes involved in how we relate to people in our social world (Moskowitz 2005). This approach thus links up with the Sapir/Whorf tradition to context, as mentioned earlier. Context for van Dijk consists of the mental models and representations speakers use to make their contribution appropriate. These mental models represent the mediating link between text and context, and between text and social structure:

> It is theoretically essential to understand that there is no other way to relate macrolevel notions such as group dominance and equality with microlevel notions of text, talk, meaning and understanding. Indeed, the crucial notion of reproduction needed to explain how discourse plays a role in the reproduction of dominance, presupposes an account that relates discourse structures to social cognitions and social cognitions to social structures. (van Dijk 1993: 280)

A mental models approach is adopted by Hart (this volume), although Hart goes further and introduces theoretical insights from cognitive linguistics. Because cognitive linguistics sees language as an integral part of cognition in general, it seeks to identify direct relations between patterns of language and patterns of thought. Perhaps the best-known example of this approach is Lakoff and Johnson's (1980) conceptual metaphor theory, which has been taken up by some discourse analysts (e.g. Charteris-Black 2004), who have sought to identify ideological patterns underlying conceptual metaphors in discourse. Hart's contribution broadens this approach away from conceptual metaphor to consider grammatical patterning and its relation to ideology, an essential component of context.

Conversation analysis

A very different model of context to that of CDA is that taken up by conversation analysis (CA). In fact, there was an important exchange of papers on this issue between Billig (1996, 1999), Schegloff (1997, 1999) and Wetherell (1998), although space precludes a discussion here. I already quoted above Waring's statement that in the CA approach to discourse analysis '[e]very current action is shaped by the context set up by the preceding action, and every current action renews the context for its next action'. While this is generally accepted by practitioners of CA, not all are in agreement as to whether this is enough. According to what might be referred to as a 'strong' view (e.g. Schegloff), if the context is significant to the participants, then there will be evidence of this in the interaction. There is no need to appeal to any further notion of context. This principle is referred to as *procedural consequentiality* (Schegloff 1987; Waring, this volume). According to what we might call a 'weaker' view, while agreeing that the immediate interactional context is essential, analysis may be enriched by appealing to the institutional context. This is the position taken by Waring (this volume), the institutional context being the classroom in her case. The issue in this debate is thus whether talk creates its own context or is additionally constrained by more distal context (Grundy 2008: 222).

Context and corpora

Firth (1957: 11) famously stated that '[y]ou shall know a word by the company it keeps', indicating that the meaning of a word is to be found in its typical co-texts. Firth's statement was later to become a guiding principle of corpus linguistics. While corpus linguistics has been critiqued for focussing on decontextualized strings of language, or *corpus lines* (e.g. Widdowson 1998, 2004), recent developments in *corpus-assisted discourse analysis* have shown its potential in the study of the relation between language and context. Typically, a corpus-assisted discourse analysis will compare the use of language in a specific target corpus of text with a *reference corpus*, usually representative of the language more generally. It can thus show how language use in a specific register, or context, varies from that found more generally.

Corpus tools can provide frequency lists of words and phrases, determine key terms in the target corpus as compared to a reference corpus, and provide concordance lines (key word in context [kwic] concordances of terms found to be of interest in the corpus).

The approach can reveal meanings present in the discourse which are not obvious to the naked eye. As an example, Baker (this volume), in his study of sexist language use in the *Daily Mail* newspaper, used corpus tools to investigate the sentence, 'gay activists are always calling for tolerance and understanding'. Baker sensed that the use of *always* in this sentence had a non-literal – that is to say context-dependent – negative meaning towards the subject of the sentence, *gay activists*. However, he had no way of demonstrating this, except with the use of corpus tools. Using a corpus of articles from the *Daily Mail*, corpus analysis demonstrated that *always* in such patterns as those in the target sentence is typically used in a negative sense, collocating with verbs such as *complaining, fighting, gambling, grumbling, lurking, moaning, niggling, quibbling* and *threatening*. Baker thus shows how a particular meaning of a given language feature, in his case *always*, may be specific to a particular context, in Baker's case, that of the *Daily Mail*. Corpus analysis is also used in the chapters in this volume by Bednarek, Cotterill and Handford. We can thus see the growing popularity of this approach in discourse analysis.

Multimodal discourse analysis

Recent years have seen the development of a rapidly developing variety of text forms associated with information and multimedia. Writing about the implications of these developments for literacy education, the New London Group (1996: 78) identify five different modes of meaning that they consider as in need of attention:1. linguistic meaning, 2. visual meaning, 3. audio meaning, 4. gestural meaning and 5. spatial meaning. With the exception possibly of the first one, these are all areas of meaning which would traditionally have been treated as different aspects of context. This shows how multimodality, as this phenomenon is referred to (Jewitt 2009), has changed how we deal with context and opened up a whole new paradigm for its study. Text is no longer considered as separate from (albeit interrelated with) context, but is instead seen as but one semiotic mode among others. O'Halloran et al. (this volume) thus write that their study of televised and online news discourse 'explores the implications of moving beyond language as an isolated semiotic system to language and semiotic resources as sets of interrelated systems which construe discourse, context and culture'. The implications of this view, as O'Halloran et al. describe them, are as follows:

> Discourse is spatially and temporally embedded in contexts which are themselves multimodal in nature; that is, the context is also a multimodal semiotic process and/or product. From this perspective, context is not external to discourse; on the contrary, the semiotic selections in discourse interact with each other and the semiotic selections in the context to construe meaning in social practices.

Multimodality thus requires a total re-evaluation of the traditional relation between text and context. The notion of figure and ground is put into question. While context was previously background, this is no longer the case; context has now become text.

Chapter template

To facilitate readers in juxtaposing the chapters in the volume and comparing and contrasting these different contexts and approaches and the application of their particular models of context, each chapter follows (grossomodo) an organizational template as follows.

1 Introduction

2 Goal(s) of the study

3 The theory/approach to discourse analysis that informs the study

4 How context is understood in the study

5 The context of the study

6 Data (what data was collected and how)

7 Analysis (how the data was analysed)

8 Findings

9 Discussion/Conclusion (including the role of context)

10 References

Brief summary of the contributions

Paul Baker's chapter, 'Considering context when analysing representations of gender and sexuality: a case study', presents a discourse analysis of an article in the British newspaper the *Daily Mail* entitled 'Why there was nothing "natural" about Stephen Gately's death' (16 October 2009), which discussed the death of Boyzone singer Stephen Gately. Baker conducts a textual analysis of the article, examining how the author uses language to construct representations of Gately and homosexuality, examining among other phenomena, use of metaphor and implicature. Using corpus linguistic techniques, Baker shows how the article references various discourses of homosexuality, as well as considering possible interpretations of such discourses. However, Baker argues, it is not possible to fully analyse the article without taking into account the numerous ways that context determined what was written, various of which are examined.

Monika Bednarek's chapter, '"*Who are you and why are you following us?*"': '*Wh*-questions and communicative context in television dialogue', explores the use of *wh*-questions in a fictional American television series. Like Baker, using corpus-assisted discourse analysis,

Bednarek investigates the frequency, distribution and variation of *wh*-questions across episodes/series in the corpus in terms of the communicative context of fictional television. By *communicative context*, Bednarek means here the relation between the media text, its producer(s) and its audience(s). Of particular importance for Bednarek's analysis in this chapter (as in some of the other chapters, e.g. O'Halloran et al.) is the concept of audience or overhearer design, which means that 'the defining characteristics of film [and television, M.B] dialogue is that it is . . . always designed "for us"' (Kozloff 2000: 121).

Drawing on a large corpus of courtroom data from English Crown Courts from the late 1990s and 2000s, **Janet Cotterill**'s chapter, 'Discourse and discord in court: The role of context in the construction of witness examination in British criminal trial talk', focuses on the ways in which both lawyers and witnesses construct, represent and frequently exploit their roles and identities through discourse. Through detailed textual analysis of aspects such as discourse markers, politeness strategies and identity construction, Cotterill provides an insight into the British courtroom context and the interplay between the legal constraints and the linguistic 'texts' which are produced. By analysing the power differential between participant dyads, predominantly lawyer/ witness (both direct and cross-examination), it is possible to understand the influence of the courtroom context on the discourse produced.

Britt-Louise Gunnarsson's chapter, 'Business discourse in the globalized economy: The construction of an attractive workplace culture on the Internet', explores multinational companies' construction of an attractive image of their staff policy and workplace culture on the internet. The goal is to explore how large business enterprises in their self-presentations on their career-oriented web pages balance between various concerns, values and interests: between global and local concerns, between economic concerns and social values, and between individual-centred and group-centred interests. Context is understood in the chapter at a macro level as dependent on various societal frameworks, at a meso level as situated within the studied company and at a micro-level as related to the analysed text with its specific goal and intended readers. A model is introduced which sets business discourse in relation to its contextual frameworks and the creation of an image of the corporate culture to the construction of an 'organizational self'.

Michael Handford's chapter, 'Context in spoken professional discourse: language and practice in an international bridge design meeting', explores the relationship between text and context through reference to a professional discourse, specifically a bridge design meeting in South Asia involving speakers from various countries, professions and institutions who use English as a lingua franca. The chapter models the relationship between the text and the context in terms of layers of practices, which, as they become more general, have a less direct relationship with the text. The main focus of Handford's study is to identify key lexicogrammatical items which directly index particular discursive practices in this meeting as genre. The analysis shows how recurrent and frequent lexicogrammatical items invoke and are constrained by the context of the meeting-as-genre.

Noting that over the last 50 years, the discussion of ethnicity and race in the United Kingdom has foregrounded a struggle between clearly demarcated dominant and subordinated racial and ethnic groups. **Roxy Harris** and **Ben Rampton**, in their chapter, 'Ethnicities without guarantees: An empirically situated approach', seek to overcome this limitation by addressing some of the ways in which race and ethnicity are indirectly evoked, performed or noted in the encounters of ordinary life, their significance held in check by a range of much more pressing everyday concerns. The chapter focuses on the interaction of a mixed group of girls in a multiethnic secondary school in London and begins the analysis with what at first looks like a racist statement. Drawing on the resources of linguistic ethnography, however, the analysis then embeds this utterance in the shifts and layering of contexts currently in play. Once these enter the reckoning, the inadequacy of the stock interpretations offered in the dominant discourses stands out.

Christopher Hart's chapter, 'Constructing contexts through grammar: Cognitive models and conceptualization in British newspaper reports of political protests', analyses, from the perspective of the Cognitive Linguistic Approach to CDA, representations of political protests in British newspapers and the cognitive models that these representations reflect and (re)construct in the minds of readers. The analysis focuses on the alternative image schemas which are available to construe protest events and how patterns of construal might index wider ideological discourses. The chapter presents a comparative analysis of online press reports of violence in the UK student fees protests on the 10th and 24th of November 2010. The chapter argues that cognitive linguistics has the potential to account for the conceptual import of various lexical and grammatical constructions.

Rick Iedema and **Katherine Carroll,** in their chapter, 'Intervening in health care communication using discourse analysis', outline an approach that regards discourse as a co-accomplished and emergent process. This process operates at the level of practice, where clinicians co-accomplish care, and at the level of research into that practice, involving researchers and research participants (the clinicians). This analytical-interventionist approach exploits the discourse analytical momentum of rendering the taken-as-given strange, to enable not just researchers but also practitioners to adopt different perspectives on practice, and hence enabling them to change practice. Framing 'context' as the domain of the taken-for-granted, the paper further explains that practice change typically relies on foregrounding aspects otherwise considered as contextual, unremarkable and given. These issues are illustrated through a case study of a recent health care communication project that drew on video to provide practitioners with practical feedback.

Jackie Jia Lou's chapter, 'Locating the power of place in space: A geosemiotic approach to context', introduces the geosemiotic framework developed by Ron and

Suzie Scollon (2003) to examine 'discourse in place'. In their work, Lou argues, the Scollons return the meaning of language and other semiosis to the most concrete, fundamental, and thus probably most often neglected aspect of context, that is, space and place. This physical grounding, however, does not exclude other kinds of context. Instead, it is conceptualized as one component of the tripartite geosemiotic aggregate, consisting of visual semiotics, interaction order and place semiotics. The chapter applies this framework to a study analysing an advertising campaign celebrating the key role a corporation played in redefining an urban neighbourhood, Chinatown in Washington, DC. The study not only shows the importance of space and place as context in shaping text, but also demonstrates the role of language as a mediator between space and place. Furthermore, it contributes to critical discourse analysis by looking at space and place as a concrete link between discursive ideology and political economy.

Anna Mauranen, in her chapter, 'Lingua franca discourse in academic contexts: shaped by complexity', notes that, with globalization affecting all walks of life, our linguistic landscapes are being shaped by the increasing use of lingua francas and that English is the most widespread lingua franca today, and the only one that is truly global. Making use of the ELFA (English as a Lingua Franca in Academic Settings) corpus of speech in university and conference settings and its written component, the WrELFA database, Mauranen looks into the specific context of English as a lingua franca (ELF) in academic contexts. Mauranen discusses the social parameters that distinguish lingua francas from other kinds of second language use, and how the complexity of a lingua franca environment shapes ELF discourse. With a relatively limited pool of shared lexicogrammatical resources, lingua franca speakers seem to draw adeptly on discourse strategies to achieve their purposes even in a heavily language-reliant context like academia.

In **Kay L. O'Halloran, Sabine Tan and Marissa K. L. E**'s chapter, 'A multimodal approach to discourse, context and culture', context is modelled as the combination of semiotic choices which construe the communicative situation for language use and discourse (spoken and written texts). The multimodal semiotic approach is demonstrated using interactive software for multimodal analysis which reveals how visual and aural choices co-contextualize and recontextualize the linguistic choices which are made in television interviews about climate change. The multimodal analysis reveals that discourse analysis based on language alone is insufficient for interpreting how meaning is created and negotiated in social situations.

David Rose and J. R. Martin's chapter, 'Intervening in contexts of schooling', draws on two complex theories of social context: the model of text-in-context developed within systemic functional linguistic theory (SFL) and the model of pedagogic contexts developed in the sociological theory of Basil Bernstein (2000). Using SFL analysis, the chapter describes an intervention in the Australian school system which involved the redesigning of curriculum genres to enhance their potential for enabling all students to achieve success. The intervention is based on an analysis of the systems of written genres involved in the research, including their social functions and staging.

Working with a conversation analytic framework, **Hansun Zhang Waring**'s chapter, 'Turn-allocation and context: Broadening participation in the second language classroom', is described as a small step towards building an empirical account of teachers' efforts to broaden participation during whole-class language-learning interactions. Context in this chapter is understood as both institutional and sequential. Institutionally, classroom interaction exhibits a clear departure from ordinary conversation. In the conversation analytic tradition, sequentially, any communicative action is both context-shaped and context-renewing within an ongoing sequence. Based on video-taped classroom interactions, the analysis shows that the teachers engage in two specific practices to broaden participation during whole-class interactions: (1) withholding selection of the first respondent and (2) selecting an alternative category. The chapter highlights how the institutional and sequential aspects of context have contributed to the analysis of the data as well as the interpretation of the findings.

The final chapter of the volume, by **Ruth Wodak**, 'Political discourse analysis – Distinguishing frontstage and backstage contexts. A discourse-historical approach', focuses on frontstage and backstage performances of a member of the European Parliament. The chapter integrates theories of performance, habitus, identity construction, genre and institutional constraints and distinguishes analytically four levels of context which are related in dialectical ways, from the sociopolitical and historical layers to the co-text of specific utterances in unique texts. The analysis indicates that politicians – although not specifically trained for their profession – have to obtain various kinds of knowledge and acquire a maximum of flexibility and competence in coping with many different immediate and frequently unpredictable events. A very close contextual analysis is necessary to be able to analyse, understand and explain the complexity of activities in the interface of politics and media, in specific countries and media traditions.

Notes

1 As Lou (this volume) notes, this view has come to be challenged more recently. Thus in Scollon and Scollon's (2003) *geosemiotics*, which is exemplified by Lou (this volume), the text is decentred in favour of a more multidimensional framework. See also O'Halloran et al. (this volume).

2 Waring notes as follows: 'While the sequential context for each utterance constitutes a decisive resource that helps me arrive at the above findings, the institutional context of a classroom makes it possible for such findings to be understood and appreciated with greater depth'.

3 This phenomenon is referred to by Bauman and Briggs as *contextualization.* They describe how it functions as follows:

> Contextualization involves an active process of negotiation in which participants reflexively examine the discourse as it is emerging, embedding assessments of its structure and significance in the speech itself. (Bauman and Briggs 1990: 69)

I prefer to use the perhaps more usual term of *metadiscourse,* at least in the discourse analysis literature, reserving the term *contextualization* for the more broader phenomenon reviewed in this section.

4 A more recent development of Grice's theory is that of Sperber and Wilson (1995), whose *relevance* model of implicature works on just one of Grice's maxims, that of relevance, interlocutors deciding what is most relevant on a cost-benefit basis.

5 I use the term 'typically', because, as Thompson (1999) has noted, these are not one-to-one correspondences.

References

Auer, P. (1992), 'Introduction: On Gumperz' approach to contextualization', in P. Auer and A. Di Luzio (eds), *The Contextualization of Language.* Philadelphia, PA: John Benjamins, pp. 1–37.

Auer, P. and Di Luzio, A. (1992), *The Contextualization of Language.* Philadelphia, PA: John Benjamins.

Baker, P. (2006), *Using Corpora in Discourse Analysis.* London: Continuum.

Bakhtin, M. (1981), 'Discourse in the novel', in M. Holquist (ed.) and C. Emerson and M. Holquist (trans.), *The Dialogic Imagination: Four Essays.* Austin: University of Texas Press, pp. 259–422.

Bateson, G. (1955), 'A Theory of Play and Fantasy'. *Psychiatric Research Reports,* 2, 39–51.

Bauman, R. and Briggs, C. (1990), 'Poetics and performance'. *Annual Review of Anthropology,* 19, 59–88.

Bhatia, V. (2004), *Worlds of Written Discourse.* London: Continuum.

Billig, M. (1996), *Arguing and Thinking: A Rhetorical View of Social Psychology* (2nd edn). Cambridge: Cambridge University Press.

—(1999), 'Whose terms? Whose ordinariness? Rhetoric and ideology in conversation analysis'. *Discourse and Society,* 10(4), 543–58.

Blommaert, J. (2005), *Discourse.* Cambridge: Cambridge University Press.

—(2007), 'Socio-linguistic scales'. *Intercultural Pragmatics,* 4(1), 1–19.

—(2010), *The Sociolinguistics of Globalization.* Cambridge: Cambridge University Press.

Chomsky, N. (1965), *Aspects of the Theory of Syntax.* Cambridge, MA: MIT Press.

Charteris-Black, J. (2004), *Corpus Approaches to Critical Metaphor Analysis.* London: Palgrave Macmillan.

de Saussure, F. (1983), *Course in General Linguistics* (1916), eds. C. Bally and A. Sechehaye and trans. R. Harris. La Salle, IL: Open Court.

Duranti, A. and Goodwin, C. (1992), *Rethinking Context: Language as an Interactive Phenomenon.* Cambridge: Cambridge University Press.

Fairclough, N. (1989), *Language and Power.* London: Longman.

Fairclough, N., Mulderrig, J., and Wodak, R. (2011), 'Critical Discourse Analysis', in T. A. Van Dijk (ed.), *Discourse Studies: A Multidisciplinary Introduction* (2nd edn). London: Sage, pp. 357–78.

Fetzer, A. (2004), *Recontextualizing Context: Grammaticality Meets Appropriateness.* Amsterdam, the Netherlands: John Benjamins.

Firth, J. R. (1957), *Papers in Linguistics 1934-1951.* Oxford: Oxford University Press.

Foucault, M. (1982), 'The Subject and Power', in H. Dreyfus and P. Rabinow (eds), *Michel Foucault: Beyond Structuralism and Hermeneutics.* Chicago: University of Chicago Press, pp. 208–26.

Gee, J. P. (1999), *An Introduction to Discourse Analysis: Theory and Method.* London: Routledge.

Giddens, A. (1984), *The Constitution of Society.* Berkeley, CA: University of California Press.

—(1990), 'Structuration theory and sociological analysis', in J. Clark, C. Modgil, and S. Modgil (eds), *Anthony Giddens: Consensus and Controversy.* London: Falmer Press, pp. 297–315.

Goffman, E. (1974), *Frame Analysis.* New York, NY: Harper & Row.

Goodwin, C. and Duranti, A. (1992), 'Rethinking context: An introduction', in A. Duranti and C. Goodwin (eds), *Rethinking Context: Language as an Interactive Phenomenon.* Cambridge: Cambridge University Press, pp. 1–42.

Gramsci, A. (1977 [1921–26]), *Selections from the Political Writings*, ed. Q. Hoare. London: Lawrence and Wishart.

Grice, H. P. (1989/1967), 'Logic and conversation', in H. P. Grice (ed.), *Studies in the Way of Words.* Cambridge, MA: Harvard University Press, pp. 22–40.

Gumperz, J. (1992), 'Contextualization and understanding', in A. Duranti and C. Goodwin (eds), *Rethinking Context: Language as an Interactive Phenomenon.* Cambridge: Cambridge University Press, pp. 229–52.

Halliday, M. A. K. (1998), 'The Notion of "Context" in Language Education', in M. Ghadessy (ed.), *Text and Context in Functional Linguistics.* Amsterdam; Philadelphia: John Benjamins, pp. 1–24.

Halliday, M. A. K. and Hasan, R. (1985), *Language, Context and Text: Aspects of Language in a Socialsemiotic Perspective.* Geelong, Australia: Deakin University Press.

Hasan, R. (2009), 'The place of context in a systemic functional model', in M. A. K. Halliday and J. J. Webster (eds), *Continuum Companion to Systemic Functional Linguistics.* London; New York: Continuum, pp. 166–89.

Holmes, J., Marra, M., and Vine, D. (2011), *Leadership, Discourse and Ethnicity.* Oxford: Oxford University Press.

Hyland, K. (2005), *Metadiscourse: Exploring Interaction in Writing.* London: Continuum.

Hymes, D. (1962), 'The ethnography of speaking', in T. Gladwin and W. C. Sturtevant (eds), *Anthropology and Human Behavior.* Washington: The Anthropological society of Washington, pp. 13–53.

Hymes, D. (1971), 'On communicative competence', in J. Pride and J. Holmes (eds), *Sociolinguistics.* London: Penguin, pp. 269–93.

Iedema, R. (2001), 'Resemiotization'. *Semiotica*, 137(1), 23–39.

Jewitt, C. (2009), *Handbook of Multimodal Analysis* (1st edn). London: Routledge.

Kozloff, S. (2000), *Overhearing Film Dialogue.* Ewing, NJ: University of California Press.

Kristeva, J. (1980), 'Word, dialogue and the novel', in L. Roudiez (ed.) and T. Gora, A. Jardine, and L. Roudiez (trans.), *Desire in Language: A Semiotic Approach to Literature and Art.* New York: Columbia University Press, pp. 64–91.

Lakoff, G. and Johnson, M. (1980), *Metaphors We Live By.* Chicago: University of Chicago Press.

Malinowski, B. (1923), 'The problem of meaning in primitive languages', in C. K. Ogden and I. A. Richards (eds), *The Meaning of Meaning.* London: Harcourt-Brace, pp. 296–336.

Moskowitz, G. B. (2005), *Social Cognition: Understanding Self and Others*. New York, NY: The Guilford Press.

Ochs, E. (1992), 'Indexing gender', in A. Duranti and C. Goodwin (eds), *Rethinking Context: Language as an Interactive Phenomenon*. Cambridge: Cambridge University Press, pp. 335–58.

Schegloff, E. A. (1987), 'Between macro and micro: Contexts and other connections', in J. Alexander, B. Giessen, R. Munch, and N. Smelser (eds), *The Micro-macro Link*. Berkeley: University of California Press, pp. 207–34.

—(1997), 'Whose text? Whose context?' *Discourse and Society*, 8, 165–87.

—(1999). '"Schegloff's texts" as "Billig's data": A critical reply'. *Discourse and Society*, 10(4), 558–72.

Shannon, C. E. and Weaver, W. (1949), *The Mathematical Theory of Communication*. Urbana, IL: University of Illinois Press.

Sperber, D. and Wilson, D. (1995), *Relevance: Communication and Cognition* (2nd edn). Oxford; Cambridge: Blackwell Publishers.

Tannen, D. (ed.) (1993), *Framing in Discourse*. Oxford: Oxford University Press.

Thomas, J. (1983), 'Cross-cultural pragmatic failure'. *Applied Linguistics*, 4(2), 91–111.

—(1995), *Meaning in Interaction: An Introduction to Pragmatics*. London: Longman.

Thompson, G. (1999), 'Acting the part: Lexico-grammatical choices and contextual factors', in M. Ghadessy (ed.), *Text and Context in Functional Linguistics*. Philadelphia, PA: John Benjamins, pp. 101–24.

Van Dijk, T. A. (2008a), *Discourse and Context: A Sociocognitive Approach*. Cambridge: Cambridge University Press.

—(2008b), 'Contextualization in parliamentary discourse: Aznar, Iraq and the pragmatics of lying', in T. A. Van Dijk (ed.), *Discourse and Power*. London: Palgrave Macmillan, pp. 237–89.

—(2009), *Society and Discourse: How Context Controls Text and Talk*. Cambridge: Cambridge University Press.

Wetherell, M. (1998), 'Positioning and interpretive repertoires: Conversation analysis and post-structuralism in dialogue'. *Discourse and Society*, 9, 387–412.

Widdowson, H. G. (1998), 'Context, community and authentic language'. *TESOL Quarterly*, 32, 705–16.

—(2004), *Text, Context, Pretext*. Oxford: Blackwell.

Wodak, R. (2002), 'The discourse historical approach'. In R. Wodak and M. Meyer (eds), *Methods of Critical Discourse Analysis*. London: Sage, pp. 63–94.

2

Considering context when analysing representations of gender and sexuality: A case study

Paul Baker

Introduction

This chapter is concerned with a discourse analysis of sexual identity in the media, using a case study which is focussed on an article (reproduced in the Appendix) in the British newspaper the *Daily Mail* entitled 'Why there was nothing "natural" about Stephen Gately's death' (16 October 2009).

Taking a feminist post-structuralist discourse analysis perspective, I first examine how the author uses language to construct representations of Gately and homosexuality, focussing on phenomena such as use of metaphor and implicature. However, I argue that it is not possible to fully interpret the article without taking into account the numerous ways that context determined what was written and how the article was received by different people. I ask how we decide what counts as 'context' and then consider a number of ways that context can be investigated. Drawing on critical discourse analytical frameworks, I consider intertextuality (e.g. how the *Daily Mail* has written about homosexuality in the past), processes of production (the political stance of the newspaper, the regulatory Codes under which it operates) and reception (how the article was received and what other texts were written about the article e.g. online comments, complaints to the PCC, the PCC's decision). I also argue that it is important to go further beyond the text itself to consider the social, historical and political context in which the article was written – considering the changing legal status for gay people, and current and recent social attitudes towards homosexuality. Finally, I consider the actual research context itself, critiquing the relationship between the researcher and the researched. I argue that this analysis of different types of wider context helps to explain and evaluate my research findings.

This study's goals and approach to discourse analysis

This study is influenced by Baxter's (2003) feminist post-structuralist discourse analysis (FPDA), a supplementary approach to discourse analysis which emphasizes that there is no such thing as a single 'truth' or correct interpretation of a text, but that instead there are potentially multiple interpretations. FPDA therefore favours combining different analytical frameworks together in a bottom-up, as-needed way, rather than following one method or set of procedures. FPDA is wary of an emancipatory agenda, arguing that there is potential danger in privileging any one point of view over others (which could result in a reconfiguring rather than a dismantling of power structures). Unlike other approaches to discourse analysis, such as critical discourse analysis, one tenet of FPDA is in viewing power as more complex than a simple hierarchy but as functioning more as a web, where even relatively powerless people may experience 'moments of power'. Baxter's approach is particularly useful in the interpretative stage of analysis because it requires the analyst to consider multiple interpretations from different types of recipients of a text. An analysis of context (particularly from an intertextual viewpoint – e.g. what other people said or wrote about the text under question) therefore fits in well with FPDA. A further facet of FPDA is researcher reflexivity, which addresses another kind of context – the context that the research is conducted in and the way that the researcher may influence the outcome of the researched.

In keeping with FPDA, I have drawn on various frameworks and theoretical perspectives where appropriate. For example, I have considered elements from Fairclough's (1989, 1995) critical discourse analysis (CDA) approach, particularly his division of analysis into three stages: description (what linguistic features occur in a text), interpretation (what those features appear to be used to achieve) and explanation (why they are used to achieve certain goals). Fairclough argues that beyond the descriptive stage, analysis of context becomes central, and he particularly advocates consideration of intertextuality (1989: 155) and social structures, practices and processes (1989: 163). I have also considered Reisgl and Wodak's (2001) and Wodak (this volume) discourse-historical analysis (DHA), which provides linguistic tools for descriptive analysis (e.g. the identification of nominational, referential and predicational strategies for social actor representation), along with the various legitimation strategies and fallacies that can be used to justify arguments. DHA also values the consideration of social and historical context. Another approach to context I have used involves corpus linguistics techniques in order to demonstrate how people in societies appear to be primed to attribute various meanings to particular words and phrases due to all of their previous encounters with such language (Hoey 2005).

Despite using some techniques from CDA, it is not a goal of this study to set out to 'prove' that the text under question represents a particular ideological position, but to instead to attempt to make sense of the different ways that the text was interpreted by readers (particularly with regard to power relations) and to explain why this was the case by referring closely to context. Therefore, I wish to demonstrate how an appreciation of context can help to take an analysis beyond description, aiding interpretation and ultimately helping analysts to explain their findings.

How context is understood in the study

For the purposes of this chapter, I view context as the constraints on a communicative situation that influence language use. Context is thus potentially far-reaching, although some contexts are more relevant than others, and so researchers need to make judicious decisions about what to include and how far to go (especially when faced with word limits). We might consider context first in terms of the immediate context that the article was written in. It occurred within the British newspaper the *Daily Mail* (and its online version *Mail Online*). It is therefore relevant to consider the *Daily Mail*, its aims and readership, and how it has written about related topics in the past. We might also look at the regulations that stipulate what can and cannot be written in the British press. Additionally, we could examine the processes that are in place if someone wants to complain about the British press.

We could also ask questions about any possible intertextual references in the text. What texts does it refer to (if any), and what texts refer to it subsequently? As the article I am analysing resulted in the largest number of complaints to the Press Complaints Commission at the time of writing, and was widely discussed on the internet in the following weeks, it is fair to say that there is a wealth of information to process, and this can be useful in telling us how the article was received.

Moreover, it is often useful to take into account the society within which the article was written. The complaints about the article took place within a society that had only recently embraced social networking media such as Facebook and Twitter. Many people were becoming linked to large, interconnected social networks which could transfer information at a rapid speed. Newspapers had only recently incorporated online versions of articles, and so it was therefore possible for the 'readership' of a newspaper to stretch far beyond people who make a decision to purchase a paper copy of that newspaper. The concept of 'audience' therefore needs to be widened to include anybody who may not normally read a newspaper but is likely to be interested if the article is seen as particularly salient.

A further consideration of society relates to the topic of the article. As Stephen Gately was gay, it is worth looking at the current and recent status of gay people in the United Kingdom. This can be achieved, for example, by examining relevant laws (and changes to laws), as well as attitude surveys. By gaining an appreciation of how British society views gay people, we are in a better position to interpret Moir's article and the responses to it.

Finally, taking FPDA's emphasis on researcher reflexivity, I view context in terms of the researcher and the research process itself. Research is not conducted in a bubble, but the person who carries out the research will have made certain decisions which will influence the outcome. The researcher is also part of a society (sometimes the same society which produced the text under analysis) and may therefore have privileged certain interpretations or perspectives over others. Towards the end of this chapter, I critically reflect on how I carried out the research, and how my own identity and 'stance' may have impacted upon the research findings.

The context of the study

This study is concerned with the analysis of an article, published in the British newspaper the *Daily Mail* (and its online version *Mail Online*) on 23 October 2009. I chose to study this article because it prompted the highest number of complaints to the Press Complaints Commission (over 25,000) ever recorded, although the complaints were not upheld. This makes it exceptionally salient for a discourse analysis relating to gender and sexuality, raising questions about why it received so many complaints and why the PCC did not uphold them.

The article was by the opinion columnist Jan Moir and was originally entitled 'Why there was nothing "natural" about Stephen Gately's death' but later relabelled in the online version as 'A strange, lonely and troubling death . . .' The article was concerned with the death of 33-year-old Stephen Gately, a member of the successful pop band Boyzone. Gately was gay and had made his sexuality known to the media in 1999. He had entered into a civil partnership with internet businessman Andrew Cowles in 2006, although the couple had also had a (non-legal) commitment ceremony in 2003. On the morning of 10 October 2009, Gately's body was found at an apartment he was staying at in Majorca. His death was determined to have been caused by a pulmonary oedema resulting from an undiagnosed heart condition. Police ruled out suicide, foul play, drugs or alcohol. At the time of the death, it appears that Gately had not been alone in the apartment, but that Cowles, and another man, a Buglarian called Georgi Dochev had spent the previous night in the apartment.

As noted above, this article about Gately's death drew more than 25,000 complaints to the British regulatory body, the Press Complaints Commission. Online media, including Facebook and Twitter, were used to draw publicity to the article, with other gay celebrities like Stephen Fry and Derren Brown becoming involved. The retailer Marks & Spencer withdrew its advertisement from the same web page as the article, issuing a statement which read: 'Marks & Spencer does not tolerate any form of discrimination'.[1] The article resulted in many other newspapers writing about it, culminating in a national debate about homophobia and media values.

Data

The primary source of data that was used in the analysis was the article by Jan Moir. The analysis of a single article can be problematic, particularly if claims about the language or discourse in the article are over-generalized. In order to make some cautious generalizations about whether the article is typical of the *Daily Mail*'s stance, I have considered other sources, such as earlier corpus research I carried out on the *Daily Mail*, as well as texts written about the article.

The article was obtained from the *Mail Online* site.[2] On the website, the article is actually the first part of a longer column by Moir, which contains a further five opinion pieces, not analysed here. Additionally, the article contains four photographs, one of Gately standing on a red carpet at a celebrity event and another of him with the other members of Boyzone. These two photos are 'posed', sanctioned photographs of Gately (who is smiling), intended for publicity purposes. The other two photographs are separately of Gately's partner Andrew Cowles and the Bulgarian man Georgi Dochev, who appear to have been photographed while walking outside and are not 'posed'. Neither man is smiling and these photographs might be viewed as rather intrusive, compared with the two publicity ones of Gately.

The web page also contains numerous links to other stories, which are regularly updated and therefore change daily. At the bottom of the page are 1,601 readers' comments (the comments page had been closed so no more comments could be added).

Other types of 'secondary' data were also considered, beyond the website where the article resided. A Google internet search of 'Jan Moir Stephen Gately' resulted in 31,000 links to other pages. Obviously, the amount of context that could be considered here is potentially enormous, and too much to do justice to in this chapter. Additional pages that appeared early in the list of web links (and were thus viewed as more relevant) included a second article by Jan Moir, which appeared a week after the original one, numerous links about the Press Complaints Commission ruling and other articles from columnists in a range of newspapers about Moir's article. Some of these pages revealed links to other sites of interest, such as the actual PCC ruling,

I have also considered other articles about homosexuality in the *Daily Mail* (based on an earlier research project I carried out, described in more detail below), the Press Complaints Commission ruling and other information with regard to the legal and social standing of gay people in the United Kingdom in the recent past.

Linguistic analysis

There is not the space to analyse the whole article, so instead I have focussed on a number of sections, particularly those which were later quoted in complaints about the article. In this qualitative analysis, I have tried to examine how Moir's stance towards Gately and homosexuality in general might be interpreted by readers. I did not begin the analysis with a predetermined list of linguistic features to isolate, but instead selected features upon reading and re-reading the article. This has led me to particularly consider metaphors, lexical choice, use of implication and generalization and legitimation strategies.

It is important to note that nowhere in the article does Moir openly state that she thinks that homosexuality is wrong. Nor does she construct Gately in an explicitly homophobic way (for example, by using a negative stance nominal like *faggot*). Early in the article, she writes that 'In the cheerful environs of Boyzone, Gately was always charming, cute, polite and funny'. These adjectives represent him positively, although it is notable how they are qualified as occurring within the specific context: 'In the cheerful environs of Boyzone'. A possible reading here is that in other environs, she may view Gately as having exuded different qualities.

Moir downplays Gately's singing abilities by saying that he was 'a popular but largely decorous addition' to Boyzone, and 'He could barely carry a tune in a Louis Vuitton trunk'. One possible reading of the description of the trunk as being Louis Vuitton (a luxury fashion brand) is that Moir is drawing on a discourse of gay men as interested in fashion, which possibly implies that gay men are feminine. However, the reference to Louis Vuitton could also or instead be linked to Gately's identity as a celebrity, and presumably his 'celebrity lifestyle'. This ambiguity between representations of 'gay lifestyle' and/or 'celebrity lifestyle' is worth highlighting, as it occurs at several points in the article.

After describing Gately and the reporting of his death, the article implies that contrary to the 'official' story, his death was drug-related.

> The sugar coating on this fatality is so saccharine-thick that it obscures whatever bitter truth lies beneath. Healthy and fit 33-year-old men do not just climb into their pyjamas and go to sleep on the sofa, never to wake up again. . . . Gately's family have always maintained that drugs were not involved in the singer's death, but it has just been revealed that he at least smoked cannabis on the night he died. Nevertheless, his mother is still insisting that her son died from a previously undetected heart condition that has plagued the family.

Moir first uses a metaphor based around the idea that the truth is a bitter taste, like a drug, and has thus been obscured by a sweeter story, just as an unpleasant pill is sugar-coated. The drug metaphor could place the idea of drugs in the mind of the reader, which are then referred to in a more literal way. Moir then casts doubt on the family's claims by her pairing of contradictory assertions which are connected by conjunctions like *but* and *nevertheless*. The phrase 'his mother is still insisting' implies that it is remarkable for Gately's mother to continue to make a claim (via the word *still*), and that also her claim is somehow unreasonable (the verb *insisting* suggests a defiant stance). As well as the link to drugs, Moir also implies that the circumstances of Gately's death involved a sexual encounter which went beyond his relationship with his civil partner.

> And I think if we are going to be honest, we would have to admit that the circumstances surrounding his death are more than a little sleazy. After a night of clubbing, Cowles and Gately took a young Bulgarian man back to their apartment.

It is not disrespectful to assume that a game of canasta with 25-year-old Georgi Dochev was not what was on the cards.

As with the implicature about the use of drugs, Moir does not explicitly say that she thinks that Cowles and Gately took Dochev back to their apartment for sex, but there are a number of clues that this appears to be the 'preferred reading' (Hall 1980) of her statement. First, she describes the circumstances as 'more than a little sleazy', as well as saying that she thinks 'a game of canasta' did not happen. However, she does not state what she thinks *did* happen, leaving this for the reader to infer, by referring back to the word 'sleazy'. Additionally, the fact that she refers to Dochev's age and also refers to him as 'young' could imply that she thinks Cowles and Gately found the man sexually attractive.

We may question why Moir chooses to imply that either Gately, Cowles or both had sex with Dochev. Sex does not appear to be linked to Gately's death, and Moir's use of *sleazy* casts a negative evaluation on what she implies has happened between the men. However, multiple interpretations are possible. Is Moir disapproving of *anyone* who has sex with someone they have just met? Is she also disapproving of *three* people being involved? And does she disapprove more because the people involved are all *men*?

Further in the article, Moir uses Gately's death in order to make a more general statement about gay relationships.

Another real sadness about Gately's death is that it strikes another blow to the happy-ever-after myth of civil partnerships. Gay activists are always calling for tolerance and understanding about same-sex relationships, arguing that they are just the same as heterosexual marriages. Not everyone, they say, is like George Michael. Of course, in many cases this may be true. Yet the recent death of Kevin McGee, the former husband of Little Britain star Matt Lucas, and now the dubious events of Gately's last night raise troubling questions about what happened.

In the above excerpt, Moir says that Gately's death 'strikes another blow to the happy-ever-after myth of civil partnerships'. It is useful to deconstruct this phrase further. The use of the adjective *another* implies that there have previously been other blows. Gately's death is therefore represented as not the first of its kind. Second, she refers to 'the happy-ever-after myth'. Her use of the definite article *the* makes this an unqualified, generic statement – she effectively labels a 'happy-ever-after view' of civil partnerships as a myth, implying that it is difficult, if not impossible, for *any* gay couple to live happily ever after. Later in this excerpt, she provides two additional examples to support her case. One is the singer George Michael (who had previously been arrested for drug offences), which she attributes to gay activists who say that not everyone is like him. A second example is the former civil partner (Moir uses the term 'husband') of a British comedian Matt Lucas, who committed suicide after the couple split up. While these are three salient and very high-profile examples of gay men who have either died or been in trouble, three cases alone do not support the argument that civil partnerships do not end happily (and George Michael is not even in a civil partnership). Moir does not refer to large-scale statistics to back up her point, nor does she consider counter-examples (from a discourse-historical analysis viewpoint, she could be said to be using the fallacy of ignoratio elenchi or ignoring the counter-proof (Reisigl and Wodak 2001: 73), sometimes referred to as 'cherry-picking'). As with Gately's mother, who is 'still insisting' that her son died of a heart condition, Moir also seems to attribute a similarly unreasonable stance to gay activists, claiming that they are 'always calling for tolerance and understanding'. It is unlikely that gay activists literally 'always' do anything, so Moir's use of this adverb of frequency must be understood in terms of what it implies, in this case, that gay activists call for tolerance and understanding a great deal, perhaps more than Moir thinks is appropriate.

The final part of the article I wish to consider is at its end:

> As a gay rights champion, I am sure [Gately] would want to set an example to any impressionable young men who may want to emulate what they might see as his glamorous routine. For once again, under the carapace of glittering, hedonistic celebrity, the ooze of a very different and more dangerous lifestyle has seeped out for all to see.

Here, Moir uses a legitimation strategy for the discourses around homosexuality that she has accessed and furthered in her article. By calling Gately a gay rights champion and saying that he would want to set an example, she attempts to justify what she is saying as for the benefit of gay men, and also something that Gately too would agree with. The final sentence begins with the words 'For once again', as with the phrase 'another blow', there is the implication that Moir has identified a pattern – that Gately's case is not an isolated incident but a sign of something more endemic. The final sentence then uses a metaphorical comparison which is similar to the sugar-coating metaphor referred to earlier. Here, Moir likens Gately's lifestyle to some sort of shelled animal (a carapace). The carapace is described as 'glittering', while inside there is 'the ooze' which 'has seeped out'. Gately's lifestyle is thus ultimately evaluated as 'different and more dangerous'. However, the word *lifestyle* itself is ambiguous. Is Moir referring to a celebrity lifestyle or a gay lifestyle or both? This is unclear, making it difficult to level a direct criticism of homophobia at Moir here.[3] One interpretation is linked to the fact that Moir mentions that Gately is a *gay rights champion.* Why would she do this if being gay was not somehow relevant to her point about dangerous lifestyles? However, it could also be interpreted that her reference of Gately as a gay rights champion is merely to demonstrate that he was a caring person.

Indeed, throughout the article, Moir is careful to avoid making explicit statements about her views on homosexuality, although the article contains numerous implicatures and statements that have multiple readings and could therefore either be read as homophobic, not homophobic or both.

Taking context into account

The linguistic analysis provides a number of clues about Jan Moir's stance towards Gately and homosexuality more widely. The fact that the analysis has highlighted a number of ambiguous statements makes it difficult to attribute a single reading to it. Here, I would argue that a consideration of wider context is necessary in order to make sense of why the article is ambiguous and why it could be interpreted in a range of different ways.

Obtaining background information:
The social and historical context

As this article is about a gay man, and it received complaints relating to the representation of his sexuality, it is worth considering the social and historical context that the article was written in, particularly in relationship to homosexuality in the United Kingdom. Researching context in this way can be a difficult and open-ended process as there are often numerous sources of information that can be taken into account. For example, how far back in time should we go when looking at laws or attitudes relating to homosexuality? For this study, I have only considered more recent context from the twentieth century.

In the United Kingdom, homosexual acts were decriminalized (for men over 21) in 1967. Before then, gay men could be imprisoned for homosexual acts and also experienced discrimination from doctors, religious groups and the general public (see Jivani 1997). In 1988, partially as a result of a moral panic related to AIDS, the Conservative government passed Section 28, a law which forbade the 'promotion of homosexuality' by Local Education Authorities, making it difficult for the subject to be discussed in schools.

In 2000, the age of consent for gay men was equalized to 16, in line with heterosexuals and lesbians. Gay men and women have also been able to serve in the army since then. Scotland repealed Section 28 in 2000, while it was repealed in the rest of the United Kingdom in 2003. In 2005, same-sex couples were allowed to form 'civil partnerships', which meant that their relationships were legally recognized by the state and they could inherit from each other. This was not viewed as the same as 'marriage', however. The changes to the law since 2000 had been made by a Labour government, and in some quarters faced opposition. For example, the equalization of the age of consent was rejected by the government's upper chamber, the House of Lords, three times.

In terms of societal attitudes, reports from the annual British Attitudes Survey suggest a softening stance towards homosexuality in recent decades (Figure 2.1).

The relevant points about social and historical context are therefore: the United Kingdom has recently experienced a period of attitudinal change in terms of softening

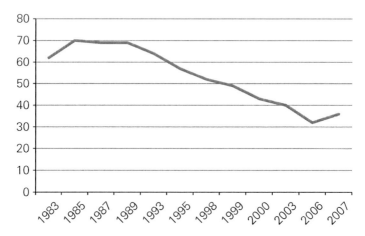

FIGURE 2.1 *Percentage of people responding that homosexuality was always or mostly wrong in the British Attitudes Surveys.*[4]

attitudes and legal change with regard to a liberalization of laws regarding homosexuality, which were enacted under Labour governments. Since around 2000, the majority of British people appear to have been accepting of homosexuality. However, is this true for the *Daily Mail* and its readers? In the following section, we will consider the *Daily Mail*'s readership, political stance and its reputation with regard to representations of homosexuality more closely.

Dog-whistle politics? The Daily Mail

The *Daily Mail* is the second most popular British newspaper (after *The Sun*), with a circulation of over 2 million and a readership of 4.6 million. It is popular with older readers, with 60.79 per cent of its readers being aged over 55.[5] Since at least 1945, the *Daily Mail* has always supported the Conservative Party in election campaigns (apart from the 1974 October election, when it supported a Liberal and Conservative coalition).[6] It has never supported the Labour Party (who did the most to liberalize laws relating to homosexuality) in this period and could therefore be viewed as a traditionally conservative newspaper, with many of its readers growing up during the period when homosexuality was illegal.

What sort of track record does the *Daily Mail* have with regard to representations of homosexuality in recent years? I carried out an earlier, corpus-based analysis of the *Daily Mail*, looking at all of its articles which contained the words *gay(s)* and *homosexual(s)* in the period 2001–2 (Baker 2005). I identified a number of common representations or discourses of homosexuality during that period, including representations of homosexuality as connected to crime and violence, gay relationships as transient, gay people as promiscuous and gay people as politically militant. Moir's article could also be read as containing traces of these discourses, as shown in Table 2.1 below.

Table 2.1 Relating Moir's article to previously identified discourses surrounding homosexuality in the *Daily Mail*. Words in bold print are most indicative of linguistic traces of discourses

Previously identified discourse	Trace of discourse in Moir's article
Homosexuality as connected to crime and violence	The **sugar coating on this fatality** is so saccharine-thick that it **obscures whatever bitter truth** lies beneath.
Gay relationships as transient	Gately's death . . . strikes another blow to **the happy-ever-after myth of civil partnerships**
Gay people as promiscuous	the circumstances surrounding his death are **more than a little sleazy** It is not disrespectful to assume that **a game of canasta with 25-year-old Georgi Dochev was not what was on the cards**.
Gay people as politically militant	Gay activists are **always** calling for tolerance and understanding about same-sex relationships.

If we understand that Moir's article is one of hundreds in the *Daily Mail* over the years which have articulated such homophobic discourses, then this could partially help to resolve or explain the ambiguity in the article. Perhaps Moir does not need to explicitly articulate homophobic discourses, because regular *Daily Mail* readers have already been primed through their encounters with other articles to accurately decode the discourses within. The term 'dog whistle politics'[7] is perhaps salient here, where a phrase like 'more than a little sleazy' can be unpacked by readers to first imply 'these men were having sex together' or even 'that's what gay men do, they're all promiscuous'.

Explaining ambiguity: Considering conditions of production

Next I would like to consider how the British press is regulated. What was Moir allowed to write in her article, and what sort of articles about homosexuality have resulted in successful complaints being made? Internet searches on terms like *British press* and *regulation* bring up a link to the website of the Press Complaints Commission, which describes itself as 'an independent body which administers the system of self-regulation for the press'. Within the Editor's Code of Practice on the PCC's website are the following sections, which were cited in a complaint to the PCC by Gately's civil partner:

1 Accuracy

i) The Press must take care not to publish inaccurate, misleading or distorted information, including pictures.

ii) A significant inaccuracy, misleading statement or distortion once recognized must be corrected, promptly and with due prominence, and – where appropriate – an apology published. In cases involving the Commission, prominence should be agreed with the PCC in advance.

iii) The Press, while free to be partisan, must distinguish clearly between comment, conjecture and fact.

5 Intrusion into grief or shock

i) In cases involving personal grief or shock, enquiries and approaches must be made with sympathy and discretion and publication handled sensitively. This should not restrict the right to report legal proceedings, such as inquests.

12 Discrimination

i) The press must avoid prejudicial or pejorative reference to an individual's race, colour, religion, gender, sexual orientation or to any physical or mental illness or disability.

ii) Details of an individual's race, colour, religion, sexual orientation, physical or mental illness or disability must be avoided unless genuinely relevant to the story.

It is possible to query the PCC's website using search terms, in order to find cases where people have complained about particular types of articles. For example, searches of the terms *gay* and *homosexual* found ten unique complaints, which were made about issues of accuracy. For example:

> Nico Juetten, Policy & Information Officer for Lesbian, Gay, Bisexual, Transgender Youth Scotland, complained that an article misleadingly gave the impression that its website targeted 13-year-olds with advice on sex. The complainant said the group worked to improve the emotional, mental, physical and sexual well-being of LGBT young people and the article's claim that it "promote[d] illegal sex" was incorrect.[8]

In cases like this, the newspaper was required to issue a retraction. Where newspapers can be shown to have made a factually incorrect statement, then they generally appear to correct the error when it is pointed out. As noted above, a complaint by Stephen Gately's civil partner, Andrew Cowles was made to the PCC about Jan Moir's article. In this case, the complaint was not upheld, although the PCC provided a 3588-word ruling to explain their decision (which was much longer than other rulings I examined at their website). I include what is (to me) the most relevant part of the ruling:

> Freedom of expression is a fundamental part of an open and democratic society. This is enshrined in the Code of Practice which states that there is a "public interest in the freedom of expression itself". Individuals have the right to express honestly-held opinions, and newspapers have the right to publish them, provided the terms of the Code are not otherwise breached.[9]

Thus, because Moir's column contained opinions, rather than statements of fact, its capacity to offend or promote prejudice was not considered to be enough for the complaint to be upheld. Taking further context into account, it is worth noting that other researchers have been critical of the PCC for not upholding complaints about opinion columns in the British press which were accused of being Islamophobic. For example, Richardson (2004: 68) argues that 'It is clear that the PCC is not an adequate bulwark against Islamophobia in the media', while Petley (2006: 61) concludes that 'the PCC is quite hopeless as a bulwark against negative representations of Muslims and Islam in the press. Since it is paid for by newspapers and its Code Committee is stuffed with editors, some of whose papers are front runners in the Islamophobia stakes, I find it extremely difficult not to regard it as part of the problem rather than part of the solution'.

An understanding then, of how the PCC operates, is crucial in interpreting Moir's stance. Moir acted within the PCC's code by expressing opinions and making use of implicatures. She would have found it difficult to make a fact-based claim like 'all gay men are promiscuous' because this could have been more easily challenged. Therefore, by considering the restrictions placed on Moir by the PCC, we have one (possible) explanation for why her article contains so few factual statements, and why she was not required to retract it.

Identifying discourse prosodies: Using a corpus of native English

A third type of context helps us to carry out a more confident interpretation of some of the words and phrases in Moir's article. Earlier I had argued that the phrase 'gay activists are always calling for tolerance and understanding' suggests that Moir thinks they do this too much due to the non-literal use of *always*. Here it is useful to consider another type of analysis, based on looking at the ways that native speakers of English normally use phrases like '[HUMANS] are always [-*ing* form of verb]'. Here, the term [HUMANS] is used to mean any word or phrase which refers to one or more human beings. What sort of contexts does such a grammatical structure tend to be used in, and are the subjects evaluated positively or negatively? This analysis thus involves an examination of discourse prosody, described by (Stubbs 2001: 65), as 'a feature which extends over more than one unit in a linear string'.

To answer this question, I consulted the British National Corpus, a 100 million word corpus consisting of 90 per cent written and 10 per cent spoken naturally occurring British English.[10] The corpus has been part-of-speech tagged so it is possible to search within it for sequences of words, grammatical parts of speech and/or both. I used the search term 'are always *_VVG' which gave me 178 concordance lines of the words 'are always' followed by an -*ing* form of a verb. I then analysed these concordance lines to see what sort of contexts this phrase occurs in.

The analysis of concordance lines suggests that authors often have a negative stance towards the subject of the sentence (60 out of 178 lines involved cases of verbs or verb phrases like *complaining*, *fighting*, *gambling*, *grumbling*, *lurking*, *moaning*, *niggling*, *quibbling* and *threatening*. It seems that one common construction of [HUMANS] are always [*ing] involves them being represented as complaining about something.

> Friends are always saying how frustrated I must feel, how unfulfilled, never to have played for England. Curiously they are mistaken.
>
> People are always complaining that they do not have enough work space/dumping space, but it may well be what they really need is better organized storage.
>
> 'Friends are always telling me to put my prices up, but I enjoy painting people, like bishops, who couldn't necessarily afford very much more,' he said.
>
> Girls are always trying to make you feel sorry for them, but they can't fool me.
>
> 'Because hasn't history proved that the English are always trying to do the Irish down?' 'No, it doesn't; don't be absurd.'

FIGURE 2.2 *Sample of cases of* are always [*ing] *in the BNC.*

Another point of note is that 25 of the concordance lines had a longer pattern whereby someone was represented as always doing or saying something, then this was followed by a statement, sometimes using the co-ordinator *but* to disagree with that statement. Five such cases are shown in Figure 2.2 below.

It would appear then that a reasonably common discourse prosody around phrases like 'people are always *ing' is that such people are mistaken. Hoey's (2005) theory of lexical priming theorizes that words are stored in people's minds along with their collocational and colligational properties, based upon our previous encounters of such words. So when native English speakers encounter a phrase like 'gay activists are always . . .' they will be primed to expect the gay activists to be described as doing something rather annoying which will be evaluated as incorrect, due to their expectations about earlier experiences of similar phrases.

Although there is not the space here, a similar form of analysis could be carried out on other words and phrases in Moir's article, such as her use of the word *insisting* in the following sentence: *Nevertheless, his mother is still insisting that her son died from a previously undetected heart condition that has plagued the family.*

Intertextuality: Looking at audience reception

It has already been noted that the article received over 25,000 complaints. In this section, I consider some of the secondary sources of data gathered from a range of internet sources, to examine possible interpretations of the article. An analysis of this type of context is useful in that it provides a range of different perspectives (which in itself can aid the original linguistic analysis[11]) but also can indicate typical and minority interpretations.

First, it is worth bearing in mind that the notion of 'audience' had changed only recently in the United Kingdom, as a result of newspapers publishing online versions of their papers, and the rise of social networking tools like Twitter and Facebook, which were relatively recent phenomena. Such tools made it easy for information to be shared among large numbers of people, as well as enabling people to find out how to complain about articles (which could also be done online via the PCC's website). While the British press have written explicitly homophobic articles in the past (see Sanderson 1995), Moir's article was one of the first to be widely circulated via social networks and scrutinized by a large numbers of people, many who will not have been traditional *Daily Mail* readers.

In order to get a better idea of how the article was received, I first examined the reader comments which appeared at the end of the original *Mail Online* article. With over 1,600 comments, this constitutes a remarkable source of reception data. It is possible for anyone who reads the page to rate comments by clicking on a green upward pointing arrow or a red downward arrow. If a comment already has a score of 60 green (positive) ratings, and I click the red arrow, it will be adjusted to show 59 positive ratings. Comments can also be displayed in terms of Best (most positive ratings from readers) and Worst (most negative ratings) Rated, for example,

Best Rated (5616 green ratings)
    What a horrible piece on the late Stephen Gately, a) the coroner stated he died of natural causes, b) he was chosen by Andrew Lloyd Webber to play Joseph therefore he must have been able to "carry a tune in a Louis Vuitton trunk"! Shame on this journalist who wrote the article and those who agree with her are just as bad. RIP Stephen.

Worst Rated (6811 red negative ratings)
Well said Jan. Couldn't agree more

In line with the 25,000 complaints, the ratings of comments indicates that a majority of people who visited the web page did not agree with Moir's position, although it is notable that the best-rated comment does not explicitly take issue with perceived homophobia but instead is critical of Moir's representation of Gately as a poor singer and the insinuation regarding the circumstances of his death.

Other than merely agreeing with Moir, what other 'minority' perspectives existed? A link to a blog entitled FleetStreetBlues[12] contains a post called 'In defence of Jan Moir and the Daily Mail'. In this article, the blogger argues that Moir is 'very good at what she does' and goes on to say that 'The point is that the *Daily Mail* connects with millions of ordinary people, and it does that by reflecting their views, telling them what they want to hear about and yes, playing on their prejudices'. The article therefore does not openly agree with a homophobic position, but argues that Moir reflects the *Daily Mail*'s readership. It is worth noting that in Figure 2.1, about 1 in 3 people in the United Kingdom viewed homosexuality as wrong or mostly wrong in the late 2000s, so even despite the softening of laws and attitudes, there still appears to be a reasonably large set of people who hold less liberal views on the subject. The fact that these people have shifted from being a majority to a minority group suggests one reason why their views do not tend to be *publicly* represented in the United Kingdom very much.

It is worth considering two further articles in the *Daily Mail*, both which were written during the following week, and refer to Moir's article. The first is by Moir herself, entitled 'The truth about my views on the tragic death of Stephen Gately'.[13] In this article, Moir addresses the criticisms made to her, writing:

> To my horror [my column] has been widely condemned as "homophobic" and "hateful." Obviously, a great deal of offence has been taken and I regret any affront caused. This was never my intention. . . . To [those close to Gately], I would like to say sorry if I have caused distress by the insensitive timing of the column, published so close to the funeral.

The apology's wording here is worth a closer look. The phrases 'I regret *any* affront caused' and 'I would like to say sorry *if* I caused distress' indicate hedging which could diminish the apology's impact. Moir could have written 'I regret *the* affront I caused . . .I am sorry *that* I caused distress'. She also writes that she regrets 'any affront caused' rather than regretting that she wrote the article.

Later in the article, Moir argues that the '"happy ever after myth surrounding" [same-sex] unions was that they can be just as problematic as heterosexual marriages. Indeed, I would stress that there was nothing in my article that could not be applied to a heterosexual couple as well as to a homosexual one'. She asserts that her criticism is of a 'louche' lifestyle rather than a gay lifestyle. Moir therefore attempts to resolve the ambiguity in her original column by claiming that the article should not have been read as homophobic.

However, the best-rated comment on this article is 'Call that an APOLOGY???' with 899 green upward ticks, suggesting that Moir's apology was not widely accepted.

The second article I wish to consider is one written in the *Daily Mail* by another female columnist, Janet Street-Porter. Porter's article is entitled 'Being gay killed a man last week – but he wasn't Stephen Gately'. Street-Porter refers to the death of a civil servant, Ian Baynham, who was kicked to death in Trafalgar Square after his assailants shouted homophobic abuse at him. Porter also writes that she was astonished by Moir's article:

> What exactly was bothering Jan? The fact Stephen was gay, the fact he was in a civil partnership, or the fact that he or his partner might have enjoyed sex with someone they had just met? . . . If Stephen and his partner went to a nightclub and returned to their flat with another man, is it really any of our business?

This article suggests that within the *Daily Mail* itself, there is a range of dissenting opinion. While the *Daily Mail* has been viewed to be homophobic in other contexts, at the time that Moir's article was published, there was at least one *Mail* columnist who was critical of her. However, the 'best rated' comment of this article implied that Street-Porter was an exception: 'Such a sensible, reasonable column seems strangely out of place in this paper. – Di, UK, 19/10/2009 09:03 I'll second that!' with 498 green upward arrows. This comment seems to suggest that Street-Porter's article was not widely taken to be typical of the *Daily Mail*'s usual stance (and it raises questions about why it appeared in the newspaper at all and at that point in time).

A final intertextual reference to the article comes from Paul Dacre, the editor of the *Daily Mail* who gave evidence to the Leveson Inquiry of 2011–12, a public inquiry into the culture, practices and ethics of the British press following a scandal involving journalists hacking into people's mobile phones. Dacre was asked about Moir's article and responded that

> My view was that perhaps when the furore – perhaps the timing was a little regrettable. I think the piece –the column could have benefited from a little judicious subediting. But I – you know, I'd die in a ditch to defend a columnist to have her views, and I can tell this Inquiry there isn't a homophobic bone in Jan Moir's body. . . . You keep using the phrase 'a lot of people' complained about this. You realise that these are all online complaints and this is an example of how tweetering can create a firestorm within hours. A well-known celebrity, who admitted he hadn't read the article, said it was unpleasant. It was then tweeted to other people who retweeted and we had a viral storm. Most of those people conceded they hadn't read the piece. That's where the 25,000 complaints came from to the PCC. . . .[14]

Dacre's commentary on the article is also ambiguous – he is not clear what the 'little judicious subediting' should have been and later claims that he did not personally approve the article because he was at the opera with his wife that evening. However, he also defends the article and Moir, and seems dismissive of the complaints because they are 'all online complaints' and 'Most of those people conceded they hadn't read the piece'. It is not clear how Dacre has acquired evidence of that though.

Conclusion

It is not the intention of this chapter to conclude with a definite answer with regard to whether Jan Moir's article was homophobic. Instead, I have aimed to show that a linguistic analysis uncovered evidence for multiple interpretations of the article, and that an analysis of context indicated that the article was interpreted as homophobic by large numbers of people. It is true that people disagreed on how the article should be interpreted and it remains unclear whether Moir intended the article to be read as a criticism of gay people or of a decadent 'celebrity lifestyle' or both. It is worth noting that the PCC would have been unlikely to condone an article that was openly critical of gay people, although this in itself should not be seen as 'proof' that Moir was writing what she felt she could get away with. The analysis of Moir's language also indicates that certain wordings draw on rather negative discourse prosodies, yet again, this does not prove Moir intended her article to be read as homophobic. Nor does the fact that the *Daily Mail's* general stance on homosexuality has been negative in the past, although other analysts may feel there is enough 'circumstantial evidence' to draw a stronger conclusion, perhaps referring to Mellinkoff's notion of 'calculated ambiguity' (1963: 450) as one interpretation of the multiple readings of the article (e.g. Moir intended to be homophobic but wanted to protect herself from criticism).

The consideration of these different types of context helps to explain why many people did feel that Moir was being as homophobic as the PCC would allow her to be. I would suggest that if Moir had not intended to be homophobic, then she was naïve not to have considered the ambiguities in her original article, and that her subsequent apology could have been better worded. The analysis of context from a legal and societal attitude perspective suggests that the United Kingdom is going through a period of relatively rapid social change, and that discourses surrounding homosexuality are therefore in flux. From an FPDA perspective of fluctuating power, Moir's (perceived) disempowering discourse of homosexuality ultimately resulted in her being disempowered herself (she later claimed to have received death threats[15]), and even the power of the PCC appears to have been compromised by subsequent criticisms of its decision.

It certainly seems to be the case that Moir and the newspaper underestimated the enormous backlash that the article caused, along with the power of newer forms of social media to mobilize large numbers of complaints. While the *Daily Mail's* traditional readership (who buy the print version of the newspaper) tends to be older, more conservative members of the United Kingdom, people who were directed to the article online are likely to have been from a wider or different demographic spread. So not only are attitudes to homosexuality changing quickly, but also people's practices in relation to new media are developing. The large number of disapproving responses to Moir's article throws these issues sharply into focus, further complicating power relationships between the media, its regulators and audiences.

A final type of context needs to be addressed – the researcher himself, and this may help to explain why I have reached such a cautious conclusion. As a gay man who is politically liberal (thus oppositional to the *Mail's* political stance), and has in the past studied the *Mail's* representation of gay people, by the time I approached this article, I was aware of the potential danger of someone who has a 'vested interest' drawing a conclusion which could be attributed to their own identity or political stance. The fact that I have tried to incorporate a post-structuralist approach to analysis has also made me more careful about privileging a single viewpoint. Instead, I have presented a range of different sorts of evidence from my own analysis of the article, as well as indicating how others interpreted the article. I am also aware that such a conclusion may be problematic to readers who may be concerned that homophobic media discourse has become more subtle and thus difficult to challenge. Despite this, my analysis demonstrates that the article was still interpreted as disempowering to gay people and the reaction to it was unprecedented. It remains to be seen how newspapers will adapt to the changing context in which they publish.

Appendix

A strange, lonely and troubling death . . . (formerly: Why there was nothing "natural" about Stephen Gately's death') (Jan Moir, *Daily Mail*, 16 October 2009)

The news of Stephen Gately's death was deeply shocking. It was not just that another young star had died pointlessly.

Through the recent travails and sad ends of Michael Jackson, Heath Ledger and many others, fans know to expect the unexpected of their heroes – particularly if those idols live a life that is shadowed by dark appetites or fractured by private vice.

There are dozens of household names out there with secret and not-so-secret troubles, or damaging habits both past and present.

Robbie, Amy, Kate, Whitney, Britney; we all know who they are. And we are not being ghoulish to anticipate, or to be mentally braced for, their bad end: a long night, a mysterious stranger, an odd set of circumstances that herald a sudden death.

In the morning, a body has already turned cold before the first concerned hand reaches out to touch an icy celebrity shoulder. It is not exactly a new storyline, is it?

In fact, it is rather depressingly familiar. But somehow we never expected it of him. Never him. Not Stephen Gately.

In the cheerful environs of Boyzone, Gately was always charming, cute, polite and funny.

A founder member of Ireland's first boy band, he was the group's co-lead singer, even though he could barely carry a tune in a Louis Vuitton trunk.

He was the Posh Spice of Boyzone, a popular but largely decorous addition.

Gately came out as gay in 1999 after discovering that someone was planning to sell a story revealing his sexuality to a newspaper.

Although he was effectively smoked out of the closet, he has been hailed as a champion of gay rights, albeit a reluctant one.

At the time, Gately worried that the revelations might end his ultra-mainstream career as a pin-up, but he received an overwhelmingly positive response from fans. In fact, it only made them love him more.

In 2006, Gately entered into a civil union with internet businessman Andrew Cowles, who had been introduced to him by mutual friends Elton John and David Furnish.

Last week, the couple were enjoying a holiday together in their apartment in Mallorca before their world was capsized.

All the official reports point to a natural death, with no suspicious circumstances. The Gately family are – perhaps understandably – keen to register their boy's demise on the national consciousness as nothing more than a tragic accident.

Even before the post-mortem and toxicology reports were released by the Spanish authorities, the Gatelys' lawyer reiterated that they believed his sudden death was due to natural causes.

But, hang on a minute. Something is terribly wrong with the way this incident has been shaped and spun into nothing more than an unfortunate mishap on a holiday weekend, like a broken teacup in the rented cottage.

Consider the way it has been largely reported, as if Gately had gently keeled over at the age of 90 in the grounds of the Bide-a-Wee rest home while hoeing the sweet pea patch.

The sugar coating on this fatality is so saccharine-thick that it obscures whatever bitter truth lies beneath. Healthy and fit 33-year-old men do not just climb into their pyjamas and go to sleep on the sofa, never to wake up again.

Whatever the cause of death is, it is not, by any yardstick, a natural one. Let us be absolutely clear about this. All that has been established so far is that Stephen Gately was not murdered.

And I think if we are going to be honest, we would have to admit that the circumstances surrounding his death are more than a little sleazy.

After a night of clubbing, Cowles and Gately took a young Bulgarian man back to their apartment. It is not disrespectful to assume that a game of canasta with 25-year-old Georgi Dochev was not what was on the cards.

Cowles and Dochev went to the bedroom together while Stephen remained alone in the living room.

What happened before they parted is known only to the two men still alive. What happened afterwards is anyone's guess.

A post-mortem revealed Stephen died from acute pulmonary oedema, a build-up of fluid on his lungs.

Gately's family have always maintained that drugs were not involved in the singer's death, but it has just been revealed that he at least smoked cannabis on the night he died.

Nevertheless, his mother is still insisting that her son died from a previously undetected heart condition that has plagued the family.

Another real sadness about Gately's death is that it strikes another blow to the happy-ever-after myth of civil partnerships.

Gay activists are always calling for tolerance and understanding about same-sex relationships, arguing that they are just the same as heterosexual marriages. Not everyone, they say, is like George Michael.

Of course, in many cases this may be true. Yet the recent death of Kevin McGee, the former husband of Little Britain star Matt Lucas, and now the dubious events of Gately's last night raise troubling questions about what happened.

It is important that the truth comes out about the exact circumstances of his strange and lonely death.

As a gay rights champion, I am sure he would want to set an example to any impressionable young men who may want to emulate what they might see as his glamorous routine.

For once again, under the carapace of glittering, hedonistic celebrity, the ooze of a very different and more dangerous lifestyle has seeped out for all to see.

Notes

1 http://news.bbc.co.uk/1/hi/uk/8311499.stm.

2 http://www.dailymail.co.uk/debate/article-1220756/A-strange-lonely-troubling-death–.html.

3 As an additional point, it is worth noting that Moir's article begins with a 'roll call' of troubled celebrities including Michael Jackson, Heath Ledger, Amy [Winehouse] and Whitney [Houston]. This could be interpreted as framing the article as being about celebrities who have 'decadent' lifestyles rather than the article as being about any perceived dangers of gay people.

4 Data from https://docs.google.com/spreadsheet/ccc?key=0AonYZs4MzlZbdHBvT19 WUWlyT3BWUElIOWE5cjdDLVE#gid=0

5 Readership and demographic stats are from http://www.mailclassified.co.uk/ circulation-readership/circulation-readership. These figures are for the paper version of the periodical.

6 http://www.guardian.co.uk/news/datablog/2010/may/04/general-election-newspaper-support

7 The term *dog-whistle politics* originated in Australia in the 1990s and refers to the act of using coded language that will have a specific meaning to a particular part of an audience, similar to the way that only dogs can hear high-frequency whistles.

8 http://www.pcc.org.uk/news/index.html?article=NDUyMw==

9 http://www.pcc.org.uk/news/index.html?article=NjIyOA==

10 I used a web-based facility called BNCweb http://bncweb.lancs.ac.uk/

11 For example, in my initial analysis of the article, I did not interpret Moir's reference to the Louis Vuitton trunk as being a possible construction of Gately as feminine, although upon reading other articles about Moir's article, I noticed that this was one interpretation that had been mentioned by others.

12 http://fleetstreetblues.blogspot.com/2009/10/in-defence-of-jan-moir-and-daily-mail_17.html.

13 http://www.dailymail.co.uk/debate/article-1222246/The-truth-views-tragic-death-Stephen-Gately.html.

14 http://www.levesoninquiry.org.uk/wp-content/uploads/2012/02/Transcript-of-Afternoon-Hearing-6-February-2012.txt

15 http://www.dailymail.co.uk/femail/article-2099110/A-girl-bullied-raped-cowardice-cyber-trolls.html#ixzz1lztRvnXB.

References

Baker, P. (2005), *Public Discourses of Gay Men*. London: Routledge.

Baxter, J. (2003), *Positioning Gender in Discourse: A Feminist Methodology*. Basingstoke: Palgrave Macmillan.

Fairclough, N. (1989), *Language and Power*. London: Longman.

—(1995), *Critical Discourse Analysis: The Critical Study of Language*. London: Longman.

Hall, S. (1980), 'Encoding/decoding,' in D. Hobson, A. Lowe and P. Willis (eds), *Culture, Media, Language*. Hutchinson: London, pp. 123–38.

Hoey, M. (2005), *Lexical Priming. A New Theory of Words and Language*. London: Routledge.

Jivani, A. (1997), *It's Not Unusual: A History of Lesbian and Gay Britain in the Twentieth Century*. London: Michael O'Mara Books Ltd.

Mellinkoff, D. (1963), *The Language of the Law*. Boston/Toronto: Little Brown and Company.

Petley, J. (2006), 'Still no redress from the PCC,' in E. Poole and J. E. Richardson (eds), *Muslims and the News Media*. London: I. B. Tauris, pp. 53–62.

Reisigl, M. and Wodak, R. (2001), *Discourse and Discrimination: Rhetorics of Racism and Antisemitism*. London: Routledge.

Richardson, R. (ed.) (2004), *Islamophobia: Issues, Challenges and Action. A Report by the Commission on British Muslims and Islamophobia*. Stoke on Trent: Trentham Books.

Sanderson, T. (1995), *Mediawatch: The Treatment of Male and Female Homosexuality in the British Media*. London: Cassell.

Stubbs, M. (2001), *Words and Phrases: Corpus Studies of Lexical Semantics*. London: Blackwell.

3

'Who are you and why are you following us?' Wh-questions and communicative context in television dialogue[1]

Monika Bednarek

1 Introduction

And more than jazz or musical theater or morbid obesity, television is the true American art form. Think of all the shared experiences television has provided for us. From the moon landing to the Golden Girls finale. From Walter Cronkite denouncing Vietnam to Oprah pulling that trash bag of fat out in a wagon. From the glory and the pageantry of the Summer Olympics, to the less fun Winter Olympics!

(KENNETH in *30 Rock*)

Recent research clearly marks television series as an emerging area of interest in Linguistics (e.g. Richardson 2010a, b; Piazza et al. 2011; Androutsopoulos 2012). This is because television has much to tell us about language use in popular culture, which may shape our identities, societies and cultures in complex and dynamic ways and can impact significantly on attitudes, beliefs and discourse itself. But before we can start analysing its impact, we need a systematic description of such language use. This chapter is a contribution to such descriptions, offering an exploratory study of 27 contemporary US television series.

2 Goals

This study aims to explore the use of *wh*-questions in contemporary American English *television dialogue* – a term I use here as a shorthand to refer to dialogue in contemporary fictional TV series such as *The Wire*, *Glee* or *The Big Bang Theory*. Questions were chosen for this exploratory study because previous corpus linguistic research suggests that they are more frequent in television dialogue than in unscripted conversation and fulfil important functions (Bednarek 2012a). More specifically, the study aims to identify and analyse the following:

- the frequency of different types of *wh*-questions;
- the distribution and extent of variation in *wh*-question usage;
- the most frequent bigrams and trigrams (combinations of two/three words) involving *wh*-questions;
- the functions of these bigrams/trigrams.

The study also aims to relate these findings to the context of television series as a mass media product, with its specific relationship between text, producers and audience.

3 Approach

This study is informed by an approach to discourse analysis that uses corpora and computer software in the analysis of discourse (e.g. Baker 2006; Partington 2006, 2008; Morley and Bayley 2009). Different labels have been attached to such an approach, such as *corpus-informed discourse analysis*, *corpus-based discourse analysis or corpus-assisted discourse studies*, to name but a few. In this chapter, I use the term *corpus-assisted discourse studies* or *corpus-assisted discourse analysis* as a cover-all for studies that combine the techniques of corpus linguistics with the analysis of discourse in various ways. This includes studies that involve in-depth discourse analysis together with corpus linguistic analysis and those that use corpus techniques to study discourse phenomena or discourse types. I choose 'corpus-assisted' over 'corpus-based' because corpus linguists frequently classify 'corpus-based' research as *deductive*, contrasting it with more *inductive,* 'corpus-driven' research (e.g. Tognini-Bonelli 2001). In other words, using the term 'corpus-based discourse analysis' might lead some linguists to expect deductive research, whereas 'corpus-assisted' discourse analysis has no such associations. In this sense, then, this study is informed by corpus-assisted discourse analysis.

4 The communicative context

In this study, the notion of context, or, more precisely, *communicative context* is understood as the relation between a media text, its producer(s) and its audience(s) (see Bednarek 2010: 14–17; Bednarek and Caple 2012: 20). I use a relatively broad definition of each of these components. That is, when we discuss the communicative context, we ask questions such as:

- How was this text produced, by whom and with what purpose?
- Who does this text address? Who is its target audience?
- How does the text mediate between its producers and its audience?
- What is the relationship between texts and ideologies (of producer/audience/ industry cultures), commercial realities, generic conventions, industry/ professional conventions, practical/technical codes, etc.?

This includes conceptualizations of the relationship between texts and audiences in mediated discourse. Relevant research proposes the notion of a 'double articulation' (e.g. Lorenzo-Dus 2009: 161; citing Scannell 1991); in the context of TV series, this means that there is an interaction between the on-screen televisual characters on the one hand, and an interaction between the characters and the audience on the other. In Bubel's (2006, 2008) model for televisual and cinematic discourse – which draws on Goffmann's (1976, 1979) distinction of listener roles as well as previous research into mediated discourse – audiences act as overhearers and are therefore unratified conversational participants (Bubel 2008: 64).[2] Others have described the audience as ratified (Lorenzo-Dus 2009: 162). Most recently, Piazza (2011) distinguishes between three audience roles for film: overhearers, targeted overhearers and undisclosed intermediaries, depending on cognitive involvement and agency. There is, however, general agreement that the audience is intended to be there and that the dialogue is designed *for* the audience – what Bubel (2006, 2008) terms *overhearer design*.

In this chapter, I do not adopt the cognitive approach that Bubel and Piazza apply and am not concerned with audience agency. Rather, I use the notion of *overhearer design* as a shorthand to refer to the fact that 'the defining characteristics of film [and television, M.B] dialogue is that *it is never realistic; it is always designed "for us"'* (Kozloff 2000:121, italics in original). Televisual dialogue is thus designed to fulfil potential functions for its audience of overhearers, although, paradoxically, the creation of 'authentic' or 'realistic' dialogue may be precisely one of these functions (Quaglio 2009: 120; Bednarek 2012a: 43).

This *overhearer design* means that the communicative context of televisual dialogue is distinctive from most other kinds of data that this edited volume tackles. What is special about American television dialogue as compared to other mediated discourse is that the kind of language that we are exposed to via US TV series reaches billions of viewers worldwide, creates global online fan communities and is heavily marketed through associated merchandise which puts the TV dialogue on public display (e.g. *The Big Bang Theory* T-shirts with quotes from the sitcom). In terms of audience reach and engagement, TV dialogue is rivalled by few other contemporary media. Many of its viewers speak English as a second language or use a different national variety of English, and are potentially influenced by what they hear on screen. Despite this, we know surprisingly little about language use in American television series. This is a significant problem, since we clearly need such knowledge for any serious academic and public debate on language use and global popular culture. Indeed, linguists are beginning to argue that 'we . . . need much more analysis of the structural characteristics of media representation of language, of different genres, formats' (Stuart-Smith 2011: 235).

In summary, a broad notion of communicative context is applied in this chapter, which includes considerations of the process of production, audiences, generic and other conventions, ideologies, commercial realities and dialogue functions. Because of the nature of my approach in this chapter, I will draw on only some of these notions when discussing my findings for TV dialogue (in § 8). I will limit this exploration to only one aspect: the use of questions.

5 Questions

Questions have attracted a vast number of researchers, mainly investigating unscripted language. I draw here primarily on Bubel's (2006: 182ff) in-depth overview of relevant research, unless otherwise indicated.

Syntactically, questions can be divided into *yes/no* interrogatives, *either-or* interrogatives, *wh*-interrogatives, tag questions and declaratives with rising intonation (Freed 1994; cited in Holmes and Chiles 2010). These can be used to elicit information, establish the truth of a proposition or the relevance of an alternative. However, there is no one-to-one relationship between form and function. For example, pragmatically questions can be used for very different speech acts such as requests, invitations and offers. Structurally, most questions form sequences and require a response, and if this is not supplied, there are consequences for conversational participants. Questions are also concerned with the negotiation of interpersonal relationships: They can indicate both power and powerlessness (depending on the context and question type; see, e.g., Wang 2006; Ehrlich and Freed 2010: 7–8), and can convey both connectedness, familiarity and separatedness, intrusion, pushiness. They can be used phatically to maintain interaction and soften disagreement; they can convey interest, involvement and support, or impatience, challenges and criticism. In sum, questions are crucial for maintaining interaction and can be associated with positive and negative aspects of interpersonal relationships. They are highly complex and multifunctional.

In the context of television dialogue, questions have been grouped alongside other features as marking 'involved' interactive texts in an analysis of *Friends* (Quaglio 2009: 61), and researchers have noted that in *Sex and the City* (Bubel 2006) and *Gilmore Girls* (Bednarek 2010) questions can be concerned with the construal of affective relationships such as friendship, hostility and conflict as well as with the expression of character emotions. The focus on questions in this chapter also arose inductively (in a 'corpus-driven' way) from an earlier study of TV dialogue (Bednarek 2012a). In this study, I found a range of words (e.g. *why*) and word combinations (e.g. *why are you*), which seemed to be associated with questions, and which were statistically speaking more frequent in TV dialogue when compared to unscripted spoken American English. The data also suggested that questions in TV dialogue can express character emotion, evaluation, confusion and conflict between characters as well as more neutral inquiries, invitations/suggestions. However, the focus of this previous study was on a range of linguistic phenomena that distinguish TV dialogue from unscripted spoken American English, meaning that questions could not be explored in depth. Further, the corpus used was limited in terms of representativeness, as it included only seven series. This chapter is a first attempt to address this issue, investigating questions in contemporary television series with the help of a more representative corpus.

6 Data

In order to compile a more representative corpus, the aim was to include dialogue from as many different contemporary television series as possible. In theory, there are various sources and methods that could be used to build such a corpus: (1) automatic extraction of subtitles, (2) collection of scripts that are available online, (3) transcription from scratch and (4) collection of online fan transcripts.

Concerning the first option, while the automatic extraction of subtitles would probably be the fastest solution, the resulting corpus might not include the names of speakers accurately (so that they might need to be checked/specified individually) and there could be a significant amount of differences between the dialogue in the subtitles and what characters actually utter on screen. In a previous comparison of a randomly selected 2.24 minute scene from *Gilmore Girls* (Bednarek 2010: 237), I found that there was a much greater number of and more significant differences in the subtitles than in fan transcripts (five times as many). In essence, the extent to which subtitles represent the dialogue uttered on screen needs to be determined for each TV series and depends on factors such as the amount of dialogue, the speed with which it is uttered and specific subtitling strategies that were adopted (e.g. standardization of dialect features). Extraction of subtitles is therefore not necessarily the best choice for data collection.

If we consider the second option, to collect scripts that are available online, this seems at first glance a better choice. Websites such as www.simplyscripts.com provide links to what appear to be official scripts of episodes for selected television series. However, there are two issues with such data. First, scripts are often only available as PDF documents (Figure 3.1).

While these can be automatically converted into files that are compatible with corpus software (here: Wordsmith, Scott 2011), such conversion is not without errors

```
INT. H&H BAGELS, NEW YORK - MOMENTS LATER

Lisa waits in a long line leading to two registers.

A GUY on a cell phone enters.  He ignores the line and
goes up to the other register.

                        LISA
          Whoa, whoa.  Excuse me.  There's a line,
          buddy.
```

FIGURE 3.1 *Script example from* 30 Rock.

and each file would have to be manually checked against the original PDF. Secondly, and most problematically, when I checked the dialogue in two collected scripts against the actual dialogue spoken by characters in the relevant episode, I found vast differences, with some script dialogue not included or phrased differently. This means that each script would have to be checked against the spoken dialogue, a very time-consuming exercise. The same applies to option 3, manual transcription from scratch. However, this would be the most accurate and transcription conventions could be applied consistently. The final option lies in the collection of fan transcripts that are already available online. These are transcripts of television episodes that are undertaken by fans, as a hobby, and are available on various websites, sometimes dedicated to a particular television series. For example, 'Ash' below administers a website (at http:// bigbangtrans.wordpress.com) featuring his transcripts for the sitcom *The Big Bang Theory*, explaining his site as follows:

> This is Ash here, and I administer this web page and also write the transcripts. . . . See, this isn't my full time job (no, duh!) It's a hobby, or labour of love, call it what you will. . . . Anyway, for a living, I am actually a performer. (Actor, comedian, writer). (http://bigbangtrans.wordpress.com/about/, accessed 19 July 2012)

This option is attractive, because these transcripts are easily accessible (usually available in html or similar formats) and reasonably accurate. For example, for a previous study (Bednarek 2012b) I checked the first scene of 17 episodes of *The Big Bang Theory* for accuracy against Ash's transcripts. The transcripts for these scenes were 99.5 per cent accurate; errors recurring most frequently concerned standardization for *wanna*, *gonna*, *gotta*, which were sometimes transcribed as *want to*, *going to* and *got to*. Such fan transcripts have also been used in previous corpus linguistic studies such as those by Quaglio (2008, 2009). Quaglio notes that the fan transcripts for *Friends* that he uses are 'fairly accurate and very detailed, including several features that scripts are not likely to present: hesitators, pauses, repeats, and contractions' (Quaglio 2008: 191–2). This was therefore the first choice for collecting data for this study. Each collected file was turned into plain text format and comprises the complete dialogue for one episode of one TV series. However, because fan transcripts are not available for all television series, additional dialogue was transcribed (orthographically) from scratch for 13 other TV series while watching the relevant episode.[3] All transcripts include only speaker names and dialogue, as illustrated in the following extract:

> Penny: Hey, guys, guys, some of the other waitresses wanted me to ask you something.
> Leonard: Oh, it's called trestling.
> Howard: It combines the physical strength of arm wrestling with the mental agility of tetris into the ultimate sport.
> Penny: Yeah, that's terrific, but what they wanted me to ask you was to cut it the hell out.
>
> (*The Big Bang Theory*, season 1, episode 16)

Finally, all files were converted into Wordsmith-compatible encoding using Wordsmiths' inbuilt Text Converter utility.

Concerning the corpus design, the corpus includes dialogue from 27 different contemporary (year of first broadcast: 2000–10) US American fictional television series. The chosen series span a variety of genres as recognized in the mainstream (represented by the Internet Movie Database at www.imdb.com). The overall aim was to include television series from the basic genres of action, adventure, comedy, crime and drama.

In order to avoid an influence of the season on the dialogue, dialogue was only collected from the first season of each series, with dialogue from episodes at the beginning, middle and end. The dialogue in the corpus thus varies in terms of 'where' in the season it was collected to ensure representation across the season, rather than over-representation of particular kinds of episodes such as pilots or season finales. Note also that the length of a season may vary – for example, the first season of *My Name is Earl* comprises 24 episodes, while the first season of *The Wire* comprises only 13 episodes. TV series also differ in the extent to which there is a developing narrative across episodes– the difference between seri*es* and seri*als*, explained for example in Bednarek (2010: 12), although in this chapter I use *TV series* as a label for both.

Table 3.1 shows the final corpus design, including the two main genres listed for each television series in the Internet Movie Database (many series are hybrids, i.e. can be categorized as more than one genre), year of first broadcast and the episode for which the dialogue was included in the corpus (all from the first season). As can be seen, taking into account the two main genres listed for each television series, there are 8 examples classified as action or adventure, 10 as comedy, 6 as crime, 19 as drama, 2 as fantasy, 1 as mystery, 1 as romance and 1 as sci-fi, with most being classified as hybrids, for example, romantic comedy, crime drama, action drama and comedy drama. In total, the final corpus comprises 117, 815 words according to Wordsmith (tokens in text). While it is thus slightly smaller than the 130,000-word corpus used in Bednarek (2012a), this corpus includes 27 instead of only 7 different series, thus being more representative and varied. For ease of reference, this corpus will from now on be referred to with the acronym TVC, for 'television corpus'.

Table 3.1 Corpus design

Name of TV series	Genre 1	Genre 2	First broadcast	Episode
Twenty-Four	Action	Crime	2001	20
NCIS	Action	Comedy	2003	1
Rome	Action	Drama	2005	11
Legend of the Seeker	Action	Adventure	2008	14
Lost	Adventure	Drama	2004	17
Tru Calling	Adventure	Drama	2003	15
Birds of Prey	Adventure	Drama	2002	1
Bones	Crime	Drama	2005	20
The Wire	Crime	Drama	2002	9
The Shield	Crime	Drama	2002	4
Breaking Bad	Crime	Drama	2008	3
Southland	Crime	Drama	2009	2
The Big Bang Theory	Comedy	N/A	2007	16
The Office	Comedy	Drama	2005	6
Desperate Housewives	Comedy	Drama	2004	19
How I Met Your Mother	Comedy	Romance	2005	12
Community	Comedy	N/A	2009	1
Entourage	Comedy	Drama	2004	7
United States of Tara	Comedy	N/A	2009	8
My Name is Earl	Comedy	N/A	2005	21
Glee	Comedy	Drama	2009	9
Dollhouse	Drama	Sci-fi	2009	6
Grey's Anatomy	Drama	N/A	2005	9
House	Drama	Mystery	2004	18
In Treatment	Drama	N/A	2008	13
Supernatural	Drama	Fantasy	2005	19
True Blood	Drama	Fantasy	2008	7

7 Analysis

This exploratory study of the TVC aims to analyse the use of *wh*-questions. *Wh*-questions were chosen because these are almost as frequent as *yes/no* questions in spoken dialogue (Holmes and Chiles 2010: 195), yet are slightly easier to identify using corpus linguistic techniques: All occurrences of *wh*-words can be automatically identified by the software, while occurrences in structures other than *wh*-interrogatives can be manually deleted by the researcher. Further, similar to other types of questions, *wh*-questions are clearly multifunctional – for example, in television dialogue the phrase *what . . . are you doing* can express surprise, provide negative evaluation or realize a neutral inquiry (Bednarek 2010, 2012a). To clarify, the approach taken here is to start from a particular syntactic form (*wh*-interrogatives) and explore its usage in TV dialogue, rather than exploring how speakers 'do questioning' (Ehrlich and Fried 2010: 5) in such dialogue in general. Of necessity, such an approach is non-exhaustive.

In this study, I make use of two corpus techniques: concordancing and n-gram analysis. Concordancing consists of the exploration of concordances, which show all instances of particular search terms or phrases together with their surrounding text. Concordancing was used to find instances for the *wh*-words *which, what, whose, who, whom, where, when, how, why*, with all instances that did not occur in a *wh*-question subsequently deleted. For example, lines 2, 4, 11, 12 and 14 in Figure 3.2 were excluded from the analysis.[4]

Concordances can also be sorted, for example alphabetically, to the right or left of the search term to find recurring patterns/usages. The concordance output, together with the various sorting options, also allows the researcher to investigate the distribution of the search term across the corpus (Figure 3.3).

The output options further permit a look at the wider co-text (using the Source Text function). Finally, concordances can also be annotated using the Set function (see further Smith et al. 2008). Again, sorting can be used to display frequencies for each annotation.

The second technique used to investigate *wh*-questions is n-gram analysis, which corpus linguists have applied to a range of spoken and written data (e.g. Aijmer 1996;

N   Concordance

1   a reasonably attractive guy. SAM: Reasonably? SARAH: Why haven't you been out and about? Another long story for
2   SARAH: It's true. I was an artist-a terrible, terrible artist. It's why I'm in the auction business. And you were pre-law? SAM
3   from Dry Doc Cleaners on 19th Street. GIBBS: DiNozzo, why are you sitting there on your ass? Get a team and go
4   wear gloves at a crime scene. DUCKY: I believe I know why there's a discrepancy in the time of death. Now since
5   see that coming. JACK: You understood us all this time? Why didn't you say anything? SUN: Your raft was already on
6   SUN: Thank you. JIN: Of course. SUN: Try this – MR. PAIK: Why is my factory closed? MR. PAIK: I'm losing millions
7   she told me I didn't check 'plus one' on the reply card. Lily: Why didn't you check 'plus... Ted: I did check 'plus one'. Lily:
8   can't be that bad. Ted: Here, Lily, you answer it. Lily: What? Why? Ted: Because this whole thing was your idea. And
9   going on with him, he's still our son and we love him Bree : Why would you say that to me? Rex : Because its obvious
10   , would you please not flirt with the ice cream man Sophie: Why not? Susan: Do you need a reason beyond the fact
11   , there's swelling, indenting the esophagus. Sean: Is that why she choked? Foreman: We'll need to do an x-ray. Naomi
12   survival rate is only about ten to fifteen percent, which is why we need to start you on chemo and radiation right away.
13   soon enough. Derek: Aren't I one of the vultures? Richard: Why do you think I want to keep an eye on you? Get going.
14   your husband dying so suddenly. But an autopsy will tell us why. Mrs. Franklin: So you think we should do the autopsy?
15   show Deputy Director Cullen is kinda gruesome. BRENNAN: Why are we meeting Cullen here? BOOTH: Because he's
16   have to check with the hospital's transplant coordinator. Why? What's going on? BRENNAN: There are indications

FIGURE 3.2 *Concordancing.*

```
1    ght there, Teri. Phil Parslow: Who the hell was that guy? To      24_S1_Ep20.txt
2    : Wait a minute. Are you sure? Who is this guy? Tony Almeida       24_S1_Ep20.txt
3    ivered by chopper. Jack Bauer: Who? Mark DeSalvo: His identi       24_S1_Ep20.txt
4    She wasn't kidding. Kim Bauer: Who? Krugman: Your friend. Th       24_S1_Ep20.txt
5    s Victor Drazen. Mark DeSalvo: Who is he? Jack Bauer: The ma       24_S1_Ep20.txt
6    ay something like that. JERRY: Who the hell are you? HELENA:       BirdsofPrey_S1_Ep1.txt
7    apped that one for you. REESE: Who are you? HELENA: I'm not        BirdsofPrey_S1_Ep1.txt
8    n the house already. KETTERLY: Who the hell are -- Helena? !       BirdsofPrey_S1_Ep1.txt
9    NAN: If BioTech doesn't exist, who sold the diseased bone to       Bones_120.txt
10   nfected know, the better. AMY: Who would do a thing like tha       Bones_120.txt
11    illegal parts to tissue labs. Who was actually doing the cu       Bones_120.txt
12    doing the cutting? BOOTH: And who was selling to hospital a       Bones_120.txt
13   e? MARTIN: No. BOOTH: No? Then who did the cutting? Who did        Bones_120.txt
14    No? Then who did the cutting? Who did the cutting of the gr       Bones_120.txt
15   stings and seven other bodies. Who do you work with? MARTIN:       Bones_120.txt
16   ous, and you didn't... CULLEN: Who was it, huh? Who the hell       Bones_120.txt
17   't... CULLEN: Who was it, huh? Who the hell did this to my d       Bones_120.txt
18   ay at least till 10. JEFF: But who studies with strangers, r       Community_S1_Ep1.txt
19   ic to be improvised. And Troy. Who cares if Troy thinks he's       Community_S1_Ep1.txt
20    one of our men. REBECCA/ECHO: Who is this? You know this m        Dollhouse_S1_Ep6.txt
21   id Sierra scream at me? BICKS: Who authorized this? I didn't       Dollhouse_S1_Ep6.txt
```

FIGURE 3.3 *A selection of concordances for the search term* who *(sorted according to file names).*

Mittmann 2004;O'Keeffe et al. 2007). N-grams, which are also known under other names (e.g. clusters, chains or lexical bundles), are recurring syntagmatic combinations of words, for example bigrams (*why not*), trigrams (*why are you*) or tetragrams (*what are you doing*). N-grams are calculated automatically by the software, which means that they do not necessarily have grammatical, semantic or pragmatic status (Stubbs and Barth 2003: 69). N-gram analysis can either be undertaken on the corpus itself (an index must be compiled first), so that lists of the 100 most frequent bigrams, trigrams, etc. in the corpus can be compiled, or it can be undertaken on concordances, so that lists of n-grams within 5 words left/right of the search word can be displayed. Deleted concordances are not taken into account in calculating these n-grams. Analysis will proceed in rather inductive/corpus-driven ways, where frequency and recurring patterns are taken as the starting point for follow-up analyses.

8 Findings

To start with frequency, Table 3.2 shows the raw frequency of *wh*-words, their frequency in *wh*-questions (after deletion of irrelevant instances such as *I don't know why*), averages (normalized per 1000 words), standard deviations and their distribution across the series in the TVC.

As can be seen, *when, which, whose* and *whom* have low frequencies, ranging from zero to ten, and occur only in zero, one, three or nine out of 27 series.[5] Next, *who* and *where* have frequencies of around 80 and a reasonable distribution – occurring in 21 and 24 of the 27 series respectively. Finally, *what, how* and *why* are most frequent and occur in *all* series, with raw frequencies of 195 (*why*), 208 (*how*) and 556 (*what*). This makes *what*-questions the most frequent question type overall. In terms of communicative context, it is unclear whether or not these proportions are unique to TV dialogue. We would need to compare these frequencies to other types of dialogue. However, Bednarek (2012a) – using keywords analysis – found that the *wh*-n-grams *what the hell, what are you, why don't you, who are you* and *why are you* are statistically speaking more frequent in the TV corpus used there than in a corpus of unscripted spoken American English.

Table 3.2 also reports averages and standard deviations for normalized frequencies (the closer to zero, the less variation in the data). Excluding the four low frequency *wh*-words, *what* shows most variation (1.492588), followed by *why* (1.094051) and then *how* (0.735539), *where* (0.616224) and *who* (0.601724). This means that we need to be aware that there is variation regarding the frequency of *wh*-questions in the TVC, even where they occur across most or all of the series.

There is also variation regarding the frequency of different *wh*-questions in episodes/series: As indicated by the lowest figures for standard deviations, *Twenty-Four* (0.851382) and *Dollhouse* (1.022049) show the least variation, while *Tru Calling* (2.4315) and *Lost* (2.726231) show the most. Such differences may arise because of the nature of the specific episode or the series or the genre. This finding confirms previous research which has suggested that there is linguistic variation between TV episodes, series and genres (Webb and Rodgers 2009; Bednarek 2011a). However, such variation needs to be explored further with a bigger corpus, as in the TVC each series is only represented by one episode. Such an exploration would also need to take into account the hybrid nature of many genres and use genre classifications other than the IMDB. Thus, in terms of communicative context, it is unclear if the variation results from the nature of the *episode*, the *series* or the TV series' *genre*.

Table 3.2 Frequency results

	Raw frequency	Final raw frequency	Average (normalized frequency)	Standard deviation (normalized frequency)	N° of series
what	955	556	4.697959	1.492588	27/27
how	338	208	1.793593	0.735539	27/27
why	259	195	1.726824	1.094051	27/27
where	149	82	0.762312	0.616224	24/27
who	222	79	0.650616	0.601724	21/27
when	196	10	0.080798	0.123469	9/27
which	37	3	0.025545	0.077941	3/27
whose	2	1	0.01261	0.065526	1/27
whom	0	0	0	0	0/27

So far this exploratory study focussed on frequency, distribution and variation. We can now turn to analysis of n-grams to tell us more about the kinds of *wh*-questions that occur in the corpus and their functions. Based on n-gram computing for edited concordances (i.e. not including any deleted ones), Table 3.3 lists the three most frequent bigrams and the two most frequent trigrams in the TVC (frequencies for longer n-grams are too low), limited to those that incorporate a *wh*-word.

There are various ways in which n-grams can be categorized, for example grammatically or pragmatically (in terms of function – see Adolphs 2008). The latter is more interesting for the purposes of this chapter. Several researchers (see Culpeper and Kytö 2010: 108–11) have classified n-grams into three main categories, although they use different labels/terms:

- Referential: relating to topics, identifying entities, conveying information, describing circumstances, etc.

- Interpersonal: relating to the speaker-hearer relationship, including the expression of emotion, attitude, modality, speech-acts, etc.

- Discoursal: relating to the organization of discourse, including turn-taking, narrative features, discourse organizers, etc.

However, there are two issues that complicate classification of n-grams according to these categories. One of the issues is multifunctionality: an n-gram frequently has multiple functions, often depending on the context but even in the same instance (Biber et al. 2004: 383–4). A second issue is that shorter n-grams are often incorporated into longer n-grams (as noted, *inter alia*, by Culpeper and Kytö 2010: 106–7). For example, in

Table 3.3 Bigrams and trigrams

	why		*how*		*What*		*where*		*who*	
bigrams	why don't	38	how do	34	what do	81	where is	23	who is	13
	why are	22	how much	21	what are	77	where are	14	who the	11
	why not/ why would	15	how did	16	what did	30	where do	9	who did	6
trigrams	why don't you	32	how do you	23	what do you	70	where is he	11	who the hell	9
	why are you	18	how am I/how did you	8	what are you	62	where is she/ where are you	8	who is this	5

the TVC, most instances of *what are* are occurrences of *what are you* and some of the latter are instances of *what are you doing*. These issues necessitate a further investigation of the n-grams in Table 3.3 using concordancing. They also require a categorization in terms of their main recurring patterns/usages (f ≥ 2) at a more detailed level, although I will later try to link these to the three-fold categorization (referential, interpersonal, discoursal) suggested above. Tables 3.4–3.8 show the results of this categorization.[6]

While I cannot discuss each n-gram in-depth, a few general points are worth making here. First, in the TVC, as in non-scripted conversation, questions are highly multifunctional, with referential, interpersonal and discoursal functions. The n-grams themselves are also multifunctional, with the same n-gram in some cases able to fulfil referential, interpersonal and discoursal functions. For example, *why don't you* can be used in an (interpersonal) suggestion/invitation/advice/insult/reproach or in a (referential) request for information or in a (discoursal) elicitation of a narrative.

Table 3.4 *Why*

n-gram	Main patterns/usages
why not	*Why not?* – mostly questioning, challenging or requesting explanation
why would	*Why would* pronoun/character name DO × (various verbs)
why don't you	Suggestions, invitations, advice, insults, reproaches, requests for information, eliciting narratives
why are you	Location (e.g. *why are you here*); mental state (e.g. *why are you so worried*); behaviour (including *why are you telling me this, why are you doing this*)

Table 3.5 *How*

n-gram	Main patterns/usages
how much	Requests for information, mainly about amounts of money or substances
how did	Either *how did you* (c.f. below) or *how did this/it happen*; *how did X go*; *how did* X DO Y (various verbs)
how do you	*How do you know* – asking about history/source of knowledge; *how do you think* – genuine requests rather than rhetorical questions (only one occurrence of the latter); *how do you feel*; *how do you* DO X (various verbs) – genuine requests for information or expressions of incomprehensibility (e.g. *How do you listen to this all day?*)
how am I	*How am I supposed to*; *How am I to*; *How am I going to/gonna*
how did you	*How did you know*; *How did you learn/figure out*; *How did you get past/get in here*; *How did you* DO X

Table 3.6 *What*

n-gram	Main patterns/usages
what did	DO: *What did I/we/he/you do* SAY: *What did you/she/I/character* name . . . *say* THINK: *What did you think* OTHER VERBS, including *what did you get*
what do you	Clear majority WANT, THINK and MEAN: *what do you want/think/mean* Plus *what do you got*
what are you	DO: *What are you doing?/*with vocative/*What are you doing here/in there?* TALK: *What are you talking about* GOING TO: *What are you . . . gonna/going to do/What are you gonna say* OTHER: *What are you (so) afraid of, What are you, gay?/what are you, my priest?*

Table 3.7 *Where*

n-gram	Main patterns/usages
where are	Entities (e.g. *where are your CDS*); People (e.g. *where are they taking* character name)
where is (s)he	*Where is (s)he?/where is (s)he,* character name?
where are you	*Where are you (now); where are you going*

Table 3.8 *Who*

n-gram	Main patterns/usages
who is	*Who is she/he/character* name?
who did	To find out who was responsible for a (mostly negative) action (e.g. crime)
who the hell	Expression of speaker emotion
who is this	*Who is this*

Figure 3.4 illustrates this multifunctionality, with examples of insults (e.g. lines 1, 4), suggestions/advice (e.g. line 32), invitations (e.g. lines 11, 14), reproaches (e.g. line 6), requests for information (e.g. line 3) and elicitations of a narrative (e.g. line 10).

There is another sense in which these n-grams are multifunctional and that is in terms of Kozloff's (2000: 33–63) functions of dialogue. Table 3.9 gives an overview of these, along with an example from the TVC where the *wh*-question seems to fulfil a particular function.

Clearly, then, *wh*-questions are important for the specific functions that dialogue fulfils *for the audience* (overhearer design) in terms of narrative (e.g. character construction) and aesthetics (e.g. humour). However, as Table 3.9 also shows, it seems that with

```
 1    be the ref, right? why don't you stand up for your fucking self? You pussy. You (
 2    : You want to help? why don't you start by leaving me alone? GARY: You know what,
 3    n good days. REESE: why don't you carry any weapons? HELENA: I am the weapon. BARI
 4    , soldier. Wake up! why don't you come here and suck my cock? GLADIATOR 2: Look, :
 5    of you guys. Artie. why don't you bring this to Principal Figgins yourself? ALL: )
 6    e excuse us, Jesus? why don't you care about this baby? Always all, tell me what I
 7    with this. BRENNAN: why don't you tell us about your relationships with BioTech? (
 8     star, right? Well, why don't you run down, see this guy as soon as you can? Tell
 9    don't have any ecs, why don't you girls have a seat. Eric: I don't care if this mo
10    o? DR. PAUL WESTON: why don't you tell me a little bit more about the boat? SOPHII
11    h, really. JEFF: So why don't you and I go study over BRITTA: Dinner? JEFF: Or dr'
12    e, sure, yeah. Roy: why don't you get on that? Jim: She's not really my type. Roy
13    ke? He was the one. why don't you get that? Lynette: Hello? it's Lynette? Hello? M
14    ve had on this job. why don't you join me for lunch? TRAPP: Be my pleasure, Mr. Pr
15    on Bree: Reverend, why don't you have a seat and I will get some refreshments Rev
16    You like that one? why don't you keep it? SHARDENE: Thank you. DANIELS: He's get1
17    lly losing it. VIC: why don't you go take a bath? I'll put the kids to bed. CORRII
18    king victor? HEARN: why don't you go paint something? Nice work, man. ECHO: where
19    : Wherever you are, why don't you just stay there tonight. WALTER: Skyler? Skyler'
20     seal. GIBBS: Okay, why don't you try it? GIBBS: Oh, wait a minute! Hey, wait! Wa'
21    e rewarding Lamont: why don't you join me? Susan: No Sophie: I'm really ticklish.
22    g spawn, all of em. why don't you and the thirteenth all line up and suck my cock
23    Play some Game Boy. why don't you watch your soap? I hear they're firing the hand:
24    h of this, alright. why don't you tell these guys how you drunk dialed Kristen an(
25    It's yours. HURLEY: why don't you try sea urchin? They got more ping. HURLEY: Hey,
26    'll be fine. MYNOR: why don't you, uh, tell me what you're looking for? PAUL: I f(
27    ncome Lynette: Then why don't you think about moving somewhere less expensive? Lil
28    ugar? Like that. So why don't you tell me about today. PAUL: The guy's name was J(
29    BE: You look tired. why don't you lie down? LUCIO: I wish I could. NEWSREADER: I
30    le of. Elliot. TRU: why don't you give me the gun, Aaron? AARON: And by the way, \
31    ive years to build. why don't you just let me mourn that loss, OK? David Palmer: I
32    again this evening. why don't you settle down? Play some Game Boy. why don't you (
```

FIGURE 3.4 *Why don't you.*

the exception of some functions such as the expression of emotion/opinion (character revelation), a *wh*-question *by itself* is not likely to fulfil one of these functions and that at least a reply is needed. Further, televisual dialogue is often multifunctional. Consider the following example from the TVC, which includes one of the rarer examples of the bigram *why don't* where it is not followed by *you*.

ABED: You know, I thought you were like Bill Murray in any of his films. But you're more like Michael Douglas in any of his films.

JEFF: Yeah, well, you have Asperger's. [exits]

ABED: What does that mean? [quietly]

TROY: [laughs] Ass burger.

ANNIE: It's a serious disorder.

PIERCE: If it's so serious, **why don't they call it meningitis**?

TROY: Yeah. [laughs]

PIERCE: Ass burger. [laughing]

TROY: Burger for your ass. [laughing]

(*Community, season 1, episode 1*)

Here, the *why*-question and its surrounding dialogue co-create humour. At the same time, the dialogue also functions to construct characters and relationships between them: we learn that Jeff is angry; how Abed is seen by Jeff, that Abed does not know what Asperger's is (the *what*-question), that Troy likes making 'stupid' jokes, and that (disapproving) Annie is more serious. We can also see Troy and Pierce momentarily bonding in co-constructing the joke.

Table 3.9 Functions

Function	Example
anchorage of the diegesis and characters: identifying time, space, characters	Nina Myers: OK. **Where are** you now? Tony Almeida: Uh, twenty, thirty minutes away. (time/space)
communication of narrative causality: clarifying connections between events	Mrs McClusky: **How did you** get in here? Lynette: Uh, Mr Mullins had a spare. (causality)
enactment of narrative events: performing key actions, for example, disclosing information, declaring love	Dr Paul Weston: **Why don't you** tell me a little bit more about the boat? (doing therapy/ probing patient – a key action in *In Treatment*)
character revelation: characterization	BARKSDALE: Man, you supposed to be the ref, right? **Why don't you** stand up for your fucking self? (Barksdale's emotion/attitude)
adherence to the code of realism: representing ordinary conversational events (e.g. ordering food)	Bree: Reverend, **why don't you** have a seat and I will get some refreshments. (conventional politeness)
control of viewer evaluation and emotions: guiding viewers' responses (e.g. suspense, attention, emotion)	CHARLIE: Jack, come on, we saw him on the beach this morning! JACK: That doesn't mean that he torched the raft. MICHAEL: Yeah, then **who did**, Jack? (end of scene; creating suspense)
exploitation of the resources of language: poetic, humorous, ironic dialogue, storytelling	Johnny: When I was on Kimmel we said the name of the place, the guy gave us the whole system for nothing. Stripper 2: **What do you mean** you were on Kimmel, is that like ecs? Turtle: No, no, it's a TV show. (humour)
thematic messages/authorial commentary/allegory: telling a moral	Dr Simpson: **Why would** you risk your career to save him? Cuddy: If you think House deserves to go, if you think I deserve to go, Wilson deserved to go, then vote yes. But if you're doing this because you are afraid of losing his money, then he's right! He does own you. You have a choice. Maybe the last real one you'll have here. [possibly a comment on capitalism]
opportunities for 'star turns': giving an actor the chance to show his/her talent	possibly as part of extended sequences or if very dramatic/emotional

To go back to discussing Tables 3.4–3.8 now: with the exception of *why don't you*, the interpersonal meanings seem related to negativity (e.g. negative emotion, confrontation, challenge) rather than positivity (e.g. friendly invitations). Even *why don't you* can be used for insults and reproaches in addition to (friendly) suggestions, invitations and

```
 1   Gross to you, dinner to me. SHANNON: Boone -- where is he? LOCKE: Don't know. SHANNON: Wha
 2   hree kids. Daddy Dearest isn't here. SAM: So, where is he? SARAH: So, what exactly is your
 3   on the way to work, then. EDUARDO: No. DUTCH: Where is he, Eduardo? How come his wife hasn
 4   old the diseased bone to the hospital? BOOTH: where is he? ALEXANDRA: Dr. Ogden had to ove
 5   No ... no! MICHAEL: No! MICHAEL: No! MICHAEL: Where is he? where the hell is he?! MICHAEL:
 6   e hell is he?! MICHAEL: where is he? MICHAEL: where is he? JACK: She doesn't understand yo
 7    where is he? where the hell is he?! MICHAEL: where is he? MICHAEL: where is he? JACK: She
 8   he doesn't understand you, man. MICHAEL: Hey! where is he? KATE: Back off. MICHAEL: No. He
 9   y God, is he okay? LYDIA: He's safe. BRIANNA: where is he? LYDIA: Children's Services has
10   ication. Security inside is very tight. PAUL: where is it? ECHO: You can't know that. You'
11   u accused me of killing Dad. Now move. CHASE: where is my family? MICHAEL: The D'Harans mo
12   say? What did she say when you talked to her? where is she? Tony Almeida: We don't know wh
13   . Earl: hey Crabman. Darnell: hey Earl. Earl: where is she? Darnell: she's in the bedroom
14   ou're lying. I'm gonna ask you one more time. where is she Earl? Earl: look Jessie, I'm th
15   did you know the Sox were gonna blow it? TRU: where is she, Gary? GARY: She went to see Wi
16   it constantly happens around here? CHARMAINE: where is she? MAX: Upstairs. CHARMAINE: You
17   Elizabeth Christianson. Tru Davies. CAMERON: where is she? PROFESSOR: Tru Davies. TRU: I'
18   almost ended our relationship. Stuart: Yeah, where is she? Ted: Um She couldn't make it.
19   Ahh you look.... Intense. Jessie: thank you. where is she Earl? You're lying. I'm trained
```

FIGURE 3.5 *Where is s/he.*

advice (Figure 3.4). In terms of communicative context, this might be a result of the professional practice of script writers who are taught to write in ways that create or heighten dramatic conflict (see Bednarek 2012a: 56–7 for further discussion).

Further, it appears that the *why*-n-grams are associated most with the interpersonal function and *where-* and *who*-n-grams most with the referential function. However, there is no one-to-one overlap. For example, *where is he* may be categorized as a referential request for information, but the fact that it occurs with a vocative (character first name), an alert such as *hey* or an expletive (*where the hell is he*) lends urgency to the request and thereby points to the speaker's emotion, an interpersonal aspect (Figure 3.5, especially lines 5, 8, 14, 19).

A final point to make with respect to Tables 3.4–3.8 concerns the category of person, where it appears that *who*-n-grams and *where*-n-grams are more associated with third person usage than the other *wh*-n-grams. This could indicate a preference for specific question types and person usage in TVC. To explore this further, I annotated the concordances (for *all wh*-questions, not just the n-grams in Tables 3.4–3.8) for explicit occurrences of:

- first or second person singular and plural subjects (e.g. *How much do* **I** *tip?*, *How* **we** *gonna waste her? How would* **you** *know?*)

- third person singular and plural subjects (e.g. *How sweet is* **that**? *How were* **they** *poisoned?*)

Table 3.10 shows the results,[7] with *wh*-questions with first/second person subjects more frequent than those with third person subjects. More specifically, while *why-*, *how-* and *what*-questions more frequently concern the addressee/s, *who* and *where-* questions are more frequently about others.

It could perhaps be argued that the use of first and second person subjects points to the involved or interactive nature of the dialogue, whereas the use of third persons is more narrative or plot-centred: Quaglio 2009 (following Biber 1988) includes the former with other features marking involved production and the latter with other features marking narrative discourse. This could indicate that televisual dialogue functions more to build characters and relationships than plot-elements. Indeed, research in media

Table 3.10 Subjects

	why	how	what	who	where
1st/2nd person (*I, we, you*)	81.6% of coded	70.6% of coded	65% of coded	23.5% of coded	37.1% of coded
3rd person (including impersonal and generic, e.g. *it, that, anyone . . .*)	18.4% of coded	29.4% of coded	35% of coded	76.5% of coded	62.9% of coded

psychology argues that in many fictional programmes it is the characters rather than the events that make viewers 'care' (see Bednarek 2011b for an overview). However, the correlation is far from perfect – *who*- and *where*-questions with third person subjects can express speaker emotion (e.g.: **Who** cares what he wanted?/Oh my god. **Who** is calling you at this hour?/**Where** is he? **Where** the hell is he?!) and *what-*, *why*- and *how*-questions with second person subjects can be about eliciting information rather than negotiating relationships (e.g.: So **what** do you know about that painting?/Sixteen years ago, **how** old would you have been?/**Why** you down at the tester line if you ain't chasing?). We thus need to find more rigorous ways of identifying 'involved' versus 'plot-centred' *wh*-questions.

9 Discussion/Conclusion

To conclude, this chapter has offered multiple avenues for future research into the use of questions in television dialogue and has come up with a number of testable hypotheses, for example:

- That *why-*, *how-* and *what*-questions function to create involvement between characters whereas *who* and *where*-questions are used for plot development (consequently, we would expect crime drama and similar genres to have more *who/where* questions than sitcoms);

- That television dialogue functions more to build characters and relationships than narratives;

- That negativity is more important than positivity;

- That there will be significant variation between episodes, series and genres.

To return briefly to the communicative context of TV dialogue, the exploratory study in this chapter only focussed on some of its aspects. Considering the first question (*How was this text produced, by whom and with what purpose?*), the study investigated the purpose of *wh*-questions in terms of their functions (for example, the creation of involvement or plot development), but did not consider processes of production/

authorship. The second question (*Who does this text address? Who is its target audience?*) could not be tackled in this study, because I would argue that each TV series has its own target audience. For such an analysis, it may be more useful to focus on individual series and explore what kind of target audience the dialogue of the respective series constructs discursively. With respect to the third question (*How does the text mediate between its producers and its audience?*), this was addressed by hypothesizing about the specific functions that *wh*-questions fulfil for the audience (such as control of evaluation and emotions). The final question or, more precisely, range of questions (*What is the relationship between texts and ideologies, commercial realities, generic conventions, industry/professional conventions, practical/technical codes, etc.?*) was only considered in the sense of analysing variation between series, which can provide useful insights into the homogeneity (or otherwise) of TV dialogue conventions. I also tried to link certain of the results to the professional practice of script writers.

Clearly, there is room for much more linguistic research into TV dialogue, including on multimodal aspects (Bednarek 2010; Richardson 2010b). But why is it important to continue with such and other research into TV dialogue? As suggested earlier, television series that are produced in the United States are a significant vehicle for transmitting 'globalised' English to audiences across the world. Despite this, we know surprisingly little about their linguistic features. Yet systematic descriptions of such language use are crucial for understanding what kind of language is promoted to global viewers, what forms televisual storytelling takes and what types of societies and cultures are constructed. Comparisons with research on unscripted dialogue will allow insights into linguistic variation, language innovation and the potential impact of popular culture to explore in how far it is indeed true that 'English is littered with telly's unsung legacies . . . Every sitcom leaves a new vernacular . . . every drama a fresh dialect' (Astle in Big Ideas 2011).

Notes

1 I am very thankful to Kay Richardson, John Flowerdew and an anonymous reviewer for their helpful comments on an earlier version of this chapter.

2 There is a long history of research on the relationship between text and audience in mediated discourse, including discussions, critiques and adaptations of Scannell's *double articulation* and Goffman's *participation framework* as applicable to traditional drama and fictional and non-fictional radio and television contexts. To review these here is beyond the scope of this chapter, but representative work in this area includes Short (1981), Bell (1991), Clark (1996), Thornborrow (1997), Tolson (2001), Montgomery (2007), Hutchby (2006) and Lorenzo-Dus (2009). Most of this research has *not* been on 'telecinematic discourse' (Piazza et al. 2011) – that is fictional televisual/cinematic texts – but rather on news, reality television, talk shows, etc. In the context of film/popular drama, Bubel (2008) provides a relevant review, while Richardson (2010b) focuses on multimodal aspects.

3 I am grateful to Cassandra Fawcett for collecting/transcribing episodes and to the University of Sydney for funding this via the School of Letters, Art and Media Research Support Scheme.

4 *Yes/no* questions were excluded (including *do you know/remember wh*-question, *can you tell/remind* person *wh*-question, *can you imagine wh*-question, *can I ask wh*-question, *does it say wh*-question, *is that wh*-question), as were other syntactic structures such as declaratives (*You don't know wh*-question? *What we want is to know wh*-question, *I'd like to know wh*-question, *He told you wh*-question, *didn't he?*), imperatives (e.g. *tell me wh*-question, *guess wh*-question, *don't ask me wh*-question), conditionals (e.g. *if you tell me wh*-question, *until I know wh*-question). Also excluded were clear usages of single *wh*-words as discourse markers (e.g. *what, are you crazy?*), vague reference (e.g. . . . *full of who knows who*), tags (*Do we got a deal or what?*) or exclamations (e.g. *What the hell!/What the fuck!*).

5 Since *whom* is associated with older varieties of English, this finding may not come as a surprise. However, at least one of the series (*Rome*) takes place in the past and another (*Legend of the Seeker*) can be classified as fantasy, a genre which may use archaic forms to evoke the past (Mandala 2010: 71–94).

6 Instances of *why don't* are mostly instances of *why don't you*; instances of *how do* are mostly instances of *how do you* (other instances include: *how do we know* or *how do we* DO X [various verbs]). Instances of *what do* are mostly instances of *what do you*; *where is* is part of the n-grams *where is/are he/she/you*; and instances of *who the* are mostly instances of *who the hell*. Further, instances of *why are* are mostly instances of *why are you*, and instances of *what are* are mostly instances of *what are you*. All these n-grams are therefore not discussed separately in the tables. Also excluded is the bigram *where do*, because it occurs mainly in one episode. (No figures are provided in these tables, because not all findings can be quantified easily without further operationalization of pragmatic categories and because boundaries between patterns/usages are not necessarily clear-cut. In addition, as noted above, some n-grams are incorporated into longer n-grams, which complicates matters further.)

7 Implicit (e.g. *How? How so?*) and unclear instances were left uncoded. The frequencies for second person subjects with *how-* and *what*-questions include four instances in total where the subject is not the addressee but rather a part of them, body or mind (*How long has **your abdomen** been like this*; *what are **your ambitions***, *what does **your instinct** tell you, what does **your heart** tell you*). These questions directly address the hearer and ask about a part of them. They are different from questions concerning others that are related to the addressee via possessive relationships but have their own agency (e.g. *your husband*). The latter were included as third person singular subjects. In any case, the frequencies for these special cases are so low as to not affect overall percentages. Concerning frequencies for *you*, all were checked for generic reference; in total, there were two generic *you* for *how*-questions and three generic *you* for *what*-questions, again very low frequencies not affecting overall percentages. For reasons of simplicity, frequencies for third person 'singular' subjects for *what-* and *who*-questions also include those where *what/who* itself is subject (e.g. *Who did it?*).

References

Adolphs, S. (2008), *Corpus and Context: Investigating Pragmatic Functions in Spoken Discourse*. Amsterdam/Philadelphia: John Benjamins.

Aijmer, K. (1996), *Conversational Routines in English: Convention and Creativity*. London/New York: Longman.

Androutsopoulos, J. (ed.) (2012), '*Language and Society in Cinematic Discourse*'. Special issue of *Multilingua*, 31(2–3).

Baker, P. (2006), *Using Corpora in Discourse Analysis*. London/New York: Continuum.

Bednarek, M. (2010), *The Language of Fictional Television: Drama and Identity*. London/New York: Continuum.

—(2011a), 'The language of fictional television: a case study of the "dramedy" *Gilmore Girls*'. *English Text Construction*, 4(1), 54–83.

—(2011b), 'The stability of the televisual character: A corpus stylistic case study', in R. Piazza, M. Bednarek and F. Rossi (eds), *Telecinematic Discourse: Approaches to the Language of Films and Television Series*. Amsterdam/Philadelphia: John Benjamins, pp. 185–204.

—(2012a), '"Get us the hell out of here": Key words and trigrams in fictional television series'. *International Journal of Corpus Linguistics*, 17(1), 35–63.

—(2012b), 'Constructing "nerdiness": Characterisation in *The Big Bang Theory*'. *Multilingua*, 31, 199–229.

Bednarek, M. and Caple, H. (2012), *News Discourse*. London/New York: Continuum.

Bell, A. (1991), *The Language of News Media*. Oxford: Blackwell.

Biber, D. (1988), *Variation across Speech and Writing*. Cambridge: Cambridge University Press.

Biber, D., Conrad, S. and Cortes, V. (2004), '*If you look at . . .* Lexical bundles in university teaching and textbooks'. *Applied Linguistics*, 25(3), 371–405.

Big Ideas (2011), '1705 Are the mass media the clearinghouses of English usage? Which has the greatest impact on the language?', ABC Radio National. 23 October 2011.

Bubel, C. (2006), '*The Linguistic Construction of Character Relations in TV Drama: Doing Friendship in* Sex and the City'. Unpublished PhD dissertation, Universität des Saarlandes, Saarbrücken, Germany. Available at http://scidok.sulb.uni-saarland.de/volltexte/2006/598/.

—(2008), 'Film audiences as overhearers'. *Journal of Pragmatics*, 40, 55–71.

Clark, H. (1996), *Using Language*. Cambridge: Cambridge University Press.

Culpeper, J. and Kytö, M. (2010), *Early Modern English Dialogues: Spoken Interaction as Writing*. Cambridge: Cambridge University Press.

Ehrlich, S. and Freed, A. (2010), 'The function of questions in institutional discourse: An introduction', in A. Freed and S. Ehrlich (eds), '*Why Do You Ask?' The Function of Questions in Institutional Discourse*. Oxford: OUP, pp. 3–19.

Goffman, E. (1976), 'Replies and responses'. *Language in Society*, 5, 257–313.

—(1979), 'Footing'. *Semiotica*, 25, 1–29.

Holmes, J. and Chiles, T. (2010), 'Is that right? Questions and questioning as control devices in the workplace', in A. Freed and S. Ehrlich (eds), '*Why Do You Ask?' The Function of Questions in Institutional Discourse*. Oxford: OUP, pp. 187–210.

Hutchby, I. (2006), *Media Talk: Conversation Analysis and the Study of Broadcasting*. Maidenhead: Open University Press.

Kozloff, S. (2000), *Overhearing Film Dialogue*. Ewing, NJ: University of California Press.

Lorenzo-Dus, M. (2009), *Television Discourse. Analysing Language in the Media*. Basingstoke/New York: Palgrave Macmillan.

Mandala, S. (2010), *Language in Science Fiction and Fantasy*. London/New York: Continuum.

Mittmann, B. (2004), *Mehrwort-Cluster in der englischen Alltagskonversation. Unterschiede zwischen britischem und amerikanischem gesprochenen Englisch als Indikatoren für den präfabrizierten Charakter der Sprache*. Tübingen: Gunter Narr.

—(2006), 'With a little help from *Friends* (and others): Lexico-pragmatic characteristics of original and dubbed film dialogue', in C. Houswitschka, G. Knappe and A. Müller (eds), *Anglistentag 2005, Bamberg – Proceedings*. Trier: WVT, pp. 573–85.

Montgomery, M. (2007), *The Discourse of Broadcast News*. London: Routledge.

Morley, J. and Bayley, P. (eds) (2009), *Corpus-Assisted Discourse Studies on the Iraq Conflict*. London/New York: Routledge.

O'Keeffe, A., McCarthy, M. and Carter, R. (2007), *From Corpus to Classroom: Language Use and Language Teaching*. Cambridge: Cambridge University Press.

Partington, A. (2006), 'Metaphors, motifs and similes across discourse types: Corpus-Assisted Discourse Studies (CADS) at work', in A. Stefanowitsch and S. Th. Gries (eds), *Corpus-Based Approaches to Metaphor and Metonymy*. Berlin/New York: Mouton de Grutyer, pp. 267–304.

—(2008) ,'The armchair and the machine: Corpus-assisted discourse studies', in C. T. Torsello, K. Ackerley and E. Castello (eds), *Corpora for University Language Teachers*. Bern: Peter Lang, pp. 189–213.

Piazza, R. (2011), *The Discourse of Italian Cinema and Beyond*. London/New York: Continuum.

Piazza, R., Bednarek, M. and Rossi, F. (eds) (2011), *Telecinematic Discourse: Approaches to the Language of Films and Television Series*. Amsterdam/Philadelphia: John Benjamins.

Quaglio, P. (2008), 'Television dialogue and natural conversation: Linguistic similarities and functional differences', in A. Ädel and R. Reppen (eds), *Corpora and Discourse. The Challenges of Different Settings*. Amsterdam/Philadelphia: John Benjamins, pp. 189–210.

—(2009), *Television Dialogue. The Sitcom* Friends *vs. Natural Conversation*. Amsterdam/Philadelphia: John Benjamins.

Richardson, K. (2010a), *Television Dramatic Dialogue. A Sociolinguistic Study*. Oxford: Oxford University Press.

—(2010b), 'Multimodality and the study of popular drama'. *Language and Literature*, 19(4), 378–95.

Scannell, P. (ed.) (1991), *Broadcast Talk*. London: Sage.

Short, M. (1981), 'Discourse analysis and the analysis of drama'. *Applied Linguistics*, 2(2), 180–202.

Scott, M. (2008), *Wordsmith Tools Version* 5. Liverpool: Lexical Analysis Software Ltd.

Smith, N., Hoffmann, S. and Rayson, P. (2008), 'Corpus tools and methods, today and tomorrow: Incorporating linguists' manual annotations'. *Literary and Linguistic Computing*, 23(2), 163–80.

Stuart-Smith, J. (2011), 'The view from the couch: Changing perspectives on the role of television in changing language ideologies and use', in T. Kristiansen and N. Coupland (eds), *Standard Languages and Language Standards in a Changing Europe*. Oslo: Novus, pp. 223–39.

Stubbs, M. and Barth, I. (2003), 'Using recurrent phrases as text-type discriminators: A quantitative method and some findings'. *Functions of Language*, 10(1), 61–104.

Thornborrow, J. (ed.) (1997), Special issue of *Text* 17 (2) on 'Broadcast Talk'.

Tognini-Bonelli, E. (2001), *Corpus Linguistics at Work*. Amsterdam/Philadelphia: John Benjamins.

Tolson, A. (2001), *Television Talk Shows: Discourse, Performance, Spectacle*. London: Routledge.

Wang, J. (2006), 'Questions and the exercise of power'. *Discourse & Society*, 17(4), 529–48.

Webb, S. and Rodgers, M. P. H. (2009), 'Vocabulary demands of television programs'. *Language Learning*, 59(2), 335–66.

4

Discourse and discord in court: The role of context in the construction of witness examination in British criminal trial talk

Janet Cotterill

Introduction and goals

The courtroom is one of the most archetypal power-asymmetric institutional contexts. In common with other settings such as the classroom or the doctor's office, the court is the site of dyadic or multiple-participant interaction involving significant levels of power asymmetry between its participants. In the contemporary adversarial trial-by-jury system, interaction is uniquely defined by its context and the rules governing engagement between the various participants. In particular, lawyer–witness interaction is constrained by a set of ancient and archaic rules and protocols which govern its shape, duration and the speech acts and roles which may or may not be adopted. The aim of this chapter is to explore the role the courtroom context plays in determining the ways in which lawyers question witnesses, and the responses which they provide. (See Bednarek, this volume, for an approach to questions in a different context.) In particular, I will discuss the extent to which lawyer–witness question and answer sequences are designed essentially as display talk, intended for a multiple audience in court, predominantly the judge and jury. In order to do this, I will examine a corpus of British courtroom data amounting to some 5 million words, employing both corpus linguistic and discourse analytic methods, and analysing a number of key phrases and expressions which indicate to the witness that responses to questions should be designed and oriented towards the members of the non-speaking jury rather than directly to the questioner, the lawyer.

The approach to discourse analysis informing the study

The data will be analysed by a hybrid combination of both discourse analysis and corpus linguistics analysis. The latter will be carried out using Laurence Anthony's *Antconc* program, v 3.3.5w[1]. The use of corpus linguistic methodology to mine the data enables the researcher to process large amounts of courtroom interaction quickly and accurately and the resulting word lists and concordances help to elucidate the processes of interaction which occur during witness examination. This must then be supplemented by a closer and more qualitative discourse analysis of the data, in order to contextualize these results.

The study is analysed within the boundaries of critical discourse analysis, as construed by Fairclough (1989, 1995), which involves three principal elements of three modes of analysis, as follows:

1 The object of analysis (including verbal, visual or verbal and visual texts), analysed and described through text analysis;

2 The processes by means of which the object is produced and received (writing/speaking/designing and reading/listening/viewing) by human subjects (processing analysis through interpretation of the data); and

3 The socio-historical conditions which govern these processes, studied through a more sociological analysis of the broader context.

In a study such as this, focusing on the courtroom as the context of interaction, this third element is particularly significant, since the discourse is only fully understandable within the context of its social setting and environment. As Eades (2010: 108) states:

the power of law is not fixed and is not restricted to the legal process. But rather, an examination of courtroom talk and its social consequences sheds light on the actual mechanisms by which societal power relations are perpetuated.

The British trial-by-jury system, which is the context of analysis in this chapter, enshrines the crucial edict for the jury, provided in the Judges Bench Book that:

the facts of this case are your responsibility. You will wish to take account of the arguments in the speech as you have heard, but you are not bound to accept them. Equally, if in the course of my review of the evidence, I appear to express any views concerning the facts, or emphasise a particular aspect of the evidence, do not adopt those views unless you agree with them; and if I do not mention something which you think is important, you should have regard to it, and give it such weight as you think fit. When it comes to the facts of this case, it is your judgement alone that counts.

(Specimen jury instruction, Judicial Studies Board 2005: I.1;
cited in Heffer 2005: 186)

Thus, the role of the jury is central to the trial process, even though in interactional terms they are non-participatory, remaining silent throughout the trial itself. It is highly unusual for a key participant with absolute power to adjudicate to remain silent and this is a significant and defining feature of the trial-by-jury process (see also Badnarek and Handford, this volume, on this).

Before presenting and analysing the data, I will explore the differences between the interactional 'rules' of casual conversation and those of the courtroom. I will discuss the three following questions:

- How does the British trial-by-jury context dictate what types of talk typically occur in court, specifically during the witness examination phase?

- How does the institutionalized and hierarchically structured environment of the courtroom influence talk by participants;

- In what respects is interaction in court similar to and different from (a) casual conversation and (b) interaction in other power-asymmetric, institutional settings?

How context is understood in the study and the context of the study

The role of context in analysing and interpreting language is crucial. As van Dijk (2008: 111) states, '[contexts] enable and constrain the production and comprehension of text and talk' and as such have a great role to play in determining the shape and nature of discourse. Contexts have the power to both influence and restrict discourse structure and content, and none more so than the courtroom setting. For van Dijk, *contextual variation* operates at a higher level than simply being based on straightforward sociological or sociolinguistic variables such as age or gender. In the case of trial talk, the institutional and power-asymmetric nature of the setting exerts a powerful influence on the speech style of its participants, which serves to affect or even to some extent neutralize the variables of age, social class and gender. In this respect, the courtroom may be considered as analogous with the workplace, where researchers such as Halford and Leonard (2006) found that workplace identities are construed and constructed not only in terms of variables such as gender, age and profession, but also in 'categories such as space and place . . . [where] many of the higher-level discourse features are controlled or controllable (e.g. choice of topics, interrupting someone, etc)' (van Dijk 2008: 115) (see also Bednarek, Gunnarson, Handford and Lou, this volume).

Control over the shape of discourse is prescribed and in some cases even legally enforceable in the courtroom context. A witness who refuses to respond to questions may be found in contempt of court and fined or even imprisoned as a result. As I discuss in Cotterill (2009), this control is not absolute, with some witnesses breaking the rules, maxims and protocols of courtroom interaction, for a variety of reasons. However, in general terms, the judge as representative of the Law has the power to require the witness to be responsive.

Courtroom interaction as a specialized genre and register is governed by a set of contextual 'rules' which determine the linguistic behaviour of its participants. In this part of the chapter, I will analyse both the macro- and micro-contexts of the courtroom. As O'Barr (1979) and others have noted, the courtroom is a highly role- and rule-governed environment. These rules control not only the laws and protocols which govern their legal behaviour, but also their linguistic interaction. This includes the relative distribution of talk between the judge, lawyers and witnesses, and also the *nature* of that talk, including interactional conventions such as the initiation and exchange of turns, and the differential use of declaratives, interrogatives and imperative forms in the courtroom (as will be seen below, specific imperative forms will be the focus of this chapter's corpus linguistic analysis).

These lines of asymmetry in the courtroom context are largely drawn up along a professional-lay cline. The trial *professionals*, predominantly the lawyers and judge, are habitually present in the courtroom as a place of work. This means that the apparently (and literally) archaic laws and modus operandi of a criminal trial are entirely familiar to the legal professionals present, whereas the witnesses who appear and jurors who sit, the *lay* participants in the process, are typically unaccustomed to such an environment and are at a disadvantage both legally and linguistically. A category of witness exists, which is commonly termed within the legal profession 'vulnerable witnesses'; this is meant to refer to witnesses (defendants and victims) such as children, the elderly or people with learning disabilities. However, I would argue that for the main part, most witnesses could be referred to as 'vulnerable' in a broader sense, since the judicial process represents a bewildering and threatening context, where the casual conversational rights of generally equal access and free negotiation of turns and turn types are suspended, to be replaced by a hierarchical system of interaction, where control and constraint is the norm. As Coulthard and Johnson (2007: 95) note, for the layperson 'the strangeness of the setting produces a sense of nervous excitement and hushed voices. One feels almost like an intruder in a private space'.

In the context of the contemporary adversarial trial-by-jury system, which is the focus of this study, the usual features of casual conversational management are, as Matoesian (1993: 79) notes, 'systematically transformed and exploited to manage the powerful interests and interactional contingencies of legal disciplinary regimes'. While interaction outside the courtroom is managed relatively spontaneously, with for example turn-taking negotiated at a local dyadic level, in the courtroom, many of these norms are predetermined, with pre-allocation of turns and turn types the rule rather than the exception (Atkinson and Drew 1979).

The expression of institutional hierarchies through control over interaction is embodied in the roles and participant configurations to be found at various stages in the criminal trial. Each of these configurations is clearly defined by the micro-context of the trial-by-jury process.

Within the courtroom context, there are a number of key individuals responsible for the majority of interaction. These include the obvious trial participants: judge, barristers (in the United Kingdom), solicitors, witnesses, defendants, interpreters and jurors. In addition, there are the more peripheral participants of court ushers, security officials, court reporters and so on. At a third level, and to some extent removed from the trial process itself, there are a number of 'unofficial' individuals or (sanctioned) overhearers in Goffman's (1981) terms. These individuals are present in an external, societal monitoring capacity. This category includes members of the public gallery, who may be relatives or friends of the victim/witness/defendant or even curious individuals including law/forensic linguistics students, who may have no direct connection to the trial itself. Rather, they are representative of 'The People' (note that in the United States, trials are referred to as *The People* versus [defendant's name]). As mentioned above, many trials have journalists attending to report on their progress, outcomes and any ensuing dramas. The journalists are ostensibly present to represent the 'public interest' dimension of significant trials, the reporting of which is seen or felt to be 'in the public interest'. The decision about what represents public interest is of course a subjective editorial decision made by news providers, but this is another way in which broader society is represented in court. All of these 'peripheral' participants are present in a nonverbal context, in other words they do not contribute to the discourse of the court and their contributions if any are not recorded on the court record. (See also Bednarek and Handford, this volume, on the roles of participants.)

It is important to note that these participants are divided into two significantly different categories, in terms of both legal training and power to engage verbally during the trial. These differences are strictly hierarchical in the courtroom context and are briefly summarized in the diagram below:

Level of legal training/seniority	*Level of interactional rights*
judge	judge
barristers	barristers
solicitors	solicitors
interpreters	expert witnesses
witnesses/defendant(s)	witnesses/defendant(s) during examination-in-chief
interpreters	witnesses/defendant(s) during cross-examination
jurors	interpreters
	jurors

There are a number of interesting aspects within this hierarchical depiction. First, it is significant that the judge, barristers and solicitors are included in the same order in both groups, in other words their interactional potential is broadly commensurate with their legal training and seniority. The second group of interactants, the *lay* people involved in the trial (witnesses/defendants), have both the least amount of legal training and the fewest interactional opportunities. Even within the category of witness, there are some significant differences, since witnesses during examination-in-chief will have greater opportunities to speak than those who are more tightly controlled during cross-examination. The category of 'expert witnesses' is a fascinating one, which is discussed in Cotterill (2003), since these individuals are necessarily 'expert' in their field of operation, but are relegated to the status of 'witness' within the trial, who normally only have the interactional right to answer questions. This apparent contradiction is generally managed by expert witnesses having a higher interactional status than regular witnesses.

It is also significant that jurors are included in both categories since their level of legal training, that is none or very little, is crucial to their role in the trial. Their status as non-legal lay people is what determines their right to function as jurors, although their interactional status during the trial is very low, almost non-existent. They are permitted to communicate with the judge, usually if a point of clarification is requested. However, this is not done in open court but rather through the use of specific written queries directed to the judge.

In this chapter, I will focus on the verbally present participants in court, and specifically the witness examination category, comprising defendant, witnesses and barristers from both sides.[2] As Heffer (2005: 47) notes, the apparently straightforward act of a question and answer sequence between lawyer and witness involves at least four principal speech participants [lawyer, witness, judge and jury] who remain 'online' during the examination, but with different speaking rights and participant roles.

Witness examination as an interactional context

One crucial feature of courtroom interaction and in particular the witness examination process is the degree to which it may be regarded as artificial to some extent, in terms of its authenticity as an information-seeking exercise. As I discuss in Cotterill (2003), from the lawyer's perspective at least the majority of the questions asked should optimally be *display questions*, in other words dealing with pre-existing knowledge on the part of the questioner, rather than *referential*, involving a genuine request for unknown information. If there is not a preponderance of display questions, this indicates that the lawyer's trial preparation has been inadequate; indeed a basic tenet for trainee lawyers is that they should never ask a question to which they do not already know the answer.

This applies both in examination-in-chief, the initial phase of questioning where so-called 'friendly' interaction takes place between the lawyer and his own witness, and in the more aggressive cross-examination phase, where lawyers from the opposing side will engage with the witness. During examination-in-chief, the witness will be asked questions which enable them to present an account of events and circumstances; as Woodbury (1984), Harris (1984), Phillips (1987) and Luchjenbroers (1997) have consistently shown, this involves the lawyer producing a greater proportion of open wh-type questions allowing the witness to present a more monologic account than in its cross-examination counterpart. Even during this apparently relatively benign trial phase however, there is nevertheless a significant proportion of closed yes/no questions which allow the lawyer to navigate the account of the crime and which limit the interactional involvement of the witness. Taken as a collective body of research, findings indicate overwhelmingly that closed questions, as indicative of lawyer's control over testimony elicitation, are the clear strategy-of-choice for criminal trial lawyers, accounting for between 64 per cent and 87 per cent of all questions in the cross-examination phase of criminal trials, and only slightly less in examination-in-chief.

Such questioning strategies can be seen in similar power-asymmetric contexts, such as TV interviews, where the interviewer will tend to speed the interviewee through the less newsworthy parts of the interview to allow for greater exploration of the juicier parts, which presumably represents one of the reasons (along with self-promotion) why the interviewee has been invited to appear. In the classroom too, teachers will employ these sorts of display-type questions; it is to be hoped that the teacher does in fact know the answers to which (s)he is seeking a response from pupils. As such, teachers will allow pupils the opportunity to display their knowledge by means of questions to which they already know the answers.

This may seem like a somewhat pointless exercise in the courtroom, in particular during the examination-in-chief phase, were it not for the group of sanctioned overhearers (the jurors) who are in contrast not familiar with the trial story, and whose difficult job it is to adjudicate between the (at least) two conflicting versions.

A useful frame within which to consider this trial-by-jury phenomenon is provided by Schiffrin (1994: 165, 169), who makes the distinction between information-*seeking* questions and information-*checking* questions. She notes that questions which function to genuinely elicit new information represent straightforward realizations of Searle's (1969) felicity conditions for questions, summarized below:

Condition	*Rule*
Speaker lacks knowledge of a particular state of affairs	Preparatory
Speaker wants (*or feigns wanting*) to gain that knowledge	(*In*)Sincerity
Speaker elicits information from hearer	Essential

The italicized portions here demonstrate the subversion of the felicity conditions for casual conversation in the context of courtroom 'display' talk (Cotterill 2003).

In the examination of witnesses, conducted predominantly by means of dialogic question-and-answer sequences, the lawyer takes on the role of questioner, a role again typically associated with the more powerful participant in power-asymmetric dyads. The lawyer can therefore be seen to function predominantly in the role of initiator of inquiry and evaluator of witness response (at the 'I' and 'F' moves of the exchange, respectively), those roles most frequently associated with interactionally powerful participants (see Sinclair and Coulthard 1975 for an initial discussion of the IRF structure).

In contrast, interactional options for the witness are severely limited. The principal role of the witness is to provide appropriate responses to the lawyer's questions (and, on occasion, those of the judge), occupying the 'R' move of the exchange, traditionally reserved for less powerful interactional participants, such as the suspect (in police interviews), the patient (in talk in medical settings), the pupil (in the classroom) or the candidate (in a job interview).

Within this dominant evidential phase, the primacy of the question-and-answer pair as the testimony elicitation technique of choice is undeniable; as Atkinson and Drew observe of witness examination, speakers' turns should be designed 'at least minimally as either questions or answers' (1979: 35).

At this micro-level of question and answer, the lawyer, and ultimately the judge, controls the interaction. In addition to controlling the content of questions, lawyers have turn-taking control over answers which are considered too lengthy, or which stray into areas which the lawyer would rather leave unexplored, since they may be damaging to their case. In both instances, the lawyer is able to limit the witness's response through the judicious and timely use of interruptions, or even through dismissal of the witness with a curt 'no further questions'.

At a macro-interactional level, the very fact that the lawyer is able to summon a witness to take the stand and give evidence at all – if necessary by subpoena – is indicative of the power asymmetry between lawyers, as representative of the judicial system, and the individual witness. As Eades (2010: 106) puts it, 'not only do lawyers have the power to control witnesses' stories, but lawyers and judges have enormous power to control witnesses in other ways – whether they stand or sit, when they can talk, what they can talk about and when they have to remain silent', as well as their basic introduction and dismissal from the dock, and by extension the trial process itself.

In summary then, witnesses are poorly placed in the interactional hierarchy of courtroom talk; they are not privy to the testimony of previous or subsequent witnesses, and have only a tightly constrained control over their own contributions. Witnesses are cast in the (R)esponse role of the exchange, in Sinclair and Coulthard's (1975) discourse analytic terms, and any attempt by them either to initiate talk occupying the 'I' position) or to provide evaluative feedback or follow-up (the 'F' position) is generally penalized. Questions posed by witnesses themselves are rare and generally limited to requests for clarification.

The data

In this chapter, I analyse data from British courtrooms. This is particularly difficult data to access in the British context, as UK courtrooms are strictly controlled in terms of the recording and broadcast of proceedings compared to many other countries (although this is currently under review). The data were collected during the late 1990s and early to mid-2000s, over a period of 10 years (1997–2007). In terms of geographic spread, the data came from Crown courts across several counties of East and South-East England (predominantly Middlesex, Norfolk and Suffolk). In order to gain access to this data, a number of court reporters were contacted. Court reporters are responsible for producing a complete record of the trial, including transcripts of the actual trial itself and any activities which occur in the courtroom such as the exchange of documents, etc.

An interesting aspect of transcripts produced by court reporters is the degree of 'completeness' which they record. For a linguist, they are lacking in several frustrating respects. First, there is obviously no recording of the intonation of utterances, making phonological analysis impossible. Furthermore, it has been noted by researchers such as Gibbons (1994), Graffam Walker (1986) Berk-Seligson (2003) and Cotterill (2003) that court reporters may hypercorrect the speech of particularly the judge and sometimes lawyers in their transcripts, correcting any language errors or anomalies. This phenomenon does not seem to occur with the language of defendants or witnesses in general. Finally, if an interpreter is involved in the trial, researchers such as Berk-Seligson (2003) and Trinch (2003) have shown that in bi- or multilingual trials involving multiple participants including interpreters, the final transcript may be stripped of certain features, such as discourse markers, which are literally lost in translation. However, all of these apparent shortcomings notwithstanding, official trial transcripts provide the opportunity to study an otherwise veiled and somewhat secret(ive) world in terms of the (mostly verbatim) language of its participants.

The data in this study span a wide range of crime types – from rape to murder, robbery to assault, theft to car crime. Since the data were obtained from court reporters, it was not possible to control the variables of collection, for example participant type, crime committed, phase of the trial transcribed. The data cover the whole trial process, from beginning opening statements by lawyers to the final sentencing speech of the judge, and also, interestingly, cover both guilty and non-guilty verdicts. As discussed briefly above, the analysis presented here will focus predominantly on the language produced by the judge, lawyers, defendant and other witnesses during the *witness examination direct* and *cross-examination* phases of the trials. It is here that the context of interaction is perhaps most clearly seen, since there is a direct clash between the language of the layperson and that of the legal professional. The rules and roles of the courtroom and trial interaction are at their most explicitly visible during these stages. The data relating to these parts of the trial amounts to some 5 million words and provides a representative overview of examination-in-chief and cross-examination in the contemporary British courtroom.

I will now move on to the analysis of the data using corpus linguistics methods, focusing specifically on the signalling of witness testimony as display talk.

Analysis and findings

'For (the benefit of) the jury'

Using corpus linguistic tools, and specifically a concordancing tool, which provides incidences of occurrence of a string of words, it is possible to elucidate some of the more explicit examples in the data of courtroom interaction as display talk. Such an analysis does not obviously highlight all instances of references to the jury; indeed, a comprehensive analysis is not possible in a chapter of this length, but a search for the phrases 'for the jury' and 'for the benefit of the jury' reveals some interesting results.

In the data, these phrases function to signal explicitly to the witness that their responses to questions are not intended primarily for the lawyer, but rather for the officially sanctioned overhearing but verbally non-participatory third party, the jury. These phrases occur with some frequency in the data. I have edited the concordance list presented below to remove procedural occurrences such as '. . . the interview has been transcribed. There are copies *for the jury*, a copy for his Honour and a copy for . . . '. The following list gives an indication of an interesting pattern of occurrence of both 'for the jury' and 'for the benefit of the jury':

'for the jury'

1 last few days, been trying to formulate a bundle *for the jury* which is in the most abbreviated form

2 Q. Describe *for the jury*, so that we all remember, where those

3 e fresher six months later? JUDGE BINNS: That is *for the jury* really. MR. FERGUSON: So be it, your

4 ou are turning towards counsel so it is difficult *for the jury* to hear. Stott telephoned you and you

5 7 o letters which your Honour has. There is no need *for the jury* to see those at this stage. JUDGE TU

6 8 they drove past as a reflex action. Describe this *for the jury*.

7 10 KEENE: That surly is simply a matter of judgement *for the jury* itself to make, is it not, Sir Ivan?

8 12 JUDGE MOSS: That is a statement. It is a question *for the jury* in due course. He has given his expla

9 13 e practicability, it is in my submission relevant *for the jury* to know what is the proportion of the

10 14 Valley and to others is a relevant consideration *for the jury*. You have just accepted my point, whi

11 21 able vagueness of what actually happened in order *for the jury*— RECORDER LAWRENCE: Why do you n

12 26 on agent provocateur? A. Yes, I have. Q. Which, *for the jury*, means what? A. It means that no poli

13 27 way. (Indicated) JUDGE DEVAUX: J. Turn it round *for the jury*. A(J). Sorry. His head was there on t

14 28? A. Yes. MR BLUNT: My Lord, it may be convenient *for the jury* to see these at this stage. MR JUSTIC

15 30 committed, if he took part (and that is a matter *for the jury*), he was acting in a state of auto-co

16 31 s. Q. When you left Manhattan's can you describe *for the jury*, in your own words, your condition th

17 35 her it is a little bit or not is perhaps a matter *for the jury*. However, scrap dealing back in July

18 36 it has been with all the witnesses in this trial *for the jury* to hear your answers. Can you please

19 37 do not think it is really necessary at this stage *for the jury* to see that. They can have it at a la

20 39 the knives. Q. It might be easier, your Honour, *for the jury* to follow this if I can hand in the b

'for the benefit of the jury'

1 Q. *For the benefit of the Jury* and I am sure my learn

2 Q. Just *for the benefit of the Jury*, your income then duri

3 can you again hold up the diagram and indicate *for the benefit of the Jury* where the bucket was

4 Would you just hold it up for moment *for the benefit of the Jury* and show them where it

In analysing the respective distribution of these phrases, it is interesting to note that the occurrences of these two phrases are almost equally split between examination-in-chief and cross-examination in the data (46% vs. 54%).

There are two occurrences of 'for the jury' in these concordance lines which refer to *spatial/auditory* matters in court. In line 18, the lawyer reminds the witness of this unusually *triadic* (lawyer–witness–jury) interactional dynamic as soon as he is sworn in, when he states:

Q. Mr Iremonger, I am going to ask you some questions. It is very important, as it has been with all the witnesses in this trial for the Jury to hear your answers. Can you please keep your voice up and notwithstanding that I am asking the questions, can you address your answers in the direction of the Jury.

A. Yes.

It is not only the lawyer's job to remind the witness to address his responses to the jury. In concordance 5, above, it is the *judge* who intervenes to remind the witness that the *jury* are the primary recipients of the response rather than the lawyer who posed the initial question:

JUDGE LANGAN:

J. What, sorry? You are turning towards counsel so it is difficult for the jury to hear. Stott telephoned you and you said something. [J.]

Auditory problems are frequent in many poorly designed court buildings not necessarily fit for purpose, many with sound absorbing wooden-panelling, and creaky wooden seats throughout.[3] One example in the data occurs where both the lawyer and judge have to remind the witness of the limitations of the courtroom layout and the technology employed within it:

Q. Mr Rowan, I shall ask you some questions to begin with. Can you keep your voice up, and can you look at the ladies and gentlemen of the Jury.

A. Okay.

Q. I want you to tell the ladies and gentlemen of the Jury where you were on the evening of 8 February 1997.

A. Well, I first started out – I arrived in King's Lynn. I went to my father's. I was on week-end leave. I went out for a couple of games of snooker. I was out in a snooker hall just down from my father's house.

Q. Now, pausing there, I am having a little difficulty in hearing what you say.

A. Sorry.

Q. That does not amplify [referring to the microphone]; it records.

JUDGE CURL:

J. That simply records. It is a bit of a trap. So, you will have to keep your voice up so that the ladies and gentlemen on the back row can hear. [J.]

MR. MORGAN:

Q. And can you speak slowly.

A. Sorry.

The hapless witness here is instructed by both lawyer and judge to address and make eye contact with the jury, as well as to raise his voice and slow down his delivery of his evidence.

One judge in the data puts it even more clearly, explicitly describing the indirect display nature of courtroom interaction:

> Q. Mr Shaw, I am going to ask you please – It is vital – that you keep your voice up, because if the Jury cannot hear you, there is not much point in your going into the witness box. [Q.] Although I am asking you the questions if you face the members of the Jury and answer directly and as clearly as you can they will be able to hear you and there will not be a problem. All right?
> A. Okay.[4]

There are also a number of occasions where problems occur of a more visuo-spatial nature, where the jury are not able to see an important element in the discussion. This occurs in concordance line 13 of 'for the jury' and lines 3 and 4 of 'for the benefit of the jury'. Thus, the witness is instructed to 'turn it around for the jury' (13) and to 'hold up X for the benefit of the jury (concordance lines 3 and 4).

'Show/tell/explain to the jury . . .'

In addition to these indications of orientation provided by both lawyer and judge to the witness, there are a plethora of examples in the data of the structure 'imperative verb + to/for the jury', whether in the form of tell, show or explain. The use of the imperative form once again indicates the relative power of the lawyer vis-à-vis the witness. Such instances clearly signal to the witness that they should orient their responses to the third-party jury and not directly to the addressee who poses the question, the lawyer. This is context-specific to the courtroom, but is also present in other multiple-participant, power-asymmetric settings. For example, in TV interviews, the interviewer may instruct the interviewee to 'tell the people at home . . .'. I will now present and discuss the relevant concordances drawn from the data which illustrate this phenomenon.

'Show the jury'

'Show the jury' clearly refers to *visual* aspects of the presentation of evidence. The majority of occurrences of this string relate to documents, maps and plans which are items of evidence, and which are referred to by (generally expert) witnesses in the course of their testimony, but this may also refer to the witness demonstrating how a blow was struck or the body language of an individual. Line 7 is an archetypical example, where the lawyer instructs the witness to 'show the jury' that once again so they can:

1 1 numbers, one at the top and one half way down just *show the jury* that please (Same handed to the jury

2 2 him that I am going to put to you in a minute and *show the jury.* [Q.] I will ask you these questions

3 that, I think it might be an appropriate moment to *show the jury* the first photograph. (Handed)

4 Q. I am going to ask the usher to *show the jury* in a moment, but that is the business

5 Photograph 13, can you hold that photograph up and *show the jury* which person you are referring to A

6 the point you say you were told to cut, and then *show the jury.* A. Right. These girders here, these

7 e, and they were in the middle of the street. Q. *Show the jury* that once again so they can see.

8 MORGAN: Let me have a look at that and then we can *show the jury* so that they can mark on their plans

9 the corner. Q. If you could hold the plan up and *show the jury*? A. Where it says on the opposite si

'Explain . . .'

The data also reveal the use of other imperative verb forms, including 'explain . . .', the majority of which occur during examination-in-chief (72%), with fewer but more adversarial examples in cross-examination (28%). During examination-in-chief, where the lawyer is questioning his own witness, 'explain' serves the function of requesting the witness to provide detail about some aspect of the case which the jury may have problems understanding. For this reason, many of the examples of this term occur during the questioning of either expert witnesses, or ordinary witnesses where a process or particular circumstance is unclear. Here, the judge poses a complex and multiple question for the witness to answer:

J. How would you explain to the jury, if you're writing to Mrs Barton at Orchard Cottage, Heacham and sending her £20, explain to the jury what you would do. What would actually go in the envelope with the property? And how would the envelope finally get to a postbox or whatever the system of posting was.
A. Right. In the envelope with the property would be the receipt . . .

In other cases, where general witnesses are questioned during examination-in-chief with the use of 'explain . . .', it is typically in the context of the co-construction of the crime narrative, as in 'Q. Would you explain to the Jury, again relatively briefly, the circumstances in which you saw a gun in the hands of Mr Browning.', where the witness is essentially prompted by the lawyer to continue his crime narrative. Note the apparent politeness of the request with 'would you explain . . .' Under control over response length with 'again relatively briefly'.

In cross-examination however, a more adversarial orientation is attached to the use of 'explain'. Opposing counsel's witness is asked to account for inconsistencies in his examination-in-chief testimony, or, for example, within his police interview. The following pair of extracts illustrates this more challenging approach adopted by the lawyer:

Extract one

Q. Explain please, if you can, why, if it all happened as you said, in your first interview you did not simply say, "Mr Gardiner gave me those cigarettes to hand to the police to give to Alan".

A. Because, to me, I didn't want – Well, for a start-off, I was arrested. Everything dashed out of my head. Everything.

Extract two

Q. Explain to the Jury please how on earth you wrote this letter if you did not have any glasses to see?

A. Because when I take my glasses off I am like that. I know what I write.

JUDGE TURNER:

J. Sorry. I do not understand what you mean.

A Without – Your Honour, when I have not got my glasses on I cannot see nothing in writing. So, therefore –

Note that in each of these examples, the imperative 'explain . . .' although accompanied by 'please', is also accompanied by intensifiers, in the first case by 'if you can' (with the implicit suggestion that he can't); in the second by the dismissive 'how on earth . . . .'. In both cases, the strategic use of a combative 'explain . . .' imperative, results in a confused and rambling response from the witness, which will presumably create a bad impression in the eyes of the jury.

'Tell the jury . . .'

In addition to these requests to show or explain particular aspects, elements or objects to the jury, the most frequently occurring string in the data is that of 'tell the jury . . .', which produces more than 50 hits in a concordance search. These occur in both examination-in-chief and cross-examination; however, the distribution of this type of string is somewhat different to that of 'show the jury . . .' and is more in the order of a ratio of one 1/3 to 2/3 – 38 per cent occurring in examination-in-chief and 62 per cent in the more aggressive and adversarial cross-examination. Because of the constraints of space, I will not reproduce the entire list of concordances, but will restrict the discussion to several instances of particular interest.

The string 'tell the jury . . .' is most frequently followed by a wh-type word, in order of frequency of occurrence: what, why, where, when and how. So, examples such as 'Tell the jury. What was his voice like?' or 'Can you tell the jury please, did you plead guilty to that' are found throughout the data, in both examination-in-chief and particularly in cross-examination. The relative function of this phrase is somewhat different dependent upon which phase of witness examination is taking place (chief vs. cross).

In examination-in-chief, the more 'friendly' interaction between counsel and witness appears to use the expression less aggressively, and although still in imperative form, they serve as an encouragement for the witness to continue with his testimony and frequently provide a reminder of the story structure to be conveyed to the jury, hence 'Q. Carry on please. Tell the jury what happened after that' and 'Q. I want you to tell the Jury what happened. Do you follow me?' These types of reminders are only of course possible when there is shared knowledge between the questioner (the lawyer) and the respondent (the witness), and as such illustrate the display talk nature of testimony particularly in direct examination. Alternatively, examination-in-chief forms of 'tell the jury' often take the form of requests for explanation and clarification, as in the following example:' 'Q. Could you tell the Jury what you mean by CIS?'.

If we contrast this with their use in cross-examination, a very different picture emerges. In this more aggressive questioning phase, lawyers use the expression to challenge the witness, either in terms of their character or in terms of the veracity of their evidence. The following extracts are illustrative of this phenomenon. It also uses the notion of shared knowledge, knowledge shared by both lawyer and witness, but which is used for a more *des*tructive rather than *con*structive purpose. In the following extract, the lawyer is incredulous about a claim made by the witness:

> Q. Are you trying to tell the Jury – This is what you are telling the Jury actually – that you thought, "Well, I'll pick that gun up, pop it in my truck. I'm going to work in two hours' time".
> A. I assume that's what I done, yeh.
> Q. Was it that you were just saying the first thing that comes into your head?
> A. Well, I'm not saying the first thing that's come into my head, no.

In the next example, the lawyer interrogates the witness about one of his previous convictions, closing down and restricting the witness' response to a series of yes/no responses. Although the witness (in this case, the defendant) is ostensibly offered the opportunity to 'tell the jury', in reality it is the lawyer himself who is providing the story, only allowing the witness to answer with brief and perfunctory affirmative responses to his specific and credibility-damaging questions:

Q. Do you want to tell the jury about your conviction for handling an offensive weapon? Just tell them what it was.

Q. You were convicted of having an offensive weapon, were you not?

A. Yes.

Q. As late as August 1995, were you not?

A. Yes.

Discussion/conclusion

The analysis of the data, involving the use of concordance lines for strings which acknowledge the presence and importance of the jury, provides a clear indication of the extent to which lawyer–witness interaction in court is at least partly a display exercise. Questions put during both examination-in-chief and cross-examination recognize the fact that the 'overhearing audience' of jurors are the primary audience for information provided in witness testimony.

This shape of interactional design is not limited to courtroom interaction; certain elements are shared by contexts such as the classroom, where the teacher already knows the answer to the question and intends to test the knowledge of the pupil and communicate that knowledge to other pupils in the class (Sinclair and Coulthard 1975). Similarly, TV chat show interviewers will generally have been provided with research which enables them and their assistants to construct appropriate interview questions, which they may also know the answers to. These are then put to guest interviewees, enabling them to provide responses which (with the notable exceptions) generally fulfil Gricean cooperative maxims and which hopefully produce an optimally entertaining interview experience for the viewing audience (Goffman 1981; Timberg 1994).

The courtroom however is uniquely positioned as a situated discourse context, both in terms of its interactional dynamics and, particularly, in terms of its significance. The court differs in a number of respects. First, each witness (vs. pupil, guest etc) is questioned by two different lawyers, first by one who is friendly, from the witness' own side, and then significantly by a second lawyer who adopts an opposing orientation towards the witness and his evidence in carrying out his cross-examination. Secondly, the structure of courtroom dynamics means that all trial talk is designed to be communicated to a different audience: the jury. Lawyers are constantly aware of this extra, although verbally non-participatory audience.

The questions in examination-in-chief are designed to elucidate and reveal the trial story, a story of which the jury are unaware at the beginning of the trial. This story should be told in as much detail as is necessary, with any technical complexities explained and any potentially damaging aspects of defendant's actions neutralized and justified. The aim of the cross-examining lawyer is of course the opposite: (s)he will attempt to portray the victim as deserving of justice and the alleged defendant as guilty of the crime. For the witness, as much a lay participant as the average juror, the context of the courtroom is a bewildering one, with all its implications of power/powerlessness (see O'Barr 1982 for a detailed discussion of this distinction).

This analysis has shown some of the ways in which lawyers from both sides go about reminding witnesses of this triadic dynamic between lawyer, witness and (especially) jury during their questioning, in an attempt to mould and shape the presentation of evidence for a third party which is relatively ignorant of the crime story and also the law surrounding it, but who occupy a uniquely powerful space in the trial context as adjudicators of the evidence. It is not possible to overstate the significance of the role played by this legally and interactionally sanctioned contextual feature of audience, as the ultimate determiners of guilt or innocence within the adversarial trial-by-jury process. Courtroom interaction represents a complex multi-party and multi-audience discourse type, with in-court participants ranging from judge to jury to public gallery, and 'external' recipients consuming journalistic reports of trial talk, as well as official documents such as judicial statements. Lawyer-witness examination is both constrained and shaped by the courtroom context, with an eye on the wider judicial and lay world who await not only the verdict, but also the preceding discourse which takes place in court.

Notes

1 The Antconc software used in this analysis is freely downloadable at: http://www.antlab.sci.waseda.ac.jp/antconc_index.html.
2 It should be noted that ostensibly non-participating observers are not always silent. In particular, it is not uncommon for there to be outbursts from interested parties from both sides, who unfortunately are often seated side-by-side in the public gallery. However, any such attempt to interact or influence the trial will result in at the very least a reprimand from the judge since these participants are strictly designed as silent observers of the trial.
3 An interesting personal observation is that when my own students are attending court in the public gallery as part of their education, they frequently report problems with hearing the testimony of witnesses, particularly women, children or elderly witnesses.
4 Even as an experienced expert witness, and an academic analyst of courtroom language, I still find this requirement somewhat uncomfortable and undoubtedly unnatural and counter-intuitive.

References

Anthony, L. *Antconc* program, v 3.3.5w (beta). Downloadable at: http://www.antlab.sci.waseda.ac.jp/antconc_index.html).
Atkinson, J. and Drew, P. (1979), *Order in Court: The Organisation of Verbal Interaction in Judicial Settings*. Macmillan: London.
Berk-Seligson, S. (2003), *The Bilingual Courtroom: Court Interpreters in the Judicial Process* (2nd edn). University of Chicago Press: Chicago.

Cotterill, J. (2003), *Language and Power in Court: A Linguistic Analysis of the O.J. Simpson Trial*. Basingstoke: Palgrave.

Coulthard, M. and Johnson, A. (2007), *An Introduction to Forensic Linguistics*, London: Routledge.

Eades, D. (1996), 'Verbatim Courtroom Transcripts and Discourse Analysis', in H. Kniffka, S. Blackwell and M. Coulthard (eds), *Recent Developments in Forensic Linguistics*. Frankfurt am Mein: Peter Lang, pp. 241–54.

—(2010), *Sociolinguistics and the Legal Process*. Bristol: MM Textbooks.

Ervin-Tripp, S. (1996), 'Context in Language', in D. I. Slobin, J. Gerhardt, A. Kyratzis and J. Guo (eds), *Social Interactions, Social Context, and Language*. Hillsdale, NJ: Lawrence Erlbaum Associates, pp. 21–36.

Fairclough, N. (1989/1995), *Language and Power*. London: Longman.

Freed, A. and Susan E. (eds) (2010), '*Why Do You Ask?': The Function of Questions in Institutional Discourse*. Oxford: Oxford University Press.

Gibbons, J. (1994), *Language and the Law*. London: Longman.

Goffman, I. (1981), *Forms of Talk*. Philadelphia: University of Pennsylvania Press.

Graffam Walker, A. (1986), 'The Verbatim Record: The Myth and the Reality', in S. Fisher and A. Todd (eds), *Advances in Discourse Processes Volume XIX: Discourse and Institutional Authority: Medicine, Education and Law*. Norwood, NJ: Ablex, pp. 205–23.

Grice, P. (1975), 'Logic and Conversation', in P. Cole and J. Morgan (eds), *Syntax and Semantics* (vol. 3). New York: Academic Press, pp. 41–58.

Halford, S. and Pauline L. (2006), 'Place, Space and Time: Contextualising Workplace Subjectivities'. *Organisation Studies*, 27(5), 657–76.

Harris, S. (1984), 'Questions as a Mode of Control in Magistrates' Courts'. *International Journal of the Sociology of Language*, 49, 5–27.

Heffer, C. (2005), *The Language of Jury Trial*. Basingstoke: Palgrave.

Luchjenbroers, J. (1997), '"In your own words . . ."': Questions and Answers in a Supreme Court Trial'. *Journal of Pragmatics*, 27, 477–503.

—(1991), 'Discourse Dynamics in the Courtroom'. *La Trobe Working Papers in Linguistics*, 4, 85–109.

Matoesian, G. (1993), *Reproducing Rape Domination through Talk in the Courtroom*. Chicago: University of Chicago Press.

Phillips, S. (1987), 'The Social Organisation of Questions and Answers in Courtroom Discourse', in L. Kedar (ed.), *Power Through Discourse*. Norwood, NJ: Ablex, pp. 83–113.

O'Barr, W. (1982), *Linguistic Evidence: Power and Strategy in the Courtroom*. New York: Academic Press.

Sinclair, J. and Malcolm C. (1975), *Towards an Analysis of Discourse*. Oxford: Oxford University Press.

Timberg, B. (1994), 'The Unspoken Rules of Talk Television', in H. Newcomb (ed.), *Television – The Critical View*. New York: Oxford University Press.

Trinch, S. (2003), *Latinas' Narratives of Domestic Abuse: Discrepant Versions of Violence*. Amsterdam and Philadelphia: John Benjamins Publishing Corporation.

Van Dijk, T. A. (2001), 'Discourse, Ideology and Context'. *Folia Linguistica*, XXXV(1–2), 11–30.

—(2008), *Discourse and Context*. Cambridge: Cambridge University Press.

Woodbury, H. (1984), 'The Strategic Use of Questions in Court'. *Semiotica*, 48(3/4), 197–228.

5

Business discourse in the globalized economy: The construction of an attractive workplace culture on the internet

Britt-Louise Gunnarsson

1 Introduction

In today's technologically advanced society, where companies rely on the internet for their externally and internally addressed information, texts on websites and other social media have come to be essential for the construction of a positive and attractive company image. It is by means of texts that the organization disseminates a picture of its history, its visions for the future and its current goals, policies and ideas. It is also by means of web texts that the company describes and promotes their available jobs. In most modern organizations, a substantial effort is put into the creation of a company image used in external and internal communication. Public relations staff are attached to the very top level of the organization, and the information policy is a part of the company's steering policies.

In this chapter, I will discuss multinational companies' construction of an 'organizational self' on the internet. I will analyse staff policy documents and career stories which were published on the websites of nine multinational companies. The goal is to explore how large business enterprises in their self-presentations on the career-oriented subpages balance between various concerns, values and interests: between global and local concerns, between economic concerns and social values, and between individual-centred and group-centred interests. Context will be understood at various levels: at a macro level as dependent on various societal framework systems, at a meso level as situated within the studied multinational company, and at a micro level as related to the analysed text with its specific goal and intended readers. Using a theoretical approach which combines sociolinguistics, sociology and organizational theory with text linguistics and narratology, I will explore which image the multinationals construct of their culture and how a positive image of the company is textually transmitted in stories featuring individual employees.

2 Business discourse in its contextual frameworks

Business discourse – as most professional discourse – is strongly related to its contextual framework. This means that successful organizations have to be flexible and open for change, also in relation to discourse. Efficient discourse has to be dynamic and continuously reconstructed in order to reflect ongoing changes at local, national and global levels. In Gunnarsson (2009a: 20–7), I develop a model for the contextual reconstruction of professional discourse, the aim of which is to provide a tool for an in-depth analysis of how and why professional discourse varies and changes. I distinguish a number of factors which relate to the various contextual frames in which professional discourse is continuously reconstructed, that is to say a situated framework, an environmental framework and four societal framework systems.

Figure 5.1 illustrates the environmental contextual framework of a large organization. Text and talk at work can be described as related to different situated communicative events. An in-depth analysis, however, must also include a *meso level*, that is to say the *environmental contextual framework* in which the communicative events, or chain of events, occur. Text and talk in a small, close-knit working group form part of traditions that evolve within an environmental structure, that is to say the small *working group* is included in a larger unit such as a *workplace*, which in its turn belongs to a *local branch* of a large *organization*. In many cases, we further find additional organizational levels,

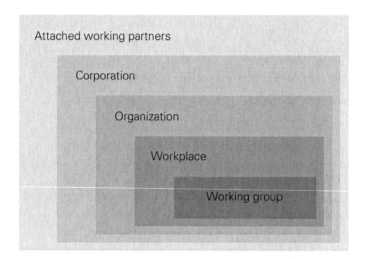

FIGURE 5.1 *The environmental contextual framework.*

that is to say the organization belongs to a *corporation,* to which there also might be *attached working partners.*

What also characterizes professional discourse is its dependence on a *macro level*, that is to say on various *societal framework systems:* (1) a *technical-economic framework*, (2) a *legal-political framework*, (3) a *sociocultural framework* and (4) a *linguistic framework* (see Figure 5.2). (1) The technical-economic framework is of course of relevance for professional discourse. We know that technology and technological advances are important for the dynamism within organizations of various kinds, as are the economy and economically driven changes. (2) Also, the legal-political framework determines discourse. It is self-evident that professional discourse is constrained by politics, laws and regulations at local, national and supranational levels, for instance in relation to education. (3) Professional discourse is further constrained by a sociocultural framework *system*. Cultural patterns, attitudes and social values are essential aspects of communication in the professions. Although we might still find professional organizations which could be described as socially homogeneous and monocultural, social diversity and multiculturalism are more characteristic of organizations today. The ethical codes adopted in a particular professional environment thus reflect, to a large extent, ideologies and ethics in this framework. (4) Fourthly, professional discourse is also dependent on the linguistic framework. The local language community, the national language community and the supranational language community establish and follow language laws and policies which directly or indirectly influence text and talk at work. Policies and practice on language dominance issues, formed within the various levels of the linguistic framework, influence communicative events for professional purposes in terms of language choice and practice.

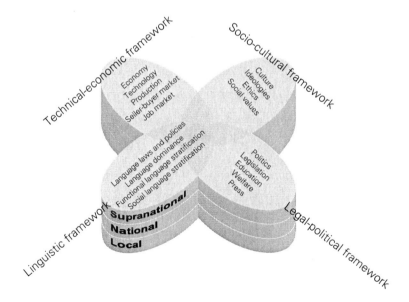

FIGURE 5.2 *The societal framework system.*

The investigation, which will be dealt with in this chapter, is based on an analysis of texts produced in large, multinational enterprises. The web texts discussed can be assumed to be either produced, or initiated and controlled by staff at the information units of these enterprises before they are disseminated to external reader groups. The contextual framework within which these texts are constructed is indeed complex. The final text is the result of a chain of communicative events, each taking place in a situated frame (related to domain, goal, time, place and tool) with a particular grouping of participants. At the same time the text has been constructed within – and dependent on – an environmental framework, which is constituted by the particular company and its partners. The texts are further related to – and constrained by – societal frameworks at local, national and global levels. As the texts discussed in this chapter are intended for prospective employees, they directly relate to several societal framework systems. All companies operate globally and employ people in different countries and different parts of the world. This means they have to relate in their discourse to technological change, economic matters and new markets, and also to workforce mobility, language dominance issues, ethnic diversity and multiculturalism. Among other things, companies' discourse on their career-oriented subpages reflect their awareness – or lack of awareness – of issues of social discrimination and marginalization, that is to say the way they handle their corporate social responsibility (Gunnarsson 2009a, 2010).

3 The construction of a company image

In Gunnarsson (2009a), I discuss the construction of a company image. I claim that the creation of an image of the corporate culture is part of the construction of an 'organizational self' in large organizations.[1] Images depict the common values of the company, which means that they show the culture and its value system both to the group itself and to those outside it. Different kinds of images exist within a company, for instance *internal images*, relating to the perception of a corporate identity, a corporate self, and *externally addressed images*, relating to the outward presentation of the corporate culture.[2]

Giving attention to company image is not a new phenomenon, and there is not anything new about the management of a company being aware of the importance of discourse for the construction of a positive presentation of its 'organizational self'. What is fairly new, however, is the use of the internet for the dissemination of both internal and external images. Previous to the internet era, large companies distributed a variety of documents on paper, each intended for one or a few specified reader groups (Gunnarsson 2000, 2009a), while the modern company relies on the internet for external and internal communication. One consequence of this change of medium relates to the readership. When a company places a text on its website, it has to count on a multiple readership, both in relation to who the reader is and in what context the reading takes place. Global accessibility – and also simultaneous access by different reader groups – is a reality for texts on websites. Another consequence of the increased reliance on the internet relates to conspicuousness. When texts are placed on the internet, the company's policy on linguistic and cultural issues becomes visible for different reader groups. For multinational companies which employ staff worldwide, the construction of an 'organizational self' does of course include an image of their workplace culture. Among other things, these projections reveal the company's interpretation of the concept of *diversity* – a key term in the modern business world. In a globalized business world, organizations have to balance between *local* and *global concerns* as well as between *economic concerns* and *social-societal values* in order to be competitive and trustworthy, which means that the construction of an 'organizational self' also reveals how the company balances between these concerns and values. As an employer of staff, the company also has to find a balance between the various interests of the individual employee, that of a professional and that of a private person.

4 Earlier studies of business discourse

Written business communication has been studied within the field of LSP (Languages for Specific Purposes), often with a focus on genre (e.g. Bargiela-Chiappini and Nickerson 1999; Bhatia 1987, 2005; Bhatia and Bhatia 2007). Much research has dealt with the genres of mission statements and annual reports (Garzone 2007; Isaksson 2005; Isaksson and Jørgensen 2011; Skulstad 1997; Swales and Rogers 1995).[3] The relationship between organizational culture and writing activities have been elucidated in a variety of studies, using methods ranging from pure survey to ethnographic observation. What characterizes the work within this area is its close connection to sociolinguistics and to work on organizations within sociology (Bargiela-Chiappini 2004). In Gunnarsson (2000, 2004, 2005, 2009a), I give an account of research related to banks and structural engineering companies in three countries, Germany, United Kingdom and Sweden. I analysed the relationship between discourse, organizations and national cultures and found that the organizational ideas and communicative policies of each enterprise mattered for the structure of discourse at the same time as national cultural patterns could be distinguished.

Many studies of business discourse concern the communicative practices within transnational companies (e.g. Haarman 2005; Harris and Bargiela-Chiappini 2003; Pan et al. 2002; Piller 2001). In Jämtelid (2001, 2002), a study of the multilingual practices of the Electrolux group in the 1990s is presented. The author found that the term *parallel writing* was relevant to describe the practices established within this transnational company for writing brochures in different languages. A common raw material was sent out from the head office in Stockholm to the selling offices throughout the world, which then could choose ideas and parts for the writing of customer brochures in their respective language and for their respective group of customers. The role of translating was thus minimized and mainly reserved for official documents like annual reports (see also Gunnarsson 2009b).

Texts on websites, however, necessitate a new type of writing and reading (e.g. Herring 2001; Kress and van Leeuwen 2001; Ylönen 2007), and also a new and challenging way of handling the complex interweaving of texts on the internet (e.g. LeVine and Scollon 2004; Norris and Jones 2005). Global accessibility – and also simultaneous access by different reader groups – is a reality for texts on websites. For the companies, this means that the specific character of each document is replaced by a possible relationship between texts on various subpages of the company website and that 'passive' reading is intermingled with interaction (Castells 1999; Lemke 2002; Qvortrup 2002; Wiberg 2004).

In today's globalized economy, when the internet is used not only to reach out to customers and producers but also to attract job seekers and shareholders, ideologies in relation to language choice and language use become socially prominent in a new and more visible way. In Gunnarsson (2009a, 2010), I present a critical, sociolinguistic study of the websites of five transnational companies, which all are major employees in Sweden. My focus was on diversity issues, that is on the companies' explicit and implicit interpretations of multilingualism and multiculturalism in texts presenting the companies' core values, in job advertisements posted on the website and in stories featuring individuals working at Swedish workplaces. Among other things, this analysis, carried out in June 2006, showed that the stories more often featured employees who had moved from one country to another during their career than on the multicultural diversity of the Swedish workplace.

5 Presentation of the study

From this review of earlier research, I will turn to a presentation of the current study. The goal of this study is to analyse the images of staff policy and company culture which are constructed in texts found on the career-oriented subpages of nine multinationals' websites. In comparison with the June 2006 analysis, one purpose of the current study is to enlarge the scope, in terms of both the number of companies and the range of job-markets they orient themselves towards, another to make an in-depth analysis of a selection of the found career stories.

Nine multinationals are included in this study, namely *Nokia, Astra Zeneca, Ericsson, Electrolux, Bosch, Siemens, ABB, Mc Donald's* and *IKEA*. The selected companies produce and sell different types of products. What they all have in common, however, is that they all are large, global companies which employ people throughout the world. The texts analysed were published on the career-oriented link found on the nine multinationals' global websites, that is to say on www.nokia.com/global/about-nokia/, www.astrazeneca.com/careers, www.ericsson.com/careers, http://group.electrolux.com/en/, etc. The corpus was collected in July–August 2011 and in September–October 2012.

In section 6, I will present a brief analysis of claimed core values in staff policy documents. I will there use the document published on Nokia's website as an example of how companies describe their staff policy and workplace culture on their websites. In Section 7, I will discuss an analysis of career stories, using examples from several websites to illustrate my findings. My research questions concern how different concerns, values and interests are textually transmitted on pages intended for prospective employees.

6 Staff policy documents on multinational companies' websites

From a text critical perspective, it is interesting to analyse what core values a company's presentation of itself as an employer include. All nine multinationals have texts on their websites which could be labelled 'staff policy document'. As an example of such a document, I have chosen the text found on the subpage 'Our people & culture' on Nokia's global website. On this subpage, we find photos of people of different gender, age and ethnicity and a text with the two subheadings 'Let's agree to disagree' and 'Doing things the Nokia Way'. For the purpose of this discussion, I have printed in italics some words and phrases, which I consider to be key terms. I will refer to these terms below.

Our people & culture

Let's agree to disagree

At the last count, the Nokia Group employed approximately 139,000 people around the world: not bad for a company that started life as a small riverside paper mill in Finland.

In 2010, the devices and services business alone employed approximately 60,000 people from around 115 *different nationalities*. And approximately 41 per cent of them were women.

Such *diversity* is crucial to our success so far – and to our continued success in the future. We're operating in more markets than ever before, and employees from *diverse backgrounds* can give us invaluable insights into our customer bases. Just as important, a *mix of cultures*, genders, age groups, beliefs, interests and opinions in the workplace helps foster *debate*, *discussion*, *ideas and innovation*. Not to mention making Nokia a more enjoyable, stimulating and *rewarding* place to spend your working day.

Doing things the Nokia Way

Commitment to *diversity* is just part of what we call the Nokia Way – the core values and shared philosophy that make our company tick. *Creativity, empowerment, openness*, *collaboration* and *consideration for people* and the environment – these are all integral to the way we do business. But above all, it's about *being human* in everything we do – *respecting and caring*, even in tough business situations.

Similar texts as this one can be found on the websites of all studied multinationals. As in the quoted Nokia text, the following five core values are stressed in all staff policy documents studied: (1) 'diversity', (2) 'respect', (3) 'development', (4) 'openness' and (5) 'creativity'.

(1) The concept 'diversity' is a core value which multinationals claim to be important in relation to the composition of their staff. In the Nokia text, the expressions 'different nationalities', 'diverse backgrounds' and 'mix of cultures' make this core value concrete. (2) In relation to the treatment of their employees, the companies stress 'respect'; in the Nokia text, this value is expressed as 'consideration for people', 'being human' and 'respecting and caring'. (3) Many staff documents also describe an interest in the 'development' of their staff, and in the quoted text, we find that working for Nokia is stimulating and 'rewarding' and combined with 'empowerment'. (4) Claims in relation to the workplace culture are also frequent in the staff policy documents. One workplace value stressed is 'openness', and in the Nokia text we find the key terms 'debate', 'discussion', 'openness' and 'collaboration'. (5) Another workplace value is 'creativity', which in the Nokia text appears as 'ideas and innovation' and 'creativity'.

7 Career stories on multinational companies' websites

The second part of my investigation focuses on career stories which are found on the multinationals' websites. Individual employees are presented in these stories, and the narratives include a description of how they have made a career, what their job is like and how they perceive of the company in question as an employer.

The career stories analysed are found on subpages entitled, 'Nokia people', 'Our people', 'Our employees', 'Working with Bosch', 'People on the move' or the like. In all, I found more than 100 'career stories' which all comprise a photo of a featured employee, his/her first or full name, some facts relating to his/her position in the company and a narrative presentation of the employee. My detailed analysis, however, concerns 27 career stories, 3 on each website of the nine companies.[4] For this analysis, I use a methodological framework which combines text linguistics – 'macro structure', 'foregrounding' and 'salience' (Gunnarsson 2009a) – with narratology – 'voice' (Mishler 1987; Vološinov 1973) and 'model reader' (Bakhtin 1986, Eco 1984, Nord 2011). My analysis includes story structure, foregrounded content and voice and salient elements.[5]

In this section, I discuss some results of my analysis of career stories. I will not give a quantitative account of my results; instead I use examples to illustrate the common features which I have found in my career stories corpus. First, in 7.1, I present my term 'career story' and give a general view of the stories' macro structure. In the following parts, 7.2–7.4, I discuss my findings on foregrounded content and voice (7.2), on salient elements in the construction of the company and its workplace culture (7.3), and on salient elements in the presentation of the employee and his/her career (7.4). Last, in 7.5, I summarize my findings on career stories.

7.1 *What is a career story?*

In order to illustrate what I mean by a career story, I will return to Nokia's subpage 'Our people and culture'. Below the staff policy document, above discussed, we find the subheading 'Nokia People'. Here we find the names of six employees, who work in Beijing, China; in Burlington, Massachusetts, USA; in Espoo, Finland; in Soho, London; in Gurgaon, India; and in Espoo, Finland. For each person, we find the name in bold, an introductory description and also a 'Read more'-link.

At the time of my study, one of the featured employees was Carol Soriano. When we click on 'Read more', we find the full name, Carol Soriano, and a picture of a fairly young woman. After a brief introduction, we then find a story featuring this employee.

Carol is the voice and force behind consumer communications, and is based in Espoo, Finland.

What do you do?
I head up the Consumer Communications team within the global communications function at Nokia. My team's responsible for putting together the relevant communications activities that relate to our introduction of new products and services to the market, along with the other functions involved in our Global Traffic Manager (GTM) programs.

How's your career progressed?
It's been anything but predictable. I trained to be a lawyer, but decided to teach medieval history at a university while working part-time at a direct marketing agency. After three years of doing both, I decided to work full-time at the marketing agency – learning everything from client service and creative development, to database management. I continued this process of evolving my marketing skills to include online and CRM consultancy for more than 10 years. In 2003, I joined Nokia as a marketing communications manager in Asia-Pacific, then became multimedia marketing director in the region. In 2006, I moved to Espoo to head up the creative team for N series, then for the whole of Nokia. In 2009, I headed the global marketing activation team to oversee implementation of campaigns across markets. And now, I manage consumer communications within the global comms team.

What do you like about your job?

For me, it was a choice of being a lawyer, a teacher or a marketer. Ultimately, they all share a trait: communicating the truth in some way. What differed was the degree of truth and the method of communication. In the end, marketing proved to be the most exciting path.

What do you like about Nokia?

First, Nokia is one of the top 10 brands in the world – what marketer can resist the chance to be a part of that? Second, it is a technology company. This means we get to experience the latest and greatest devices and services as part of our job. Third, it is a truly global company. You work with people from all over the world, and you get to hear – and appreciate – many different points of view. And last, but not the least, it is a company that stands for something. I still get inspired by the fact that our company has enabled people to connect with one another in so many new and different ways. Coming from the Philippines – an emerging market where landlines were difficult to access up until five years ago – I have witnessed first hand how mobile phones (the ones that Nokia has developed and brought to market) can make a real difference in people's lives. Whole villages and industries are transformed as a result of connectivity. It's not a cliché, it is a reality. And the company – which I work for – has made that happen.

How do you help Nokia?

My work in marketing and comms does not involve putting technology in place, or building a smartphone. But a well-crafted ad or a perfectly-timed press release from the marketing or comms teams can convince a consumer to buy a Nokia product, or an investor to buy Nokia stock. Our job is to clearly communicate the benefits of Nokia and its products. That is our contribution to the company's mission.

How has Nokia helped you?

In a lot of ways. From a career perspective, Nokia has allowed me to experience different aspects of marketing (from creative development to implementation) in different locations (from local to global). This experience has broadened my skill set, and deepened my knowledge of the company and the industry.

When you're not working, what are you doing?

I am probably in front of another screen: either watching TV shows or playing video games. Probably with my seven-year old son, my hubby and my pug sharing the screen. And internet access is a pre-requisite for our choice of holiday destinations – yes, I am a nerd, and my family is too.

As we can see, this career story follows a question-answer pattern. The questions (marked in bold in the text) structure Carol's story. The story moves from a description of her job at Nokia (What do you do?), to her career (How's your career progressed?), to her views on her job (What do you like about your job?) and on the company (What do you like about Nokia?). The following question concerns her role in the company (How do you help Nokia?) and the next question how Nokia as an employer has made her develop (How has Nokia helped you?). The last question then concerns her private life (When your're not working, what are you doing?). We do not know who is posing these questions, nor who has written the text. In the answers, however, the voice of the employee, Carol Soriano, is made explicit by the use of 'I', 'me' and 'my' throughout the story; 'I head up the Consumer Communications team', 'My team's', 'I trained to be a lawyer', 'I decided to work' and so on. – All career stories on Nokia's website are structured in the same way as Carol Soriano's story. After the brief introduction, the text is organized following a question-answer pattern.

If we then look at the entire career story corpus, the majority of the stories could be said to follow a similar news article pattern. All have a heading and a brief introduction, either summarizing/asking a question/giving a perspective or quoting what the employee said. Some stories have a longer introduction or an abstract. The macro structure of the text bodies either follows a thematic/partly chronological pattern or a question-answer/statement-quotation pattern. What is worth noting, however, is that we do not get to know *who* has posed the questions or made the statements. The interviewer is unknown to the reader, as is also the author of the stories. I will come back to this fact later on.

7.2 *Foregrounded content and voice*

My next focus is on the relationship between the foregrounded content and voice. When I began analysing career stories, I expected to find several voices in the texts, that of the employee, that of company representatives, that of the interviewer and writer and also that of colleagues and maybe also customers. To my surprise, however, I have only found one distinct voice, namely that of the employee. This voice is explicitly heard in the career stories, both in the presentation of the company and of the employee him or herself: all texts quote the employee, often using first person pronouns: 'I', 'me' and 'my'. In most stories, there are also quasi-neutral passages which describe the company and sometimes also the employee. Although the company's voice is not heard explicitly in the same way as that of the employee, that is to say no manager or other company representative is quoted, I have chosen to refer to these quasi-neutral passages as the company's voice. In order to avoid misunderstandings, I should add that my use of the term 'voice' is not related to any analysis of authenticity. I do not know if the text quotes the employee literally, and neither what has been omitted.

I will begin with the 'voice of the company'. As example passages where the 'voice of the company' is heard, I have chosen two extracts from a career story published on the website of the pharmaceutical multinational company AstraZeneca. The story features Britt-Marie Stålbom, who judging from the picture, is a middle-aged woman.

The first passage foregrounds the company. Without references to any source, the reader gets to know that the personnel collaborate with scientists and commercial colleagues globally, and also that the staff is technically skilled.

> Personnel at the Regulatory Affairs department work together with scientists and commercial colleagues to support the development of new drugs and to maintain marketing licenses worldwide.
> It s a cross functional and global work with many points of contacts. At Regulatory Affairs technically skilled staff is working with compiling application files, project managers are coordinating cross functional contributions to . . .

The second passage foregrounds the employee. Also this passage is written in a 'quasi-neutral' way. Britt-Marie Stålbom's broad experience within the field, her years with the company and her career are summarized without any direct quotations from her or any other references.

> Britt-Marie Stålbom has a broad experience within the regulatory field and has worked for AstraZeneca over 10 years, in a number of different positions within Regulatory Affairs. Today Britt-Marie is working with knowledge transfer and internal trainings for her co-workers at Regulatory Affairs.

All stories have shorter passages as the ones in the examples above, for instance in the introduction, as was the case in the Nokia story of Carol Soriano. Statements are made, facts are listed, summaries are given and questions are posed without any explicit sender or any reference to a representative of the company or any document.

Let us next turn to some passages where the 'voice of the employee' is explicitly heard. The relationship between content and voice is here more complex, as these passages from a career story published on Ericsson's website illustrate. The career story has the heading 'Meet Yu who joined Ericsson in 2007'. We do not get to know the full name of Yu but on the photo attached to the story we see a young man. Let us look closer at three passages from this text, in which the voice of Yu is heard.

The first extract begins with a sentence in which the company, its products and customers are foregrounded. The next sentence, where the voice of Yu is heard, describes how he sees the 'customer-first aspect' as a challenge in his job.

> Ericsson does not only provide world-class products to the customers but also world-class services. As an instructor, the customer-first aspect is always the most important thing but also the greatest challenge in my job.

In the second extract, we also hear the voice of Yu. He describes his view on Ericsson's policy towards staff and customer. The core value 'respect', which is stressed in Ericsson's staff policy document, is by Yu said to permeate the whole organization.

I have always considered respect as Ericsson's most attractive characteristics. The respect permeates the whole organization as well as respect towards our customers. My managers always delegates (sic) me the jobs I am competent for, and coach me on the jobs I am not that familiar with. The fact that we respect our customers from our hearts is the foundation for them trusting us as a supplier.

In the third extract, we find Yu telling us about his ambitions and why he chose to apply for a job at Ericsson. The following sentence describes Ericsson as an employer who encourages and develops the talents of its staff.

During that time I realized that influencing people is what I really like and something I am good at as well, so I applied for an internal job as an instructor and got it. Ericsson really encourages all employees to constantly look for new challenges and new positions in the organization to enable each person to develop his/her talent.

In all three extracts, the use of pronouns indicates that we here hear the voice of the employee, Yu. He constructs a positive image of the company at the same time as he is presenting himself as a professional. First person pronouns, 'I', 'my', 'me', are used in all three extracts. We can also note the intertwinement of (1) a description of the company and its products, (2) of Yu as a professional, that is in his role as instructor, (3) of his possibility to advance and (4) the company's general treatment of his staff. We get to know through Yu that Ericsson delegates and coaches its staff and shows them respect, and also that Ericsson encourages their employees to look for new challenges and positions.

Although the career story on Ericsson's website gives an impression that we hear Yu's voice, we do not get to know anything about his family and private life. In other stories included in my corpus, we also get glimpses from the featured employee's life outside the job. For instance, in the earlier discussed career story featuring Carol Soriano, the last question posed to her concerned her private life, that is what she is doing when she is not working. In the answer to this question, we hear Carol's voice telling us something about her family and her life outside the job. Also the career stories on the websites of Electrolux, ABB and Bosch include passages where the employee's voice is heard about private matters in addition to the job and company related ones.

7.3 *Salient elements in the construction of the company and its workplace culture*

My next set of questions concerns salient elements in the stories. I will first summarize my results with a focus on how the company and its workplace culture are constructed in the texts. My focus will be on elements which reveal how the company balances (1) between global and local concerns and (2) between economic concerns and social values on staff and workplace culture. I will below give examples of how different elements are highlighted in the stories.

(1) Global and local concerns

As could have been expected, all nine multinational companies are constructed as global companies in the career stories published on their websites. In the story featuring Carol Soriano, she mentions, among the things she likes about Nokia, that 'it is a truly global company. You work with people from all over the world, and you get to hear – and appreciate – many different points of view'. Also Yu highlights the global character of the company: 'Ericsson is a truly global company with presence in 175 countries which gives me as an employee a lot of opportunities to work with people from all over the world'.

The company's local concerns are stressed in some stories but not in all. In Carol Soriano's story, for instance, Nokia is constructed as a company that makes a difference for people in Asia.

(2) Economic concerns and social values

Excellence is indeed strongly related to economic concerns. The companies' excellent products, excellent services and economic success are highlighted in one way or the other in the career stories. Nokia is said in Carola Soriano's story to be 'one of the top 10 brands in the world' 'with the latest and greatest devices and services'. Ericsson is described, through the voice of Yu, as a company which 'not only provide world-class products to the customers but also world-class services'.

Not infrequent in the stories in the corpus is reference to an interesting and creative environment, for instance in this story featuring Magnus Ruth at Astra Zeneca: 'The advanced scientific level, the interesting interactions with different people and the creative environment is constantly motivating me to drive research forward. To have the opportunity to work with world class scientists is very inspiring'.

Social values are stressed in many of the stories. The companies are described as employers which give their staff training and support. In the earlier discussed story on Ericsson's website, we hear Yu's voice saying: 'Ericsson really encourages all employees to constantly look for new challenges and new positions in the organization to enable each person to develop his/her talent'; 'My managers delegate me the jobs I am competent for, and coach me on jobs I am not familiar with'. Also Nokia is constructed as an employer which gives its staff a possibility to develop, for instance in Carol Soriano's story: 'From a career perspective, Nokia has allowed me to experience different aspects of marketing (from creative development to implementation) in different locations (from local to global)'.

Marco Rebuli, featured on Electrolux' website, stresses 'the creative spirit' of Electrolux. The text quotes him as saying: 'Electrolux is a company that fosters innovation by affirming and encouraging employees to take ownership of their own ideas. This means not only coming up with an idea, but being involved in seeing it through.' In order to pass the innovative spirit along, Rebuli claims that he has supported others: 'Sometimes innovation can come out of very simple ideas, and I try to relate this to employees when I run change projects—that innovation doesn't have to be intimidating. When employees can then see their ideas are taken seriously and implemented, they are inspired to innovate even more.'

Many career stories focus on the workplace culture, for example, on dimensions like 'openness' and 'respect for the individual'. As we remember, Yu claimed that at Ericsson 'Respect permeates the whole organization'. Social values and company culture are also stressed in the career story featuring Zhang Wei Ping on Siemens' website. The headline of this story is 'Can a company be a good company?' and the first paragraph highlights social values and corporate culture: 'When you work for a company, it's not just its reputation or remuneration that matter. So do its values and the people you work with every day. Whether they're in the office next door or on another continent, the way people deal with each other makes the difference for a corporate culture.' The combined nature of a company's training and support of staff is further focused on in this story. Zhang Wei Ping, who spent a period in Germany as a trainee, says that she profited a lot from this period personally, but that it also helped her do a better job. 'It's a combined thing, really,' she adds. 'Siemens helps you to develop yourself while you help develop the Siemens business.'

7.4 Salient elements in the presentation of the employee and his/her career

From the stories' construction of the company, I will turn to salient elements in the presentation of the employee and his/her career. Many career stories include background details about the employee's education and earlier jobs. Age is seldom mentioned explicitly, but as all career stories include a picture, the readers get a general idea of the individual's age. I will leave these background data aside and instead focus on what is highlighted in relation to the employee's career and his/her profile. My focus will be on the following salient elements which construct the featured employees as important professionals within their companies: (1) their successful career within the company, (2) their interest in other people and skill as team leaders and (3) their open-mindedness and flexibility.

(1) Successful career within the company

Most career stories include information about when the employee joined the company or how many years he or she has been employed. 'Loyalty with the company' is thus an element which is highlighted in the presentation of the featured employees and their successful careers.

The employee's current position and earlier career within the company are, of course, highlighted and described in a positive way in the stories. All stories feature individuals who appear to be successful within their fields of expertise. Carol Soriano, who joined Nokia in 2003, heads a creative team. Britt-Marie Stålbom, who has worked 10 years for Astra Zeneca, is presented as a person 'with a broad experience within the regulatory field' who 'is working with knowledge transfer and internal trainings for her co-workers at Regulatory Affairs'. Yu is described as an 'experienced instructor' working in Beijing, China. He joined Ericsson in 2007 and was 'awarded best employer in 2008'. Zhang Wei Ping, featured on Siemens' website, has also had a successful career within her company. She 'leads a sales team at Siemens Energy in Shanghai' and 'is responsible for a number of tasks, ranging from license control to strategic support'.

(2) Interest in other people and skill as team leaders

Many stories feature managers and team leaders who are interested in other people. Several stories tell about individuals who like to develop and support other employees. Nikki Craddock, featured on IKEA's website, describes his attitudes towards his job as development coach like this:

> Now I am Competence Development Coach for Sales in the UK. I realised I have a lot of passion for helping people develop. I have learned that people come in all shapes and sizes. And I have learned to appreciate that fact.

The featured employees' interests in networking and interacting with people are highlighted in various ways in the stories, for instance, on the subpage 'Working at Bosch' on Bosch's website. Here we find a picture of Rogerio Nakamuro with the following text.

> *Success stories don't just happen. They are made.*
> "Everyday I interact with co-workers."
> Brazilian Rogerio Nakamuro is a specialist involved in the product creation process in the Gasoline Systems division. The passionate soccer fan is currently stationed in Stuttgart.

However, I have also in my corpus one career story which features an employee at IKEA in Germany who stepped down from a position as team leader, as she found the workload too heavy. In the story featuring Silvia Soekeland, currently business navigator, she says:

> In 1993 I became team leader for my group. It was a great time, but after about three years I decided to give up the personnel management. The main reason was the heavy workload. When I left, I got very positive feedback from my co-workers. What they said has stayed with me until this day – it feels like we are really close.

In the next paragraph, Silvia tells about her interest in variation and also in interaction with others: 'During these 20 years, no day has been like the day before. To handle change and to work in the right way, I always discuss things with my colleagues. We talk, talk, talk'.

(3) Open-mindedness and flexibility

As all the studied companies are multinationals, it might not come as a surprise that many career stories focus on the international experiences of the featured individuals. On Electrolux's website, there is a subpage entitled 'People on the move' where we find a number of career stories which present employees who have moved from one country to another. For instance, the story featuring Kristoffer Ljungfelt, a Swede who has worked seven years for Electrolux, tells us that he has held several positions in different countries in Europe during these years: in Denmark, in Italy and in Sweden, and that he is now moving to Singapore. Tomas Dahlman, another Swede working for Electrolux, has recently made a move from Stockholm, Sweden, to Charlotte, USA. In the career story featuring this individual, one question posed to him is what cultural adjustments he has had to make. His answer can be seen as an example of how successful employees, and also their families, are presented as open to change:

> The most exciting thing has been to learn more about the US, exploring business life and meeting new people. My family has been very well taken care of among colleagues, neighbors and school – everyone has reached out and made us feel welcome.
>
> Of course there are many practical differences when you move to a new country. But we like to try new things and see it as one big experience, like what's involved in getting a drivers licence. However, I must admit we are happy that we have an IKEA in Charlotte. When we get cravings for Swedish food we go there for candy, chocolate and of course the world famous Swedish meatballs!

The featured employee's appreciation of the chance for international experience which working for the company has given them is also stressed in several of the stories published on Nokia's, Ericsson's, IKEA's, ABB's and Bosch's websites.

In many career stories, open mindedness and flexibility are connected with a willingness to take on new responsibilities and an interest in professional growth and development. The following story, found on IKEA's website, illustrates this connection. The story features Aziza Nathan, who works for IKEA in the Netherlands. The headline presents her ideas on 'employability': 'You have to be open minded, adaptable and able to take risks . . .', and the last paragraph of the story summarizes her view: 'If you are adaptable and willing to take calculated risks, I would recommend you to explore the opportunities within IKEA. It would help you grow further, learn new skills and embrace new cultures and different ways of living altogether!'

Another story which makes this connection explicit is found on Electrolux' website. The text tells us that Sara Menis has returned home to Italy after an eight-year assignment in Belgium with Electrolux. She describes her experiences as a 'fresh perspective': 'Somehow living abroad gives you the chance to restart, create new habits, and find a new balance'. The story attributes Sara Menis' 'successful professional development' to 'her willingness to be flexible, seek out opportunities and take on new positions, even when it meant packing up and leaving her home country'.

7.5 Summary

The studied career stories balance between a description of the company, its policy and culture, and the featured employee. The voice of the employee is often made explicit – by pronouns and quotations – in the construction of the company, while the voice of the company is heard only indirectly. The interviewers and the writers are anonymous. All stories construct the company as global and economically successful. The company's social policy in relationship to staff is also stressed in many stories, where, for instance, the readers get to know that the company offers its company's offering employees good training, support and a possibility to bring family to new countries. The positive workplace culture is further highlighted in the stories, that is to say the workplace climate is described as friendly, informal and allowing much discussion and good teamwork. The salient elements in the construction of all featured employees are open-mindedness and flexibility; they are described as open to new challenges, new responsibilities and international experience. Most employees are also presented as ambitious, that is to say with a wish to develop and grow as professionals and as individuals. Many stories further stress the employees' interest in other people; they are educators, leaders of teams, in frequent contact with customers and colleagues. A divide is between stories where the model reader[6] is a well-educated, skilled person, and those where the model reader is an unskilled person open for education within the company. Another divide is between stories which include information about the employee as a private person, that is to say a person with a family and children to take care of, with hobbies and with interest in new cities, and the stories which only tell about a skilful, professional person.

8 Discussion

In this chapter, I have explored staff documents and career stories on the websites of nine multinationals. These texts can be assumed to be either produced, or initiated and controlled, by staff at the information units of these companies before they are published on the internet, which means that they form part of the companies' construction of a positive image of their culture and 'organizational self' (see § 3). The texts studied here, both the staff policy documents and the career stories, must be considered as mainly *externally addressed*. The reliance on the internet for disseminating company images, however, entails a complexity. As the image of the company's organizational policy and practice becomes visible both for 'outsiders', that is for prospective employees and other readers outside the organization, and for 'insiders', that is managers and employees, the external marketing of the company is often intertwined with the internal marketing. The border between externally addressed images and internal images is therefore not always clear.

9 Conclusion

The conditions for business discourse have been influenced by a series of changes taking place in recent decades. New technology, workforce mobility and a globalized job market have transformed many workplaces to bilingual and multicultural settings. Lifelong learning, flexibility, mobility and diversity have come to be key values in the global economy.

Let us return to the earlier introduced model of the contextual reconstruction of professional discourse. The contextual framework for texts on multinationals' websites is indeed quite complex. Although this investigation has not dealt with the writing processes as such, we can assume that all texts analysed, both the staff policy documents and the career stories, are the final result of a chain of communicative events involving several individuals (Figure 5.1).

As the texts discussed are intended for prospective employees, they directly relate to several societal framework systems (Figure 5.2). The *technical–economic framework* is indeed reflected in the nine multinational companies' reliance on the internet for their presentation of staff policy and company culture and also for the featuring of successful employees. All companies operate globally and employ people in different countries and different parts of the world. The texts on the career-oriented subpages reflect this global orientation. In their staff policy documents, the companies present themselves as global and stress the fact that they employ people all over the world. Also the career stories reflect this global orientation, and employees featured have different backgrounds and work in different regions. Mobility, flexibility and the employees' interest in international experience are also found among the elements highlighted in the presentation of successful employees.

Also the *sociocultural framework* is reflected in the texts. Both the staff policy documents studied and the career stories explicitly highlight social and ethical values. 'Diversity' and 'respect' are core values claimed by all companies in their staff policy documents, and when they describe their company culture, social values like 'openness', 'development' and 'creativity' are found. Also the career stories highlight these social values. The stories describe how the companies give their staff possibilities to develop and grow, that the workplace culture is open and team oriented, and that working for the company is stimulating and varied.

Turning next to the *legal-political framework*, there are of course a number of legal and political constraints on business discourse both globally and locally. What my data reflect is a concern for – or an awareness of – the so-called corporate social responsibility. In their staff policy documents, the companies make claims that show that they wish an image of their company culture which allows for diversity instead of social discrimination and marginalization.

Lastly, I wish to discuss my results in relation to the *linguistic framework*. Although diverse background, different nationalities and mix of cultures are highlighted in the studied documents and stories, the multilingual issue is strikingly absent. The multinational companies' global websites clearly reflect the use of English as a global business language. None of the staff policy documents studied mention languages, that is to say the companies' diversity concept includes mix of cultures, different nationalities, different backgrounds but not different languages. And although it is obvious that English must be a second language to several of the featured employees, the language issue is not brought up as a topic in the career stories.[7] We do not either get to know if employees who have held positions in different countries, for example, in Germany, France or Italy, have had to make efforts to learn the local majority language. For the multinationals studied, the language issue does not seem to be important for the image they wish to transmit to prospective employees. For a linguist, this fact is of course worth noticing.

Notes

1   According to Hofstede (1994: 16–17), imagery is connected to the company culture.

2   There are also images which are created outside the company. These images reflect the views of the company which are held by 'others' – by those not directly involved. Such *externally constructed images*, which are obviously not always favourable, quite often function as counter-images to the internally constructed ones, and one of the essential aims of conscious image construction within a company is to change such negative, externally created images (Gunnarsson 2000, 2005).

3   A survey of the field 'professional communication' is found in Gunnarsson (2007). A survey of studies on 'discourse in organizations' and 'discourse and technology' is also included in Gunnarsson (2011).

4   The detailed analysis of the websites was carried out in July and August 2011.

5   In a paper at AILA 2011 in Beijing, China, I presented a preliminary analysis of the career stories.

6   In Nord (2011: 279–80), the following definition of 'model reader' is found: 'The reader construed within the text, i.e. it is not a physical, empirical reader, but a text-internal representation, an aspect of the "addressivity" of the text (Bakhtin 1986). The model reader is, in a way, a representation of the "ideal" reader – the reader most loyal to the stance taken in the text'.

7   The stories on the subpage "People on the move" on Electrolux' website have a fact square, and among the facts listed in this square is found languages, that is the languages which the featured employee knows.

References

Bakhtin, M. M. (1986), 'The problem of speech genres', in *Speech Genres and Other Late Essays*. Austin: University of Texas Press, pp. 60–102.

Bargiela-Chiappini, F. (2004), 'Language at work: Meeting the challenge of inter-disciplinarity', in C. Gouveia, C. Silvestre and L. Azuega (eds), *Discourse, Communication and the Enterprise. Linguistic Perspectives*. Lisbon: University of Lisbon Centre for English Studies, pp. 3–16.

Bargiela-Chiappini, F. and Nickerson, C. (eds) (1999), *Writing Business: Genres, Media and Discourses*. New York: Longman.

Bhatia, V. K. (1987), *Analysing Genre: Language Use in Professional Settings*. London and New York: Longman.

—(2005), 'Genres in Business Contexts', in A. Trosborg and P. E. Flyvholm Jørgensen (eds), *Business Discourse. Texts and Contexts*. Bern, Berlin, Frankfurt am Main: Peter Lang, pp. 17–39.

Bhatia, V. K. and Bhatia, A. (2007), 'Global Genres in Local Contexts'. *Linguistic Insights – Studies in Language and Communication*, 14, 263–81.

Castells, M. (1999), *The information age. Economy, Society and Culture* (vol. 1–3). Oxford: Blackwell Publishers.

Eco, U. (1984), *The Role of the Reader. Explorations in the Semiotics of Text*. Bloomington Indiana University.

Garzone, G. (2007), Annual Company Reports and CEOs' Letters: Discoursal Features and Cultural Markedness. *Linguistic Insights – Studies in Language and Communication*, 14, 311–41.

Gunnarsson, B.-L. (2000), 'Discourse, Organizations and National Cultures'. *Discourse Studies*, 2(1), 5–34.

—(2004), 'The multilayered structure of enterprise discourse'. *Information Design Journal + Document Design*, 12(1), 36–48.

—(2005), 'The Organization of Enterprise Discourse', in A. Trosborg and P. E. Flyvholm Jørgensen (eds), *Business Discourse. Texts and Contexts*. Bern, Berlin, Frankfurt am Main: Peter Lang, pp. 83–109.

—(2007), 'Professional Communication', in N. Van Deusen-Scholl and N. H. Hornberg (eds), *Encyclopedia of Language and Education: Second and Foreign Language Education* (2nd edn, vol. 4). New York: Springer Science, pp. 83–95.

—(2009a), *Professional Discourse*. London and New York: Continuum.

—(2009b), 'Discourse in Organizations and Workplaces', in L. Wei and V. Cook (eds), *Contemporary Applied Linguistics: Linguistics for the Real World* (vol. 2). London: Continuum, pp. 121–41.

—(2010), 'Multilingualism within transnational companies. An analysis of company policy and practice in a diversity perspective', in H. Kelly-Holmes and G. Mautner (eds), *Language and the Market*. Basingstoke and New York: Palgrave-MacMillan, pp. 171–84.

—(2011), 'Applied Linguistics', in J.-O. Östman and J. Verschueren (eds), *Pragmatics in Practice. Handbook of Pragmatics Highlights 9*. Amsterdam/Philadelphia: John Benjamins Publishing Company, pp. 23–45.

Haarman, H. (2005), 'Multiple Foreign Languages Choices in Response to Varied Economic Needs'. *Sociolinguistica*, 19, 50–7.

Harris, S. and Bargiela-Chiappini, F. (2003), 'Business as a Site of Language Contact'. *Annual Review of Applied Linguistics*, 23, 155–69.

Herring, S. C. (2001), 'Computer-mediated discourse', in D. Schiffrin, D. Tannen and H. Hamilton (eds), *The handbook of discourse analysis*. Oxford: Blackwell Publishers, pp. 612–34.

Hofstede, G. (1994), *Cultures and Organizations: Software of the Mind: Intercultural Cooperation and its Importance for Survival*. London: Harper Collins.

Isaksson, M. (2005), 'Ethos and Pathos Representations in Mission Statements: Identifying Virtues and Emotions in an Emerging Business Genre', in A. Trosborg and P. E. Flyvholm Jørgensen (eds), *Business Discourse. Texts and Contexts*. Bern, Berlin, Frankfurt am Main: Peter Lang, pp. 111–38.

Isaksson, M. and Flyvholm Jørgensen, P. E. (2011), 'The rhetoric of corporate mission statements: Virtues and emotions for the market', in H. Kelly-Holmes and G. Mautner (eds), *Language and the Market*. Basingstoke and New York: Palgrave-MacMillan, pp. 226–37.

Jämtelid, K. (2001), 'Multilingual text production at an international company', in F. Mayer (ed.), *Language for Special Purposes: Perspectives for the New Millenium* (vol. 2). Tübingen: Gunter Narr Verlag, pp. 797–805.

—(2002), *Texter och skrivande i en internationaliserad affärsvärld. Flerspråkig textproduktion vid ett svenskt storföretag*. Acta Universitatis Stockholmiensis. Stockholm Studies in Scandinavian Philology. New Series. 27. Stockholm: Almqvist & Wiksell International.

Kress, G. and Van Leeuwen, T. (2001), *Multimodal Discourse. The Modes and Media of Contemporary Communication*. London: Arnold.

Lemke, J. L. (2002), 'Travels in hypermodality'. *Visual Communication*, 3, 299–325.

LeVine, P. and Scollon, R. (eds) (2004), *Discourse and Technology. Multimodal Discourse Analysis*, Washington, DC: Georgetown University Press.

Mishler, E. G. (1987), 'The interactional construction of narratives in medical and life-history interviews', in B.-L. Gunnarsson, P. Linell, and B. Nordberg (eds), *The Construction of Professional Discourse*. London and New York: Longman, pp. 223–44.

Nord, A. (2011), 'The reflective cultivator? Model readers in eighteenth century Swedish garden literature', in B.-L. Gunnarsson (ed.), *Languages of Science in the Eighteenth Century*. Berlin and New York: De Gruyter Mouton, pp. 279–301.

Norris, S. and Jones, R. H. (2005), *Discourse in Action. Introducing mediated discourse analysis*. London and New York: Routledge.

Pan, Y., Scollon, S. W. and Scollon, R. (2002), *Professional Communication in International Settings*. Malden, MA and Oxford: Blackwell Publishers.

Piller, I. (2001), 'Identity Constructions in Multilingual Advertising'. *Language in Society*, 30(2), 153–86.

Qvortrup, L. (2002), *The Hypercomplex Society*. New York: P. Lang Publishing Co.

Skulstad, A. S. (1997), *Establishing Emerging Business Genres. Genre Analyses of Corporate Annual Reports and Corporate Environmental Reports*. Ph.D. dissertation, Department of English, University of Bergen, Bergen, Norway.

Swales, J. M. and Rogers P. S. (1995), 'Discourse and the Projection of Corporate Culture: The Mission Statement'. *Discourse & Society*, 6(2), 223–42.

Ylönen, S. (2007), 'Culture Specific Differences in Business Communication with New Media?', in J. Murath, and À. Olàh-Hubai (eds), *Interdisciplinary Aspects of Translation and Interpreting*. Wien: Praesens Verlag, pp. 337–66.

Vološinov, V. N. (1973), *Marxism and the Philosophy of Language*. New York & London: Seminar press.

Wiberg, M. (ed.) (2004), *The Interaction Society. Theories, Practice and Supportive Technologies*. Umeå: Umeå Universitet.

6

Context in spoken professional discourse: Language and practice in an international bridge design meeting

Michael Handford

Introduction

The role and nature of context in discourse is complex, elusive and contested. According to Cook (1989: 1), the 'infinitely expandable' nature of context in authentic situations is one of the reasons that analysts need to forego claims of objectivity and completeness in describing a context. Contexts are infinitely expandable because the analyst cannot be certain some potentially salient aspect of the context, such as the weather or a previous discussion in a different setting, is indeed relevant to the language in question. Therefore, a more realistic goal is to achieve a plausible, rather than a comprehensive and incontrovertible, interpretation.

This chapter, like the others in this volume, is concerned with context from two, related, perspectives: in what situation is the discourse produced, and how is context construed by the analyst. Specifically, this chapter analyses English as a lingua franca discourse from a bridge design meeting held in South Asia[1], and it should be noted that the analysis of professional discourse presents particular challenges in terms of interpreting context and exploring the relationship between text and context (Charles and Charles 1999). The underlying conceptualization of context here is that it is in a reflexive relationship with the language: context, in the form of practices, constrains and enables what language is appropriate and therefore produced; also, the language reproduces, maintains and may alter the context. Without a context-specific situation and contextual appreciation, language lacks meaning (Gee 2005).

Goals of the study

As stated above, this collection focuses on two aspects of context in discourse, the role it plays and how it is construed. This chapter therefore seeks to explore the role context plays in a bridge design meeting, with particular foci on viewing the meeting as genre and on the lexicogrammar that indexes discursive practices. In so doing, it will be possible to see to what extent this professional context differs from other professional contexts and what features it shares. Specifically, three questions will be addressed:

1   What can corpus-informed genre analysis tell us about this professional meeting?

2   What are important lexicogrammatical features that index repeated discursive practices in this meeting?

3   Are there any generalizations can be drawn about the discourse?

The theory/approach to discourse analysis that informs the study

Analysing spoken professional discourse presents particular yet fruitful challenges when exploring the relationship between the text and context (Charles and Charles 1999). To achieve a plausible interpretation of the data or, as Bhatia (2004) puts it, to see the whole of the elephant, it is necessary to use a variety of tools. Therefore, an interdisciplinary approach is taken here, drawing on methods and insights from corpus linguistics (McCarthy 1998; Stubbs 2001; Flowerdew 2005; Baker 2006; Hunston 2011), genre analysis (Swales 1990; Bazerman 1994; Bhatia 2004, 2008; Koester and Handford 2011), discourse analysis and professional discourse analysis (Gee 2005; Gee et al. 1996; Holmes and Stubbe 2003; Koester 2006; Handford 2010) and construction communication (Emmitt and Gorse 2003; Dainty et al. 2006; Handford and Matous 2011).

Each of the above approaches can provide different discursive insights: genre analysis illuminates the relationship between participants' goals, their involvement in a community and the overall participatory framework; corpus linguistics provides a pathway into the data and can unearth previously unforeseen findings, while providing a degree of objectivity that may be lacking in some discourse analyses; Gee's approach to discourse analysis brings to light the nature and function of practices and power, through the combination of emic and etic insights, and Gee's notion of 'situated meanings' (2005) shows how linguistic forms employed in a specific context can index practices (see Figure 6.1 below) and thus achieve meaning in that context (also see Ochs 1996); professional discourse analysis explores the constrained nature of the discourse among those at work, especially in terms of lexicogrammar and pragmatic

Discourse:	being a Chair
Social practice:	managing a construction project
Professional practice:	problem-solving
Discursive practice:	clarifying direction of discussion
Text:	*So thank you and er (2.0 seconds) now er do you want to discuss main bridge or er start with RTW take the decision and then?*

FIGURE 6.1 *The relation between language and practice.*

features; and construction communication provides insights on the wider professional context from the perspective of the construction industry. While the combination of these approaches illuminates more parts of the elephant than a single approach would permit, the data could also be analysed from various other perspectives to let us see more. These include intercultural communication, gender studies, management studies and social network theory.

How context is understood in the study

Conversational analysts persuasively caution against 'bucket' approaches to context (Drew and Heritage 1992), that is, those which assume the relevance of external contextual features without showing their relevance in the data and which ignore the reflexive, dynamic relationship between language and context. While the approach to understanding context in this study is very much grounded in the textual features of the interactions, to offer plausible interpretations of *professional* communication it is often necessary to consider a wider range of potential contextually relevant features than is evidenced in the transcripts. This is not only because the researcher tends not to be an 'insider', but also because much of what is said can be interpreted from several points of view, and various candidate explanations can be offered given the multiple overt and covert communicative goals in professional settings, several of which explanations may be simultaneously valid.

For instance, in the meeting analysed below, certain utterances are ostensibly addressed to the Chair, but in fact may be uttered for the benefit of other members of the meeting, or for the 'audience', which in this meeting is made up of the financiers of the project sitting at the back of the room who take no active part in the meeting itself. As such, this meeting shares certain contextual features with media discourse despite being a 'private' meeting. However, to offer a plausible account of the possible intended audience(s) of an utterance, it is necessary to go beyond the transcript and to conduct ethnographic-style research into the background context. Even then, we need to remember we are at best working at the level of inference, as our understanding of context and goals is inevitably incomplete (Cook 1989; McCarthy 1998), speakers may not in retrospect accurately link goals and communication (Hopper and Drummond 1990), and professional discourse is inherently multifunctional (Holmes and Stubbe 2003; Handford 2010).

The relationship between the text and the context in this study is modelled in terms of layers of practices (Handford 2010, 2012; Handford and Matous 2011), which as they become more general have a less direct relationship with the text (see Bhatia 2004). Figure 6.1 shows how an utterance can be interpreted using this approach, with the arrow indicating the ever-widening context which the text reflexively constitutes. In other words, we (and the participants) make sense of the utterance through making such contextual factors relevant.

The context of the study

Typically, construction projects can be broken into two parts: the project design phase and the actual construction phase (Emmitt and Gorse 2003). The meeting analysed here is part of the latter stages of the design phase of a bridge construction project in South Asia; it is the eleventh gathering in the design process, the first having taken place two years earlier.

In this extract, there are several parties present at the meeting: the design consultants (DC), the national bridge association (NBA) representatives and the head of the national construction ministry, the panel of experts (PoE) including the Chair, an independent checking engineer and the financiers. There are two representatives of the (American multinational) design company: one designer who is German and another who is from New Zealand (the only L1 speaker of English in the meeting). There are several members from the national bridge association, all of whom are from the host nation. The independent checking engineer is from Denmark, and the PoE is made up of a mixture of experts from the host nation, Colombia, Japan and Norway. The PoE have various areas of expertise including structural engineering, environmental issues and resettlement. In total, there are 15 active participants in the meeting from seven countries. The financiers, from various banks such as the Asian Development Bank, while present do not actually speak at all during the meeting. All the participants in the meeting were male, mainly in their 50s or 60s, although a couple of the participants including the Chair were in their 70s.

Each group has a different function in the meeting, with differing and sometimes conflicting goals, leading to divergent communication, which again is typical of large construction projects (Emmitt and Gorse 2003). The DC have to prepare a design for the bridge which the construction companies can bid for, and then construct; the NBA's is concerned with ensuring this design suits their domestic needs; the PoE was hired by the financiers to make sure the DC designs an appropriate bridge – appropriate in terms of structure and safety, and in terms of the needs of various stakeholders, including those who may not have a voice, such as the residents of the affected area who are

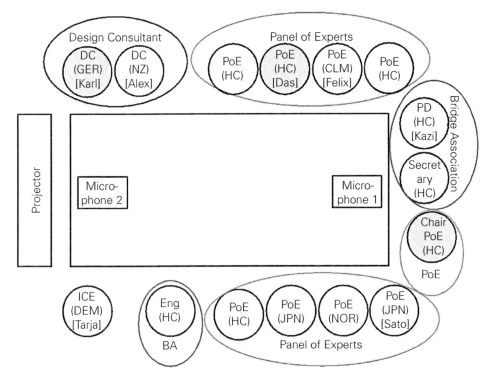

FIGURE 6.2 *Seating plan.*

to be resettled; the independent checking engineer's function overlaps with that of the PoE and is there to check that the bridge design meets various criteria[2]; the financiers are observing the meeting to check whether the project in which they have invested is progressing as expected. Figure 6.2 shows the seating arrangements around the table. The financiers sat at the back of the room in a row behind the DC.

The presence of the financiers cannot be ignored, for while they do not actively take part in the discussions, according to the participants in follow-up interviews at least some of the contributions were for their benefit. As such, the meeting is in some ways unusual in that discussions are directed at the other members around the table. Here, however, the meeting is somewhat similar to media discourse in that it is, at least sometimes, for the benefit of a passive audience.

Data

The data used in this study can be broken into two types: primary data, for instance recordings of the meeting and written documents which are referred to during the meeting, and what might be termed 'reference data', which include reference corpora and background literature from the civil engineering field.

Primary data

There were several types of primary data that I was able to collect. These include written documents; an audio recording of the whole meeting, which was then transcribed; observation notes and interviews. This section will outline these types of data in more detail, and how they were collected.

1. Audio recordings and transcription

Digital recorders were placed at either end of the table where the participants were seated to capture all the discussions that took place (see Figure 6.2). There were four meetings spread over the two days, and this chapter analyses the second of the four meetings, comprising 41,207 words, and which took place at the beginning of the second day. Once recorded, the meetings were then fully transcribed, then checked and anonymized by two transcribers. Because the main linguistic focus for the text analysis in this research project is lexicogrammar, prosodic features were not transcribed.

2. Written documents

I was able to obtain several written documents related to the project from my colleague on the PoE several weeks before the meeting took place, which provided a lot of background information on the project. These included the bridge design documents made by the DC and several technical documents. While the former were reasonably accessible, the latter were more specialized in nature and meant I had to have discussions with relevant experts.

   In addition to the above documents, the meeting minutes of the preceding ten gatherings were also made available. These again not only contained a lot of technical information, but also showed who had attended the meetings, and how certain themes continued through several meetings. For instance, there was ongoing discussion from the first meeting about what system should be used for supporting the bridge design – geobags or rocks to support the bridge structures along the riverbed. The DC were proposing using geobags (heavy duty bags containing sand or silt), whereas several members of the PoE were critical of this proposal. In interviews with the DC members, it seems one reason for the PoE's stance was that they had not used this technique on earlier projects. In the meeting analysed here, an agreement to use geobags is in the process of being reached, although the divergent goals of the groups in terms of their preferences may account for the evaluative (Hunston 2011) and at times divergent (Handford and Koester 2010) language evidenced below.

3. Observation notes

As I was allowed to sit in during the meeting at the back of the room, I was able to make notes of the proceedings, make diagrams of seating arrangements, list the stages, phases and moves of the meeting as they unfolded, make a note of any particularly interesting exchanges and note any problematic terms, discussions or references that I did not understand or which seemed particularly important. The participants could then be approached straight after the meeting about such issues, while they were still fresh in their minds.

4. Interviews, emails, etc.

Apart from the immediate follow-up interviews, I was able to conduct several interviews prior to the meeting and have remained in contact with selected members of the meeting. This means I can email the participants about any queries and also ask representatives of the differing organizations and groups the same question to see compare responses.

Reference data

In addition to these primary data sources, there are also 'reference data'. What I mean by this are the reference corpora that are used to provide a benchmark against which the recordings can be compared. In this case, the CANCODE[3] and VOICE[4] corpora were used to discover statistically significant keywords, and the CANBEC[5] and the British National Corpus were used for more general comparisons. Literature on 'construction communication' could also be included as reference data, especially the book-length studies by Emmitt and Gorse (2003) and Dainty et al. (2006), and research by Loosemore (e.g. Trajkovsk and Loosemore 2006; Loosemore and Galea 2009).

Analysis

As stated above, this is an interdisciplinary study employing tools and insights from several fields. The analysis itself is divided into two parts: a brief outline of the meeting as genre and a corpus-driven analysis of important lexicogrammatical items and the discursive practices they invoke. The genre analysis unveils the overall structure and goals of the meeting, and the corpus analysis pinpoints some of the items that invoke recurrent discursive practices that make up the genre.

Genre analysis is a powerful approach for analysing professional data because it ties together several pertinent areas, including the participants, their goals and the structure of the event. Swales much quoted definition of genre analysis specifies these:

> genre comprises a class of communicative events, the members of which share some set of communicative purposes. These purposes are recognised by the expert members of the parent discourse community, and thereby constitute the rationale for the genre. This rationale shapes the schematic structure of the discourse and influences and constrains choice of content and style. (Swales 1990: 58)

While this definition will be applied in the next section to the data, it is worth exploring in more detail the notion of constraint in professional genres. This is because constraint means constrained context and language: what is permissible and appropriate, and what is not. Bhatia (2004: 23), in his analysis of written professional genres, explains how constraint and convention are recurrently realized in lexicogrammatical and discursive form, areas which corpus linguistics can also help clarify (Tribble 2002; Baker 2006; Handford 2010). Genre analysis thus illuminates the relationship between the language interlocutor's use and the contexts they invoke, repeat and sometimes challenge. The key benefit of professional genre analysis to this study is through this clear conceptualization of constraint in professional settings. A central assumption is that, as the participants are all 'experts', this is an 'expert performance' of the genre (Bazerman 1994); from this we can infer that, unless otherwise signalled in the text or the interviews, the descriptive and the normative merge. In other words, what these experts *do* (with language) is what they *should do* in this context.

Following the brief analysis of the meeting as genre, a corpus-driven discourse analysis will be conducted. According to Tribble (2002), corpus tools, such as the Wordsmith keyness tool version 5 (Scott 2011),which pinpoints statistically significant items when compared to a reference corpus, can shed light on the constraints of the social context of a given genre by pinpointing recurrent and therefore appropriate, lexicogrammatical items. Also of interest are 'negative' keywords, that is, words that occur with a less than random frequency in comparison with the reference corpus. In this study, the main reference corpus is the three-million word social and intimate spoken communication sub-corpus of the CANCODE corpus. This allows us to see how our meeting data compares to 'everyday English'. As CANCODE is primarily made up of L1 users of English, and the meeting mainly involves L2 users (14 out of 15 speakers), the one million VOICE corpus of ELF interactions has also been used as a reference corpus. Interestingly, the results from both reference corpora for positive and negative keywords show a very high degree of overlap, suggesting that the negative and positive keyword findings are not strongly influenced by the fact that the speakers are L2 users, but may be influenced by other factors such as their profession and their stance. The results outlined below are taken from the CANCODE comparisons.

While keyword analysis is an excellent method for pinpointing statistically significant items in relation to a reference corpus, pure frequency lists can also show what are typical items in the data. This is particularly the case with clusters, that is lexicogrammatical items of more than one word in length (Handford 2010). These longer items are of interest because they often convey a context-specific (constrained) pragmatic intent, as in the common business chunk *you have to*. Analysis of the CANBEC corpus reveals that, depending on the relationship of the speakers, the meaning conveyed by this item can be quite different: it can be used to direct subordinates, or it can offer friendly advice to associates (Handford 2010).

Another interesting aspect of the analysis of clusters is at the paradigmatic level: from a semantic perspective, it seems feasible that speakers may choose to use synonymous phrases such as *you must* rather than *you have to*. However, whereas there are several hundred instances of *you have to* in CANBEC, there are hardly any examples of *you must*. This can be explained in terms of the potential face threat which might be interpreted by the use of *must*; *(you) have to*, in contrast, has a more objective and arguably institutional semantic prosody. The use of deontic modal forms in the context of our bridge meeting will be explored below.

The lexicogrammatical analysis will thus employ a corpus-driven approach, the only expectation of which being that it will throw up some interesting findings. Nevertheless, this is not to suggest that recurrence of use is the only measure of importance in discourse, as of course there are other types of items could be pinpointed in a longer study (see Handford 2010), such as those that have been shown to be of interest in other, related studies, and those that are culturally key. An example of the former might be the use of metaphors and idioms in business (e.g. Handford and Koester 2010), which because of their variety do not appear on blunt statistical lists, and an example of the latter in a professional setting might be *goal*. In business, there are many items that may be used in everyday language and therefore do not show up in keyword comparisons, like *goal*, but they have a constrained meaning in a business context (Nelson 2000).

As stated above, this corpus analysis can unearth areas of interest from an indexical (Ochs 1996) perspective: the situated meanings (Gee 2005) of keywords and clusters in the context of this meeting index discursive practices which can help us better understand what the interlocutors are doing in this specific context, and how the interaction relates to the wider context (Handford 2010). The analysis is iterative, in that it moves from the lexicogrammatical findings to the background data and back again to offer plausible interpretations of what the interlocutors are doing.

Findings

1. Genre analysis

The categories of Swales' (1990: 58) definition are applied to the design meeting (see Table 6.1) through a combination of the background interviews and notes, and the corpus-informed textual analysis. The schematic structure of the meeting follows that developed in Handford (2010: 61–70).

Despite the fact that various topics are covered at the differing phases of the meeting, certain themes run throughout. These include the issue of whether the project should use geobags or rocks to support the structure and the riverbed (as mentioned above in the primary data discussion). Also, after each report was made, there was some discussion of the points raised by particular participants. For example, following the first report on resettlement compensation, there were some further points raised by the government minister. On several occasions, such discussions became somewhat fractious, and they were occasionally punctuated by humorous asides, thus demonstrating both divergent and convergent communication respectively. For instance, one of the goals of this

Table 6.1 Genre breakdown

Class of communicative events: business meeting

Communicative purposes: address issues of tardiness of project; receive reports on resettlement, and environmental impact study; begin to draw up document for tender

The discourse community: the participants in the meeting (PoE, DC etc)

Evidence of constraint of content and style: see section 2 below

The schematic structure of the discourse:

Stage pre-1: Small talk

Transition move: Chair moves to opening meeting

Stage 1: Opening of meeting

Apologies

Stage 2: Discussion of the agenda

i) Chair invites the following reports:

    1a. report on resettlement by PoE resettlement expert

    1b. discussion of 1a

    2a. update on environmental issues by PoE environmental consultant

    2b. discussion of 2b

    3a. report on structural concerns by PoE structural expert

    3b. discussion of 3a

    4a. design consultants respond to various concerns

    4b. discussion of 4a

ii) Meeting returns to previous day's topic of river training.

iii) Topic moves on to discussion of tender works and tender document.

Stage 3: Closing of meeting: at lunchtime.

meeting is to speed up the design construction process. In extract 1 (during phase 4b of stage 2), we see the senior design consultant ($5) sardonically commenting to the Chair ($1) on the possibility of the process taking 'another five years', which provokes widespread laughter.

Extract 1
<$1> There is no possibility of going beyond six point one five.
<$5> Correct.
<$1> That length+
<$5> Yeah.

<$1> +takes into account additional erosion. Okay.
<$5> Unless it takes another five years to award the contract.
<$12> I I.
<$1> Don't say that.
<$5> The you know.
(Laughing)

The meeting progresses in terms of presentations and reports by experts or relevant people invited by the Chair, which are then discussed by the other participants. Thus, the meeting is made up of several long uninterrupted turns, with no back channelling, followed by discussion. For instance, there are seven monologic turns of more than 500 words, with the longest comprising 2262 words, lasting about four and a half minutes. In a separate study on this same data set, Tsuchiya and Handford (in preparation) analyse the length of all turns in the meeting and find that, per speaker, the average number of words per turn varies from 13 words to 106 words. As for the number of turns taken, the Chair takes 32 per cent of all turns although the average length of a turn is only 20 words, indicating how active a role he plays in managing the meeting without dominating the discussions.

A defining feature of any genre is its communicative purpose (Swales 1990), and the primary purposes of this meeting are to discuss the bridge project's delay and address the concerns of the PoE. Nevertheless, there are other rather more covert goals, which might include allaying any fears the observing financiers may have about the proposed process and proving to the financiers that the PoE, and indeed the other parties, are fulfilling their professional roles. As discussed earlier, as it is impossible to categorically state that communication is caused by one or other goal, it is therefore more prudent to allow for multiple goals affecting the discourse.

2. Lexicogrammatical analysis

Keywords

From the keyword comparison with the CANCODE (and VOICE) corpus, one of the striking findings is the very high number of nouns in the top 300 keywords, even when compared to other keyword lists of spoken professional interactions (e.g. Nelson 2000; Handford 2010). There are around 80 per cent of noun keywords, whereas in the CANBEC keyword list (made up of mainly L1 meetings), approximately 60 per cent of the keywords are nouns. Given that the comparison with the ELF VOICE corpus also threw up a very high number of (largely the same) nouns (again around 80 per cent), the suggestion that this very high nominal density is down to the speakers being L2 users of English can be discounted. It is also considerably higher than a study of ELF interactions on a construction site (Handford and Matous 2011). From these comparisons, we can tentatively infer that this 'nominal tendency' is specific to this context of the bridge design meeting, rather than being shared among ELF, business or construction industry interlocutors.

Table 6.2 Keyword nouns in the bridge meeting

Engineering process nouns: design (0.32), construction (0.15), checking (0.07)

Engineering object nouns: geobags (0.20), bridge (0.22), mattress (0.10), fascine (0.11), concrete (0.09)

Physical environment nouns: scour (0.21), rock (0.16), apron (0.10), earthquake (0.08)

River-related nouns: velocity (0.06), flow (0.06), bank (0.15), slope (0.13)

Organizational abbreviations: (N)BA, DC, POE (0.02)

Finance-related nouns: payment (0.05). compensation (0.05), financiers (0.02), cost (0.08)

General occupation nouns: layer (0.22), contractor (0.20), layers (0.18), report (0.13), consultant (0.07), combination (0.07), tender (0.05), contract (0.09), formula (0.05)

General nouns: alternative (0.06), combination (0.07), factor (0.06), transition (0.04), analysis (0.04), discussion (0.05), solution (0.03), suggestion (0.02), prediction (0.02), decision (0.04), criteria (0.02), effect (0.05)

Evaluative nouns: issue (0.10), flexibility (0.08), issues (0.07), impact (0.06), evaluation (0.02), concerns (0.02), uncertainty (0.02)

Vocative nouns: Sir (0.12), Professor (0.05), Mr (0.07), Dr (0.03)

Table 6.2 provides a categorization of selected keyword nouns (compared to everyday English), with the figure in parentheses representing the frequency of the item in terms of percentage. So *design* accounts for 0.32 per cent of all words in the meeting.

The above categorization can be further broken into two: nouns that are related to engineering and the project (for instance engineering process nouns, or organizational abbreviations), and nouns that are more generally related to work. Even within this latter category, there are fuzzy boundaries, as general and evaluative nouns can also be used in non-professional settings. However, it is important to reiterate that the keyword analysis explicitly tells us that these items are more typical of this professional context than everyday situations.

Of further note is the high number of evaluative nouns, which again did not tend to appear in the CANBEC comparison to CANCODE (Handford 2010). There are also several evaluative adjectives and adverbs on the keyword list (see Table 6.3 below), which further add to the evaluative tone of much of this meeting. Extract 2 shows how the evaluative noun *flexibility* is used by the Colombian structural engineer on the PoE ($12). He is categorically telling the DC that the whole section much be completed in one working section, and that there is no 'flexibility' over that.

Extract 2
<$12> Yeah. I want er I only want to add that flexibility is flexibility but where there is not this flexibility that any part south or north has to be completed as a whole in one single season.

<$5> Yes.
<$12> There is no flexibility.
<$1> Oh yes.

The evaluative nature of the communication and the stance and relationships of the participants was very apparent in the interviews I conducted before and after the meeting, with many interviewees commenting on the sometimes fractious nature of the communication and the diverging goals of the different parties. Interestingly, the evaluative nature of the discourse tended to be framed rather formally, for instance in terms of the tendency to use nominalizations and formal terms of address, which is discussed further below.

Several of the 'general' and 'evaluative' keyword nouns have verb forms, for instance *suggestion*, *prediction* or *evaluation* (or adjectival forms, such as *flexible*). Given that one of the differences between spoken and written language is that verbs tend to be preferred to nouns (Carter and McCarthy 2006), we might expect that in other spoken contexts the verb form might be preferred. In systemic functional linguistics, the use of nouns where verbs may be more congruent, or vice versa, is termed 'grammatical metaphor' (Halliday 1985), and one attraction for speakers is that it achieves a degree of succinctness that is not usually possible with the verb form. Furthermore, the process to which it refers can be placed in various syntactic positions in the clause, and the process to which it refers can become a participant in other processes. For these reasons, it tends to be found in formal written styles (Biber 1988). More generally, nominalization allows speakers 'to withhold identity of agents and causality of events' (Jaworski and Coupland 1999: 497). At the end of this section, such lexicogrammatical tendencies and discursive practices will be explored in a short extract from the meeting.

Another contextually interesting finding from the noun keyword list was the use of vocatives. In the meeting, the person's title followed by the family name is often used, signalling a high degree of formality and a large social distance (Carter and McCarthy 2006). Vocatives are often used as part of turn management in the meeting, for example the Chair's discursive practice of nominating the next speaker:

Extract 3:
< $1> Er Mr Tarja? Are you aware of the responsibility of looking at the specifications? Er.

However, apart from the independent checking engineer (Mr Tarja) and the senior DC, the other Western members of the committee are referred to or spoken to by their given name, for instance in extract 4 where the Chair asks the DC for his response.

Extract 4:
<$1> Yes. Karl?

Also, some of the junior members of the NBA are referred to only by their family name. The two individuals who are referred to only by their titles are the Chair and the government minister. Some of the participants from the host country (in South Asia) used 'Sir' when addressing the Chair, even when the message was clearly intended for the whole audience or at other members of the group. For instance in extract 5, the speaker is apparently addressing the Chair about his concerns over the direction of the discussion, whereas in fact it is the design consultant who has reopened the issue of geobags vs rocks.

Extract 5
<$13> Sir sir I I'm I'm getting disturbed. What are we discussing? We have agreed to go for geotextile bags.

The evaluative role of adjectives and adverbs is well documented in corpus studies (e.g. Conrad and Biber 2000; Hunston and Sinclair 2000; Hunston 2011), and Table 6.3 shows that several such items recur in the meeting for example, *robust*, *critical* and *correctly* (see Table 6.3). While most of the items are used by a variety of speakers, *frankly*, except for one instance, was used wholly by a single participant (which highlights dispersion issues with a small data set). In addition, there were several verbs in the top keywords that are metalinguistic performatives: *suggest*, *consider*, *propose* and so on. Metalinguistic performatives tend to be the marked form in business interactions and metalanguage in general is an explicit marker of power in professional discourse (Koester 2006; Handford 2010), as indeed are evaluative terms and the discursive practice of evaluating they invoke.

Table 6.4 groups some of the remaining keywords that are not content words, but which instead play a more interpersonal or textual role. The one exception is the definite article *the*, which accounts for 5.88 per cent of all words in the meeting. This is a very high percentage in spoken language (in CANBEC meetings, the percentage is 3.7 per cent) and is far closer to written language (in the 90 million word written sub-corpus of the BNC, the percentage is around 6.1 per cent). The indefinite article *a* is somewhat surprisingly on the negative keyword list, which contains items significantly less likely to occur in the meeting in comparison with everyday speech. As *the* often indexes already shared knowledge, whereas *a* tends to introduce new or unknown content, we can conclude that such statistical differences indicate a very high degree of shared knowledge and references between the speakers. This can be explained by the fact that the participants have regularly gathered on this project over a period of two years, and that many of the participants have known each other for far longer than that.

As for the interpersonal and textual items, several of these items and the categories to which they belong are also found in other business meetings, for instance the pronoun *we* (fulfilling the discursive practice of signalling relationships and identities), the modal verbs *will* and *should* (used to negotiate power over actions), and the hedge *er*. Also, while deictic terms signalling place are not typical in business meetings, they were found to be statistically significant in on-site interactions in the construction industry (Handford and

Table 6.3 Keyword verbs, adjectives and adverbs

Verbs: is (2.40), agree (0.11), agreed (0.08), have (1.21) has (0.29), are (0.73), propose (0.04), placed (0.04), consider (0.04), discussed (0.03), include (0.03), accept (0.03), suggest (0.02)

Adjectives: critical (0.06), conservative (0.04), robust (0.02), correct (0.05), temporary (0.03), provisional (0.02)

Adverbs: basically, correctly (0.03), reasonably (0.03), frankly (0.02)

Table 6.4 Miscellaneous keywords

Discourse markers: okay, so

Article: the (5.88)

Pronouns: we (1.87)

Modal verbs: will (0.48), cannot (0.04), should (0.18), may (0.06)

Deictics: this (1.18), that (1.99), these (0.23)

Conjunctions: also (0.28), so (1.27)

Hedge: Er (4.01)

Matous 2011). That they occur in a sit-down meeting in a room, as opposed to outside on a construction site, highlights the physical nature of construction communication, even when the actual physical context is displaced in terms of time and location, as here.

It is of note, however, that there are no back channels on this list, as they are a key feature in other business meetings (Koester 2006; Holmes and Stubbe 2003; Handford 2010). This relative dearth of back channels is partly explained by the long monologues which are a recurrent feature of this meeting. The practice of evaluation that forms such a theme of the meeting can also help explain the lack of back channels: as back channels tend to evidence supportive listenership (McCarthy 1998), their absence suggests a more critical stance. Another interpersonal feature common to meetings but absent here is the use of vague language (e.g. vague category markers like *and stuff like that*), which is often used in business to create a sense of shared knowledge in an informal way (Handford 2010). Its absence may be attributable to transactional and interpersonal reasons: the need for extremely clear meanings in the context of bridge design (given issues like safety implications) and the overall evaluative, formal and somewhat critical or divergent tone of the meeting.

Clusters

Clusters are of particular interest in studies of discourse, because they can invoke recurrent discursive practices (Handford 2010). Table 6.5 is a categorization of the most frequent two and three-word clusters[6] and the primary discursive practices they index. Instead of giving percentages (which in many cases are very low), the figures in parentheses represent the number of occurrences in the meeting. The most frequent clusters in business meetings tend to be interpersonal (Handford 2010), and in this highly transactional meeting we also find many interpersonal clusters; Table 6.5 shows there are very few recurrent noun phrases. Notwithstanding this, there are five instances of the phrase *preposition + definite article* among the top 15 two-word clusters, which in total account for 1.7 per cent of all words in the meeting, and are further evidence of the high degree of nominalization (in CANBEC, the same five clusters accounted for 0.99 per cent of all words). Also of note is the frequency of the clusters involving the 'dummy subject' *there is/are*, which is often used to frame evaluations (Hunston and Sinclair 2000).

From an interpersonal perspective, it is interesting to compare the frequent deontic modal clusters here and in the CANBEC corpus, as all the items listed here are also among the most frequent in the larger corpus. Such a finding suggests there is overlap at the lexical and discursive levels between English L1 and ELF professional contexts (a similar finding was reported in Handford and Matous 2011). Deontic modals are used to negotiate power over actions, and, as stated above, while there are a wide range of such modal and semi-modal verbs, there is a strong preference for some and not others: both here and in CANBEC, *need, have to, should* and *can* are very common, but clusters involving *must, ought to* and *had better* are rarely or never used. This may be due to the face-threat implicated by *must*, and the more objective nuance of *have to* and *need to* (McCarthy and Handford 2004). Also, it is noteworthy that the more

Table 6.5 Cluster categories and main discursive practices

Preposition + definite article: of the (188); in the (146); for the (121); on the (109); to the (76)

Practice: outlining processes/relating concepts and objects

Existential 'there + be': is (102); There are (53); There will be (19)

Practice: presenting information as fact

Hedges, indirect expressions: I think (105); you know (53); sort of (33); kind of (25); I mean (15)

Practice: negotiating power over knowledge/negotiating threats to face

If + pronoun: if you 68 (0.18) if we (29); so if (17); if it (15); if I (14)

Practice: Problem-solving/Suggesting

Modal forms: have to (55); we can (41), you can (35); need to (34); we should (20); we have to (20); we need to (14)

Practice: negotiating power over action

Noun phrases: the South Bank (23); the river training (18); the main bridge (15); the design consultant (13)

Practice: communicating ideational content

collaboratively framed *we need to* and *we have to* are more frequent that the *you need to* and *you have to*, and most of these uses are inclusive, for example, *Er but we have to move forward now.*

In extract 6 (taken from the beginning of phase 2b from stage 2 of the meeting), we see several of the categories and practices discussed so far at work. Here the DC is responding to the criticism from the environmental engineer (Henrik) that the DC has not responded to requests to have an environmental expert draw up a short report comparing geobags with rocks.

Extract 6
<$5> Yes er (*Clears throat*) sorry. Um yes the intention always was to arrive at um hopefully a um a final decision um today er on the extent of geobags versus rock um incorporating the works and we'll see what flows from that. And as Henrik says very correctly umer if the decision is made um to go for a anoption incorporating substantial number of geobags. The potential e= um effects of that needs to be examined. And so we would propose once that decision is made to um er get our environmental team to review that and produce a um I think the easiest way to do it is a is a supplement erto the existing report.
(3.5 seconds)

There are several instances of nouns being used in the subject and complement positions, along with the use of passive rather than active forms of verbs. This leads to a depersonalizing of the discourse, which simultaneously objectifies it and reduces the degree of agency, thus enabling the responsibility for the inaction to be framed in terms of processes rather the responsibility of agents (in this case, the DC). The use of a metaphor to provide an indirect evaluation (we'll see what *flows* from that) is also a common feature of other meetings (Handford 2010). The extract includes several items pinpointed in the corpus searches: types of nouns, of both an engineering and more general nature (*geobags, supplement, effects*); contrasting uses of *we*, indexing an inclusive identity (*we'll see . . .*), and an exclusive one (*we would propose*); power-indicating evaluations such as performative verbs (*review, propose*), and evaluative adverbs and adjectives (*correctly, easiest, substantial*); the frequent deontic modal form *need to* which indexes obligatory action; a convergent vocative (Henrik); the use of *if* to hypothesize about a possible outcome, and that of *will* to frame a future event. These items and practices combine to shape a response to the criticism that both acknowledges the criticism, thus achieving a degree of convergence, and proposes a professionally appropriate and confidently worded response.

Conclusion

This analysis has attempted to show how recurrent and frequent lexicogrammatical items invoke and are constrained by the context of this meeting as genre. This meeting features several types of items that Koester (2006: 129–31; also Handford and Koester 2010) terms 'emphatic markers of subjective stance', that is items that frame the discourse as less convergent than might otherwise be the case. These include the surprisingly high degree, in comparison with other studies of meetings, of evaluative language, particularly nouns, adjectives and adverbs, as well as metalinguistic performative verbs. Also, the relative infrequency of certain interpersonal items commonly associated with convergent business communication (vague language, hedges, back channels) adds to the forthright context of much of the communication. This frankness is combined with a high degree of formality, evident in the forms of address, and the heavy nominal density, which are more typical of formal writing registers. Nevertheless, while the overall context can be categorized as frank yet formal, the meeting is punctuated by moments of humour, and there is evidence of convergence, as in the choice of deontic modals and inclusive *we*. Therefore, in answer to the question, how does this meeting compare to other professional contexts in terms of discursive practices and the language used to invoke them, evaluating appears more commonplace, overt and cumulative (Hunston 2011), and while negotiating power over actions and knowledge are evident in all meetings, such practices are less hedged in this meeting. Furthermore, the forthright baldly evaluative tone apparent in the meeting contrasts with many other studies of business English as a lingua franca (e.g. Rogerson-Revell 2008), but has been described in other studies of international construction communication (Emmitt and Gorse 2003).

Notes

1 The actual location will not be stated to protect the confidentiality of the participants.
2 In interviews with the participants, this overlapping of goals was seen as a potential source of conflict, as the independent checking engineer might resent having his role duplicated. Given that conflict is usually attributed to conflicting goals, it is interesting to see that the same goals can also cause conflict in professional discourse.
3 Cambridge and Nottingham Corpus of Discourse English, copyright Cambridge University Press. Project directors Profs Ronald Carter and Michael McCarthy.
4 Vienna and Oxford International Corpus of English, http://www.univie.ac.at/voice/page/what_is_voice.
5 Cambridge and Nottingham Business English Corpus, copyright Cambridge University Press. Project directors Profs Ronald Carter and Michael McCarthy.
6 Only two and three-word clusters are examined because of space constraints.

References

Baker, P. (2006), *Using Corpora in Discourse Analysis*. London: Continuum.
Bazerman, C. (1994), 'Systems of genres and the enhancement of social intentions', in A. Freedman and P. Medway (eds), *Genre & New Rhetoric*. London: Taylor & Francis, pp. 79–101.

Biber, D. (1988), *Variation Across Speech and Writing*. Cambridge: Cambridge University Press.

Bhatia, V. (2004), *Worlds of Written Discourse*. London: Continuum.

Bhatia, V. (2008), 'Towards critical genre analysis', in V. Bhatia, J. Flowerdew and R. Jones (eds), *Advances in Discourse Studies*. Abingdon: Routledge, pp. 166–77.

Charles, M. and Charles, D. (1999), 'Sales Negotiations: Bargaining through Tactical Summaries', in M. Hewings and C. Nickerson (eds), *Business English: Research into Practice*. London: Longman, pp. 71–99.

Conrad, S. and Biber, D. (2000), 'Adverbial markers of stance in speech and writing', in S. Hunston and G. Thompson (eds), *Evaluation in Text: Authorial Stance and the Construction of Discourse*. Oxford: Oxford University Press, pp. 56–73.

Cook, G. (1989), 'Transcribing infinity: Problems of context presentation'. *Journal of Pragmatics*, 15, 1–24.

Dainty, A., Moore, D. and Murray, M. (2006), *Communication in Construction: Theory and Practice*. London: Taylor and Francis.

Drew, P. and Heritage, J. (1992), 'Analysing Talk at Work: An Introduction', in P. Drew and J. Heritage (eds), *Talk at Work*. Cambridge: Cambridge University Press, pp. 3–65.

Emmitt, S. and Gorse, C. (2003), *Construction Communication*. Oxford: Blackwell.

Flowerdew, L. (2005), 'An integration of corpus-based and genre-based approaches to text analysis in EAP/ESP: Countering criticisms against corpus-based methodologies'. *English for Specific Purposes*, 24, 321–32.

Gee, J. P. (2005), *An Introduction to Discourse Analysis*. Abingdon: Routledge.

Gee. J. P., Hull, G. and Lankshear, C. (1996), *The New Work Order: Behind the Language of the New Capitalism*. London: Allenand Unwin.

Halliday, M. (1985), *An Introduction to Functional Grammar*. London: Edward Arnold.

Handford, M. (2010), *The Language of Business Meetings*. Cambridge: Cambridge University Press.

Handford, M. and Koester, A. (2010), 'It's not Rocket Science': Metaphors and Idioms in Conflictual Business Meetings. *Text & Talk,* 30(1), 27–51.

Handford, M. and Matous, P. (2011), 'Lexicogrammar in the international construction industry: A corpus-based case study of Japanese – Hong-Kongese on-site interactions in English'. *English for Specific Purposes*, 30(2), 87–100.

Holmes, J. and Stubbe, M. (2003), *Power and Politeness in the Workplace*. London: Longman.

Hopper, P. and Drummond, K. (1990), 'Emergent goals and relational turning point: The case of Gordon and Denise', in K. Tracy and N. Coupland (eds), *Multiple Goals in Discourse*. Avon: Multilingual Matters, pp: 39–65.

Hunston, S. (2011), *Corpus Approaches to Evaluation*. Abingdon: Routledge.

Hunston, S. and Sinclair, J. (2000), 'A local grammar of evaluation', in S. Hunston and G. Thompson (eds), *Evaluation in Text: Authorial Stance and the Construction of Discourse*. Oxford: Oxford University Press, pp. 74–101.

Jaworski, A. and Coupland, N. (1999), 'Introduction to Part Six', in Jaworski, A. and Coupland, N. (eds), *The Discourse Reader*. London: Routledge, pp. 495–501.

Koester, A. (2006), *Investigating Workplace Discourse*. Routledge: London.

Koester, A. and Handford, M. (2011), 'Spoken Professional Genres', in J. P. Gee and M. Handford (eds), *The Routledge Handbook of Discourse Analysis*. Abingdon: Routledge, pp. 252–69.

Loosemore, M. and Galea, N. (2008), 'Genderlect and conflict in the Australian construction industry'. *Construction Management and Economics*, 26, 125–35.

Trajkovski, S. and Loosemore, M. (2006), 'Safety implications of low-English proficiency among migrant construction site operatives'. *International Journal of Project Management*, 24(5), 446–52.

McCarthy, M. (1998), *Spoken Language and Applied Linguistics*. Cambridge: Cambridge University Press.

McCarthy, M. and Handford, M. (2004), '"Invisible to us"': A preliminary corpus-based study of spoken business English', in U. Connor and T. Upton (eds), *Discourse in the Professions: Perspectives from Corpus Linguistics*. Amsterdam: John Benjamins, pp. 167–202.

Nelson, M. (2000), '*A Corpus-based Study of Business English and Business English Teaching Materials*'. Unpublished PhD Thesis. Manchester: University of Manchester.

Ochs, E. (1996), 'Linguistic resources for socializing humanity', in J. Gumperz (ed.), *Rethinking Linguistic Relativity*. Cambridge: Cambridge University Press, pp. 407–37.

Rogerson-Revell, P. (2008), 'Participation and performance in international business meetings'. *English for Specific Purposes,* 27, 338–60.

Scott, M. (2011), *Wordsmith Tools, Version 5*. Oxford: Oxford University Press.

Stubbs, M. (2001), 'On inference theories and code theories: Corpus evidence for semantic schemas'. *Text*, 21(3), 437–65.

Swales, J. (1990), *Genre Analysis*. Cambridge: Cambridge University Press.

Tribble, C. (2002), 'Corpora and corpus analysis: New windows on academic writing', in J. Flowerdew (ed.), *Academic Discourse*. London: Longman, pp. 131–49.

Tsuchiya, K. and Handford, M. (in preparation), Not 'letting it pass' in an ELF business meeting in South Asia: A time-aligned corpus based approach.

7

Ethnicities without guarantees: An empirically situated approach

Roxy Harris and Ben Rampton[1]

1 Introduction and goals

What can the close study of the everyday interactional life in a multi-ethnic urban setting reveal to us about contemporary ethnicity?

Over the last 50 years or so in the United Kingdom, the discussion of race and ethnicity has centred, often with very good reason, on conflict, discrimination, racism and anti-racism, placing ongoing struggle between clearly demarcated dominant and subordinated racial and ethnic groups in the foreground. But the public and academic discourses that describe this environment rarely look beyond explicit statements to *non-propositional* expression and its capacity to evoke and engage with contexts which push racial antagonism into the background. This limitation seriously skews the empirical account of ethnic difference as a context for everyday interaction, and in consequence, social science often struggles to produce empirical analyses of the conditions that facilitate the emergence of 'new' and 'convivial' ethnicities, unobstructed by the splits and divisions emphasized in the dominant idiom (Hall 1988; Gilroy 2006).

This chapter seeks to overcome this limitation by addressing some of the ways in which race and ethnicity are indirectly evoked, performed or noted in the encounters of ordinary life, their significance held in check by a range of much more pressing everyday concerns. It focuses on the interaction of a mixed group of girls in a multiethnic secondary school in London and begins the analysis with what at first looks like a racist statement. But it then turns to linguistic ethnography, itself a relatively recent synthesis of US linguistic anthropology and British applied linguistics, tuned to the interdisciplinary imperatives of contemporary UK social science (cf Rampton 2007; Rampton, Maybin and Tusting 2007, *www.uklef.net*). In doing so, it embeds the apparently racist statement in the shifts and layering of contexts currently in play – the institutional and social network relations among the participants and their histories of interaction together, the types of activity they're engaged in, their positioning in and around institutional discourses and circumambient ideologies, and what's just been said and done. Once these enter the reckoning, the inadequacy of the stock interpretations offered in the dominant discourses stands out, alongside the contribution that the close study of everyday interactional life can make to a better understanding of contemporary ethnic relations.

2 The context of the study: Old and new thinking about race/ethnicity

What we are calling the dominant idiom on race/ethnicity has been influential throughout the period from 1945 to the present day, and with a little arbitrary license, we can divide this into three phases: 1945–75, 1975–97 and 1997–2008.

The phase **1945** to **1975** began with the dominance of social, economic and political systems which were explicitly committed to racial hierarchy, sustained by direct colonial rule in the European Empires (British, French, Dutch, Belgian, Portuguese, etc.), by segregation (USA) and by apartheid (South Africa). The challenge to these systems increased throughout the period and culminated in their overthrow or serious weakening. There was an important warrant for this process of change in the rhetorical claim that the allies were fighting World War II to preserve freedom and democracy – in 1941, Churchill and Roosevelt had initiated The Atlantic Charter, a ringing declaration that democracy and human rights for all were essential international requirements. In London in 1944, black and brown colonial subjects responded with a Charter for Coloured Peoples which they circulated worldwide, demanding that the British state make good its Atlantic Charter commitments (Ramdin; 1987). The following year, the historic 5th Pan-African Congress was held in Manchester to articulate a demand for colonial freedom (Adi and Sherwood 1995), and after World War II, challenges to the explicit systems of racism took a variety of forms. There were (i) *Independence struggles*, movements for independence from colonial rule taking the form of mainly mass movements of civil protest (e.g. the Caribbean, West Africa, India); (ii) *Liberation movements*, armed struggles for independence from colonial rule (e.g. Kenya, Malaya, Mozambique, Angola, Guinea Bissau); and (iii) *Civil Rights movements*, particularly in the United States (e.g. Martin Luther King, the Black Power Movement [Black Panthers + Malcolm X]).

Changing gear away from attempts to suppress these challenges, in the phase **1975** to **1997** a settlement emerged in the United States and United Kingdom acknowledging that racial discrimination existed, was wrong and should be countered (as a minimum) by state interventions in support of (nominal) racial equality and against discriminatory practices (cf. the UK Race Relations Acts 1965, 1968, and the comprehensive 1976 Race Relations Act). The definition of *institutional racism* provided by Stokely Carmichael and Charles V. Hamilton in the United States played a key part precipitating this change:

> "Racism is both overt and covert. It takes two, closely related forms: individual whites acting against individual blacks, and acts by the total white community

against the black community. We call these individual racism and institutional racism. The first consist of overt acts by individuals, which cause death, injury or the violent destruction of property. This type can be recorded by television cameras; it can frequently be observed in the process of commission. The second type is less overt, far more subtle, less identifiable in terms of *specific* individuals committing the acts. But it is no less destructive of human life. The second type originates in the operation of established and respected forces in the society, and thus receives far less public condemnation than the first type." (1967, 1969: 20 [Original emphasis])

This stimulated the idea that state institutions could counter racism with systems of ethnic monitoring for all official bodies. Monitoring would provide a ready and practical way of disclosing racially inspired discrimination and disadvantage, leading in turn to remedial action, at least by implication. Critics would argue that state interventions of this kind were only ever symbolic, tokenistic and deliberately designed to leave racially constructed power structures and relations intact. Nevertheless, these schemes typically involved special funding allocations, building on the racial/ethnic classifications and labels through which the obligatory ethnic monitoring procedures were conducted. From **1997** in the United Kingdom, the Labour Government consolidated legally backed actions against institutional racism, as in, for example, the relatively comprehensive Race Relations Amendment Act (2000). This was supported by moves to strengthen the visibility of black and brown people in Parliament and at the highest levels of the governmental apparatus, and more generally, their appearance in wider spheres of public life has become more normal.

Throughout the post–World War II period, group classifications have been highly problematic. The British Empire was deft at using both *racial* and *ethnic* categories. On the one hand, notions of race reinforced a commonsense in which 'white European' was superior, 'black' was inferior and 'brown' was in between (as in the North American rhyme 'if you're white you're all right, if you're brown stick aroun', if you're black get back'), while on the other, ethnicity was deployed as a subtle tool to divide and rule subordinate colonized populations (e.g. within Africa, Asia or the Caribbean). With ethnic monitoring in the period from 1975 onwards, 'ethnicity' started to displace race as the pre-eminent discursive construct, but there was still a tension between a residual concentration on relations of dominance (race) and the emerging focus on relations of difference (ethnicity). Monitoring itself tended towards a tripartite conceptualization of '*white*' (the majority of the British population), '*black*' (people of Caribbean and/or African descent) and '*Asian*' (Indian, Pakistani, Bangladeshi), and there was often a confusion of *colour* (with implied notions of biological race – 'White', 'Black'), *nationality* ('Pakistani', 'Bangladeshi') and *ethnicity* ('Asian'). Even policy-makers acknowledged the practical problems involved in ethnic monitoring, with 'other' and 'unclassified' becoming an increasingly significant category in survey returns (more than a third in e.g. the monitoring of schools – DfE 1995, Harris 1997: 16–18).

More fundamentally and whatever the labelling used, there was an essentialist tenor to all of these discourses, and for different reasons this was widely accepted by both the dominant majority and subordinate minorities (cf e.g. Bauman 1996). The crucial *break* with these modes of thought and action came with Stuart Hall's seminal 1988 formulation of a 'new ethnicities' perspective and with Paul Gilroy's critique of ethnic absolutism (1987), extended more recently in his conceptualization of urban 'conviviality'.

Insisting that race and ethnicity have 'no guarantees in Nature', Hall challenges the dominant idioms of classification and sees the search for 'goodies' and 'baddies' as limiting. He argues for

> "the 'end of innocence', or the end of the innocent notion of the essential black subject. . . . What is at issue here is the recognition of the extraordinary diversity of subjective positions, social experiences, and cultural identities which compose the category 'black'; that is, the recognition that 'black' is essentially a politically and culturally *constructed* category, which cannot be grounded in a set of fixed transcultural or transcendental racial categories and which therefore has no guarantees in Nature. What this brings into play is the recognition of the immense diversity and differentiation of the historical and cultural experiences of black subjects . . .
>
> Once you enter the politics of the end of the essential black subject you are plunged headlong into the maelstrom of a continuously contingent, unguaranteed, political argument and debate: a critical politics, a politics of criticism. You can no longer conduct black politics through the strategy of a simple set of reversals, putting in the place of the bad old essential white subject the new essentially good black subject." (1988: 254–5)

In the perspective that Hall develops, discourse and context play a crucial role (1988: 253–4), and picking up this view of ethnicity as discursively constituted and situationally contingent, Gilroy considers the implications for everyday life in British cities:

> "Largely undetected by either government or media, Britain's immigrants and their descendants have generated more positive possibilities. Other varieties of interaction have developed alongside the usual tales of crime and racial conflict. These patterns emerge, not from a mosaic pluralism along US lines, in which each self-sustaining and carefully segregated element is located so as to enhance a larger picture, but with an unruly, convivial mode of interaction in which differences have to be negotiated in real time . . .
>
> Recognising conviviality should not signify the absence of racism. Instead, it can convey the idea that alongside its institutional and interpersonal dynamics, the means of racism's overcoming have also evolved . . . In this convivial culture, racial and ethnic differences have been rendered unremarkable, . . . they have been able to become 'ordinary'. Instead of adding to the premium of race as political ontology and economic fate, people discover that the things which really divide them are much more profound: taste, life-style, leisure preferences." (2006: 39–40)

At the same time, it is very difficult for social science to describe in any detail how convivial culture actually works (Gilroy 2006: 28), and indeed Hall also admits "that 'new ethnicities' (like almost everything I have ever written) was not very empirically based" (2007).

This is where our work seeks to make a contribution, and in what follows later, we outline linguistic ethnography and the analysis of ordinary interaction as productive ways of describing the kinds of ethnicity identified by Gilroy and Hall. But first, here is some data.

3 Data: An interaction involving text messages, mobile phones and racial statements

The data in this section come from the project 'Urban Classroom Culture and Interaction', which sought to explore the dynamics of contemporary urban schooling from the students' perspectives. The project followed nine adolescents (5F and 4M) over two years in a London secondary school, and data collection involved participant observation, interviews, radio-microphone recording (180 hours) and playback interviews focusing on the radio-mic data. To set the scene for the interactional episode which follows, two points are in order.

First, the episode is not particularly unusual in the attention that the girls give to popular and new media culture (PNMC) in general, and to text messages in particular. In an observational survey of kids' involvement with PNMC at school, we listened to 80hrs of radio-mic recordings of 5 pupils over 2 years (3F and 2M), identifying over 530 episodes in which they audibly used, referred to or performed: music, TV, mobiles, mp3s, PSPs, PCs, internet, electronic games, magazines, newspaper, fashion, body care, 'recreational food' and sport (cf Dover 2007; Rampton 2006: ch. 3). There was considerable variation between individuals – 237 episodes with one girl, 24 with another – and there were also striking differences in how (and with what degrees of success) young people drew popular and new media culture into the negotiation of their school and peer group relationships. Even so, these five youngsters' involvement with non-curricular, popular and digital culture at school averaged about 7 episodes an hour, and for Habibah, one of the main protagonists in the transcript below, there were 122 episodes in 16 hours of radio-mic recording.

Second, although we were on the alert for any evidence corroborating the dominant idiom on race and ethnicity (and had four minority ethnic researchers in our team of six), we found very little in our 100 + days of observation and radio-mic recording to justify the emphasis on racial/ethnic trouble. Adolescents certainly recognized ethnic differences – in Nadia's friendship group, for example, whiteness had lesser value in popular culture contexts, and in looks, mixed race and light brown rated highest. But this wasn't a crisis. References and allusions to ethnic difference featured as subsidiary issues in conversations addressed to far more insistent concerns – friendship responsibilities, male-female relations, popular media culture, etc. – and indeed there is evidence of this in episode that follows.

In this interaction, some 14-year-old working class girls of South Asian and Anglo descent are talking about boys, text messages and phoning, and in the course of their conversation, one of them says:

> "I don't mix with [kɑḻe:] ((= 'black boys' in Punjabi)) I don't like [kɑḻe:], cos they...cos you know what they're like...that's why I don't like them." (lines 92–5 below)

What significance can we attach to this? Within the dominant discourse, the temptation would be to jump in and accuse the girls of making a 'racist' statement, but the ethnographic discourse analysis we are proposing cautions against taking words too literally, insisting instead on paying serious attention to the discursive and social contingencies involved. To start building an understanding of these situated contingencies, here is quite an extensive transcript of the episode in which this statement was made.

An episode in which ethnicity becomes salient

Participants (all pseudonyms)*:* Habibah (Indian descent), Lily (White British), Masouda (Pakistani descent) (and Mena, who makes a brief appearance around line 97).

Background: Wednesday 18 May 2005 – Habibah is wearing a lapel radio-microphone. A drama lesson, in which as a 'treat', the class is watching a video because quite a lot of pupils are absent at a residential week. But Habibah and Lily aren't interested and have instead been chatting near the door, singing duets for the last 10 minutes or so. At the start of the episode, they are joined by Masouda, who has left the video viewing, motivated, it seems, by a text message she's just received on her mobile from a boy. So far this morning, Habibah and Lily's relations with Masouda have been strained, following a falling out over recent weeks, and later on, Habibah and Lily say it's been about a week or two since they've spoken with her.

Transcription conventions:

[text	overlapping turns
[text	
text=	two utterances closely connected without a noticeable overlap, or different parts of a single speaker's
=text	turn
( )	speech that can't be deciphered
(text)	analyst's guess at speech that's hard to decipher

((*italics*))	stage directions
(2)	approximate length of a pause in seconds
e::xt	the colons indicate that the word is stretched out
>text<	words spoken more rapidly
TEXT	capitals indicate words spoken more loudly
[kɑ̩le:]	phonetic transcription of Punjabi
text	text message read out loud
text	singing
text	speech in an Indian English accent

1	Habibah:	((*referring to trainers which they've found in a boy's*
2		*bag by the door:*)) he's got some big feet boy (.)
3		((*Masouda comes up with her mobile*))
4	Habibah:	[fuck you scared me
5	Masouda:	[( ) pick it up and say "Um she left my phone with you"
6		I was so fuckin scar[ed
7	Habibah:	[>woa::h<((*sounds excited*))
8		who is it (.) who is it
9	Masouda:	I just got this text (.)
10	Habibah:	sha' I answer it (.)
11		((*proposing a response:*))
12		"well can you fuckin fuckin stop callin' my fuckin phone
13		what the fuck is your problem bitch="
14	Lily:	= >no no< I'll do it I'll do it
15	Masouda:	I'm gonna missed call the person
16		I don' wanna look
17		I'm so scared now (.)
18	Habibah:	((*reading the text message slowly and in monotone:*))
19		**"do you (want) me**
20		**I [want you**
21	Masouda:	[I don't like this black boy
22	Habibah:	**"(it's) me** ((*Lily joins in the reading:*)) **(the black boy)**
23		**[come to (my house) my name is**
24	Masouda:	[I don't know who the FUCK he is he knows who I am

25   Habibah: "ANDREW"

26   Lily: ["black boy come to=

27   Habibah: ["call me [or

28   Lily: ["see me I

29   Habibah: "me and you can do something today

30   so call me

31   you've seen me

32   and I want you to be [(   )"

33   Masouda: [give me it

34   Habibah: what

35   I know what number it is

36   Lily: missed call him then init=

37   Masouda: =yeah

38   Lily: and then if he-

39   when he ring[s I'll answer

40   Masouda: [Lily I want you to do it

41   I'm so scared

42   I ain't jokin I'm so scared

43   Lily: I'll do it

44   I'm a gangster

45   I'll do it

46   (.) [gangsta

47   Habibah: [what shall I say

48   can I do it

49   [I know I know

50   Masouda: [any of you two

51   as long as one of you two do it

52   Lily: [let me do it let me do it

53   Habibah: [yeh go on

54   what you gonna say

55   Lily: I'm gonna say (   )-=

56   Habibah: =shall I fuck him off

57   (.)

58   boy him off

59   Lily: no I'll [(fucking   )

```
60   Habibah:           [((rehearsing reply:)) "cn can you stop fucking
61                 fucking calling my phone yeh
62                 [don't fucking call my phone"                    01.08
63                 [((some conversation in the background too))
64   Masouda:   I missed called him ([and it's gonna          )
65   Lily:                          [when it ring yeah
66                 I'll go like this yeah
67                 I'll go "hello (West   ) yeah
68                 Masouda left her phone"
69                 can [I-
70   Masouda:      [NO no
71                 he doesn't know my name
72   Lily:      [alright
73   Masouda:   [my name     he thinks my name is Aisha
74                 yeh
75   Lily:      alright=
76   Masouda:   =Aisha
77                 Alright I'll say 'hi'>yeah yeah yeah<
78   Habibah:   ((directing her attention to Masouda in particular:))
79                 see! [kɑḽe:] (('kale:'='black boys'))
80                 [that's it           you're gone
81   Lily:      [why d-you why d-you keep ringin' me
82   Masouda:   ((responding to Habibah:))
83                 NO I didn't
84                 no::
85                 I I know one of his friends
86                 that's why
87                 (.)
88   Lily:      that's a [lie
89   Masouda:          [I know one of his friends
90                 I don't- I d-
91                 Ha- Ha- Habibah
92                 I don't mix with [kɑḽe:]
93                 I don't like [kɑḽe:]
94                 cos they're cos you know what they're like
```

```
 95                that's why [I don't like them
 96                          [((A banging of the door opening and closing))
 97   Lily:       ((addressing Mena, the girl causing the banging?:))
 98                stop stop stop
 99                (Miss ) gonna come (.)
100                I'll say why-
101   Masouda:    >Mena stop it<
102   Habibah:    Mena stop
103   Masouda:    [cos they're tryin to-
104   Lily:       [(              )plea:se
105                (.)
106   Masouda:    I've got credit ((for the phone))
107   Habibah:    ((singing to herself:)) "when you're not here
108                I sleep in your T-shirt"
109   Masouda:    don't understand (why)
110   Habibah:    (eh) eh speak speak ((is Habibah referring to the radio-
                   mic?))
111   Lily:       "ello Moto"
112   Habibah:    Masouda say something (.) ((into the radiomicrophone))
113   Masouda:    oh
114   Lily:       "ello Mo[to"
115   Habibah:            [((laughs))
116                >no no don't take it off< (('it'=the radio-mic?))
117                (.)
118                ((sings: )) "when you're not here
119                I sleep in your T-shirt"
120                (.)
121   Masouda:    [that's why I don't like [kɑḽeː] man
122   Habibah:    [ wish you were here [ to sleep in your T-shirt"
123   Masouda:    [oh            [
124   Lily:                      [there's some buff black boys man
125                seriously
126   Habibah:    half-caste (I go)
127   Masouda:    [>half-caste<
```

```
128  Lily:       [na na

129  Masouda:    [yeah but this guy is blick

130              this er- bu- [not

131  Lily:                    [na blood

132              I'm not fucking about (.)

133              [(d-you know that   ) buff man     that boy

134  Masouda:    [he's burnt toast

135  Lily:       that tall black boy is

136              (.)

137              buff

138              don't fuck about

139  Masouda:    ((with a hint of laughter in her voice)) he's bu::rnt
                 toast man

140              ((in a constricted voice:)) he's burnt toast

141  Lily:       ((exhaling:)) na::

142  Habibah:    fucking why's it not ringing

143  Lily:       ((quieter, with the argument dying down:)) he's bu:::ff

144              ((very quietly:)) (buff)

145              (.)

146  Habibah:    how the fuck did he get your number

147  Masouda:    I don't know

148              (.)

149              cos I don't- [

150  Habibah:                 [((singing:))  "I wish you were here

151              to sleep in your T Shirt

152              (.)

153              then we make lo::ve

154              (.)

155              I sleep in your T-shirt"

156  Masouda:    (he picked up (('he' = Andrew, returning the missed-call))

157              ((half-laughing:)) (jus as you were singing)

158  Lily?:      did he pick it up

159  Masouda:    yeh he picked it up (.)

160              just (killed it)
```

161		(4.0) ((*teacher talking in the background*))
162	Lily:	mad cow
163	Habibah:	does he go to this school
164	Masouda:	no
165		(2.0)
166		somewhere in (Shepherd's Bush)
167		(5.0)
168	?Masouda:	is it ringing
169	Habibah:	how the fuck do you get
170		yeh- pass-
171		(.)
172	Masouda:	yeah (just) flash (('*flash*' = *let the phone ring once and hang up*))
173		[(cz my minutes)
174	Lily:	[(that's what I thought)
175		and then I go
176		"eh eh (.) (ex-blood)"
177		(.)
178	Habibah:	Say ((*in Indian English*)) **"hell:o who this calling me**
179		**don't call me next time"**
180	Lily:	I'll go like this
181		((*carrying on in Indian English*)) **"eh hello please**
182		**who you ringing**
183		**this my phone (not)**
184		**gil[this ol lady"**
185	Masouda:	[and (wants) to
186		come to ((St Mary's)) on Friday
187	Habibah:	((*laughs*))
188	Lily:	((*continuing in IE*)) **"this is ol' lady"**
189	Habibah:	((*deeper voice, with an Elvis impersonation?*)) 'hello hello'
190	Lily:	I'll be like [hello
191	Habibah:	[shall I do that
192		do you dare me to
193		((*deeper voice, Elvis impersonation?*))'hello'

```
194  Lily:      [(     )
195  Masouda:   [(    [      )
196  Habibah:      [((continuing the rehearsal in IE:))  "this is her dad
197                leave her alone"
198  Girls:     [((loud laughs))
199  Habibah:   [((not in IE:)) "I'm gonna kill [you"
200  Lily:                                      [let do
201             do you dare me to do that-
202             do you dare me to do that
203  Habibah:   yeh go on
204             if you can but don't laugh
205  Lily:      ((more rehearsing Indian English for the phone-call:))
                "hello hello
206             this her dad
207             how can I help you
208  Girls:     ((laughter))
209  Lily:      okay bye bye"
210  Girls:     ((laughs & giggles))
211  Habibah:   no let's talk normal
212  Lily:      yeh >I'll be like<
213             hi (.)
214             yeah (.) yeah I-
215  Habibah:   >>oh he's (ringing)<<
216  Masouda:   pick it up
217  Lily:      (J    ) (it's flashed) again
218  Masouda:   oh you fucking shit
219             is that the number though that he (gave) me?
220  ?:         (I bet-)
221  Masouda:   Yeah this is what Asif sent to me (.)
222             ((discussion turns to the text message sent by another
                boy))
```

Presented in a fuller context like this, it isn't so straightforward reading racism into Masouda's original statement about not liking 'kale'. But are the prospective gains made in moving past a simplistic interpretation immediately cancelled out by the rather daunting task of trying to get to grips with everything else that seems to be going on in this episode? This is where linguistic ethnography and interactional discourse analysis can help, providing relatively systematic frameworks and procedures for working one's way through the complicated organization of an episode like this *without* losing sight of all the situated and emergent particularities, which, if we follow Hall and Gilroy, are actually crucial to the meanings of ethnicity.

4 Our approach: Linguistic ethnography

Contemporary linguistic and interactional ethnography generally takes a 'practice' view of identity, concentrating on how identities affect and get configured in people's social activity together. In studying the embedding of *ethnicities* in everyday life, the aim is to understand their significance without either exaggerating this or ignoring the flexible agency with which people process ethnicities in everyday encounters. Analysis starts with careful description of real-time interactional discourse, but from there it looks to the relationship between communicative practices, social actors, and the institutional processes in which they are participating. So race and ethnicity can be conceptualized and empirically explored in three closely interlocking 'sites':

- If the analyst's main interest is in *social actors,* then ethnicity is construed as those aspects of a person's (semiotically manifest) resources, knowledge, capacities, dispositions and embodiment that have been shaped over time in networks regarded as distinctively different from others in the locality.

- When *institutional processes* are the central concern, race and ethnicity are treated as elements in well-established ideologies which frame the situations in which social actors find themselves, inclining them to particular kinds of action and interpretation before, during and/or after an encounter.

- Where the interest is in *communication* itself, race and ethnicity are located in the semiotic activity – in the signs, actions and practices that reflect, invoke or produce the resources, capacities and ideologies associated with actors, networks and institutions.

At the same time, however, even in highly racialized and ethnically marked situations, racial and ethnic identifications exist alongside a myriad of other role and category enactments, and it is in their dynamic interaction with these other identity articulations that much of the meaning of ethnicity and race takes shape. Zimmerman (1998) usefully suggests at least three kinds of identity at play in any social encounter:

- *discourse (or interactional) identities*, such as 'story teller', 'story recipient', 'questioner', 'answerer', 'inviter', 'invitee', etc., which people are continuously taking on and leaving as talk progresses;

- *situated (or institutional) identities*, such as 'teacher', 'student', 'doctor', 'patient', which come into play in particular kinds of institutional situation;

- *'transportable' identities* which are latent, travel with individuals across situations, and are potentially relevant at any time (e.g. 'middle-aged white man', 'working class woman', 'adolescent black boy', etc.)

These identities can either be 'oriented to', actively influencing the way that people try to shape both their own actions and the subsequent actions of others, or they may be merely 'apprehended' – tacitly noticed but not treated as immediately relevant to the interaction on hand. And the interactional and institutional identities that a person projects at any moment may be ratified, reformulated or resisted in the immediately following actions of their interlocutors.

To see how different kinds of identity get activated, displayed and processed in situated interaction, the analysis of interactional discourse focuses on the ways in which participants handle a wide range of linguistic/semiotic materials in their exchanges together – pronunciations, accents, words, utterances, gestures, postures, ways of speaking, modes of address, texts, genres and so on. But – and here we return again to the contingency emphasized by Hall and Gilroy – the meaning and interpretation of a linguistic or semiotic form is always influenced by the way in which people read its *context*, with context minimally understood as

  i the *institutional and social network relations* among the participants and their *histories of interaction* both together and apart (here institutional and 'transportable' are most immediately relevant);

  ii the *type of activity* in which participants are currently engaged, the stage they've reached in the activity, and their different interactional roles and positionings within it (cf. institutional and interactional identities);

  iii their position and manoeuvring in and around institutional *discourses* and circumambient *ideologies* (institutional and transportable identities);

  iv what's just been said and done, and the options for doing something right now *(the moment-by-moment unfolding of activity)* (interactional identities).

Of course it is often hard knowing exactly *which* aspect of context is relevant to an utterance (and how), and it only takes a small shift in how you conceive of the context to change your understanding of what an utterance means. But this is an issue that participants themselves have to address throughout their interaction together, and so to prevent the analysis becoming an interpretative free-for-all, researchers can try to track the way in which participants develop, monitor and repair an inter-subjective understanding together from one moment to the next.

Putting all of this together, we can see that in the interactional negotiation of meaning, things move very fast, and people are extraordinarily adept at using very small pieces of linguistic/semiotic form to guide or challenge the understandings of the world emerging in the talk – the choice of one word rather than another can introduce a different issue, a particular pronunciation can reframe the significance of what's going on, a shift in facial expression can convey a specific stance or attitude. And so as well as looking closely at semiotic forms and slowing things down to capture the processes of adaptive improvisation from one moment to the next, analysts also need a lot of background knowledge of the local contexts if they are to have any chance of picking up and understanding what it is that these crucial nuances and intimations are pointing to. People generally do manage to communicate fairly well together, but they don't just go around expressing themselves in explicit, well-formed and readily quoted sentences.

This perspective is consonant with Gilroy's interest in 'mode[s] of interaction in which differences have to be negotiated in real-time', 'largely undetected by government and media' (see above), and our contention is that for a fuller – or indeed maybe for even only an *adequate* – understanding of what people mean when they speak, the combination of linguistics, interaction analysis and ethnography provides valuable support. To illustrate this, it is worth now returning to the episode in Section 3.

5 An initial analysis of the girls' interaction

Analysts interested in race and ethnicity could, of course, draw attention to a number of different aspects of this episode, and there are many ways in which the girls are living the historical and institutional effects of large-scale racial/ethnic processes well beyond what they are either consciously aware of or actually discuss. Nevertheless, to illustrate our larger point about the importance of meanings that are not explicitly stated, it is worth focusing on two fairly conspicuous sequences in the interaction when the girls themselves orient actively to ethnicity:

- *Focal sequence* 1: lines 78–95 and 121–40, from Habibah's 'see! *Kale*' to Masouda's 'he's burnt toast'
- *Focal sequence* 2: lines 178–211, when the girls switch into Indian accented English ('IE') in their rehearsals of speaking to Andrew over the phone

Following Hall and Gilroy's injunctions, as well as the methodological tenets of linguistic ethnography, these moments of racialization/ethnification need to be situated in their contexts, taking context as

- i the institutional and social network relations among the girls, and their (recent) histories of interaction together,
- ii the types of activity they are involved in,

iii the broader discourses, ideologies and moralities they live amidst, and

iv the acts and utterances immediately leading up to and following ethnifying utterances.

The tables below take the first three of these as the point of entry into analysis of '*kale*', the Indian English voicing and of the episode as a whole. They explicate in a little more detail both how and where these contexts are relevant to the interaction, and try to show how one might start to navigate the structuring of this episode while also beginning to reckon with some of its vital particularities.

This description is very preliminary and says hardly anything about the turn-by-turn sequencing in the interaction ('context [iv]' above). But it already opens several potentially productive lines into the investigation of contemporary ethnicities, and we might dwell, for example, on the resonance of African American popular culture (Habibah's humming and singing), processes of ethnic boundary crossing (the acceptability of Lily's Indian English impersonations), or new technologies and the renegotiation of sexuality, gender and generational relations. But rather than elaborating on these here (cf Harris 2006; Rampton 2005), the argument in this chapter dictates that we turn instead to the types of interpretation *eliminated* by data and analyses like ours.

6 Implications for the interpretation of this episode

If we allowed our interest in ethnicity to take us straight to '*kale*' and the Indian English voicing, hurrying past the contexts of activity, interactional history, network relations and circumambient discourse sketched out in Tables 7.1–7.3, we might find it hard to

Table 7.1 Institutional and social network relations, histories of interaction etc.

Institutional identities	Schoolgirls in Year 9 (aged 13–14)
Family networks	Family links with different countries: Habibah (India); Masouda (Pakistan); Lily (white, England);
Peer relations & recent interactional history	Habibah and Lily are good friends, and they spend a lot of time together talking about boys. Masouda has recently fallen out with them, but is keen to re-establish friendship (later during break, she gets a friend to tell Habibah that she wants to say sorry for anything she's done, but Habibah tells the friend not to interfere and to get lost).

Table 7.2 Types of activity

	Lines
THE MAIN ACTIVITY IN THIS SEQUENCE	
RESPONDING TOGETHER TO A TEXT MESSAGE FROM A MEMBER OF THE OPPOSITE SEX – Masouda, Habibah and Lily. The girls are active protecting this from potential interruption/disruption by the teacher or others.	5–219
SUBSIDIARY ACTIVITIES (These are either abbreviated or ignored as the girls' attention shifts back to texting/phoning, the main activity)	
AVOIDING INTERRUPTION FROM THE TEACHER	96–102
RESUMING A DISPUTE (Habibah & Masouda) Prompted by the discovery that Masouda has actually played an active part in soliciting the text message (telling the boy she was called Aisha), Habibah puts an accusation to Masouda ('See! [*kale*] That's it, you're gone') which Masouda denies. (see Table 7.3 below for further discussion)	78–95, 109, 121–40, 146–9, 169
SOLO-HUMMING & SINGING – Habibah Habibah sings snatches of a song by Destiny's Child to herself ('T shirt')	107–8, 118–19, 122, 150–5
BEING RESEARCHED – Habibah, Lily, Masouda	110–16

Table 7.3 Ideologies and institutional and moral codes variously in play in the episode

THE PROPRIETIES & POSSIBILITIES OF CONDUCT & CONVERSATION DURING LESSONS:

These are largely **suspended** (though there is a risk of their being reasserted at any time)

THE CONVENTIONS AND EXPECTATIONS OF FRIENDSHIP:

For the most part, these are **enacted** – they are implied, negotiated or indeed questioned in the way these girls initiate, reciprocate or refuse actions and activity together.

But drawing on our ethnographic knowledge of Habibah's friendship with Masouda, as well as on what she says later, there is a good case for saying that issues of friendship and loyalty are central to Habibah's 'See! [*kale*] That's it, you're gone' in lines 78–80. Later in the recording (not in this extract), Habibah says: 'that was funny, boy . . . see, see, how the fuck did she get in contact with those boys, and then she calling me a whore'. So it looks as though her 'See! – *kale*' alludes to the defamatory claims that Habibah thinks Masouda has made about Habibah's contact with black boys in particular. 'See!', in other words, seems to be implying that Masouda is a hypocrite. In the event, of course, Masouda's response in lines 82–95 fails to address these rather inexplicit accusations of defamation & hypocrisy, and instead she responds by denying an interest in black boys. But Habibah never explicitly accepts this, and she never lets her off with for example an 'okay'. Instead, she carries on with questions about the contact ('how the fuck did he get your number' [146, 169]), and then she blanks Masouda's answer in lines 147–9 by singing to herself (150–5).

THE PROPRIETIES & POSSIBILITIES OF CONTACT BETWEEN GIRLS & BOYS/WOMEN & MEN.

These are **explicitly debated in talk, written in text messages and sung** – they constitute topics that all the girls are interested in, and that serve as a source of laughter, excitement, stories, argument (both more & less light-hearted), etc. Within this broad field of interest, ethnically marked moral codes also become salient. . . .

5–222

(Continued)

Table 7.3 (Continued)

PUNJABI PROHIBITIONS ON GIRLS ASSOCIATING WITH (BLACK) BOYS	
are **evoked** by the introduction of elements from the Punjabi language (vocabulary and pronunciation).	
But the girls shift their stance on the (relatively stable) view that Asian girls shouldn't associate with black boys. In the 'kale' sequence, Masouda appears to accept the prohibition and denies that she has transgressed, but in the phone voicings, the prohibition is subject to comic impersonation and implicit ridicule. These shifts are an effect and articulation of fluctuations in the spirit of Habibah's relationship with Masouda.	78ff
Focal sequence 1: Habibah: 'See! *Kale*' (('*kale*' = '*black boys*' in Punjabi)).	
• Habibah's switch to Punjabi introduces a co-ethnic angle on her 'See! That's it – you're gone'. This seems to be forceful. Rather than responding to Habibah's 'See!' with 'So what?', or to 'you're gone' with 'why?' or 'how', Masouda dwells on the issue of black boys in her rebuttal, first appealing to a shared ethnic understanding ('I don't like '*kale*' cos you know what they're like') and then claiming that Andrew is 'burnt toast' (134, 139, 140).	
• But there is a strong case for saying that Habibah is more concerned with Masouda's hypocrisy about Masouda's own contacts with black boys and with her gossiping, than she is with the notion of contact with boys of the wrong race and colour *per se* (see above). Indeed, in a subsequent playback interview, Habibah made it clear that she likes black boys ('I think they're buff, innit'), Masouda confirmed this, and talking to the researcher (who is a black woman), both of them were embarrassed about having used the word '*kale*'.	
Focal sequence 2: *Rehearsing for the phone conversation with Andrew with Indian English accents – Habibah & Lily.*	178ff
• Indian English is widely used as a stereotypic voice, even by Lily who's white British – as Masouda comments in a playback interview, 'Lily uses it A LOT. I've got this video clip in my phone – oh my gosh – she done this Indian accent, it was so funny'.	
• More than that, Habibah had previously been seen being severely reprimanded by her father for being alone with some boys from school, and his reproachful injunction 'don't look at em' has temporarily become a jocular Indian English catch-phrase directed at Habibah by her peers.	
• So Habibah's dad doesn't like her hanging around with boys – indeed, he doesn't allow her a mobile and he has cut back on her MSN contact list. *But* he doesn't actually speak English with an Indian accent – 'my dad don't speak like that, my dad speaks proper English' (playback interview). In addition, Habibah also says subsequently that she partly understands his views – 'it looked wrong [being alone with the boys], but still… I wasn't doing anything wrong'. Overall, she considers her parents 'not strict, they have- we have limits like', and her mum 'understands everything. . . she knows I won't do anything wrong'.	

resist several stock interpretations from a rather well-rehearsed repertoire of racial/ethnic analyses.

- In lines 78–80, Habibah's 'See *kale!* That's it, you're gone' might be treated as the expression of ethno-moral purism, upholding traditional values in the face of Masouda's alleged deviation. Linguistic ethnographic description, though, makes it clear that instead of reflecting the irrepressible dictates of a compelling ethno-moral conscience, '*kale*' points to the fragility of the girls' on-and-off friendship and constitutes a moment of retaliation to the moral character assassination that Habibah thinks Masouda's been engaged in.

- In lines 92 and 93, Masouda's 'I don't mix with "*kale*," I don't like "*kale*"' might be read as straight racial hostility. But even a cursory reading of the transcript shows that this is a defensive protestation, and our wider ethnographic knowledge repositions this in the very active interest in black boys that Masouda, Habibah and Lily all share.

- The shift in tone between our focal sequences – the switch between the rather serious argument about '*kale*' and the very light-hearted Indian English voicings – might be viewed as a contradiction or confusion in the girls' ethnic ideologies and perspectives on Punjabi/South Asian sexual codes, tempting us into a 'caught-between-cultures' formulation. But if we reckon with the interactional purposes driving these invocations of ethno-morality at the particular moments when they're produced, then the girls' utterances seemed perfectly coherent, very effective (in terms of their impact on the recipients) and actually rather assured. If there is trouble and contradiction, it has far less to do with East vs West than with (a) Habibah and Masouda's friendship and (b) the general business of male-female relations among adolescents.

In saying all this, we are certainly not denying that the episode reveals ethnically linked differences in sexual morality, as well as ethnically inflected conflict between the peer group and home-based proprieties. If it were not for these tensions, then as rhetorical actions, the switches into Punjabi and Indian English would have been entirely inert. *However,* it cannot be claimed that conflict around race and ethnicity was the girls' principal preoccupation in this episode, or that it somehow incapacitated them. Instead, they were obviously much more concerned with the tensions and excitement of prospective boy-girl relations and the vicissitudes of adolescent female friendship, and rather than being disempowering, ethno-moral conflict featured as a resource that the girls exploited quite skilfully in pursuit of their really pressing interests.

In fact, even though there were lots of allusions and evocations of the kind shown here, it was very rare in our data set of 180 hours of radio-microphone recordings to see race or ethnicity pushed into the foreground as the central issue in an interaction. Contrary to the claims of what we have characterized as the dominant idiom, race and ethnicity featured for the most part as subsidiary and incidental issues, very much in the 'unruly convivial mode of interaction' identified by Gilroy and illustrated in Section 3. And indeed all this points to one of the most general ways in which our data and analysis can contribute to wider discussions of ethnicity and race. Holding closely to the contexts of everyday life, linguistic ethnography helps get ethnicity and race *into perspective,* as significant but by no means all-encompassing processes, intricate but much more ordinary and liveable than anything one might infer from the high-octane, headline representations of the political and media arena.

7 Discussion

As the work of Hall and Gilroy amply demonstrates, linguistic ethnographies of routine practice certainly aren't the only path to this kind of perspective – participant observation in non-linguistic ethnography is another route, as is first-hand experience of everyday urban life. But our account does raise quite serious questions about the adequacy of the standard social science interview as a means of assessing the significance of race and ethnicity amidst all the other social relations that people live (see also Savage 2007: 893–4).

In the transcript we have presented, (i) the talk is jostling, allusive, multi-voiced, partisan and interwoven with physical movement and action; (ii) ethnic issues are introduced amidst a range of other concerns, contested and collaboratively reformulated over time (and across settings); and it is obvious (iii) that you need a lot of contextual knowledge to understand what's going on. In contrast, research interviews typically privilege (a) orderly progression, explicitness, relatively detached (and detachable) commentary, illustrative narrative and speech separated from movement and action; (b) they seldom serve as sites for the contestation of identity claims against a background of shared knowledge; and (c) researchers often lack the local understanding to pick up on allusions, looking for quotably literal encapsulations instead (see also Georgakopoulou 2008).[2]

All this favours the dominant idiom in the representation of ethnicity and race. If researchers don't grasp (i), (ii) and (iii) – if they lack access to local activities and to the ongoing co-construction/renegotiation of racial or ethnic meanings among everyday associates amidst a host of other concerns – then the accounts of context produced in interview research are not only likely to be limited. There is also a risk that in trying to identify a context for what interview informants say, researchers draw on (and position their informants 'inter-textually' within) only the most obvious discourses at large. Unfortunately, these tend to be essentialist and crisis-oriented, and if these are used as the main framing for the utterances of interviewees, then research cedes the terms of engagement to dominant formulations. This makes it much harder to pick up on the articulation of alternative/different agendas, and more likely for research to find itself confined to 'the strategy of a simple set of reversals' (Hall, cited above).

When we presented our perspective at a seminar on ethnicity organized by the Identities Programme, Hall agreed that it represented an empirical advance.[3] But he also wondered 'how you ever get back to the larger field' from all the contingent detail.

As both of us are committed to using fine-grained data to address much bigger questions (about e.g. ethnicity, race, class, education and contemporary culture), we see this is a vital question, and elsewhere, we have made extended attempts to address it (Harris and Rampton 2002; Harris 2006; Rampton 2005, 2006, 2007, 2011). Nor, as we said at the start, do we want to underplay the significance of contemporary racism, and we know that in order to address it, sometimes it certainly is necessary to go straight to the big concepts, in acts of strategic essentialism. So we are not advocating a retreat from larger generalizations about ethnicity and race in contemporary society, either in analysis or in politics. We do hold, though, that in the process of abstracting and simplifying, it is vital to refer back continuously to what's 'lived' in the everyday, and that ultimately both academic and political generalizations must be made accountable to the kinds of activity represented in the transcript in Section 3.

Without that anchoring – without a sense of how in one way or another, most people *do* manage in the generally rather low-key practices of the day-to-day – it is impossible to identify changes in the terms of everyday ethnic/racial encounters, and discussion is left vulnerable to the dramatizations of the dominant idiom, panicked and unable to imagine how anyone copes. And we're also not convinced that on its own, talk of 'multiple, fluid, intersecting and ambiguous identities' provides recovery from this, assuming as it often does (a) that the identities we mention all count, and (b) that it's really hard working out how they link together. In our view, it is essential to look searchingly at how in their everyday practices, people do make sense of things, work them through, and bring quite a high degree of intelligible order to their circumstances. This sometimes reveals that people aren't as preoccupied, fractured or troubled by particular identifications as we initially supposed, and that they are actually rather adept at negotiating 'ethnicities without guarantees', inflecting them in ways that are extremely hard to anticipate in the absence of close empirical observation. And then this in turn prompts some crucial critical reflection on the relationship between political, academic and everyday constructs and practices. Of course there are no pure truths or easy readings in/of the everyday – no 'guarantees' – and its empirical study and representation require a host of historically located interpretative frameworks and procedures, as we've tried to illustrate. Still, we see ordinary activity as a vital resource and reference point for discussion about identities in general, quite often cutting the ground from dominant accounts, pointing in new or different directions.

Notes

1 The ethnographic fieldwork and data collection for the chapter was carried out by Lauren Small, and as well as drawing on Lauren's work, we are highly indebted to other members and associates of the Urban Classroom Culture and Interaction project team – Alexandra Georgakopoulou, Constant Leung, Caroline Dover and Adam Lefstein. An earlier version of this paper appeared in M. Wetherell (ed.) (2009), *Identity in the twenty-first Century: New Trends in Changing Times* (Palgrave), a volume containing papers from the 2005 to the 2008 ESRC Identities & Social Action Programme.

2 We recognize, of course, that interviews take many shapes, are often embedded in ethnography and can themselves be productively analysed as culturally situated interactional events. Indeed, when we interviewed senior teachers in this school and conducted focus groups with others, ethnicity didn't emerge as more of a pressing issue than in our recordings of youngsters' spontaneous interaction, and in this regard, the interview and radio-mic data are complementary. Still, though our characterization may be a little too stark, we don't think it completely misses the mark, and it actually also extends to survey questionnaires.

3 '[W]hat I have heard is a very substantial deepening of the [new ethnicities] paradigm. . . . I think the move to ethnography, the move to discursive analysis, discourse analysis of interviews, is a way of methodologically exemplifying the conceptual complexity that the paradigm talked about. . . . I hope you learn very much more exactly what it means to say the end of the essential social subject – how to look at this question when we don't have fixed, essentialised subjects who are the endless bearers of these positionalities whether they are race identity, ethnic identity, etc. What that actually means methodologically and conceptually – very important work' (Hall in an unpublished ESRC ISA Programme transcript of the Ethnicities Workshop held at the London School of Economics, 21st June 2006).

References

Adi, H. and Sherwood, M. (1995), *The 1945 Manchester Pan-African Congress Revisited.* London: New Beacon Books.

Blommaert, J. (2005), *Discourse: A Critical Introduction.* Cambridge: Cambridge University Press.

Bradley, H. (1996), *Fractured Identities: Changing Patterns of Inequality.* Cambridge: Polity Press.

Bauman, G. (1996), *Contesting Culture: Discourses of Identity in Multi-ethnic London.* Cambridge: Cambridge University Press.

Carmichael, S. and Hamilton, Charles V. (1967), *Black Power.* Harmondsworth: Penguin.

Department for Education (DfE) (1995), *Ethnic Monitoring of School Pupils: A Consultation Paper.* London: DfE.

Dover, C. (2007), 'Everyday talk: Investigating media consumption and identity amongst schoolchildren'. *Participations,* 4.1. At www.participations.org.

Georgakopoulou, A. (2008), '"On MSN with buff boys": Self- and other-identity claims in the context of small stories'. *Journal of Sociolinguistics,* 12(5), 597–626.

Gilroy, P. (1997), *There Ain't No Black in the Union Jack.* London: Hutchinson.

—(2006), 'Multiculture in times of war: an inaugural lecture given at the London School of Economics'. *Critical Quarterly,* 48(4), 27–45.

Hall, S. (1988), 'New Ethnicities', in J. Donald and A. Rattansi (eds), *1992 'Race', Culture & Difference.* London: Sage, pp. 252–9.

Harris, R. (1997), 'Romantic bilingualism?: Time for a change', in C. Leung and C. Cable (eds), *English as an Additional Language: Changing Perspectives.* Watford: NALDIC, pp. 28–39.

—(2006), *New Ethnicities and Language Use.* Basingstoke: Palgrave.

Harris, R. and Rampton, B. (2003), 'Creole metaphors in cultural analysis: On the limits and possibilities of (socio-)linguistics'. *Critique of Anthropology,* 22(1), 31–51.

Ramdin, R. (1987), *The Making of the Black Working Class in Britain.* Aldershot: Gower.

Rampton, B. (2005), *Crossing: Language and Ethnicity among Adolescents* (2nd edn). Manchester: St Jerome Press.

—(2006), *Language in Late Modernity: Interaction in an Urban School*. Cambridge: Cambridge University Press.

—(2007), 'Linguistic ethnography and the study of identities'. *Working Papers in Urban Language & Literacies*, 43. At www.kcl.ac.uk/ldc.

—(2011), 'Style contrasts, migration and social class'. *Journal of Pragmatics*, 43, 1236–50.

Rampton, B., Harris, R. and Small, L. (2006), 'The meanings of ethnicity in discursive interaction: Some data and interpretations from ethnographic sociolinguistics'. At www.ling-ethnog.org.uk/documents/Ethnicity_in_sociolinguistic_ethnography.pdf.

Rampton, B., Maybin, J. and Tusting, K. (eds) (2007), *Linguistic Ethnography: Links, Problems and Possibilities*. Special issue of *Journal of Sociolinguistics*, 11(5), 575–695.

Savage, M. (2007), 'The coming crisis of empirical sociology'. *Sociology*, 41(5), 885–99.

Zimmerman, D. (1998), 'Identity, context, interaction', in C. Antaki and S. Widdicombe (eds), *Identities in Talk*. London: Sage, pp. 87–106.

8

Constructing contexts through grammar: Cognitive models and conceptualization in British newspaper reports of political protests

Christopher Hart

1 Introduction

In this chapter, I investigate, from the position of the Cognitive Linguistic Approach (CLA) to Critical Discourse Analysis (CDA), the conceptualization of violence in British media discourse on political protests. Specifically, I analyse the image schemata and construal operations grounded in the system of attention which contribute to the construction of event models in the student protests against higher tuition fees which were held in the United Kingdom in 2010. In doing so, I show how the Cognitive Linguistic Approach, which shifts the locus of investigation in Critical Discourse Analysis to the interpretation stage, can engage theoretically with a broader socio-cognitive perspective (Van Dijk 1998, 2002, 2010). In Section 3, I outline the Cognitive Linguistic Approach to CDA. In Section 4, I discuss the role of mental models in the discursive construction of contexts and relate the Cognitive Linguistic Approach to CDA to the Socio-Cognitive Approach. In Section 5, I briefly sketch previous research on discourse and civil disorder. In Section 6, I introduce my data. In Section 7, I present a qualitative analysis demonstrating the ideological qualities of alternative event models. In Section 8, I present a more quantitative analysis of alternative conceptualizations of violence across online British press reports of the student fee protests. And, finally, in Section 9, I offer some conclusions.

2 Goals

The goals of this study are twofold. First, I aim to advance the Cognitive Linguistic Approach to CDA by aligning it with the socio-cognitive approach and arguing that the mental models postulated in the Socio-Cognitive Approach can be theorized in terms of conceptual structures and construal operations described in Cognitive Linguistics. Specifically, I aim to show that grammar plays an important part in the discursive and ideological construction of contexts as alternative grammatical patternings invoke alternative conceptualizations of events. Secondly, I aim to conduct an empirical study of the grammatical patterns that occurred in online reports of the 2010 student fees protests in Britain and thus the way that this particular context was constructed by the press.

3 The cognitive linguistic approach

As a multifarious practice consisting of several analytical traditions, including Critical Linguistics and the Discourse-Historical Approach, Critical Discourse Analysis has, over the last decade, witnessed the development of a Cognitive Linguistic Approach (CLA).[1] One major advantage of this approach is that it shifts the focus of investigation in CDA to the interpretation stage – something which, on the assumption that the discursive construction of contexts ultimately takes place in the minds of interacting members (see § 4), provides a significant 'missing link' in mainstream CDA (cf. Chilton 2005).[2]

To a very large extent, this approach has been focussed on metaphor as a site of ideological reproduction (e.g. Koller 2004; Musolff 2004). However, this approach has more recently been turned to address the role of grammatical patterns in guiding understanding of socio-political contexts (Hart 2011a/b, 2013).The second major advantage of the CLA, then, is that it functions as a lens through which a broad base of linguistic (lexical and grammatical) phenomena can be analysed, at the interpretation stage, within a unified theoretical framework (cf. Widdowson 2004). The CLA can thus be characterized as addressing the conceptual import of various strategies in texts and in this way accounting for the discursive construction of contexts.[3] Within this framework, several construal operations are described, including metaphor but also, inter alia, schematization, focus, profiling and scanning. Construal operations are indexed in text and realize discursive strategies when they are invoked in discourse processing to constitute readers' conceptualizations.[4] Since Cognitive Linguistics assumes that language is not an autonomous faculty but is rather 'in touch' with other domains of cognition (Croft and Cruse 2004), these construal operations rely on non-linguistic cognitive abilities. The relationship between particular construal operations, discursive strategies and non-linguistic cognitive systems is shown in Figure 8.1.

Structural configuration is the strategy by means of which speakers (intentionally or not) impose upon the scene a particular image-schematic representation which constitutes our basic understanding of the whole event-structure. The strategy

System / Strategy		Gestalt	Comparison	Attention	Perspective
Structural Configuration		Schematization			
Framing	Construal operations		Categorization		
			Metaphor		
Identification				Focus	
				Profiling	
				Scanning	
Positioning					Deixis
					Modality

FIGURE 8.1 *Typology of construal operations.*

is realized through *schematization* and grounded in an ability to analyse complex events in terms of gestalt structures. Framing strategies concern how the actors, actions, relations and process that make up events are attributed more affective qualities as alternative categories or conceptual metaphors, which carry different evaluative connotations or entailments, are apprehended in their conceptualization. Framing strategies are therefore grounded in a general ability to compare domains of experience.[5] Identification strategies concern which social actors are selected for conceptual representation and to what degree of salience they are represented relative to one another. Identification strategies are rooted in attentional abilities, then, and are realized in various construal operations which Langacker (2002) groups together as 'focal adjustments'. Lastly, positioning strategies are grounded in our ability to adopt a particular perspective in how we conceive of a given scene. Specifically, positioning strategies concern where we situate other actors and events relative to ourselves (deictic) and where we situate propositions relative to our own conceptions of reality (epistemic) and morality (deontic).[6]

In this chapter, we concentrate on schematization and those construal operations grounded in the system of attention.[7] Based in the Gestalt system, schematization is a construal operation which enables us to 'make sense' of objects and events in the world in terms of a finite set of image schemata. According to Cognitive Linguistics, such image schemata are abstract, holistic knowledge structures which arise from repeated patterns of early experience as 'theories' or 'models' of the world. These models, in turn, serve to delimit experience, expression and reason.[8] As Johnson (1987: 42) puts it: 'patterns of typical experiences . . . work their way up into our system of meaning and into the structure of our expression and communication . . . [T]hese

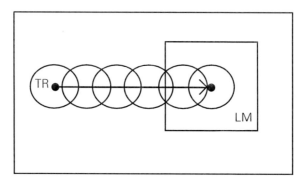

FIGURE 8.2 *Image schema for enter or [NP [VP [into NP]]].*

image-schematic gestalt structures constrain and limit meaning as well as patterns of inference'. Image schemas, then, constitute the meaningful basis of lexical items and grammatical constructions. Language is thus viewed as a system of form-meaning pairs.[9] The conceptual counterparts in these form-meaning pairs are called up in discourse to conceptualize the objects and events described. For example, one event regularly encountered would be that of a smaller object following a path of motion to enter a larger object. The resultant schema, depicted in Figure 8.1, is invoked in discourse by both the lexical item *enter* and the grammatical structure [NP [VP [*into* NP]]].

Language has the further facility to direct attention to different aspects of the active schema. Construal operations of *focus, profiling* and *scanning* affect the distribution of attention in different ways to realize identification strategies. As Langacker states, what we actually see when we construe a scene 'depends on how closely we examine it, what we chose to look at, which elements we pay most attention to and where we view it from' (2008: 55). These conceptual parameters are indexed in linguistic expressions which, in turn, serve as access points to particular facets of the evoked schema. Construal operations of focus, profiling and scanning are the conceptual reflexes of information structure, agent deletion (through ergativity or agentless passivization) and nominalization, respectively. The agentless passive construction in (1), for example, profiles only a particular part of the schema depicted in Figure 8.2, namely the PATH and GOAL.

(1) *The building was entered.*

The rest of the schema remains active in the *scope of attention* but is conceptually less salient than the profiled portion designated by the clause.[10] The construction in (1) invites a version of the schema such as represented in Figure 8.3.

The argument I wish to make in this chapter is that construal operations of this kind play a fundamental part in the discursive construction of contexts. More specifically, I am suggesting that the event models made appeal to in the Socio-Cognitive Approach as necessary mediations between texts and ideologies may take the form of image schemata as theorized in Cognitive Linguistics.

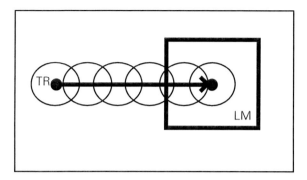

FIGURE 8.3 *Image schema for The building was entered.*

4 Contexts as mental models

Researchers in Critical Linguistics have traditionally used Halliday's functional grammar as a lens through which patterns of belief and value (ideologies), reflected in the grammatical patterns of texts reporting on particular contexts, can be brought to bear and be systematically analysed (Fowler 1991: 67). Elements of the grammar found to be particularly significant in the expression of ideology include transitivity and grammatical metaphor. These systems allow for semantic concepts such as agency and action to be realized in different (ideologically motivated) ways within the clause. As Fowler (1996: 5) points out, however, Critical Linguistics has had a very high mileage out of a restricted set of linguistic notions such as transitivity and nominalization (as only one particular form of grammatical metaphor). Moreover, functional grammar is a speaker-oriented and process-focussed model of text production. Consequently, it is not well-placed to serve interpretation-stage analysis in CDA, which, it has been argued, warrants a more detailed treatment (O'Halloran 2003; Chilton 2005; Hart 2010). Interpretation-stage analysis is necessary if one wants to account for the discursive construction of social and political contexts since contexts are ultimately constructed in the cognitive systems of interacting group members (Van Dijk 2010). It therefore necessarily also requires a cognitive theory of discourse processing. According to O'Halloran, however, 'anything to do with cognition at the interpretation stage has not received comprehensive scrutiny' (2003: 3).

One major exception to this last observation is Van Dijk's work in the Socio-Cognitive Approach. Van Dijk (e.g. 1998, 2002, 2010) has extensively argued that any account of the discursive construction of political contexts presupposes an account which relates structures in text to structures in social cognition. These latter structures are discussed, within the Socio-Cognitive Approach, in terms of 'mental models' (Van Dijk 2011).

According to Van Dijk, mental models are the cognitive architectures stored in social cognition which enable us to understand situations or events, including as they are described in discourse (Van Dijk 2011). Van Dijk (1999) distinguishes between three types of mental model: *event models*, *experience models* and *context models*. Experience models represent personal, participatory experiences. Context models are a particular type of experience model which represent the communicative episodes in which we participate. Event models, by contrast, represent situational contexts not personally experienced but largely learnt about through discourse. They may be constructed, however, in terms of experience models. There are clear parallels here with the theory of image schemas in Cognitive Linguistics. As Van Dijk states:

> Model structures should be seen as the strategic schemata people use in the fast interpretation of the events in their daily lives, and it is not surprising that such schemata would also shape at least some of the structures of the discourses engaged in by speech participants when talking or writing, reading or hearing about such events. (Van Dijk 1997: 191)

For Van Dijk, 'event models represent the subjective interpretation of discourse, the mental starting point of production, and what people later (correctly or falsely) remember of a discourse' (1999: 125). Information represented in event models, then, provides the basis of shared understanding and is reflected in discourse. Crucially, though, event models are also derived from discourse, as well as shared cultural norms and values, and, through generalization and abstraction, constitute sociocultural knowledge (ibid.). Such models are reflected in, and constructed by, 'the characteristic semantic structure of complex propositions as well as the case structure and ordering of syntactic structures in discourse' (Van Dijk 1997: 191).

Despite rather extensive work on mental models, however, Van Dijk points out that 'an explicit theoretical account of their internal structures has so far not been provided' (1998: 190). He suggests that mental models are made up of at least two components: the semantic and the affective (see also Koller 2011). 'People not only build and use models of events in order to represent their knowledge about such events, but also in order to represent their opinions about them' (Van Dijk 1997: 192). Event models, then, are not only likely to contain some semantic representation of the context in question but also some reactive, evaluative information. We will leave aside the evaluative dimension of event models for present purposes and focus here on their semantic dimension.[11]

Van Dijk suggests that event models are hierarchically organized. He distinguishes between the macro-structure and the micro-structure of such models. The macro-structure of the model is more abstract while specific details concerning participants, process, etc. are represented in the micro-structure. Thus, for any mental model of a given situation or event, we may distinguish between information characterizing the generic situation- or event-type and information detailing the particular participants and circumstances involved. At the macro level, Van Dijk argues that mental models are 'probably organised by a limited number of fixed categories that make up an abstract form or "schema," *a model schema*' (2010: 65, original emphasis). These categories include, at least, participants, process and circumstance (or setting) but also more abstract concepts such as agency, intention, and causation (ibid.). Now, Van Dijk assumes, 'lacking alternative formats of representation', that these schemata are propositional in form (1997: 191). As noted earlier, however, research in Cognitive

Linguistics suggests that our mental models of situations and events may in fact be imagistic rather than propositional in nature. In other words, the event models which constitute our understanding of particular contexts may be theorized in terms of image schemas and construal operations grounded in the system of attention as described in Cognitive Linguistics. These image schemas, through abstractions made across repeated instantiations, contribute to the construction of superordinate *frames* for similar events. That is, models built for specific events become idealized in more general cognitive models which in conceptual clusters or networks underpin discourses or ideologies. As Van Dijk articulates it:

> Particular models represent unique information about one specific situation, for instance the one "now" being processed. General models may combine information from several particular models about the "same" or the same "kind" of situation . . . General models that appear to be socially relevant may be transformed to frames or scripts in semantic (social) memory, for example by further abstraction, generalisation and decontextualisation. (Van Dijk 1985: 63)

In this chapter, we therefore conduct an analysis of the different image schemata and attentional distributions which alternative grammatical constructions impose on the reader's conceptualizations of particular protest events.

5 Context of study: Political protests

Much has been written in Critical Linguistics concerning the representation in media discourse of political protests and civil disorder. This research has demonstrated the significance of grammar as a site of ideological difference. Systematic asymmetries are found in the distribution of grammatical patterns which, upon analysis, seem to reflect the ideological frameworks in which alternative news institutions operate (Trew 1979; Montgomery 1986; Toolan 1991; Van Dijk 1991; Macleod and Hertog 1992; Hacket and Zhao 1994). In the UK context, the right-wing press especially have been found to favour grammatical patternings which contribute to the construction of discourses or ideologies in which protestors are seen as violent deviants while authorities are seen as moral defenders of civil order (Montgomery 1986; Van Dijk 1991).

Various discursive strategies have also been shown to relate to ideological positions with regard to international geopolitical contexts. For example, Lee and Craig (1992) investigated 'us versus them' patterns in US press reports of labour disputes in Poland and South Korea. They found that, through this dichotomy, in the case of Poland, a communist country at the time investigated, blame for the disputes was attributed to communism itself. By contrast, in the case of South Korea, a country whose political system is much more closely aligned with that of the United States, blame was attributed to the protestors, thus constructing a discourse more in line with the domestic narrative in which civil action is seen as a deviation from normative behaviour

(Hall 1973). In a similar vein, Fang (1994) analysed representations of international political protests in the Chinese state newspaper *Renmin Ribao* from the perspective of Functional Grammar. She found that patterns in both lexical and grammatical choice depended on whether the country in question was deemed hostile or sympathetic towards the People's Republic of China. Representations of political protests, however, have not been investigated at the interpretation stage or through the analytical lens of Cognitive Linguistics (though see Hart 2013). Cognitive linguistics, however, can not only shed light on the conceptual import of those grammatical choices typically dealt with in CDA but can also reveal the ideological effects of a further range of linguistic phenomena (Hart 2011a/b).

In the remainder of this chapter, we analyse representations of violence in contemporary political protests from the perspective of the CLA. We focus on differences in event-construal which are interpreted as indexical of alternative ideological positions.

6 Data

On 10th and 24th November, two major student protests took place in London against rises in tuition fees for Higher education in England and Wales. The first protest was attended by between 30,000 and 52,000 people.[12] On both occasions, police used a controversial crowd control technique known as 'kettling'.[13] On both occasions, violent encounters between police and protestors were witnessed.

A total of 12 articles (two per paper) were collected from across the online editions of British broadsheet and mid-market newspapers. The articles were published in the immediate aftermath of the student fee protests on 10th and 24th November 2010. British newspapers can be divided on a vertical axis according to 'quality' or a horizontal axis according to left or right alignment on the political spectrum. The statistics for the corpus are given in Table 8.1. Table 8.2 shows the orientation of the different newspapers.

Table 8.1 Protest corpus

Paper	Words
Guardian	1700
Independent	1661
The Times	593
Telegraph	1096
Mail	2618
Express	996
	Total: 8664

Table 8.2 UK Newspapers by quality
and political alignment

Guardian	The Times
Independent	Telegraph
	Mail
	Express

The data is by no means exhaustive of the discourse on political protests but is sufficiently representative to demonstrate the effects of different grammatical patterns in constructing the same situational context in alternative ways (with alternative associated axiological values).

7 Analysis

7.1 *Schematization*

Image schemas arise in basic domains of experience like ACTION, SPACE, MOTION and FORCE. They are derived, then, from early, embodied experiences. However, they later come to constitute experience as they are apprehended in discourse to conceptualize situations and events in particular ways.[14] Image schemas impose upon the scene a particular configuration which defines the basic event type and structure. For example, the same event can be construed in terms of an ACTION schema or a MOTION schema. Within each of these domains there then exists a 'grammar', which can be exploited in different ways to invoke alternative conceptualizations. For example, the grammar of ACTION allows for an event to be construed in terms of an *asymmetrical* or a *reciprocal* action chain. Schemas in the domain of ACTION are especially significant to structural configuration strategies in protest reporting (see Hart 2011b on the grammar of FORCE in immigration discourse).

Action chain schemas represent the transfer of energy between participants in an event, often resulting in a change in state to a participant 'downstream' in the energy flow. There are various action chain schemas available to construe the same event and in selecting one over the other we necessarily close down alternative conceptualizations. There are options, for example, in how many participants are covered within the *scope of attention* and which are in turn focussed on or *profiled* (see below). However, one fundamental distinction concerns whether we conceive of an event in terms of an asymmetrical or a reciprocal action chain.

In an asymmetrical action chain, the event is construed in terms of a unidirectional flow of energy from an AGENT to a PATIENT (sometimes via an INSTRUMENT or THEME which for present purposes we will gloss over). By contrast, a reciprocal action chain construes the event in terms of a bidirectional flow of energy so that one participant cannot be ascribed the status of AGENT and the other PATIENT but rather both entities are active participants in the event. By way of example, consider the difference between (1a) and (1b):

(1a) A number of police officers were injured after they **came under attack from** youths, some wearing scarves to hide their faces. (*Telegraph* 10th November)

(1b) Activists who had masked their faces with scarves **traded punches with** police *(Guardian*, 10th November)

The construction in (1a) construes the event in terms of the action chain schema modelled in Figure 8.4 whereas the construction in (1b) construes the event through the schematization modelled in Figure 8.5.

The alternative conceptualizations invoked by (1a) and (1b) carry significant ideological consequences. In schematizing the event in terms of an asymmetrical action chain, as in (1a), responsibility for the violent action is attributed to only one participant, the sole source of energy flow in the event, in this case the protestors. In schematizing it in terms of a reciprocal action chain as in (1b), by contrast, responsibility for the violence is shared.

Alternatively, the same kind of events may be construed in terms of FORCE or MOTION. Construing the event in terms of force reduces the intensity of the process so that the

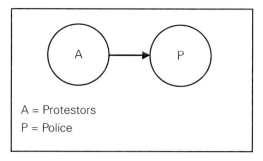

FIGURE 8.4 *Asymmetrical action chain.*

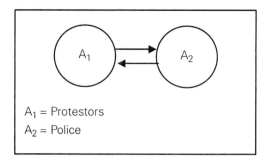

FIGURE 8.5 *Reciprocal action chain.*

event becomes one of 'balance' (and its modulation) rather than violence. That is, an event is understood as a force event rather than an action event when it is an entity's location or freedom to move that is at issue. Of course, it is impossible to clearly delineate with absolute confidence the distinction between action, motion and force domains.

In exploiting the grammar of FORCE, the event can be further subject to construal as it is 'viewed' from the perspective of the AGONIST or the ANTAGONIST depending on deixis.[15] In this way, structural configuration strategies interact with identification and positioning strategies. In (3), for example, there is a shift in viewpoint from protestors (AGONIST) to police (ANTAGONIST). Notice, however, that in both clauses the protesters are cast in the role of AGONIST whereas police are the ANTAGONIST attempting to maintain the 'equilibrium'. Although there is a difference in perspective, then, FORCE schemas applied in this way serve to legitimize the role of the police as defenders of civil order.

(3)   Pockets of demonstrators **pushed forward** and were **held back** by police (*Independent*, 24th November)

The same kind of event can further be conceived as one in which the 'equilibrium' is successfully maintained as the AGONIST is prevented from realizing their force tendency or one in which the 'balance' shifts in favour of the AGONIST who is able to overcome the ANTAGONIST and realize their force tendency.[16] Consider (4) compared to (3):

(4)   [P]rotesters **burst through** police lines to storm the Conservative party headquarters. (*Guardian*, 24th November)

The contrast between (3) and (4) can be modelled in terms of two types of FORCE schema: a steady-state schema versus a shift-in-state schema respectively. The schema in Figure 8.6 depicts an interaction between ANT and AGO in which the AGONIST has a tendency towards force (>) but is kept 'in check' by the stronger (+) ANTAGONIST resulting in equilibrium (O). The schema in Figure 8.7 depicts an interaction in which

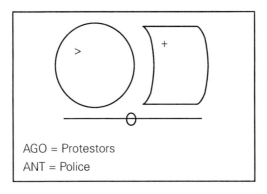

FIGURE 8.6 *Steady-state schema.*

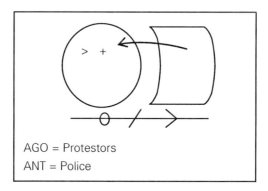

FIGURE 8.7 *Shift-in-state schema.*

Table 8.3 Semantic inventory

Action		Force		
Reciprocal	**Asymmetrical**	**Steady-state**	**Shift-in-state**	**Motion**
scuffle	attack	push	break through	move
clash	hit	hold	burst through	charge
confrontation	punch	contain	overcome	surge
encounter	strike	detain	penetrate	enter
trade	throw	corral	breach	lead
exchange	launch	enclose	escape	go
	hurl	block		

the balance of strength shifts onto the AGONIST previously kept in check by a stronger ANTAGONIST but now able to express their force tendency as in example (4).

Construing the event in terms of MOTION still further reduces the intensity of the process and serves in framing strategies of euphemization. Crucially, in MOTION schemas the process is not a transactive one. There is no transmission of energy between entities but rather a motion path of one entity (the TRAJECTOR) is delineated relative to another entity (the LANDMARK). The 'vector' in the process represents the *trajectory* of the TRAJECTOR (in this case also an AGENT) rather than a *transfer of energy*, with the 'endpoint' a LOCATION rather than a PARTICIPANT. Consider (5) as an example. The schema it invokes is the one modelled earlier in Figure 8.2.

(5) About 50 riot police **moved in** [to the area] just after 5 p.m. (*Independent,* 10th November)

The alternative schemas, as well as the further construal operations we deal with in section 7.2, constitute Cognitive Grammars of ACTION, FORCE and MOTION exploited in different ways in discourse on political protests. The lexical and grammatical forms that these meanings are paired with can be inventoried to serve as search words in a future, larger-scale corpus investigation. Table 8.3 is illustrative of such an attempt.

7.2 *Focus and profiling*

Within RECIPROCAL ACTION and FORCE schemas, there are further means by which alternative, ideologically vested conceptualizations may be invoked. Here the strategy of structural configuration overlaps with identification strategies grounded in the cognitive system of attention as different participants can be in and out of *focus* relative to one and other. Identification strategies group together strategies of topicalization (Van Dijk 1991) and exclusion (van Leeuwen 1996).

Focus pertains to the degree of attention afforded to those entities explicitly selected for representation, relative to one and other. It is a fundamental feature of cognition that in perceiving any scene, one entity, the FIGURE, stands out relative to another, the GROUND. The FIGURE is perceptually more prominent than the GROUND, which serves as a point of reference for the FIGURE. FIGURE/GROUND alignment features in several aspects of discourse, including descriptions of spatial relations, metaphor and presupposition (Talmy 2000; Langacker 2008). However, one important dimension of discourse which can be said to manifest a FIGURE/GROUND construal is *information structure*, where entities introduced earlier in the clause are conceptually more salient, and thus function as FIGURE, relative to entities subsequently introduced, which function as GROUND. According to Talmy (2000: 12), for example, 'the entity that functions as the figure of situations attracts focal attention and is the entity whose characteristics and fate are of concern'. Focus is therefore the conceptual process involved in realizing topicalization strategies as it, experientially, accentuates the role of one particular participant in the event. This can be most clearly seen in reciprocal actions chains.[17] Consider the contrast between (6a) and (6b):

(6a) There were some minor **scuffles between protesters** and **police** in Bristol
(*Express*, 24th November)

(6b) **[P]olice** wielding batons **clashed with a crowd** hurling placard sticks, eggs
and bottles (*Guardian*, 10th November)

Conceptually, this contrast can be modelled as in Figures 8.8 and 8.9 where the bolder lines represent the foregrounded entity within the schema.[18]

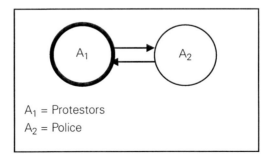

A_1 = Protestors
A_2 = Police

FIGURE 8.8 *Focus (6a).*

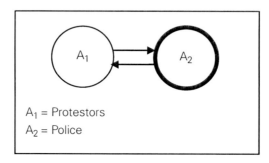

FIGURE 8.9 *Focus (6b)*.

Profiling can be seen as an extension of focus (Langacker 2008). The distinction between them is that in the case of focus both entities receive linguistic representation. In profiling, one entity is left implicit. Conceptually, they are both based on the same cognitive principles but are distinguished according to the difference in degree of attention. Focus is a matter of 'fine-tuning' one's attention whereas profiling involves a starker contrast. Profiling is the conceptual reflex of exclusion in discourse (van Leeuwen 1996). Exclusion can be seen in a range of linguistic phenomena, including ergativity/metonymy, nominalization and agentless passivization. Exclusion, it is argued, allows speakers to obfuscate participants in actions which are incommensurate with the normative system in which the speaker operates. According to Reisigl and Wodak, exclusions in discourse 'enable speakers to conjure away responsible, involved or affected actors (whether victims or perpetrators), or to keep them in the semantic background' (2001: 58). It has been questioned, however, whether absences at the level of text necessarily result in any mystification at the level of cognition (Billig 2008; O'Halloran 2003; Widdowson 2004). Cognitive grammar, though, in which language is seen to be based on known principles in other domains of cognition, suggests that exclusions in discourse can at least keep actors in the 'semantic background', experienced conceptually in terms of salience. Consider the examples in (7a) and (7b):

(7a)   London Ambulance Service confirmed that eight people had been **injured** during the demonstrations in the capital (*Telegraph*, 24th November)

(7b)   Eight people were taken to hospital with **injuries** after the violence flared at Millbank Tower. (*Telegraph*, 10th November)

In (7a) 'injured' is used in the agentless passive voice with no mention of the manner in which the injuries were sustained or who caused the injuries. The valence of the verb dictates that there must have been some CAUSE(R) and so it remains within the *scope of attention* but conceptually backgrounded relative to the PATIENT. As Langacker (2008: 384) puts it, 'when one participant is left unspecified, the other becomes more salient just through the absence of competition. On the other hand, augmenting the salience of one participant diminishes that of others (in relative terms)'. To the extent to which salience and relevance are related (see Maillat and Oswald 2011), readers are likely not to attend to the backgrounded element in the action chain in sufficient detail to critically question (ibid.) how the injuries were sustained or who caused them.[19] The schema invoked by (7a) is modelled in Figure 8.11 where only part of the schema is profiled. This can be seen in contrast to the schema in Figure 8.10 where, invoked by the canonical transactive clause, the whole structure is profiled. The stepped arrow indicates a change in state to the PATIENT.

(7a) at least designates a process. In (7b), 'injuries' excludes agency through nominalization. Conceptually, nominalization invokes a *summary scanning* of the scene which again precludes hearers from properly attending to details such as PLACE, MANNER and CAUSE.[20] According to Cognitive Grammar, we conceptualize events by mentally scanning the series of relations obtaining between participants at different (continuous) stages in the process that constitutes an event. However, there are two different modes of scanning: sequential and summary. In sequential scanning, 'the various phases of an evolving situation are examined serially, in noncumulative fashion' (Langacker 2002: 78–9). Thus, sequential scanning lends itself to the conceptualization of complex events and is the mode of scanning indexed in and invoked by a transactive clause. In summary scanning, by contrast, the various facets of an event are examined cumulatively so that the whole complex comes to cohere as a single gestalt (ibid.). That is, we see an event as an OBJECT or THING rather than as a series of INTERACTIONS or PROCESSES. And since 'things do not pertain to time, we do not scan their internal

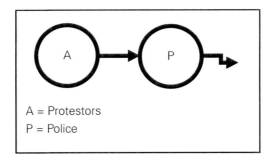

A = Protestors
P = Police

FIGURE 8.10 *Full action chain.*

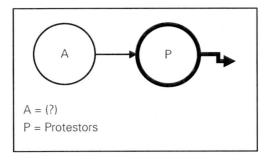

A = (?)
P = Protestors

FIGURE 8.11 *Profiling.*

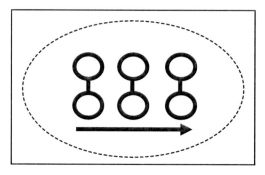

FIGURE 8.12 *Sequential scanning.*

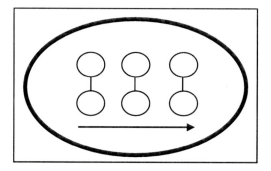

FIGURE 8.13 *Summary scanning.*

component states sequentially but see all of them accumulated' (Radden and Dirven 2007: 80). The two alternative conceptualizations can be modelled as in Figure 8.12 and 8.13. In sequential scanning, it is the relationships held between entities at different moments in the evolving event that is profiled. In summary scanning, it is the event as a whole, atemporal thing that is profiled and its internal structure thus backgrounded.

Crucially, the selection of alternative patterns across the grammars of ACTION, FORCE and MOTION constructs for readers alternative conceptualizations of the same situational context. Indeed, for Langacker (1991: 295), 'it is precisely because of their conceptual import – the contrasting images they impose – that alternate grammatical devices are commonly available to code the same situation'. In the final section, then, we investigate how the context of the student fees protests in the United Kingdom was constructed across the British press.

8 Findings

The twelve articles which formed the data for this study were closely read and all 'hard news' instances of interaction between police and protestors were extracted. The analysis therefore excludes actions directed at buildings and other material objects. Rather, it focuses specifically on conceptualizations of violence between two opposing groups – those empowered by the state and those protesting against the state (see also Fang 1994). The analysis also excludes any commentary or reported clauses in the article as well as reports of interactions at previous protests such as the G20 protests in 2009. The extracted data was then manually compared for grammatical differences within the parameters discussed above in Section 7.

Tables 8.4 and 8.5 show the total number of interactions in which police and protestors are agentive. Results are expressed both in absolute numbers and as a function of the total number of transactive processes extracted from the relevant sub-corpus. The total number of interactions in which police and protestors are agentive is then broken down into event type – action, force or motion. Results in these columns are expressed both in absolute numbers and as a function of the total number of interactions in which the relevant participant is agentive.

Several things can be garnered from these results. Comparing the total number of interactions in which police versus protestors are agentive in Tables 8.4 and 8.5 shows that *The Times*, the *Telegraph* and the *Express* code protestors as agentive more frequently than they do the police and more frequently than do the *Guardian*, the *Independent* or the *Mail*, in which the opposite is seen. On first glance, then, it might be tempting to conclude that the *Guardian*, the *Independent* and the *Mail* all construct the context in a way which pays heed to police violence and deligitimizes the

Table 8.4 Police as agentive

	ACTION	FORCE	MOTION	Total
Guardian	6 (0.55)	3 (0.27)	2 (0.18)	11 (0.58)
Independent	3 (0.18)	12 (0.71)	2 (0.12)	17 (0.68)
The Times	1 (0.2)	4 (0.8)	–	5 (0.36)
Telegraph	4 (1)	–	–	4 (0.36)
Express	1 (0.5)	1 (0.5)	–	2 (0.25)
Mail	2 (0.12)	10 (0.59)	5 (0.29)	17 (0.71)

Table 8.5 Protestors as agentive

	ACTION	FORCE	MOTION	Total
Guardian	6 (0.75)	1 (0.125)	1 (0.125)	8 (0.42)
Independent	7 (0.875)	1 (0.125)	–	8 (0.32)
The Times	7 (0.78)	2 (0.22)	–	9 (0.64)
Telegraph	7 (1)	–	–	7 (0.64)
Express	6 (1)	–	–	6 (0.75)
Mail	5 (0.71)	2 (0.29)	–	7 (0.29)

authorities' handling of the events. However, comparing across event types reveals that both the *Independent* and the *Mail* construe events in which the police are agentive as FORCE interactions or MOTION events significantly more frequently than ACTION events. The same is not seen in Table 8.5 in which all papers conceptualize events in which protestors are agentive more frequently as ACTION events.

Schematizing events in which police are agentive as a MOTION event, as in examples (8a–c), invokes a conceptualization of the event in which no physical effect is felt by another participant and therefore legitimizes police actions as largely peaceful.

(8a) The volatile situation started to calm down at about 4.30 p.m. when the Metropolitan Police **sent in** hundreds of riot officers (*Daily Mail*, 10th November)

(8b) Officers **led** them [protestors] down from various floors of the seven-storey building (*Daily Mail*, 10th November)

(8c) By mid-afternoon, police had given up trying to **disperse** the crowds (*Daily Mail*, 24th November)

Schematizing events as FORCE interactions in which the police are the ANTAGONIST and protestors the AGONIST, as in (9a–c), further legitimizes police action by presenting the police not as perpetrators of violence but as moral upholders of civil order – the last barrier between normality and chaos.

(9a) The 20 officers lining the route at Millbank faced an impossible task of trying to **hold back** thousands of demonstrators (*Daily Mail*, 10th November)

(9b) About 25 students remained **detained** inside a police cordon (*Independent*, 10th November)

(9c) The police slowly **forced** the remaining protesters out of the courtyard of Millbank Tower (*Independent*, 10th November)

By the same token, schematizing events as FORCE interactions in which protestors are the AGONIST delegitimizes their actions by presenting them as instigators of force interactions, bent on bringing chaos and therefore in need of controlling. FORCE schemas also have an inherent topology which construes the event as a conflict between two opposing sides. The conceptualization particularly lends itself to metaphorical extension framing the event as a 'battle', as in (10). This metaphorical extension further serves to legitimize police action and delegitimize protestors' actions through counterpart correspondences in a conceptual blend (see Hart 2008, 2010) between the valiant soldier and the police on the one hand and the defiant aggressor and protestors on the other.

(10) One constable suffered a broken arm and a second officer was knocked unconscious as he **battled** to contain protesters outside the Foreign

Office . . . Huge crowds had attempted to break the security cordon outside the building but the line of police was quickly bolstered to ensure the **barricades** were not **breached** (*Daily Mail,* 24th November)

With the exception of the *Telegraph,* all papers are more likely to frame police processes in terms of FORCE or MOTION than protestor processes. Again, however, a closer look reveals further ideological qualities. ACTION events in which the police are agentive in the *Telegraph* are always conceived as either reciprocal or retaliatory, whereas protestor actions are construed as reciprocal in only three out of seven instances and never as retaliatory. Consider (11a–c).

(11a) The Metropolitan Police confirmed that three protestors have been arrested in London for violent disorder and theft, while a further two arrests were made during **scuffles** with the police in Cambridge (*Telegraph,* 24th November)

(11b) A number of police officers were injured after they came under **attack** from youths (*Telegraph,* 10th November)

(11c) Rocks, wooden banners, eggs, rotten fruit and shards of glass were **thrown** at police officers trying to **beat back** the crowd with metal batons and riot shields (*Telegraph,* 10th November)

In (11a), the event is construed in terms of a reciprocal action chain in which both police and protestors are agentive. In (11b), the protestors alone are designated as agentive. In (11c), the police are construed as agentive but only *in response to* protestors' unprovoked actions.

By contrast, the *Guardian* designates a higher degree of agency to police as in (12) compared to (11c). And although five out of six events in which police are agentive are construed as reciprocal action events, protestors' actions are also construed in terms of reciprocal action schemas an equal five out of six times.

(12) [P]olice **wielding** batons clashed with a crowd hurling placard sticks, eggs and bottles. (*Guardian,* 10th November)

A similar pattern to that found for the *Telegraph* is repeated across the rest of the corpus. Table 8.6 shows the total number of reciprocal action schemas in each paper as a function of the total number of ACTION events in which the police versus protestors are agentive (see Tables 8.4 and 8.5). Overall, then, the *Guardian* construes the violence as more two-sided than the other papers in the corpus.

There is also a difference in focus of attention between newspapers when construing events in terms of a reciprocal action schema. In (11a) compared to (12), for example, the protestors versus the police are in focus, respectively. Table 8.7 shows the total number of reciprocal action schemas across the corpus broken down into police-in-focus, protestors-in-focus and nominalizations in which no particular entity

Table 8.6 Reciprocal action schemas

	Reciprocal action schemas		
	% Police action events	% Protestor action events	Total
Guardian	83	83	5
Independent	67	29	2
The Times	100	14	1
Telegraph	75	43	3
Express	100	17	1
Mail	50	20	1

Table 8.7 Focus in reciprocal action schemas

	Reciprocal action schemas		
	Police focussed	Protestor focussed	Unknown	Total
Guardian	1 (0.2)	2 (0.4)	2 (0.4)	5
Independent	–	–	2 (1)	2
The Times	–	–	1 (1)	1
Telegraph	1 (0.33)	1 (0.33)	1 (0.33)	3
Express	–	1 (1)	–	1
Mail	–	1 (1)	–	1

is in focus. Here, although the numbers are small, we can see that when the clause structure permits one entity to be in focus relative to the other, it is more frequently protestors.

Profiling, recall, is an extension of focus and is involved in the conceptualization of agentless passive constructions and, through summary scanning, nominalizations. It has the effect of obscuring cause or agency in action events. Focussing specifically on injuries sustained by police and protestors, we can glean from Table 8.8 that there is a general tendency towards grammatical patternings which invoke alternative mental models for events in which police or protestors receive injuries. The *Guardian* is the exception whereby the causes of injuries to both parties are obscured. When police are reported as receiving injuries, then, the full action chain is profiled as in (13a–b).[21] By contrast, when protestors are reported as sustaining injuries, only the resultant of the interaction or a reification of the process is profiled, thus precluding attention to the causes of injuries as in (14a–b).

Table 8.8 Causes of injuries

	Police injured		Protestors injured		
	Cause specified	Cause mystified	Cause specified	Cause mystified	Total
Guardian	—	2	—	2	4
Independent	1	—	—	1	2
The Times	1	1	—	1	3
Telegraph	3	—	—	5	8
Express	2	—	—	2	4
Mail	3	—	—	1	4

(13a) A number of **police officers** were **injured** as they came under attack from the **protesters** (*The Times*, 10th November)

(13b) A number of **police officers** were **injured** after they came under attack from **youths** (*Telegraph*, 10th November)

(14a) The demonstration followed a day of action two weeks ago that saw 60 arrested and dozens **injured** when a riot broke out at the Conservative Party headquarters (*Telegraph*, 24th November)

(14b) At least 14 people were treated for their **injuries** in hospital and 32 arrested (*The Times*, 10th November)

9 Conclusion

The analyses of schematization and attentional distribution given in this chapter further support the claim that grammar is a locus of ideology. However, they go beyond description of the text to address the interpretative dimension of discourse and demonstrate that grammar not only encodes ideology but also enacts it as alternative patternings evoke alternative mental models of the context described. In this way, grammar constructs contexts. These event-models, I have further suggested, feed into more general frames or discourses.

In the chapter, I have had both theoretical and empirical goals. Empirically, the results point to the *Guardian* being the only newspaper which draws any significant, explicit attention to police violence and calls into question police actions in the student fees protests. The other newspapers, by contrast, promote 'preferred models' (Van Dijk 1998) of events in which, through strategies of structural configuration and identification, police actions are legitimated while protestors' actions are delegitimated.

This ultimately constructs for readers a frame in which civil action is seen as a deviation from normative behaviour and is therefore associated with moral wrong-doing (Hall 1973), which state authorities are there to defend against.

Theoretically, I have tried to further develop both the Socio-Cognitive and the Cognitive Linguistic Approaches to CDA by suggesting a synergy between them. Specifically, I have suggested that the mental models necessarily predicated in the Socio-Cognitive Approach may be best theorized in terms of conceptual structures and construal operations described in Cognitive Linguistics. Cognitive Linguistics, I have argued, has the potential to account for the conceptual import of various lexical and grammatical constructions. Cognitive Linguistics is pattern-focussed and hearer-oriented (Nuyts 2007) and therefore, in fact, perfectly positioned to provide an analytical lens on the conceptual processes involved in ideological reproduction.

Notes

1 The need for a Cognitive Linguistic Approach and the benefits it brings to CDA have been extensively argued for and elaborated elsewhere. I will not repeat the arguments here. For details see, for example, Chilton (2004, 2005) and Hart (2005, 2010, 2011a)

2 This is not to detract from the contribution of Systemic Functional Grammar in CDA which, has proved particularly useful at the description-stage (e.g. Fairclough 1989; Fowler 1991)

3 It should be noted that in its current guise, the Cognitive Linguistic Approach offers only hypotheses as to the conceptual import of grammatical structures. The next stage in this research programme would be to experimentally validate the claims being made.

4 'Strategy' is defined, following Reisigl and Wodak (2001), as a more or less intentional or institutionalized plan of discourse practices. See Koller (forthcoming) for an alternative definition of discursive strategy.

5 It should be noted that while strategies of structural configuration and framing are functionally different and can be isolated for analytical purposes, they are closely connected and not easily separable in the practice of discourse. Indeed, all of these strategies can be seen to interact with one and other in the complex of discourse.

6 The conceptual structures involved in realizing such positioning strategies have been most concisely theorized, from a Cognitive Linguistic perspective, in terms of 'discourse worlds' (see Chilton 2004 and Cap 2006).

7 These construal operations have received relatively little attention within the Cognitive Linguistic Approach. By contrast, although the relevant authors would not necessarily situate their analyses with respect to this taxonomy or the broader Cognitive Linguistic Approach envisaged here, metaphor in particular has been much studied from a Cognitive Linguistic perspective (see, e.g., Charteris-Black 2004; Koller 2004; Musolff 2004). Deixis and modality have also been investigated within CDA from a Cognitive Linguistic perspective (e.g. Chilton 2004; Cap 2006; Marin Arrese 2011).

8 In Cognitive Linguistics, this is known as the 'embodiment thesis' (Evans and Green 2006).

9   In Cognitive Linguistics, this is known as the 'symbolic thesis' (Evans and Green 2006).

10 Salience is experienced on the longitudinal axis (Talmy 2000).

11 The affective component may be best modelled in terms of the categories of evaluation delineated in Martin and White's (2007) Appraisal Theory (Koller 2011). Within the Cognitive Linguistic Approach to CDA, the categories of evaluation found within Appraisal Theory could be characterized as construal operations grounded in the perspectival system and realizing effective positioning strategies (cf. Marin Aresse 2011).

12 Source: http://www.guardian.co.uk/news/datablog/2011/mar/28/demonstrations-protests-uk-list. Figures unavailable for second protest.

13 Kettling involves police partial cordoning of protestors within a designated area leaving only one route open or complete enclosure by police cordon for given periods of time, often without access to toilets and water etc.

14 It is worth noting that the domains of SPACE, MOTION and FORCE often act as source domains in metaphoric constructions of experience (Lakoff and Johnson 1999; Talmy 2000).

15 In the grammar of FORCE, the AGONIST is 'the entity whose circumstance is at issue' and is determined by the relative 'strength' of the ANTAGONIST (Talmy 2000: 415). Note that these participant categories are distinct from AGENT and PATIENT.

16 See Hart (2011b) for a detailed treatment of FORCE schemas.

17 It can also, of course, be seen in active versus passive constructions for asymmetrical action chains.

18 Notice that laterality is irrelevant here. Figure/ground alignment operates on salience, which we tend to experience on the longitudinal axis (Talmy 2000).

19 This is not to say that readers are not capable of such critical analysis (see Chilton 2005) but that in normal conditions to do so would exceed the 'resource-bound efficiency constraint balancing cognitive effort and contextual effects' (Maillat and Oswald 2011: 69) which operates on information processing.

20 The abstract, metaphorical agent in 'violence flared up' would presumably invoke a similar conceptualization.

21 Note that causal information in an adverbial clause is represented in the event-structure (though it is defocussed relative to information in the main clause).

References

Billig, M. (2008), 'The language of critical discourse analysis: The case of nominalization'. *Discourse & Society*, 19, 783–800.

Cap, P. (2006), *Legitimisation in Political Discourse: A Cross-Disciplinary Perspective on The Modern US War Rhetoric*. Newcastle: Cambridge Scholars Press.

Chilton, P. (2004), *Analysing Political Discourse: Theory and Practice*. London: Routledge.

—(2005), 'Missing links in mainstream CDA: Modules, blends and the critical instinct', in R. Wodak and P. Chilton (eds), *A New Agenda in (Critical) Discourse Analysis: Theory, Methodology and Interdisciplinarity*. Amsterdam: John Benjamins, pp. 19–52.

Croft, W. and Cruse, D. A. (2004), *Cognitive Linguistics*. Cambridge: Cambridge University Press.

Evans, V. and Green, M. (2006), *An Introduction to Cognitive Linguistics*. Edinburgh: Edinburgh University Press.

Fairclough, N. (1989), *Language and Power*. London: Longman.

Fang, J. Y. (1994), '"Riots" and demonstrations in the Chinese press: A case study of language and ideology'. *Discourse & Society*, 5(4), 463–81.

Fowler, R. (1991), *Language in the News: Discourse and Ideology in the Press*. London: Routledge.

—(1996), 'On critical linguistics', in C. R. Caldas-Coulthard and M. Coulthard (eds), *Texts and Practices: Readings in Critical Discourse Analysis*. London: Routledge, pp. 3–14.

Hackett, R. and Zhao, Y. (1994), 'Challenging a master narrative: Peace protest and opinion/editorial discourse in the US press during the Gulf War'. *Discourse & Society*, 5(4), 509–41.

Hall, S. (1973), 'A world at one with itself', in S. Cohen and J. Young (eds), *The Manufacture of News: Deviance, Social Problems and the Mass Media*. London: Constable, pp. 147–56.

Hart, C. (2005), 'Analysing political discourse: A cognitive approach'. *Critical Discourse Studies*, 2(2), 188–95.

—(2010), *Critical Discourse Analysis and Cognitive Science: New Perspectives on Immigration Discourse*. Basingstoke: Palgrave.

—(2011a), 'Moving beyond metaphor in the cognitive linguistic approach to CDA: Construal operations in immigration discourse', in C. Hart (ed.), *Critical Discourse Studies in Context and Cognition*. Amsterdam: John Benjamins, pp. 171–92.

—(2011b), 'Force-interactive patterns in immigration discourse: A Cognitive Linguistic approach to CDA'. *Discourse & Society*, 22(3), 269–86.

—(2013), 'Event-construal in press reports of violence in political protests: A Cognitive Linguistic Approach to CDA'. *Journal of Language and Politics*, 12(3), 400–23.

Johnson, M. (1987), *The Body in the Mind: The Bodily Basis of Meaning, Imagination, and Reason*. Chicago: University of Chicago Press.

Koller, V. (2004), *Metaphor and Gender in Business Media Discourse: A Critical Cognitive Study*. Basingstoke: Palgrave.

—(2011), 'How to analyse collective identity in discourse: Textual and contextual parameters'. *CADAAD*, 5(2), 19–38.

Lakoff, G. and Johnson, M. (1999), *Philosophy in the Flesh: The Embodied Mind and its Challenge to Western Thought*. New York: Basic Books.

Langacker, R. W. (1991), *Foundations of Cognitive Grammar, vol. II: Descriptive Application*. Stanford: Stanford University Press.

—(2002), *Concept, Image and Symbol: The Cognitive Basis of Grammar* (2nd edn). Berlin: Mouton de Gruyter.

—(2008), *Cognitive Grammar: A Basic Introduction*. Oxford: Oxford University Press.

Lee, J. and Craig, R. (1992), 'News as an ideological framework: Comparing US newspapers' coverage of Labor strikes in South Korea and Poland'. *Discourse & Society*, 3(3), 341–63.

Macleod, D. and Hertog, J. (1992), 'The manufacture of "public opinion" by reporters: Informal cues for publication perceptions of protest groups'. *Discourse & Society*, 3(3), 259–75.

Maillat, D. and Oswald, S. (2011), 'Constraining context: A pragmatic account of cognitive manipulation', in C. Hart (ed.), *Critical Discourse Studies in Context and Cognition*. Amsterdam: John Benjamins, pp. 65–80.

Marin Arrese, J. (2011), 'Effective vs. epistemic stance and subjectivity in political discourse: Legitimising strategies and mystification of responsibility', in C. Hart (ed.), *Critical Discourse Studies in Context and Cognition*. Amsterdam: John Benjamins, pp. 193–224.

Martin, J. R. and White, P. R. R. (2007), *The Language of Evaluation: Appraisal in English*. Basingstoke: Palgrave.

Montgomery, M. (1986), *An Introduction to Language and Society*. London: Routledge.

Musolff, A. (2004), *Metaphor and Political Discourse: Analogical Reasoning in Debates about Europe*. Basingstoke: Palgrave Macmillan.

Nuyts, J. (2007), 'Cognitive linguistics and functional linguistics', in D. Geeraerts and H. Cuyckens (eds), *The Oxford Handbook of Cognitive Linguistics*. Oxford: Oxford University Press, pp. 543–65.

O'Halloran, K. (2003), *Critical Discourse Analysis and Language Cognition*. Edinburgh: Edinburgh University Press.

Radden, G. and Dirven, R. (2007), *Cognitive English Grammar*. Amsterdam: John Benjamins.

Reisigl, M. and Wodak, R. (2001), *Discourse and Discrimination: Rhetorics of Racism and Antisemitism*. London: Routledge.

Talmy, L. (2000), *Toward a Cognitive Semantics*. Cambridge, MA: MIT Press.

Toolan, M. J. (1991), *Narrative: A Critical Linguistic Introduction*. London: Routledge.

Trew, T. (1979), 'Theory and ideology at work', in R. Fowler et al. (eds), *Language and Control*. London: Routledge and Keegan Paul, pp. 94–116.

Van Dijk, T. A. (1985), 'Cognitive situation models in discourse production: The expression of ethnic situations in prejudiced discourse', in J. P. Forgas (ed.), *Language and Social Situations*. New York: Springer, pp. 61–79.

—(1991), *Racism and the Press*. London: Routledge.

—(1997), 'Cognitive context models and discourse', in M. Stamenow (ed.), *Language Structure, Discourse and the Access to Consciousness*. Amsterdam: John Benjamins, pp. 189–226.

—(1998), *Ideology: A Multidisciplinary Approach*. London: Sage.

—(1999), 'Context models in discourse processing', in H. Oostendorp and S. Goldman (eds), *The Construction of Mental Models during Reading*. Mahwah, NJ: Erlbaum, pp. 123–48.

—(2010), *Discourse and Context: A Socio-Cognitive Approach*. Cambridge: Cambridge University Press.

—(2011), 'Discourse, knowledge, power and politics: Toward a critical epistemic discourse analysis', in C. Hart (ed.), *Critical Discourse Studies in Context and Cognition*. Amsterdam: John Benjamins, pp. 27–64.

Van Leeuwen, T. J. (1996), 'The representation of social actors', in C. R. Caldas-Coulthard and M. Coulthard (eds), *Texts and Practices: Readings in Critical Discourse Analysis*. London: Routledge, pp. 32–70.

Widdowson, H. G. (2004), *Text, Context, Pretext: Critical Issues in Discourse Analysis*. Oxford: Blackwell.

9

Intervening in health care communication using discourse analysis

Rick Iedema and Katherine Carroll

Introduction

This chapter describes an application of discourse analysis that intervenes in the way hospital services are provided. It is important to engage with hospital services because clinical work is becoming more and more complex. This is thanks to the technologization of care, the rising turn-over clinical staff, the rising numbers of older patients who seek care for multiple diseases, the mobility of patients and the difficulty of establishing clinical histories, and the slowing growth in resource investment per patient across most industrialized countries (Sorensen and Iedema 2008). These factors create numerous risks in care, and particularly in hospitals, where the use of invasive procedures and dangerous technologies is common. These risks create many failures in care, as is evident from reports that analyse the rates and frequencies of 'iatrogenic' (hospital/clinician-caused) errors (Baker and Norton 2004; UK Department of Health 2000; US Institute of Medicine 1999) and which publish the results of enquiries into clinical failures (Hindle, Braithwaite, and Iedema 2004).

Goals

Engaging with how clinicians operate in these complex environments is therefore critical. Researchers need to better understand the complexity of care, and such research may assist clinicians in 'taming' that complexity. The present chapter will contend that discourse theory harbours a principle that is central to responding to the *in situ* complexity found in health care and hospitals in particular. As this chapter will argue and demonstrate, discourse theory is critical for doing health service research because it is grounded in the principle of *relativization*; that is, a practice, meaning or feeling has a relational dimension in that it becomes meaningful by distinguishing itself from what it is not, relative to other practices, meanings and feelings. Such relativization makes it possible for these practices, meanings and feelings to become different. In the work presented here, relativization is achieved by capturing *in situ* activities on video and showing them back to professionals. This is referred to as video-reflexive ethnography. The chapter demonstrates the links between discourse analysis and video-reflexive ethnography, and the impact these can have on *in situ* practice.

The theory and approach that inform this study

Existing health service research operates largely on the medical test model: subject a large enough sample of 'subjects' to a treatment, evaluate its effectiveness and implement the treatment for everyone globally if it proves to be effective for the sample. This approach is problematic for two reasons. It denies the importance of local difference, and it glosses over the need for constant adaptation of existing rules and resources to suit complex situations. The present chapter mobilizes discourse theory as a means for clinicians to re-engage with their here-and-now. While the solutions produced 'scientifically' through large sample studies cannot be dismissed as unimportant, the complexity of care is increasingly demanding that frontline clinicians become engaged themselves in producing emergent solutions for their increasingly unique patients.

To connect with frontline health care professionals, the research presented here hones in on the here-and-now as the site of maximum complexity; the site where frontline professionals make decisions and enact care, and the site where change will occur, if it occurs at all (Iedema and Carroll 2010). The theory that underpins this work is that, to intervene in our (organizational, professional, clinical) habits, we need to find ways of interrupting them (Dewey 1922; Shusterman 2008). Such interruption is achieved here through the use of 'reflexive video' (Iedema, Mesman and Carroll in press; Iedema, Long, Forsyth and Lee 2006). Reflexive video ensures that one's own activities and relationships are brought into view. Once a previously unrecognized aspect of what is enacted, meant or felt is allowed to come into view in this way, the original practice, meaning and feeling may reveal their local peculiarity and historical contingency. This means the practice, meaning and feeling may lose their status as being natural, necessary and normal (Iedema 2007).

The present chapter equates that which is seen or experienced as natural, necessary and normal, as the *contextual*. Context, in this sense, is that which is delegated to the periphery of, or that which is entirely excluded from, people's attention. Reflexive video assists in retrieving that which is treated as contextual and rendering it focal. In this way, reflexive video interrupts taken-as-given ways of acting, speaking and thinking, and opens us up to new ways of acting, speaking and thinking.

What now is the connection between reflexive video and discourse analysis? Well, an important premise of discourse research is that what people do and say is not objectively out there ('labeling reality'), nor a transparent articulation of their thoughts and intentions ('constructing reality') (Iedema 2007). Instead, what people do and say is 'citational' (Butler 1997); that is, people's agency involves instantiating and perturbing more or less settled and habituated social practices. In everyday work, and for the people doing it, this citational aspect tends to be remain hidden in a double sense. On the one hand, the *everyday* naturalizes and normalizes what people do, think and say: 'this is how things are done here'. On the other hand, *commonsense* feeds the assumption that people intend what they do, think and say in a transparent and self-evident way. In using the term 'citation', we signal that agency – that is, what people do, think and say – may be beholden to everyday norms and prevailing commonsense, rather than to principles and practices that we have rationally established, critically assessed and pro-actively shaped.

The citational perspective on practice is relevant here for another reason too. Critical analyses of health care have revealed that clinicians' agency is frequently caught up in and therefore determined by seemingly unchallengeable (health) professional traditions and conventions. These traditions actively prevent revisiting and revising the principles and practices informing and structuring clinical practice (Degeling, Maxwell, Kennedy, and Coyle 2003). In our work, we deploy reflexive video to alert clinicians to the citational dimensions of what they do, think and say – dimensions that might otherwise remain contextual to how these people understand their own impact on the world and their role in everyday practice. Put differently, reflexive video sets in train a 'decontextualisation' of the taken-as-given. As we shall see, this has the practical effect of enabling actors to reconfigure their practices and some of the principles that underpin them.

How context is understood in this study

As noted, we understand context as the domain of the taken-as-given, or that domain that does not warrant our immediate attention. Rather than defining context in spatial terms ('the area that surrounds where we are'), in cultural terms ('these are the practices that inform how we act') or in semiotic terms ('the meaning making resource available to us'), this chapter regards context as the periphery (and beyond) of everyday sociocultural processes. These processes shape what we can turn our attention to, and what we are to leave undiscussed, unrepresented, out of consideration. In part, of course, these processes are political and cultural, as they pertain to what we can do, think and make explicit on the one hand, and to what we cannot do, say and question, on the other hand.

Context plays a critical role in video-reflexive ethnography. Video renders context visible as those phenomena that professionals take as given: everything they treat as contextual to the real business of doing clinical work. What is relegated to the status of context is a critical issue in health. This becomes clear when we consider that patients' needs and personal preferences have for many decades been regarded as peripheral or secondary to the real business of health care. As Armstrong notes, 'the clinical teaching manuals that were published in the nineteenth and early twentieth centuries reflected the dominance of [clinical] signs in medical diagnosis, barely mentioning the process of obtaining reports of symptoms ["the medical history"] from the patient' (Armstrong 2002: 59). For many decades since the birth of the clinic, patients were only partially or not at all informed about their doctors' decisions, even when these decisions or diagnoses pertained to their own impending death (Glaser and Strauss 1965). Here, the patient as person remained 'contextual' to the business of medical-clinical practice *per se*.

Challenging health professionals' assumptions about the position of the patient meant challenging what they regarded as contextual and what as central to their practice. To achieve this, conventional health services research has proceeded largely on the basis of formal arguments and numerical statistics. It is thought that formal evidence will enable professionals to alter their view of what is important to patients, and this will lead to changes in care, benefiting patients. And yet, even after numerous publications announcing that patients are treated in ways that are unsafe and disrespectful of patients' views and knowledge about what is good and safe care, health reform in this respect has proceeded at a snail's pace, if at all (Vincent, Aylin, Dean Franklin, Holmes, Iskander, Jacklin and Moorthy 2008).

Our approach engages directly with how professionals enact care in the here-and-now and it confronts them with their own taken-as-given principles and practices. Video-reflexive ethnography shows professionals footage of themselves at work. Viewing such footage interrupts their sense of who they are and what they do (Iedema, Long, Forsyth, and Lee 2006). By being videoed (ethnographically) and then being invited to observe their own practices, meanings and feelings, people's 'citations' become visible, and this renders these 'citations' available for evaluation, exploration and experimentation.

Video is crucial here. The moving image produces an 'othering' visualization of what we say and do. Indeed, moving images effect 'a continuous displacement of the subject, the object and their general relation . . . it is an opening onto a space of transformation' (Massumi 2002: 51). Engaging with ourselves through video harbours the possibility of transformation, precisely because video interrupts the relationship between what we hold as focal in what we do, say and think, and what we regard as contextual. The video screen flattens and foregrounds relationships in ways to contravene our assumptions about how practice works and about how we fit into practice. This creates an effect that we have described elsewhere as the emergence of 'a new structure of attention' (Iedema, Jorm, Wakefield, Ryan and Sorensen 2009; Thrift 2004a).

The context of the study

The focal concern of the present chapter is to describe how such a new structure of attention results from practitioners' engagement in video-reflexive ethnographic research. To address this concern, the chapter describes an instance of discourse research that sought to privilege two principles. First, discourse analysts locate themselves in the midst of constantly emerging organizational discourses and practices. This involves confronting the dilemma that the contemporary complexity and fluidity of social and organizational structures require a strategic and flexible stance on the part of the researcher. Second, discourse analysts are not just suppliers of theoretical and methodological expertise, but people who exploit their ability to recognize the contextuality of and thereby the relativity inherent in situated practice, including their own. This recognition, if shared with practitioners, makes it possible for all involved to move into new roles, cross professional-organizational boundaries and become co-productive of new professional-organizational realities.

To exemplify what such stance looks like in practice, the chapter presents two empirical case studies where these principles were realized. The first case study is sited in an out-patients spinal clinic in a local metropolitan teaching hospital. Here, we will consider how the researcher's interpretation of who she is and what she understands about spinal care is affected by the spinal clinicians' appropriation of her visual data for reconceptualizing cross-infection in their unit. The second case study is sited in an intensive care unit at a regional hospital, where the negotiation over what to film, what to screen back and how to interpret the footage harboured unanticipated risks, intensities and outcomes for both the researcher and the clinicians.

Data

Case study 1: The spinal clinic

The spinal clinical team participated in a three-year study[1] that centred on filming the team doing their everyday work. The filming was done to understand how staff come to embody, enact and manage the increasingly complex processes that are typical of contemporary health care provision. Central to the project were filming of clinical practices and showing the footage back to clinicians to learn together (researchers and clinicians) about what was going on, a process then referred to as 'video reflexivity'. We saw such learning as crucial for clinicians and consumers due to the rising complexity of contemporary health care. In spinal care in particular, this rise in complexity results to an important extent from medical technologies enabling clinicians to do much more for patients now than they could twenty or even ten years ago (Brown and Webster 2004).[2]

The development of care further means that the provision of health services is creating a growing population of chronically ill patients who are, in different ways, dependent not only on sophisticated kinds of expert medical care, but also on increasingly specialized nursing care, allied health care and community care.

Further adding to this complexity, patients themselves are increasingly keen and called upon to 'co-produce' the treatment of their own precarious health through self-care, requiring them to be knowledgeable about their condition, treatment, pharmaceutical dependencies and biophysiological needs (Iedema, Sorensen, Jorm, and Piper 2008).

As far as the spinal clinic is concerned, complexity is inherent in spinal patients' frequently developing pressure sores from lying still over extended periods of time. These sores often get infected with multi-resistant organisms (MROs) that are transmitted by clinicians who carry them on their clothes and hands. Indeed, cross-infection in hospitals counts among the most serious and costly kinds of clinician-caused incidents (Duerden 2005; Pittet 2005), with the cost of in-hospital acquired infections estimated at US $17–29 billion yearly in the United States and at £1billion in the United Kingdom (Pittet 2005). Invasive infections with MROs such as 'methicillin resistant staphylococcus aureus' or MRSA are associated with high levels of preventable morbidity and mortality (McLaws and Taylor 2003). For that reason, the accelerating spread of these hospital-acquired infections (Whitby, McLaws, and Berry 2001) calls for intensified 'surveillance' of clinicians' practices to minimize cross-infection. Alongside intensive care units and emergency departments, spinal units are cross-infection hotspots (Vidal 1991).

The screening back of footage showing everyday practice at the spinal unit led to two unexpected developments. First, an infection control nurse who happened to see the footage at a feedback meeting realized that the visual data harboured information that she had not noticed when surveilling people's practices 'live' on the ward. Although hospital-caused cross-infection was not a predetermined focus of our study, we began working with this nurse to draw out the implications of the infection risks that were evident in the footage (Iedema and Rhodes 2010). The infection control nurse requested to see more footage of clinicians dealing with patients who had infected wounds, enabling her to identify numerous previously unrecognized cross-infection vectors. Where before she had to spend hours on the ward with a clipboard to rate clinician compliance with rigid personal-protective equipment and hand-washing rules, she was now, by viewing practice on the video screen, able to identify (for herself and for us) how infections can travel across bodies (from one wound to another on the same body), tools (through handling of mobile phones, referral letters) and spaces (from beds across consult rooms into corridors).

Second, the infection control nurse insisted on using the video footage to engage the spinal clinicians in discussions about infection control risks. During the bi-monthly video reflexivity meetings, the clinical team thus became involved in focusing on cross-infection risks affecting their practices. Footage was shown of clinicians examining patients' wounds and then leaning on the bed rail, transferring potentially infectious material to a place where other people could pick it up and carry it further again (Visual 9.1). Other footage alerted the clinicians to the risk of overflowing bins – items that had not been noticed before because they had become taken-as-given and no-longer-noticed elements of the ward environment (Visual 9.2).

VISUAL 9.1 *Clinician leaning on handrail.*

VISUAL 9.2 *Bin overflowing with potentially infectious material.*

Analysis

How should we analyse this data? On the whole, discourse research has encompassed two overarching approaches. The first is one that emerged from linguistics some time ago (Harris 1952) and which edged up from the sentence analysis towards analysis of 'the whole text' (Coulthard 1977; de Beaugrande and Dressler 1981; Stubbs 1983; van Dijk 1977), including spoken exchanges (Berry 1981) and eventually also visual and other semiotic aspects of text and interaction (Kress and van Leeuwen 2001). This strand is focused on understanding patterns of language use in different forms of linguistic and textual practice. Enquiry here centres on developing generalizations about text patterns and types, sentence constructions and registerial phenomena (see Martin 1992 for an overview).

This strand can also be said to encompass work initiated during the 1970s by a group of UK researchers called 'critical linguists' (Fowler, Hodge, Kress and Trew 1979).

These critical linguists fused linguistic analysis and critical theory. The purpose was to link language patterns to political ideologies (Hodge and Kress [1979] 1993). This strand was further bolstered when it began to cross-fertilize with the lexicogrammatical analyses developed by Michael Halliday ([1985] 1994), producing a rich vein of politically motivated discourse analysis (Martin 1985). When in the late eighties Norman Fairclough expounded the theoretical bases of a critical approach to discourse analysis (published as Fairclough 1995), seeds were sewn for an influential paradigm that capitalized on the combined strengths of analytical and critical enquiry: critical discourse analysis (Fairclough 1992). Its concern with social practices proved fertile ground for critical discourse analysis to harness multimodal theory to its investigations and critiques of meaning-making phenomena (Kress 2010).

The second main strand of discourse research centres on profiling the socio-political aspects of contemporary social practices. Placing less emphasis on the analyses of specific empirical objects, this research regards as its main task the identification of broad social domains of practice (Foucault 1972; Laclau 2005). The aim here is to bring into view and thereby denaturalize the principles and assumptions that underpin social practices in general (Thrift 1997).

What unites these two strands of discourse enquiry is interest in the socially constructed and therefore potentially changeable nature of social life (Phillips and Hardy 2002). In that sense, *discourse* acts as banner for work that seeks to challenge taken-as-given practices and associated understandings about and perspectives on the real.

While both strands of discourse theory conduct critical analysis in the interest of social change, limited evidence exists of researchers engaging with the institutions and practices sought out for critique. This observation becomes acute in the light of the 'liquid' (Bauman 2000) or 'foamy' ontology of contemporary post-industrial societies (Sloterdijk 2004; Sloterdijk 2005). The terms 'liquid' and 'foamy' refer to the rapidly shifting knowledge-base of late-modern social life, and the increasingly complex and multi-faceted nature of power, control and practice, both in organizations (Clegg, Courpasson, and Phillips 2006) and in society generally (Sloterdijk 2005). This liquid or foamy state is certain to affect discourse, whether defined as meaning making practice or as a broadly ideological configuration.

This liquidity or foaminess also raises questions about the ponderous analyses proposed by discourse research when dealing with fast-paced social and organizational change. It further raises questions about the usefulness and durability of the generalizations produced by these analyses. It is not insignificant in this regard that prominent social theorists like Nigel Thrift and Nikolas Rose, for whom 'discourse' represented an important theoretical tool in the 1990s (Rose 1996; Thrift 1997), are now actively pursuing *prediscursive* concerns focusing on the neurological and affective dimensions of social and organizational phenomena (Rose 2004; Thrift 2004b). Besides their interest in the non-representational dimensions of being, these more recent writings bear out sensitivity to the tentative nature of knowledge and the inherent changeability of practice.

For these reasons, the empirical material presented here evoked a form of discourse research that privileges co-accomplished sense-making of practice involving researcher and researched, or, if you like, research participant (Karnieli-Miller, Strier and Pessach 2009: 281). Without losing sight of the analytical-critical moments that have thus far driven discourse analytical endeavours, we use empirical description to explore what it means to move from discourse analysis as the deployment of a pre-designed analytical framework and critical objectives towards a stance that creates 'sites of engagement' (Latour 2004). In such forums of engagement, the researcher and research participant pursue not 'matters of fact, but matters of concern' (Latour 2004). Put differently, they partake in the co-construction of discourse as a dynamically emerging practical reality.

What should be evident now is that our concern is not to analyse 'found practices' using standard discourse analytical techniques. Rather, we seek to make sense of what is going on in collaboration with practitioners, and, through this feedback and dialogue, co-produce new practices and meanings. This approach echoes Luke's point 'that if we are to take the axiom of 'what is to be done' seriously in current conditions, critical discourse studies must turn towards a reconstructive agenda, one designed towards redress, reconciliation and the rebuilding of social structure, institutional lives and identities' (Luke 2004: 151). Luke's call for 'a flexible analytical toolkit' (Luke 2004: 151) also mirrors Sarangi's recent conceptualization of a hybrid critical-reconstructive praxis that involves the researcher and the research participant in shared sense-making about practice (Sarangi 2006). Sense-making, if read in the context of Weick's work (Weick 1995), is a practice that is not just retrospective, but also prospective and creative, leading to:

> inquiry in which participants and researchers co-generate knowledge through collaborative communicative processes in which all participants' contributions are taken seriously. The meanings constructed in the inquiry process lead to social action, or these reflections on action lead to the construction of new meanings. (Greenwood and Levin 2000: 96)

Finally, shared sense-making (of video footage) further references Deleuze's notion of sense and not the linguistic concept of sense. Instead of understanding sense as a function of how we refer to phenomena, Deleuze treats sense as an affective value or a general mood that *colours* events (Williams 2008). Similarly, when put to work in our video-reflexive research, sense-making does not refer to interpreting or analysing what is in the footage, but to the dynamics of stakeholders becoming involved, interested and enabled through viewing the footage. The footage and the alternative way of seeing it may afford 'make sense' when they reverberate on through what people say, think and do next.

In sum, the approach to discourse analysis utilized here accords the participation, insights and creativity of professional practitioners a central role. Indeed, the approach stakes its success on whether professionals themselves are willing and enabled to apprehend their own principles and practices 'from under a different aspect' (Wittgenstein 1953), and whether they will mobilize that realization to achieve *in situ* practice reform. Our research targets not existing patterns in practice or speaking *per se*, nor does it seek to achieve particular patterns or predetermined structures. Rather, its findings and achievements are defined by and contingent on the extent to which professionals are and feel enabled to reform how they work together and, in our case, provide care for patients (Iedema 2011).

Findings

Upon viewing the infection control footage described above, one of the clinicians comments as follows (I = infection control nurse; D = doctor):

Extract 1: Reflexive feedback meeting (15/2/05)

8:20[3] I. it's really exciting, it's great

8:25 D. I think it will give us an idea as to whether or not we're bringing the multi-resistant bugs into the ward from clinic, and whether or not those bugs are evolving and getting more and more resistant as [name patient] comes into contact with other patients. I think they're the sorts of things we want to know, as objective outcomes, but I guess the other thing is the behaviour that may be contributing to that, and what that is.

This exchange foregrounds two issues of interest. First, it evinces the video footage's capacity to produce new ways of seeing, and that this new way of seeing in turn creates interest among those present (Iedema, Forsyth, Georgiou, Braithwaite, and Westbrook 2007): 'it's really exciting' (8.20) and 'they're the sorts of things we want to know' (8.25). Second, it shows the clinicians engaging with the problems high-lighted in the footage and thinking through what these insights mean for their practice: 'it will give us an idea as to whether or not we're bringing the multi-resistant bugs into the ward from clinic' (8.25).

To us, the researchers, the clinicians' involvement in exploring practical implications of what they had seen was not a predetermined outcome from a complex process of negotiation. That is, the reflexive session was preceded by a range of complex dynamics: the researcher negotiating with clinicians what to film and what to screen back; the infection-control nurse picking out specific footage and requesting that more comparable footage be identified; the clinical team being comfortable with the infection-control nurse driving a particular set of interpretations of the footage[4]; and the researchers enabling the clinicians to 'take over' when it came to determining the implications of what was shown for their own practice.

In the extract below (extract 2), taken from the same meeting transcript as extract 1, the researcher who led the reflexive sessions (see Visual 9.3) admits to having 'crossed

VISUAL 9.3 *Video-reflexive feedback meeting in the spinal unit.*

boundaries'. She points to how important crossing boundaries are to enabling specific issues to drop out from the video-reflexive meetings and to be pursued by those present. The point of the discussion shown in extract 2 is that both researchers and clinicians should be able to let go of their conventional professional identity. Equally, they are to let go of their expectation of autonomy and self-completion, in order to engage with the full impact and implications of reflexive practice. For the researcher, this means allowing the research participant to co-determine what is important and why (Karnieli-Miller, Strier and Pessach 2009: 281). For the clinicians, this means acknowledging that there are patient safety risks that may not be visible to them when they are 'in the thick of things', caught up in the 'hurly-burly' of everyday practice, their experience and training notwithstanding.

Extract 2: Reflexive feedback meeting (researcher speaking to clinicians; 15/2/05)

4:33 We had a meeting with the infection control people, and I wasn't completely aware of what we were doing, and I feel a little bit nervous about crossing boundaries and working both outside my area of expertise and in what I'm supposed to do, and I'm very excited by the opportunities that the infection control stuff is creating for us . . . And we went down there and [name doctor] said "[name researcher] do you want to chair this", and I immediately went "I don't know what I'm doing" . . . And it was a confidence issue – it was me being very, very nervous about not wanting to overstep my boundaries, and having an enormous amount of faith in [name doctor]'s ability, more confidence in [name doctor]'s ability to handle the situation than mine, so yeah, I'm not pointing fingers at anything I haven't done myself. But I think it is something, that if [name doctor] genuinely wants to devolve responsibility, and if the rest of the team genuinely feel that that is an important thing for the clinic – and if you don't maybe that's a conversation that needs to be had, but if you do, then strategies for both the passing over and the receiving [of responsibility] are probably worthwhile discussing.

Crossing boundaries (i.e. relaxing rules around who is researcher and who is not) enables the researcher to be told what is important in the data that was captured, and why this was considered important. For the clinicians, boundary crossing (i.e. speaking and thinking like a researcher) makes clinical practice visible 'from under a different aspect' (Wittgenstein 1953). This, in turn, entrains new sensibilities and responsibilities with regard to heretofore invisible problems, errors and infection risks. Put in these terms, viewing the real 'from under a different aspect', the discourse analytical move *par excellence*, is not achieved here thanks to painstaking analysis, but through the tactics of relaxing rules and boundary-crossing. As we suggest below, these tactics are in fact crucial to clinicians enacting patient safety: new ways of seeing engender a new inter-professional communicative space where previously unnoticed material-clinical risks become visible, discussable and alterable.[5]

Case study 2: The intensive care unit

The second case study was conducted in a regional intensive care unit (ICU) as part of the same project that funded the spinal unit work discussed above. This part of the study involved working with clinicians on their ICU communication practices. Through discussing with them what they saw as issues of concern, one of the things we agreed to pay attention to was their medical information hand-over sessions or 'ward rounds' (Carroll, Iedema and Kerridge 2008). To make aspects of this practice visible, a 15-minute DVD was edited from the 11 hours of footage collected and this DVD was shown at a reflexive session (Visual 9.4). As with the spinal clinicians discussed above, viewing the DVD enabled the ICU doctors to see aspects of their own work they had not seen before, despite, or perhaps thanks to, being deeply embedded in ICU practice.

VISUAL 9.4 *Negotiating hand-over practices in ICU.*

But this novel seeing is not automatic. It is contingent on a complex process of negotiation between the researcher and the clinicians preparing for sometimes quite confronting insights:

"I . . . realised there was quite a complex flow of information going on as there were several contributors about each patient but there was talking at different levels about different things, there were fragments of things that people needed to say and then the big picture about this, and then suddenly a small detail issue . . . and they leapt from one to the other and then back to the big picture. There is no build up . . . they just get thrown in as fragments from one to the other." (Intensivist, 26/10/05)

Besides commenting on the organizational complexities embedded in ward round handovers, this intensivist also focuses on the interpersonal challenges:

"The things that I was noticing . . . was this is quite daunting for the junior doctors. I realized there was a semi circle of people standing in front of them . . . it looked quite an intimidating situation . . . they were forced to try and create and maintain peoples' attention . . . they had to put on an act to try and get people not to be bored . . . other people were struggling to maintain interest by bed 14 . . . not only is it a daunting role but to have to put on a show to try and get people to listen to them. . . . I hadn't realized it was an acting skill as much as a communication skill." (Intensivist, 26/10/2005)

As the researcher who initiated this process explains, deciding what to show back to clinicians is not unproblematic, because inevitably interpersonal issues arise alongside organizational ones. Clinicians' responses to such a range of issues are therefore not necessarily predictable:

In the process of video reflexivity the researcher and her video ethnographic gaze are exposed to the experts of the field, resulting in the researcher not only looking alongside clinicians as they interpret the visual footage but also being available for both direct criticism and praise in this creative research space. (Carroll 2009: 103)

The video-reflexive moment takes place in an uncertain and potentially creative space where the researcher's tentative portrayal of clinical practice seeks to dialogue with clinicians' often quite fixed understandings, priorities and concerns. To the extent that clinical work itself is unpredictable and 'messy', and clinicians' interpretations of what is 'good care' often diverge (Iedema, Jorm, Braithwaite, Travaglia and Lum 2006), choosing what to portray of the clinical work is complex. Such portrayal runs the risk of privileging one particular perspective over others, or erasing from the reflexive discussion some people's interpretations and concerns because they missed out on being screened (Iedema, Long, Forsyth, and Lee 2006). On the other hand, video footage is rich in what it captures, and, as with the infection control nurse seen above, its impact cannot easily be predetermined. Hence, screening back visual data situates the researcher in a space of uncertainty and risk:

> Although this is the more difficult research route, accepting the uncertainty and the "mess" that comes with this creative space also means facilitating the side-benefit of creativity and innovation for clinician-participants. (Carroll 2009: 108)

For those willing to negotiate over what to film, what footage to screen back, how to see the footage and what conclusions to draw from it can create a new vitality; that is, a 'new potential for interaction' (Massumi 1995: 96). This new potential for interaction emerges from putting at risk that which to date was made to appear natural, necessary, 'automatic', and not worthy of our attention because *contextual*. As with the first case study, the risks inherent in boundary-crossing here are therefore not principally sacrificing theoretical and methodological integrity, but, by having one's assumptions and starting points challenged through seeing them 'from under a different aspect', having to co-negotiate new communicative spaces, discursive opportunities and practical ways 'for going on'.

Discussion

The analysis above sought to demonstrate that discourse research can deploy data and methods to perturb taken-as-given professional practices and spaces. The analysis also showed that such an approach may lead to the researcher being affected and her approach itself being perturbed. The negotiation over what to visualize, how to read the footage and where to take these reflections made it possible for the researchers and clinicians alike to enter a not-yet-experienced communicative space. In this space, researchers and clinicians created a new potential for interaction. They risked engaging with a vitality whose orientation and effect were unpredictable and uncharted. In negotiating over what to film, what footage to show and how to respond to it, researchers and clinicians confronted what had until then been natural and necessary, a part of everyday (professional and research) business. In capturing these taken-as-given aspects of practice on video, both parties came to apprehend themselves as at once self and other, as practitioners whose academic and clinical routines and identities were now no longer unquestioned and unquestionable.

Central here we suggest is the visualization of practice. Visualization de-objectifies objects, bringing newly to the fore the agency of handrails in infection, as well as that of bins, ward rounds and other phenomena that populate everyday clinical work. Visualization also de-subjectifies subjects, denaturalizing the roles, functions and status of spinal specialists, infection control nurses, ward round leaders and researchers. In effect, visualization makes questions possible about how subjects have come to act and speak as they do, and about how objects have come to be used the way they are and about how all this has been allowed to appear natural and necessary by being framed and rendered stable discursively.

Critical to the argument of this chapter is that the transformations accomplished in both case studies are the discursive analytical move *par excellence* (Iedema 2007): reframing what appears to be marginal (contextual) or essential (focal) to everyday practice renders both contingent and therefore 'discourse'. The notion discourse does not function here as label for particular objects (language, visuals, spaces of meaning making and so on) that can be collected, analysed according to a schema and judged against standardized criteria (power, emancipation, practice improvement). Rather, discourse is a way of seeing and sensing. Discourse is a *stance* vis-à-vis the practices, meanings and feelings that populate our lives – a stance that allows experience to be de-automatized and thereby become revitalized.

To be sure, the recent emphasis on the pre-discursive, affective and neurological dimensions of co-existence (Thrift 2004) is to acknowledge that practice and discourse may be hostage to a multiplicity of automatized phenomena whose origin and logic need to be located elsewhere than in representation. Explaining discourse or practice may need to involve referencing biophysiological and mimetic processes that we have little to no conscious control over (Damasio 1994; Ledoux 1996).

> The fact that emotions, attitudes, goals, and the like are activated automatically (without any conscious effort) means that their presence in the mind and their influence on thoughts and behaviour are not questioned. (Ledoux 1996: 63)

One way for discourse research to work with rather than ignore the limits of discourse is by confronting and transgressing socially and organizationally sanctioned boundaries, such as those that are inscribed into theoretical frameworks, methodological routines and organizational spaces. Specifically, by de-automatizing the conducts that commonly define discourse research as 'discipline', researchers may enter *discursive praxis*. This praxis mobilizes rather than erases the pre-personal dimensions of the research relationship, allowing unpredictability and messiness into the research process, and affording indeterminate outcomes rather than theoretically and methodologically predetermined ones.

In this, the visual representation of practice may play the role of catalyst. As discourse that decontextualizes context and that places the taken for granted 'under a different aspect', visualization helps perturb relationships between what is focal and what is contextual.

The argument developed here does not involve suggesting that we discard approaches to discourse research that involve data collection and analysis to realize particular descriptive or critical objectives. What the argument does mean to imply is that we begin to ask questions about discourse theory and analytical frameworks; questions that discourse research in general and critical discourse research in specific have to date not adequately addressed. For example, how confident can we be in reading the meaning(s) of social practice off from discursive objects when we know that these objects themselves are becoming increasingly unstable (Iedema 2007)? Similarly, what relevance do generalizing theoretical and analytical frameworks have for engaging with social practices that are becoming increasingly dynamic thanks to intensifying modes of feedback and rising rates and speeds of change and innovation (Sloterdijk 2005)?

Indeed, the turn-over of repertoires of (discourse) practice is now so fast-paced that some have begun to speak about a 'runaway society' (Giddens 1991). Its people face 'a permanent emergency' forcing them to adopt a 'hair-trigger responsiveness to adapt to the expectedly unexpected' (Thrift 1999: 674). In health care, this 'hair-trigger awareness' manifests not just in 'emergency' (rather than 'casualty') now being the principal entry point into the contemporary hospital, but also in 'constant vigilance' being advocated to limit the spread and rise of clinical failures and errors (Reason 2004). Seen against this background, could it be that theoretical frameworks and disciplinary approaches, beyond mapping what is, in fact constrain what could be? Could it be time to take stock of that which has come to define discourse research, and engage with challenging viewpoints, such as Luke's preference for a 'reconstructive agenda', to revitalize taken-as-given assumptions and practices?

Offering one step in that direction, the present chapter exemplifies what engaged discourse research may look like. Involving research participants in the construction of research outcomes (practice interpretations, workplace changes, research papers), this approach calls existing boundaries between discourse analysis and social practice into question. This questioning occurs at different levels: who determines what is data; how data is gathered and what is done to it; who decides what the practices and discourses portrayed in that data mean; what do such interpretations entrain as outcomes, to name but some.

Both cases described above involved crossing taken-as-given boundaries, with the visualization of practice exploited here as catalyst. By mobilizing the effects of video, this approach to discourse research refers the meaning of 'discourse' on to its Latinate origins: '*Dis-cursus* – originally the action of running here and there, comings and goings . . .' (Barthes 1978). Rather than defining and privileging fixed patterns, structures or relationships, this approach regards discourse as a dynamic at the heart of contemporary complexity. Rather than privileging static data, analytical theory and pre-established methodology, we situate discourse as *in situ* performance, creativity and enactment; not a fixity, but a movement of construals, experiences, perspectives, feelings and intensities. Likewise, the outcomes sought here are not principally analytical-factual descriptions and conclusions, but snapshots, emblematic narratives, doing no more than freeze-framing shifting social entanglements and evolving practices.

Conclusion

This chapter has presented two case studies describing the re-construction of a local praxis involving the research participant, that is, the producer of what is at interest for the discourse researcher. This approach to discourse research pursues the emergence of social phenomena and relationships in the first instance, de-emphasizing methodological routines and analytical conclusions in the interest of acknowledging that, when placed 'under a different aspect', practices, meanings and feelings may emerge in unexpected ways and appear very different. This approach to discourse research treats its resources and principles as springboards for initiating and exploring relationships, rather than as analytical-critical courses of action that predetermine outcomes and effects.

Framing research as emergent practice, we contend that the study of discourse benefits from entanglement with the people and the contexts where discourse is produced. Here, the production of discourse does not reference the object of meaning or feeling into which the analyst proceeds to invest knowledge. Instead, discourse refers to a process of realization: what was once assumed to be natural and necessary is now discourse, moveable, reconceivable and changeable. Here, analysis vacillates between a feedback device that enables both research participants and researchers to re-appraise their and each other's practices, and a knowledge recording device that captures these practices and the changes to these practices that result from the research.

No doubt, the paradigm presented here challenges discourse analytical conventions as much as it upsets social scientific expectations about appropriate methodologies, authoritative findings and generalizable outcomes. But if discourse analysis is to have relevance in the contemporary world, it will only do so if it can capitalize on its most significant achievements: the relativization and historization of practices, identities, knowledges and values, and the building of solidary relationships that will afford transformation.

Notes

1 Australian Research Council Discovery Project 0450773. This project had ethics approval from the University of NSW, the University of Technology Sydney and from the health departments where the research was done.

2 Up until 20 years ago, most patients with spinal fractures simply died.

3 These figures refer to transcript number and place in the transcript.

4 We report on other outcomes from this project elsewhere (Iedema, Forsyth et al. 2007; Iedema, Long et al. 2006; Iedema and Rhodes 2010).

5 There is widespread evidence that clinicians refuse to report problems to or errors made by colleagues. Medicine places a high premium on 'medical autonomy . . . and has a historical lack of inter-professional cooperation and effective communication' (US Institute of Medicine 1999: 142). Consequently, 'even when problems are noticed . . . such as the disturbingly high yet stable incidence of nosocomial [hospital-induced] infections . . . remedial actions such as hand washing occur with modest frequency' (Weick 2004: 189).

References

Armstrong, D. (2002), *A New History of Identity: A Sociology of Medical Knowledge*. Basingstoke: Palgrave.

Baker, G. R. and Norton, P. (2004), 'Patient Safety and Healthcare Error in the Canadian Healthcare System: A Systematic Review and Analysis of Leading Practices in Canada with Reference to Key Initiatives Elsewhere.' Health Canada, Ottawa.

Barthes, R. (1978), *A Lover's Discourse: Fragments*. New York: Hill and Wang.

Bauman, Z. (2000), *Liquid Modernity*. Cambridge: Polity Press.

Berry, M. (1981), 'Systemic linguistics and discourse analysis: a multi-layered approach to exchange structure,' in M. Coulthard and M. Montgomery (eds), *Studies in Discourse Analysis*. London: Routledge & Kegan Paul, pp. 120–45.

Brown, N. and Webster, A. (2004), *New Medical Technologies and Society: Reordering Life*. Cambridge: Polity Press.

Butler, J. (1997), *Excitable Speech: A Politics of the Performative*. London: Routledge.

Carroll, K. (2009), 'Unpredictable Predictables: Complexity Theory and the Construction of Order In Intensive Care (unpublished Ph.D. thesis).' Centre for Health Communication, University of Technology Sydney, Sydney.

Carroll, K., Iedema, R., and Kerridge, R. (2008), 'Reshaping ICU ward round practices using video reflexive ethnography.' *Qualitative Health Research*, 18, 380–90.

Clegg, S., Courpasson, D., and Phillips, N. (2006), *Power in Organizations*. Thousand Oaks, CA: Sage.

Coulthard, M. (1977), *Introduction to Discourse Analysis*. London: Longman.

Damasio, A. (1994), *Descartes' Error: Emotion, Reason and the Human Brain*. London/ New York: Penguin.

de Beaugrande, R. and Dressler, W. (1981), *Introduction to Text Linguistics*. London: Longman.

Degeling, P., Maxwell, S., Kennedy, J., and Coyle, B. (2003), 'Medicine, management and modernisation: a "danse macabre"?' *British Medical Journal*, 326, 649–52.

Dewey, J. (1922), *Human Nature and Conduct: An Introduction to Social Psychology*. New York: H. Holt & Company.

Duerden, B. (2005), 'Out of the Shadows: Raising the Profile of HCAI,' vol. 2006.

Fairclough, N. (1992), *Discourse and Social Change*. Cambridge: Polity Press.

—(1995), *Critical Discourse Analysis: The Critical Study of Language, Language in Social Life Series*. London: Longman.

Foucault, M. (1972), 'The Discourse on Language,' in M. Foucault (ed.), *The Archeology of Knowledge*. London: Tavistock Publications, pp. 215–38.

Fowler, R., Hodge, B., Kress, G., and Trew, T. (1979), *Language & Control*. London: Routledge & Kegan Paul.

Giddens, A. (1991), *Modernity and Self-Identity*. Cambridge: Polity Press.

Glaser, B. and Strauss, A. (1965), *Awareness of Dying*. London: Weidenfeld and Nicholson.

Greenwood, D. and Levin, M. (2000), 'Reconstructing relationships between universities and society through action research,' in N. K. Denzin and Y. S. Lincoln (eds), *Handbook of Qualitative Research*. London: Sage, pp. 85–106.

Halliday, M. A. K. ([1985] 1994), *An Introduction to Functional Grammar*. London: Edward Arnold.

Harris, Z. (1952), 'Discourse Analysis: A sample text.' *Language*, 284, 474–94.

Hindle, D., Braithwaite, J., and Iedema, R. (2004), 'Patient Safety Research: A Review of Technical Literature.' Centre for Clinical Governance Research, The University of New South Wales, Sydney.

Hodge, B. and Kress, G. ([1979] 1993), *Language as Ideology*. London: Routledge & Kegan Paul.

Iedema, R. (2007), 'Essai: On the materiality, contingency and multi-modality of organizational discourse.' *Organization Studies*, 28, 931–46.

—(2011), 'Creating safety by strengthening clinicians' capacity for reflexivity.' *BMJ Quality and Safety*, 20, S83–6.

Iedema, R. and Carroll, K. (2010), '"Discourse research that intervenes in the quality and safety of clinical practice.' *Discourse & Communication*, 4, 68–86.

Iedema, R., Mesman, J., and Carroll, K. (2013), *Visualising Health Care Improvement: Innovation from Within*. Oxford, UK: Radcliffe.

Iedema, R., Forsyth, R., Georgiou, A., Braithwaite, J., and Westbrook, J. (2007), 'Video-research in health: Visibilizing the effects of computerizing clinical care.' *Qualitative Research Journal*, 6, 15–30.

Iedema, R., Jorm, C., Wakefield, J., Ryan, C., and Sorensen, R. (2009), 'A New Structure of Attention? Open Disclosure of adverse events to patients and families.' *Journal of Language & Social Psychology*, 28, 139–57.

Iedema, R., Jorm, C. M., Braithwaite, J., Travaglia, J., and Lum, M. (2006), 'A root cause analysis of clinical errors: Confronting the disjunction between formal rules and situated clinical activity.' *Social Science & Medicine*, 63, 1201–12.

Iedema, R., Long, D., Forsyth, R., and Lee, B. (2006), 'Visibilizing clinical work: Video enthography in the contemporary hospital.' *Health Sociology Review*, 15, 156–68.

Iedema, R. and Rhodes, C. (2010), 'An Ethics of Mutual Care in Organizational Surveillance.' *Organization Studies*, 31, 199–217.

Iedema, R., Sorensen, R., Jorm, C., and Piper, D. (2008), 'Co-producing care,' in R. Sorensen and R. Iedema (eds), *Managing Clinical Processes in Health Services*. Sydney & London: Elsevier, pp. 105–20.

Karnieli-Miller, O., Strier, R., and Pessach, L. (2009), 'Power Relations in Qualitative Research.' *Qualitative Health Research*, 19, 279–89.

Kress, G. (2010), *Multimodality: A Social Semiotic Approach to Contemporary Communication*. London: Routledge.

Kress, G. and Van Leeuwen, T. (2001), *Multimodality*. London: Sage.

Laclau, E. (2005), *On Populist Reason*. London: Verso.

Latour, B. (2004), 'Why has critique run out of steam? From matters of fact to matters of concern.' *Critical Enquiry*, 30, 225–48.

Ledoux, J. (1996), *The Emotional Brain: The Mysterious Underpinnings of Emotional Life*. New York: Simon & Schuster.

Luke, A. (2004), 'Notes on the future of Critical Discourse Studies.' *Critical Discourse Studies*, 1, 149–52.

Martin, J. R. (1985), *Factual Writing: Exploring and Challenging Social Reality*. Geelong, VC: Deakin University Press.

—(1992), *English Text: System and Structure*. Amsterdam: Benjamins.

Massumi, B. (1995), 'The autonomy of affect.' *Cultural Critique*, 31, 83–109.

—(2002), *Parables for the Virtual: Movement, Affect, Sensation*. Durham, NC: Duke University Press.

McLaws, M. L. and Taylor, P. C. (2003), 'The Hospital Infection Standardised Surveillance (HISS) programme: analysis of a two-year pilot.' *Journal of Hospital Infection*, 53, 259–67.

Phillips, N. and Hardy, C. (2002), *Discourse Analysis: Investigating Processes of Social Construction*. London: Sage Publications.

Pittet, D. (2005), 'Infection control and quality health care in the new millenium.' *Am J Infect Cont*, 33, 258–67.

Reason, J. (2004), 'Beyond the organizational accident: the need for "error wisdom" on the frontline.' *Journal of Quality and Safety in Health Care*, 13, 28–33.

Rose, N. (1996), *Inventing Ourselves: Psychology, Power and Personhood*. Cambridge: Cambridge University Press.

—(2004), 'Becoming Neurochemical Selves,' in N. Stehr (ed.), *Biotechnology, Commerce And Civil Society*. Piscataway, NJ: Transaction Press, pp. 89–128.

Sarangi, S. (2006), 'The conditions and consequences of professional discourse studies,' in R. Kiely, P. Rea-Dickens, H. Woodfield, and G. Clibbon (eds), *Language, Culture and Identity in Applied Linguistics*. London: Equinox, pp. 199–220.

Shusterman, R. (2008), *Body Consciousness: A Philosophy of Mindfulness and Somaesthetics*. Cambridge: Cambridge University Press.

Sloterdijk, P. (2004), *Sphären III: Schäume*. Frankfurt Am Main: Suhrkamp.

—(2005), *Im Weltinnenraum des Kapitals: Für eine philosophische Theorie der Globalisierung*. Frankfurt am Main: Suhrkamp.

Sorensen, R. and Iedema, R. (2008), *Managing Clinical Processes in Health Care Services*. London and Sydney: Elsevier.

Stubbs, M. (1983), *Discourse Analysis: The Sociological Analysis of Natural Language (Language in Society No. 4)*. Oxford: Blackwell.

Thrift, N. (1997), 'The Rise of Soft Capitalism.' *Cultural Values*, 1, 29–57.

—(2004a), 'Intensities of feeling: Towards a spatial politics of affect.' *Geografiska Annaler*, 86B, 57–78.

—(2004b), 'Movement-space: the changing domain of thinking resulting from the development of new kinds of spatial awareness.' *Economy and Society*, 33, 582–604.

UK Department of Health (2000), 'An organisation with a memory: Report of an expert group on learning from adverse events in the NHS chaired by the Chief Medical Officer.' London: The Stationery Office.

US Institute of Medicine (1999), *To Err is Human: Building a Safer Health System*. Washington, DC: National Academy Press.

Van Dijk, T. A. (1977), *Text and Context: Explorations in the Semantics and Pragmatics of Discourse*. London: Longman.

Vidal, J. M. S. (1991), 'An analysis of the diverse factors concerned with the development of pressure sores in spinal cord injured patients.' *Paraplegia*, 29, 261–7.

Vincent, C., Aylin, P., Franklin, B., Bryony, H., Alison, I., Sandra, J., Ann, and Moorthy, K. (2008), 'Is health care getting safer?' *British Medical Journal*, 337, 1205–7.

Weick, K. (1995), *Sense-making in Organisations*. London: Sage Publications.

Whitby, M., McLaws, M. L., and Berry, G. (2001), 'Risk of death from methicillin-resistant Staphylococcus aureus bacteraemia: a meta-analysis.' *Medical Journal of Australia*, 175, 264–7.

Williams, J. (2008), *Gilles Deleuze's Logic of Sense*. Edinburgh: Edinburgh University Press.

Wittgenstein, L. (1953), *Philosophical Investigations*, trans. G. Anscombe. Oxford: Blackwell.

10

Locating the power of *place* in *space*: A geosemiotic approach to context[1]

Jackie Jia Lou

Introduction

In discourse studies, the physical circumstance of language use has always been considered an essential part of its context. In Dell Hymes (1974)'s SPEAKING grid, a mnemonic summary of the eight essential contextual components in ethnographic approaches to communication, the letter 'S' stands for 'setting and scene', with 'setting' referring to 'the time and place of a speech act, to the physical circumstances' and 'scene' referring to the 'the cultural definition of an occasion' (55). This distinction made between these two terms echoes the extensive discussion regarding the differences between *space* and *place* in other social scientific disciplines around the same time, particularly in human geography (Tuan 1977).

The word *space* in its ordinary sense conjures up an image that is empty yet at the same time everywhere. Its own definition depends on the existence of other tangible objects. It is the 'thing' between the surface of the earth and the moon; it is the distance between two buildings; and it is the small amount of white between words and lines on this page. Given its primordial, physical and natural quality, it is thus not too surprising that, for a long time, *space* was not at the centre of social scientific consciousness (Soja 1989). In Foucault's words, 'Space was treated as the dead, the fixed, the undialectal, the immobile' during the nineteenth century, when scholars were preoccupied with time and history (quoted in Soja 1989: 4). The second half of the twentieth century, however, witnessed a gradual movement of *space* to the foreground in various social scientific disciplines (Soja 1989; Low and Lawrence-Zúniga 2003). During this period, space has become not simply a subject of investigation but more importantly a model of conceptualization. Bourdieu (1991), for example, suggests 'sociology presents itself as a *social topology*. Accordingly, the social world can be represented in the form of a (multi-dimensional) space constructed on the basis of principles of differentiation or distribution . . .' (1991: 299; original emphasis). In anthropology, this new focus on *space* invites researchers to examine the formerly neglected location of culture and rekindles a sense of critical reflectivity on the relationship between the anthropologists and the people whom they study (Rodman 1992). As Low and Lawrence-Zúñiga (2003) observe, 'Anthropologists are rethinking and reconceptualizing their understandings of culture in spatialized ways' (1). The term *place* then becomes particularly relevant for the study of the cultural meanings of *space*.

In this chapter, I follow human and cultural geographers' definitions of these two terms. *Space* is defined to be the physical location of objects in the world and the objective and natural context of human activities (Entrikin 1991 cited in Johnstone 2004: 67). For example, Chinatown in Washington, DC can be cartographically defined as the physical space enclosed by Massachusetts Avenue, K Street, G Place, 5th Street and 8th Street.[2] *Place*, on the other hand, refers to the subjective experience of *space*, socially constructed (Entrikin 1991 cited in Johnstone 2004: 67). Thus, the place of Chinatown can be discursively formulated as 'a historical ethnic enclave', 'the center of downtown DC' or 'a gentrified urban neighborhood'.

How context is understood in this study

From the above discussion, it seems evident that researchers who study language use in its social context have an important contribution to make in improving our understanding of how *space* is imbued with social–cultural meaning and thus transformed into *place*. As the human geographer Yi-Fu Tuan (1991: 684) remarks:

> Words alone, used in an appropriate situation, can have the power to render objects, formally invisible because unattended, visible, and impart to them a certain character: thus a mere rise on a flat surface becomes something far more – a place that promises to open up to other places – when it is named "Mount Prospect."

In fact, research in sociolinguistics, discourse analysis and linguistic anthropology in general has moved towards a dialogical view of context (summarized in Goodwin and Duranti 1992; also Flowerdew, this volume). It no longer seems sufficient to conceive space as a neutral container of talk and place merely a location where language is sampled (Eckert 2004; Johnstone 2004). Instead, linguistic practice is an important kind of such human interaction, as Johnstone (2004) explains:

> A space becomes a place through humans' interaction with it, both through physical manipulation, via such activities as agriculture, architecture, and landscape, and symbolically, via such activities as remembering, "formulating" (Schegloff 1972), depicting, and narrating. (p. 68)

While most work on language and space is located in linguistic anthropology (summarized in Keating 2000), discourse analysts are mainly interested in how place is represented and constructed in language. Flowerdew (2004) for example is a critical discourse analysis of how a government branding campaign constructs Hong Kong as Asia's World City. In this growing body of work, *place* has moved to the foreground of research, that is, *place* itself has become the text (cf. Jaworski and Thurlow's (2010) discussion of the concept of *landscape*).

It is against this background of research that this chapter introduces Ron and Suzie Scollon's geosemiotic framework (2003) as a fresh approach to context, because it not only acknowledges the importance of *place* but also returns *space* to *context* and provides a way for us to analyse the dialogical interaction between them.

Goals of the study and approach to discourse analysis that informs the study

The main purpose of this chapter is to introduce to the reader the geosemiotic framework (Scollon and Scollon 2003). It will then demonstrate how it can be integrated with other approaches to context in an analysis of an advertising campaign attempting to legitimize the rapid gentrification that has transformed the Chinatown neighbourhood in Washington, DC. Through this empirical study, the chapter argues that taking the spatial context of language seriously could in fact illuminate how one particular ideology of *place* (i.e. legitimized gentrification) gains power.

Introducing *geosemiotics*

Coined and developed by Scollon and Scollon in their book *Discourses in Place: Language in the Material World* (2003), *geosemiotics* provides a useful framework for understanding the importance of the physical, material, spatial context for the meaning of language and signs. In geosemiotics, *place* is conceived as a 'geosemiotic aggregate', defined as 'multiple semiotic systems in a dialogical interaction with each other' (12), including 'interaction order', 'visual semiotics', and 'place semiotics'.

The first semiotic system in the framework is *interaction order*, a term borrowed from Goffman (1983) but also intended here to include any analytical tools concerned with 'the current, ongoing, ratified (but also contested and denied) set of social relationships we take up and try to maintain with the other people who are in our presence' (Scollon and Scollon 2003: 16). For example, in a coffee shop, we can observe many different types of interaction order. There is the *line* or *queue* running either parallel or perpendicular to the cashier; there is, of course, the service encounter between the customer and the cashier; there is the *with*, two or more people engaged in interactions with a common focal point; there is the *single*, an individual appearing

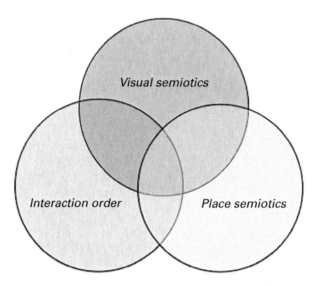

FIGURE 10.1 *The Geosemiotic Aggregate. (Scollon and Scollon 2003)*

not to interact with anyone else, for example, reading a newspaper; then, when there is anyone with a markedly loud voice or making unusual comments, everyone's attention temporarily shifts towards this person, who, in Goffman's words, would have staged a *platform event*, however fleeting it may be. Scollon and Scollon reminded us that, it is important to recognize interaction orders also as semiotic signs, which 'give off' (Goffman 1959) social information about social actors. In addition to these 'units of interaction order', Scollon and Scollon also include the five types of perceptual spaces developed by Edward T. Hall (1966) under *interaction order*. Because different sensory perceptions of a place also imbue it with meaning, in this study, they have been moved under the heading of place semiotics, which will be discussed later.

The second component system in the geosemiotic framework is *visual semiotics*, referring to as 'the ways in which pictures (signs, images, graphics, texts, photographs, paintings, and all of the other combinations of these and others) are produced as meaningful wholes for visual interpretation' (Scollon and Scollon 2003: 8). Here the Scollons opt for a narrower definition of the term as used in Kress and van Leeuwen (1996). A broader definition of visual semiotics includes 'all of the ways in which meaning is structured within our visual fields' (Scollon and Scollon 2003: 11), which would significantly overlap with the other two component systems, as interaction order and place semiotics can also be perceived as visual signs. The current study adopts the broader definition and includes the verbal along with the visual image.

As the third system of geosemiotics, *place semiotics* is coined by the Scollons in an attempt to connect studies in fields such as urban planning and cultural geography to studies of micro-level social interaction and language use. It is concerned with the meaning system of spatial organization or inversely defined as 'the huge aggregation of semiotic systems which are not located in the persons of the social actors or in the framed artifacts of visual semiotics' (Scollon and Scollon 2003: 8). Place semiotics includes things such as a typology of spaces according to their uses, for example, frontstage versus backstage (see Wodak, this volume), private versus public and display space versus passage space. As mentioned in the discussion of interaction order earlier, I would also include Hall's typology of spaces (1966) according to the five kinds of sensory perceptions under place semiotics. A modified outline of geosemiotics and its component systems is presented in Table 10.1 below.

It can be seen from the above summary that geosemiotics is a framework that integrates other approaches to discourse in context rather than excluding them. Looking at *interaction order*, it is drawing upon interactional sociolinguistics, an approach examining how language shapes and is shaped by the relationships between and the identities of participants. Looking at *visual semiotics*, it is drawing upon social semiotics and critical discourse analysis, both of which explore how the use of language and signs reflects and reproduces ideology and power. Looking at *place semiotics*, it is drawing upon humanistic geography and architectural studies, in which place and space are seen as dynamically influencing and being influenced by human actions, including linguistic and semiotic practices. Thus, context, in geosemiotics, is not the background of text. Rather, it is an organic whole, of which text is a part. What Scollon and Scollon (2003) seem to be trying to do with geosemiotics is to introduce a multidimensional framework, which decentres the text and transcends the long-standing dualistic model in which text is seen as the 'focal event' and context the background (see Goodwin and Duranti 1992 for a summary of this conceptual model that underlies most approaches to discourse analysis; also see Flowerdew, this volume).

Table 10.1 A modified geosemiotic framework

Geosemiotics		
Interaction Order:	**Visual Semiotics:**	**Place Semiotics:**
1. Interpersonal distance (intimate, personal, social, public) 2. Personal front (appearance, behaviour) 3. Units of interaction order (single, with, file or procession, queue, contact, service encounter, conversational encounter, meeting, people-processing encounter (interview, screening, examination), platform event, celebrative occasion)	1. Pictures (represented participants modality, composition, interactive participants) 2. Material aspects of visual semiotics (moved from *place semiotics*):code preference, inscription, emplacement	1. Perceptual spaces (moved from *interaction order*): visual, auditory, olfactory, thermal, haptic. 2. Use spaces: frontage or public (exhibit/display, passage, special use, secure), backstage or private, regulatory spaces (vehicle traffic, pedestrian traffic, public notice), commercial space (e.g. holiday market), transgressive space (e.g. homeless hangouts).

Context of the study: Corporatizing Chinatown

To demonstrate how these three components can be integrated to illuminate the complex interaction between language, space, and place, this study analyses an advertising campaign of a corporation located in Washington, D.C.'s Chinatown that attempts to legitimize its gentrification.

Since the mid-1980s, the Chinatown in Washington, DC has undergone rapid urban redevelopment. Language has become one of the few available means for the community to preserve and revitalize the neighborhood's ethnic characteristics, albeit also commoditizing it in the process. A small downtown neighbourhood with most ethnically Chinese-owned businesses concentrated on one block of H Street, its size has been continuously shrinking. At the same time as the residential pattern of Chinese immigrants shifted to the suburbs, more non-Chinese American (e.g. AT&T) and transnational chains (e.g. McDonald's) have moved into this downtown neighbourhood. Facing the challenge of Chinatown disappearing completely, Chinatown Steering Committee, formed in 1986 by a group of local Chinese-American entrepreneurs, has devised and implemented a policy in conjunction with the Office of Planning of Washington, DC Government to mandate all stores in the officially designated Chinatown area to carry Chinese-English signs on their storefronts. The result of this policy is a unique linguistic landscape which is not observed in other major North American Chinatowns: Chinese characters are inscribed not only on Chinese restaurants but also seen on the outside of American businesses such as Starbucks and AT&T. This phenomenon has generated much discussion in the local press (e.g. Moore 2005; Gillet 2007), which describe the Chinatown covered by mandatory bilingual shop signs as 'varnish' or more bluntly 'fake', and also in sociological (Pang and Rath 2007) and sociolinguistic (Lou 2007; Leeman and Modan 2008) studies, which largely interpret the mandatory bilingual landscape as symbolic commodification of ethnicity and urban space.

However, ethnographic studies of the neighbourhood (Lou 2009, 2010a and b, 2012, 2013) reveal a much more complicated picture, particularly the roles played by the municipal government and large corporations in changing Chinatown both materially and symbolically. An analysis of place names in Washington, D.C.'s urban planning policies (Lou 2013), for example, has shown that the D.C. government has adopted an increasingly agnostic stance towards the neighbourhood's preservation by reshaping and reducing the area indexed by the place name 'Chinatown' and labelling it with other neighbourhood names such as 'Penn Quarter'. In addition, corporations also seek to make their imprint on Chinatown's linguistic landscape while complying with the mandatory bilingual signage policy, through semiotic strategies such as minimizing the visual prominence of Chinese characters and maintaining corporate chromatic schemes in shop signs. Corporations also employ other forms of discourse to legitimize their presence in Chinatown (Lou 2012a and b, 2013). This chapter continues to examine the corporatization of the neighbourhood by analysing an advertising campaign in its geosemiotic context.

Data

Data in this study are an advertising campaign consisting of 14 billboard advertisements to celebrate the tenth anniversary of Verizon Center. The Verizon Center is a 20,000 seat multifunctional arena 'located in the heart of Chinatown' in downtown Washington, DC (Verizon Center 2008; also see Map 1 in Figure 10.2), owned and operated by Washington Sports and Entertainment, LP. Until 5 March 2006, this arena was named MCI Center, which had been the arena's name for more than eight years since its opening in 1997, and which is still often used by many long-time residents and office workers in the area. After Verizon Communications closed their $6.7 billion acquisition of MCI Communications in January 2006, the name change took place swiftly on all signs at the arena.

Launched on 27 September 2007, this year-long campaign began with a project named 'station domination', which means all advertising spaces in Gallery Place-Chinatown Metro Station, the closest metro station to the arena, would be covered with this campaign for two months (Verizon Center 2007). The campaign included 14 advertisements, each of which portrayed one or two individuals with a block of text next to their photos. The people featured in these advertisements included not only local political figures and celebrities, for example, Washington, DC Mayor Adrien Fenty and Washington Mystic's All Star player Alana Beard, but also many 'friends of the neighborhood' (Verizon Center 2007), for example, farmer's market organizers, a bartender, a chef, the Spy Museum director and even a costumed Shakespeare from the Shakespeare Theatre. Each of them wears a tattoo of the Verizon Center's 10th Anniversary logo. During the two months leading to the anniversary on 2 December 2007, these advertisements were lined up on both sides of the corridors connecting the

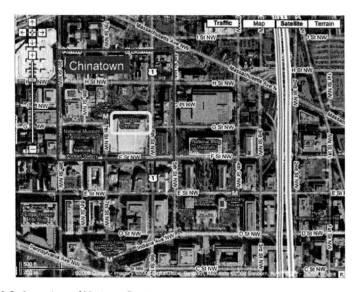

FIGURE 10.2 *Location of Verizon Center.*

underground metro turnstiles and the street-level entrances and occupied all available advertising space inside the station. In addition, the campaign also appeared outside the Verizon Center in the form of banners attached to street lamp posts.

Methods of analysis

The advertising campaign was first noticed and photographed during my fieldwork in the Chinatown neighbourhood, the focus of which was on its bilingual linguistic landscape, including mostly shop signs. The campaign caught my attention, as it skilfully employed a multitude of visual and textual resources to extol the role of the corporate in urban revitalization. In a previous article (Lou 2010), I have analysed one advertisement directly relevant to Chinatown. In the current study, the entire campaign will be examined, in order to better understand the multiple layers of context. I will first do a visual semiotic and critical discourse analysis of the 13 advertisements and then apply the geosemiotic framework to analyse its physical context. I will conclude with the contributions of geosemiotics to the analysis of text in context, especially regarding the concrete connection this framework enables us to draw between power and ideology.

Findings

Visual semiotics

As introduced earlier, the visual semiotic component of the geosemiotic aggregate includes not only the image but also the verbal text. Therefore, when analysing how the advertising campaign represents Chinatown, I draw upon both Kress and van Leeuwen's (1996) grammar of visual design and critical discourse analysis informed by the systemic functional approach to language (Halliday 1978; Eggins 2004; Fairclough 2003).

First, advertisements in the campaign represent social events in which Verizon Center has brought positive change to the community or provided opportunity to individuals. The ad featuring then-Mayor of DC, Adrien Fenty, contains the following text (Figure 10.3).

The first clause represents a RELATIONAL PROCESS ('catalyst for urban revitalization', in which 'Verizon Center' is the CARRIER with ATTRIBUTE ('incredible' and 'dynamic'), and 'in the District of Columbia' as CIRCUMSTANCE. The second sentence of the text represents the same event as two MATERIAL PROCESSES, viz. 1) 'the heartbeat (ACTOR) that has pumped (PROCESS) life (AFFECTED) into downtown Washington (CIRCUMSTANCE), 2) and 'brought (PROCESS) a renewed sense of pride (AFFECTED) about everything our great city has to offer (CIRCUMSTANCE). All of these three processes represent the social events (i.e. the actual, concrete changes caused by

FIGURE 10.3 *Advertisement featuring then-Mayor of D.C., Adrien Fenty.*

the Verizon Center) at a high level of abstraction (Fairclough 2003: 138), first through nominalization as in 'urban revitalization' and second through a metaphor as in 'the heartbeat that pumped life into downtown Washington'.

Such abstract representations provide a stark contrast to the text in the following two advertisements, the first of which carries a quote by Steve Buckhantz, a play-by-play announcer for the cable TV network, Comcast:

> Sitting courtside and broadcasting a game for the team I grew up rooting for is the most exhilarating experience I've never known. From the minute I walk into the arena, my heart pounds with anticipation. Bright lights, rabid fans and the best athletes in the world, who could ask for more? (Ad #11)

The main clause in the first sentence of the text represents the RELATIONAL PROCESS in which 'sitting courtside and broadcasting a game' is the 'most exhilarating experience' (CARRIER + PROCESS + ATTRIBUTE). The second sentence metaphorically represents the MENTAL PROCESS (i.e. excitement) of the sports announcer as a MATERIAL PROCESS, in which 'my heart (ACTOR) pounds (PROCESS) with anticipation (CIRCUMSTANCE)'. Note here the Verizon Center only appears as 'the arena', the circumstantial element of the adverbial clause. Similarly in the following text quoting EZ Street, a local radio personality, Verizon Center is represented as CIRCUMSTANCE of a RELATIONAL process:

> Some of the best concerts I have ever seen are at the Verizon Center. Where else can you go in the city to see everything from Beyonce to Aerosmith? I've probably seen a hundred shows here and they've all been incredible. I've also met a lot of interesting people. It's just a great place to go if you want to be entertained! (Ad #12)

In addition, some ads in the campaign contain both kinds of representation as analysed above. For instance, the ad featuring a bartender working in Matchbox, a pizzeria located a block away from sport arena carries the following short text:

> **Verizon Center** has made a big impact on the community and on me personally. It has totally changed the face of Penn Quarter. Nothing was here before and now new businesses are coming in. I started out working at **Verizon Center** and it led me to Matchbox, which is my passion. I recently bought a condo nearby. I just love this place!

The first occurrence of 'Verizon Center' in the text is a grammatical ACTOR in a rather abstract MATERIAL PROCESS of making 'a big impact on the community', and the second occurrence is the spatial CICUMSTANCE of a more concrete MATERIAL PROCESS of 'working'.

Table 10.2 below summarizes the ideational representations of Verizon Center in the text of the advertising campaign. A large number of occurrences represent the sports arena as the ACTOR in relatively abstract MATERIAL or RELATIONAL processes of change.

Table 10.2 Representations of Verizon Center in the copy texts of the campaign

	VC as ACTOR	VC as LOCATION	VC as AFFECTED
Abstract	9	0	0
Concrete	3	4	2
Total number of occurrences of VC	12	4	2

It should also be noted here that in the clauses in which the Verizon Center is represented as a catalyst for urban revitalization, a variety of place names are assigned to the community that is said to have benefited from this change (the AFFECTED), ranging from Chinatown to Penn Quarter, which will be further discussed in the section on place semiotics, in connection with indexicality.

Among the occurrences of Verizon Center as ACTOR, it is personified to various extents: it is the catalyst for change (ads 2 and 4), benefactor (ad 13), impact-maker (ad 1), and giver of opportunities (ads 6 and 7) to both the community and the individual. It is also 'hailed' as 'neighbor and most friend' in the ad quoting a costumed Shakespeare (Figure 10.4):

In contrast, the other occurrence of Verizon Center as object in the text simply represents it as what it is, a sports arena and company built by its owner Abe Pollin, as in the following ad featuring two organizers of the neighbourhood's farmers' market.

Thereby it also reveals the identity of the person whom the Verizon Center is represented as in the earlier discussion. The clearest instances of personification are the campaign slogans that appear on every individual ad: 1) A Passion that Shows, and 2) Happy 10th Birthday, Verizon Center!

Visually, however, the processes of development, the agent of change (Verizon Center itself, or its owner) the neighbourhood where the arena is located do not appear in the images of the campaign. Instead, we see smiling individuals wearing Verizon's corporate colour scheme, black-and-red, against place-less white background, and temporary tattoos designed specifically for the 10th anniversary on their arms or hands. The only other discernable corporate identity is the use of the Verizon logo in the happy birthday wish that appears on every ad of the campaign. Much larger than the text, photos of happy faces provide a visual evaluation of the events represented in the text and legitimize gentrification of the neighbourhood as positive transformation that benefits everyone.

FIGURE 10.4 *Advertisement featuring 'Shakespeare'.*

FIGURE 10.5 *Advertisement featuring organizers of farmers' market.*

Interaction order

Thus, it would seem that people featured in the ads are speaking to Verizon Center or the man who built it. Yet, the visual representation makes it appear otherwise. As illustrated in farmer's market ad (Figure 10.5 above), the medium shot shows the featured individuals from waist above or higher, creating a 'far personal distance', defined by Edward Hall as the distance at which 'subjects of personal interests and involvements are discussed' (cited in Kress and van Leeuwen 1996: 130). Their eyes place a direct *gaze* upon the imagined reviewer, and their spoken words placed at the level of their mouths, reminiscent of speech bubbles, engaging the viewers directly on an equal footing.

Visually, Goffman's (1981) three production formats are also unified in these photographic portraits. They appear to be not only *animator* of these quotes, but also *author* and *principal,* but as we will see in the following analysis of the textual cohesion in the advertising campaign, these individual voices are infused with a strong corporate voice.

The 14 individual advertisements are linked together by several visual and linguistic ties. First, the intertextual cohesion among them is achieved by repeating the slogans 'A Passion That Shows' and 'Happy 10th Birthday, Verizon Center'. Second, the entire campaign uses Verizon Center's corporate colour palette of black, red and white. In fact, the individuals featured in the campaign were invited to the photo shoot wearing any of these corporate colours (interview with Stephanie Cheng, the daughter in ad shown below in Figure 10.6). The last visual device for cohesion among the ads is the tattoo. Everyone in the ad wears a temporary tattoo of the 10th anniversary logo, on the back of their hands, on their arms or even on their chest.

Within each individual ad, there is also a strong level of cohesion through the repetition of several campaign keywords. Take the word 'passion' for example. It not

FIGURE 10.6 *Advertisement featuring the owner of a Chinese restaurant, Tony Cheng and his daughter.*

only appears prominently in the slogan vertically placed on the left edge of every ad, but is also found in the quotation texts of five ads, as listed below.

> Ad #1: . . ."I started out working at Verizon Center and it led to Matchbox, which is my passion. . . ." (Layla Nguyen, Bartender at Matchbox)
>
> Ad #5: "Abe Pollin showed his passion for the city when he built Verizon Center, sparkling revitalization . . . (Ann Harvey Yonders & Bernadine Prince, co-directors, Freshfarm Markets)
>
> Ad #6: "Verizon Center gives me the arena to showcase my skills and express my passion for the sport . . ." (Alana Beard, Washington Mystics All-Start)
>
> Ad #7: "My passion is my family and **Verizon Center** provides numerous opportunities for us to spend time together . . ." (Angie Reese with Daughter Anjali, Age 4)
>
> Ad #8: "I'm blessed by the commitment Verizon Center and the Wizards have shown to us. They share our passion for giving . . ." (Wenners Ballard II, Director, The Salvation Army)

In these examples, except Ad #5, the passion is that of the quoted individual, for their work, for the sport, for their family; Ad #5 refers to the passion of a non-present third individual, Abe Pollin, the owner and founder of the company. All of these individual passions are in various ways enabled by the Verizon Center: it led Layla to Matchbox, it gave Alana the arena to play basketball, it provided the mother opportunities to spend more time with family and it shared the passion of the Salvation Army in giving. In Ad# 5, a cause-effect relationship is implied between the construction of Verizon Center and revitalization of the city, the passion of Abe Pollin. In short, the word 'passion' in the rather abstract slogan is made concrete through these individual experiences, while at the same time the individual passions are made possible by the corporate benefactor.

The repetition of words such as 'passion', along with other visual cues such as the bolding of 'Verizon Center', suggests that there is a much more complicated production format than what appears on the surface. Although, visually, the quotation texts are represented as 'reported speech', they are in fact 'constructed dialogues' (Tannen 1982). Based on information gathered during the interview, Verizon Center's public relations department invited these individuals to photo shoots in a studio and conducted the interviews with them. Their answers were written down in a notebook. It is beyond the scope of the current study to find out how many edits and changes were made between the interviews and the printing of the ads, but it is clear that the Verizon Center corporation is at least part of the *author* and *principal* of these texts.

To recapitulate, the foregoing analysis shows a strong corporate voice permeating the ideational, interpersonal and textual meanings of the text. As Bakhtin (1981) points out, different texts are dialogical to various extents. Although the campaign features 16 individuals in 14 ads, the polyphonic individual voices are deployed to construe a similar story in which the Verizon Center is personified as an agent of urban revitalization, which has benefited not only the city but also the individuals. The key underlying assumption here is that urban revitalization has been necessary and beneficial. This positive appraisal of gentrification is then animated by neighbourhood figures visually represented in close, friendly interaction with the viewers of the advertisements.

Place semiotics

Having analysed how the images and texts of the advertising campaign represent the neighbourhood as a *place* that has benefited from gentrification, now I will turn to its physical, spatial context and discuss how, as a kind of material resource, it is employed by the corporation to legitimize their presence in the neighbourhood.

As mentioned earlier in the chapter, this advertising campaign inundated the Gallery Place – Chinatown Metro Station for two months before its 10th anniversary. It was seen on the wall of the corridors between the ticketing gate and the exit, on the pillars next to the escalators inside the station, as well as light boxes on the platform. It also appeared on lamp posts above the ground, just outside the station and on the high-definition scoreboard hanging from the ceiling inside the arena. In Scollon and Scollon's geosemiotic framework, these spaces are part of the place semiotics, in a complex dialogical relationship with visual semiotics and interaction order. Here, I would like to suggest that these two other components could also be linked with the ideational, interpersonal and textual meanings of the campaign text and will illustrate how in the following analysis.

It might seem natural that the main target location of the advertising campaign was the closest Metro Station, but the fact that the metro station is also located in Chinatown, as indicated in the hyphenated station name – 'Chinatown – Gallery Place', presents an intriguing contradiction to the array of place names assigned to the neighbourhood in the ideational representation. Among these other neighbourhood names, Penn Quarter appeared in four ads. Take the quote by the chief chef at Zola for example (Figure 10.7):

FIGURE 10.7 *Advertisement featuring the chief chef of Zola.*

The indexical 'here' is highly ambiguous, depending entirely on the position of the speaker. Since this ad was seen on the wall of the metro station, the 'here' then physically indexes the area that emanates from the station. At the same time, the cohesive chain within the text names it as 'Penn Quarter'. The metro station is also a *passage space*, 'designed to facilitate or allow passage from one space to another' (Scollon and Scollon 2003: 214). One exit of the station connects to Verizon Center, and another exist leads up to 7th and H Streets, the centre of Chinatown, where the Friendship Archway stands. Thus, the emplacement of the ad in the metro station creates an exophoric link between the ad and its geographic surrounding, making the ads spatially relevant to the passers-by and visitors in how they make sense of the places that they are going to see, are seeing or have seen.

In the analysis of the visual representation in the ads, we have seen how gaze and size of frame are used to represent the participants in a direct conversation with the viewer of the ad, whereas the speech event in which the narrative was originally created involved the publicist of the Verizon Center as the audience and co-author. A stretch of spoken discourse is 'resemiotized' (Iedema 2001, 2003) into a written text, resulting in an illustrative example of *secondary orality*: 'even when printed it affects the style of personal spoken communication' (Cook 1992: 24). The illusory immediacy of interaction is further enhanced by the physical space. Following the analysis of Scollon and Scollon (2003), the metro station combines multiple kinds of semiotic spaces in one and shapes an *interaction order* (Goffman's term re-introduced in Scollon and Scollon 2003) that is particularly conducive to the circulation of commercial discourse (e.g. Lock 2003). First, the metro station is a kind of *exhibit-display spaces*, that 'are simply to be looked at as we do other things in them or as we pass through them' (Scollon and Scollon 2003: 170). Compared with the vast array of competing visual messages above the ground, the corridor's grey cement walls provide a monotonous background against which the ads would stand out. The dim lighting in the corridor also limits the interaction among passers-by, and their attention is instead led to the illusory participants by the dim lighting.

Lastly, the ads are printed on glossy paper, framed in black metal and firmly mounted onto the wall of the corridor between the metro station and the street level, which further 'indexes a longer time of preparation and a greater expense in production' (Scollon and Scollon 2003: 136). Whether mounting the advertisement as a billboard on the wall of the metro station or showing it on the screens inside the arena requires material and spatial resources that are only affordable by big corporations such as Verizon Center. With these material resources, the ad is concretely emplaced in the very physical *space* that it seeks to construct as a particular kind of *place*, stamped with its corporate identity.

Conclusion

In his synthesis on symbolic power, Bourdieu (1991) cautions us against 'a pure and purely internal analysis (semiology)' of 'ideological productions as self-sufficient, self-created totalities' (169). Instead, he argues, 'symbolic power, a subordinate power, is a transformed, i.e. misrecognizable, transfigured and legitimated form of the other forms of power' (170). Thus, it is the task of the analyst to describe how other kinds of capital are transformed into symbolic capital. Geosemiotics provides one answer to the call by locating the symbolic power of place in its concrete spatial context. The analysis presented in this chapter has first shown how an advertising campaign effectively personified the corporation as a friendly agent of welcoming urban change, representing neighbourhood figures sharing a homogeneous voice, and ultimately branded the neighbourhood with a corporate logo. The strategic deployment of indexical words in the text and the material resources for acquiring the advertising space made it possible for the campaign to redefine the neighbourhood that it was located in. In other words, in the geosemiotic framework, *space* is not simply considered as the geographic and physical context of the campaign, but as a kind of material resource, which reinforces the corporate ideology of *place*.

Marchand (1998) observes that the public relations department of giant American corporations during the first half of the twentieth century evoked 'countless touching instances, in both sacred and secular lore, of powerful figures bestowing tender and beneficent attention upon frail subjects' (1), and at that time, how corporations needed to create fictional towns and communities to 'afford them a gratifying sense of rootedness and legitimacy' (Marchand 1998: 1). Over the past century, this image of corporation as powerful yet benevolent figure is increasingly built upon real cities and neighbourhoods, resulting in what Klein (2000) calls 'the branding of the cityscape' (35–8). This chapter demonstrates how Scollon and Scollon (2003)'s geosemiotic framework (2003) can help us understand the corporatization of urban space both discursively and materially.

Analysing the data in their visual, interactional and spatial contexts, the study finds that *space* is employed as a key material resource in the redefinition of *place*. It thus not only shows the importance of *space* and *place* as context in shaping text but also demonstrates the role of language as a mediator between space and place. Lastly, it contributes to critical discourse analysis by looking at space and place as a concrete link between discursive ideology and political economy.

Notes

1 I sincerely thank John Flowerdew, Adam Jaworski and the anonymous reviewer for their careful reading of the chapter and most helpful comments. Any errors that remain are entirely my own.

2 However, we will not be able to talk about 'space' without language, either. This cartographic definition of Chinatown's boundary is also discursively constructed and changes over time with the shift of urban planning priority. Thus, the distinction between space and place is not absolute, but the former emphasizes the physical quality of space and the latter emphasizes the cultural meaning of space.

References

Bakhtin, M. M. (1981), *The Dialogic Imagination*, trans. C. Emerson and M. Holquist. Austin, TX: University of Texas Press.

Bourdieu, P. (1991), 'Language and Symbolic Power', *Social Space and the Genesis of "classes"* (Vol. Language and Symbolic Power, pp. 229–51).

Center, V. (2007), 'Verizon Center Launches 10th Anniversary Campaign with a Community Service Day Makeover at Spingarn High School'.

Cook, G. (2001), *The Discourse of Advertising*. London: Routledge.

Eckert, P. (2004), 'Variation and a sense of place', in C. Fought (ed.), *Sociolinguistic Variation: Critical Reflections*. Oxford and New York: Oxford University Press, pp. 107–18.

Eggins, S. (2004), *An Introduction to Systemic Functional Linguistics*. New York and London: Continuum.

Fairclough, N. (2003), *Analysing Discourse: Textual Analysis for Social Research*. London and New York: Routledge.

Flowerdew, J. (2004), 'The discursive construction of a world-class city'. *Discourse & Society*, 15(5), 579–605.

Gillette, F. (2003), 'Year of the Hooter: The District's Chinese character gets lost in the translation'. *Washington City Paper The Fake Issue–Keepin' It Unreal*, 22(52).

Goffman, E. (1959), *The Presentation of Self in Everyday Life*. New York: Anchor Books.

—(1983), 'The interaction order'. *American Sociological Review*, 48(1), 1–17.

Goodwin, C. and Duranti, A. (1992), 'Rethinking Context: Language as an Interactive Phenomenon'. *Rethinking Context: An Introduction* (Vol. Rethinking Context: Language as an Interactive Phenomenon Cambridge). Cambridge University Press, pp. 1–42.

Hall, E. T. (1966), *The Hidden Dimension*. Garden City, New York: Doubleday.

Halliday, M. A. K. (1978), *Language as Social Semiotic: The Social Interpretation of Language and Meaning*. Baltimore: University Park Press.

Hanks, W. F. (2001), 'Indexicality', *Key Terms in Language and Culture*. Oxford: Blackwell, pp. 119–21.

Hymes, D. (1974), *Foundations in Sociolinguistics: An Ethnographic Approach*. Philadelphia: University of Pennsylvania Press.

Iedema, R. (2001), 'Resemiotization'. *Semiotica*, 137(1), 23–39.

—(2003), 'Multimodality, resemiotization: Extending the analysis of discourse as multi-semiotic practice'. *Visual Communication*, 2(1), 29–57.

Jaworski, A. and Thurlow, C. (2010), 'Introducing semiotic landscapes', in A. Jaworski and C. Thurlow (eds), *Semiotic Landscapes: Language, Image, Space*. London and New York: Continuum.

Johnstone, B. (2004), 'Place, globalization, and linguistic variation', in C. Fought (ed.), *Sociolinguistic Variation: Critical Reflections*. Oxford, England: Oxford University Press, pp. 65–83.

Keating, E. (2000), 'Space'. *Journal of Linguistic Anthropology*, 9(1–2), 234–7.

Klein, N. (2000), *No Logo: Taking Aim at the Brand Bullies*. New York: Picador.

Kress, G. and Van Leeuwen, T. (1996), *Reading Images: The Grammar of Visual Design*. London: Routledge.

Labov, W., Ash, S., and Boberg, C. (2006), *The Atlas of North American English: Phonetics, Phonology and Sound Change: A Multimedia Reference Tool*. Berlin and New York: Mouton de Gruyter.

Leeman, J. and Modan, G. (2009), 'Commodified language in Chinatown: A contextualized approach to linguistic landscape'. *Journal of Sociolinguistics*, 13(3), 332–62.

Lock, G. (2003), 'Being international, local and Chinese: Advertisements on the Hong Kong Mass Transit Railway'. *Visual Communication*, 2(2), 195–213.

Lou, J. J. (2007), 'Revitalizing Chinatown into a heterotopia: A geosemiotic analysis of shop signs in Washington, DC's Chinatown'. *Space and Culture*, 10(2), 145–69.

—(2009), *Situating Linguistic Landscape in Time and Space: A Multidimensional Study of the Semiotic Construction of Washington, DC Chinatown*. Ph.D. thesis, Georgetown University, Washington, DC.

—(2010a), 'Chinese on the side: The marginalization of Chinese in the linguistic and social landscapes of Chinatown in Washington, DC', in E. Shohamy, E. Ben-Rafael, and M. Barni (eds), *Linguistic Landscape in the City*. Bristol, Buffalo, and Toronto: Multilingual Matters, pp. 96–114.

—(2010b), 'Chinatown transformed: Ideology, power, and resources in narrative place-making'. *Discourse Studies*, 12(5), 625–47. doi: 10.1177/1461445610371055

—(2013), 'Representing and reconstructing Chinatown: A social semiotic analysis of place names in urban planning policies of Washington, DC', in C.-M. Pascale (ed.), *Representing and Reconstructing Chinatown: A Social Semiotic Analysis of Place Names in Urban Planning Policies of Washington, DC*. Thousand Oaks, CA: Sage.

Low, S. M. and Lawrence-Zuniga, D. (2003), 'The Anthropology of Space and Place: Locating Culture', in S. M. Low and D. Lawrence-Zuniga (eds), *Locating Culture: The Anthropology of Space and Place*. Malden, MA: Blackwell, pp. 1–47.

Marchand, R. (1998), *Creating the Corporate Soul: The Rise of Public Relations and Corporate Imagery in American Big Business*. Berkeley, CA: The University of California Press.

Moore, J. (2005), 'Beyond the Archway: D.C. Chinatown debate: Vanish vs. Varnish'. *Washington Asia Press*, 1.

Pang, C. L. and Rath, J. (2007), 'The force of regulation in the land of the free: The persistence of Chinatown, Washington DC as a symbolic ethnic enclave', in M. Ruef and M. Lounsbury (eds), *The Sociology of Entrepreneurship*. New York: Elsevier, pp. 195–220.

Rodman, M. (1992), 'Empowering place: multilocality and multivocality'. *American Anthropologist*, 94(3), 640–56.

Scollon, R. and Scollon, S. (2003), *Discourses in Place: Language in the Material World*. London: Routledge.

Soja, E. W. (1989), *Postmodern Geographies: The Reassertion of Space in Critical Social Theory*. London and New York: Verso.

Tannen, D. (1982), 'Oral and literate strategies in spoken and written narratives'. *Language*, 58(1), 1–21.

Tuan, Y.-F. (1977), *Space and Place: The Perspective of Experience*. Minneapolis, MN: University of Minnesota Press.

—(1991), 'Language and the making of place: A narrative-descriptive approach'. *Annals of the Association of American Geographers*, 81(4), 684–96.

11

Lingua franca discourse in academic contexts: Shaped by complexity

Anna Mauranen

1 Introduction

Josef Albers showed it with colour: context makes the object. If you keep your original object constant, as he did with his sheets of coloured paper, the effect of bringing it into new contexts is dramatic, even if the new contexts are nothing more than other sheets of coloured paper.

Using language, or 'languaging', is just as context sensitive as colours. Speakers respond to their environments intuitively and spontaneously, even though they may not be consciously aware of doing so. The environments for humans, however, are more complex than those for coloured paper. Some classic twentieth-century distinctions made by linguists who were influenced by social sciences established a fundamental analytic separation between the social setting and the linguistic environment, like J. R. Firth's (1968) distinction of 'context of situation', 'context of text' and Hymes's (1972) more elaborate list of similar categories with additional 'participant' variables. Such work played an important part in widening linguists' awareness of the social context as closely intertwined with language use. Along these lines, this paper looks into speakers' use of a lingua franca at the cross-section of two kinds of contextual parameters: those of the social environment, in this case academia, and those of the linguistic environment, a highly complex language contact, English as a lingua franca.

2 Goals of this study

This study is concerned with how contextual features manifest themselves in the forms that language use takes. It is concerned with the intersection of two contextual parameters: a social environment and a linguistic environment. The social environment, academia, has a comparatively clear hierarchy in terms of institutions and of roles for individuals; the linguistic environment, which uses English as its lingua franca, is a site of very complex language contact. Both are suffused by the realities of the globalized world. The analyses tackle three questions: how languages other than English are negotiated in the lingua franca context, how English is negotiated and how English is manipulated to meet the speakers' needs for communicative progress.

3 Discourse: Cooperative interaction

In this study, discourse is understood as interactive spoken activity. Written discourse is excluded only for reasons of space. In spoken interaction, participants need to negotiate meaning, and in the course of this negotiation they manage turn-taking, changes of topic and the interrelations among shorter chunks and longer stretches in the flow of language. Conversation is co-operative, with speakers both helping each other and competing with each other. It puts pressure on the interactants' real-time processing: turn-taking is often rapid and frequent, so that participants need to negotiate speaker and hearer roles constantly, and alternate in both roles. At the same time, they are actively involved in co-constructing the unfolding discourse. Successful communication is participants' joint achievement, but the requisite cooperation need not mean consensus. Disagreement and conflict are also speakers' co-constructions. In ELF conversations, the commonly found cooperativeness (e.g. House 2002; Seidlhofer 2006) thus applies at the level of discourse construction. It does not imply that all ELF discourse should have a constructive, collaborative feel or be unusually consensual.

In the complex language contact that lingua francas are, much work needs to be done by participants for 'matching speaker perspectives' (Mauranen 2012) in terms of linguistic, cultural and contextual expectations. To achieve this, speakers rely on two principal linguistic strategies: first, they make prospections on the basis of the preceding language, the unfolding context that changes with every increment as speakers make their contributions (cf. Sinclair and Mauranen 2006). These prospections are based on chunking the incoming information into manageable portions and will be either confirmed or adjusted as the conversation progresses. Such prospections must tolerate a good deal of fuzziness to accommodate the many approximations observable in ELF speech. The other kinds of strategies that speakers fall back upon operate beyond the boundaries of clauses or sentences: enhancing clarity and explicitness, such as rephrasing, metadiscourse and syntactic explicitation like 'headers' and 'tails' (see e.g. Carter and McCarthy 2004; also known as 'left or right dislocation'). While both kinds are normal in spoken discourse, they achieve special prominence in ELF, where uncertainties and unpredictability are typical situational parameters; lingua francas, English in particular, are often used in ad hoc encounters between people unknown to each other, and even when this is not the case, speakers' command of English can be asymmetrical, and shared knowledge limited.

4 Context as a social and linguistic phenomenon

Context at a general level is here understood to be the environment that an object is embedded in or part of; in the case of language use, the two most relevant contexts are the social environment and the linguistic environment, although the comparative neglect of visual, physical and perhaps technological contexts may not be based on very good reasons (but see e.g. papers by Bednarek, Gunnarson, Lou, and O'Halloran, Tan, and E. this volume on some of these contexts).

The social environment can be seen to involve several layers, or levels, from macro-social comprising entire societies to micro-social interaction between individuals. Although distinguishing such levels is a matter of analytical choice, since all of these levels co-exist simultaneously, layering is a convenient way of conceptualizing the social environment, because we cannot focus our attention on all levels simultaneously with equal force or sharpness. Different levels of social formations also warrant different analytical instruments and methodological approaches for analysing them, as do linguistic formations. The same is true of modelling the use of language as part of the social context.

Lingua francas are sites of complex language contact, and the differentiation of relevant levels is taken on board major models of language contact: Weinreich (1953) in his classic work on bilingualism distinguished between transfer at the level of the individual ('speech') and at the level of society ('language'). Transfer in the former was to trickle gradually into the latter through repeated use, connecting the speech of individuals to language in society. Along similar lines, Jarvis and Pavlenko (2007) make a distinction between 'cross-linguistic influence' at the level of the individual and 'transfer' at the level of society. For many sociolinguists, the crucial distinction is between the societal level of the language community and the individual level of speakers in interaction (e.g. Milroy 2002; Trudgill 1986, 2011). Drawing on these key distinctions, we arrive at three interrelated levels: the societal or macrosocial, the individual or cognitive, and the inter-individual microsocial level of face-to-face interaction. In the present view, all three are interconnected, with social interaction in face-to-face conversation as the mediating level between the societal and the individual. It is also assumed that connections work bidirectionally at each interface, constituting a dynamic whole.

Lingua francas arise in contexts where speakers of different first languages need a means to communicate. Although speakers use one language, they do not shed their other languages, but all other language resources participants have between them maintain a presence. Lingua franca environments are thus inherently multilingual (see for instance House 2003; A. Firth 2009), what Mortensen (2013) calls 'lingua franca scenarios'. This multilingualism, given in the social situation, tends to manifest in ELF discourse not only by different languages surfacing, but also in participants talking about the language being used and problems with it, thus indicating language awareness, as will be seen in Section 8 below. Facets of context, such as goals, can be drawn on to explain seemingly contradictory findings: Mortensen (2013) shows how different degrees of misunderstanding in ELF conversations found in House (1999) and Mauranen (2006) could be reconciled by observing the different settings the data came from: House's context was simulated conversations, whereas Mauranen's was actual academic discussions. Speaker goals were thus arguably different, and different interests were at stake.

5 The particular context: ELF in academia

The context in the present study is academia in a matrix culture where the main national language and the general language of higher education is Finnish (in part also Swedish), but where international study programmes, conferences and some other event types are carried out in English. The focus here is on the linguistic context, with English used as the lingua franca in every event, but where other languages also make their presence felt every now and then.

At the outset, some major contextual determinants of language use in this environment can be outlined as follows: First, the predictability of what language resources are shared is low. Secondly, there is a constant presence of several languages, incorporated in the multilingualism of the participants even when it does not surface openly. Third, English in some ideal form, as spoken by the 'educated native speaker', looms somewhere in the background and occasionally gets drawn on as a reference point. Finally, perhaps as a result of these other factors, we can expect a heightened awareness of language among speakers – seen in the common metalinguistic comments they make (Hynninen 2013, and see below § 8), including those on their own English.

ELF speaking environments are complex sites of language contact, where speakers' Englishes reflect the diverse language backgrounds they come from. There is thus much in common with dialect contact: speakers use the same language, but in systematically different ways. Yet ELF also diverges from dialect contact in important respects. Dialects evolve in local communities, in speakers' interaction with each other, and develop identifiable features that distinguish the community from others of the same language. Like dialects, different L2 Englishes have identifiable characteristics, as evidenced in learner language research (e.g. Ringbom 1992; Granger 1998), and known in popular parlance by nicknames like 'Spanglish' or 'Dunglish'. However, such similarities within particular first-language groups can be traced back to cross-language influence: the similarities within speaker groups develop in parallel rather than in mutual communication. I have therefore suggested (Mauranen 2012) the term 'similect' for such group similarities. Similects are, then, L1-based group lects that derive from parallel cross-linguistic influence in individual speakers, identifiable as similar features in their second language repertoires. Encounters in ELF consist of speaker mixes where each individual may represent a different hybrid. Therefore, we can characterize ELF as what could perhaps best be called 'second-order language contact': a contact between hybrids.

ELF is used in communities that are typically non-local and context-driven, as for instance net-based communities (Mauranen 2013), which gather around common pursuits (like Communities of Practice, cf. Lave and Wenger 1991), can be short-lived and have many characteristics of imagined communities (Anderson 1991). They consist of mobile speakers who shuttle between locations, contracting numerous weak ties (Granovetter 1973) and carrying along linguistic influences (e.g. Milroy and Milroy 1985). A vital characteristic is the multilinguality of ELF communities. By definition, a lingua franca is used between people who do not share a first language – therefore they necessarily have at least one other language in their linguistic repertoires. Any social context or community with multilingual participants is, of course, itself necessarily multilingual.

6 Data

The present data is drawn from the ELFA corpus (*English as a Lingua Franca in Academic Settings*, www.helsinki.fi/elfa), which comprises a million words of spoken English in university contexts: academic speech events (seminars, lectures, doctoral defences) in four Finnish universities and in international conferences (presentations, discussions). The ELFA corpus project started at the University of Tampere, with the first recordings made in 2001, but shifted its home to the University of Helsinki in 2005, where it was completed in 2008. The corpus consists of recordings in authentic speech events as they were running their normal course, and recording was as unobtrusive as possible. Transcriptions made use of field notes from the recording sessions and were checked and revised three times by different transcribers.

To capture authentic ELF use, no events are included with same-L1 speakers, and to avoid a language learner perspective, no EFL classes are included. There is a deliberate bias for dialogic events, and in practice most events are polyadic, that is, have several participants engaged in discussion.

Corpus compilation criteria can be related to setting and to participants. The setting-related choices were primarily 'external', which means that the prominent genres, or event types, were identified on a social basis, not language-internal, which would imply selection based on linguistic features. The speech event types reflect the naming practices of the discourse community, resulting in event types named and identified by the users themselves. Many of the event labels ('seminar', 'thesis defence') were used across the institutions.

The basic unit of sampling was the 'speech event type', along the lines used in the MICASE corpus (http://quod.lib.umich.edu/m/micase/). The term is looser than 'genre', and perhaps more appropriate, because the naming practices varied somewhat across the four universities and also because some of the event types were more firmly established as genres (e.g. lectures) than others (e.g. panel discussion). The commonest event types were well-established and central in their institutional contexts. The aim was to capture a wide coverage of types, and therefore events were recorded outside the major types as well.

Compiling an ELF corpus in an environment where English is not universally used as a language of teaching or administration cannot assume the same event type selection as a single-university corpus in an ENL context. It was therefore felt that disciplinary areas from more than one university should be included so as to get a better-balanced selection into the corpus. In addition to the universities of Helsinki and Tampere, events from two technological universities were recorded (the Helsinki University of Technology and the Technological University of Tampere). Even with the involvement of four universities, the selection of disciplinary domains remains somewhat arbitrary. However, it is hard to conceive of a 'correct' basis for the distribution of disciplines, and therefore a wide coverage of both 'hard' and 'soft' sciences is the most realistic solution.

Some compilation criteria were related to participants, or speakers, rather than the setting. This meant that despite the general aim of prioritizing language-external criteria, some language-internal ones were also used. The first was to capture as much variation in language backgrounds for the database as possible and to keep the proportion of Finnish L1 speakers below 50 per cent. Both goals were successfully met: 51 typologically highly diverse first languages are represented (for a list, see Mauranen et al. 2010), and the proportion of Finns is a little over a quarter (28%) of the speakers. The position of ENL speakers in ELF has been much debated, with some definitions confining ELF to non-native speakers only (e.g. A. Firth 1996; House 1999). ELFA adopted a broad approach, which accepts ENL speakers as a natural part of ELF communication. This is more realistic in view of the actual circumstances of use: native and non-native speakers intermingle in ELF encounters. ENL speakers are nevertheless confined to participants in multiparty conversations, and they were not recorded in performing long monologues such as lectures or presentations.

The other language-internal criterion was a deliberate bias for 'dialogic' events, in effect polyadic events with several speakers, which comprise two-thirds of the database. Even though monologic discourses serve many vital functions in academia, they are not able to provide answers to questions that are crucial to understanding language change and linguistic self-regulation in groups. Interactional discourse is a fundamental form of language, and it is above all in interaction that we can see language and norms in the making (e.g. Milroy 2002; Mauranen 2012; Hynninen 2013). These are among the most intriguing questions to be answered in ELF research, and the database must obviously answer to this need.

Speech event types in ELFA thus result from considerations of the discourse communities' self-perceptions and the kinds of research questions that the database was set up to answer. For more detailed information on the corpus, see for instance Mauranen et al. (2010) or Mauranen (2012).

In this paper, subsamples of ELFA were made for analysing discourse in interaction, and the whole corpus was used either as a first step in sampling or for some item searches. I looked into 10 seminar and conference discussion sessions (about 17h of recordings) for the surfacing of other languages than English (tagged FOREIGN), that is, code-switching. I also kept an eye on mentions of 'English'.

For analysing discourse features that speakers resorted to in negotiating intelligibility, I used other subsamples of the ELFA corpus: the preliminary work was done by going through the first half a million words of the ELFA corpus. For refining the categories, three samples were chosen for closer scrutiny from the final corpus: all conference presentations were taken as one sample, all conference discussions as another and six select seminar discussions as a third. The seminar discussions were selected to cover different disciplines.

7 Analysis

The analyses made use of the corpus in different ways. For some analyses, corpus methods were employed, and for others, detailed analyses of subsamples carried out. The third main type of analysis was a mixture of these two, as for instance in the case of code-switching, where corpus searches were first run in order to select the transcripts; these were then searched for certain tags, and the surrounding text analysed in detail for the functions for which non-English items were inserted.

The overall approach is data-driven, which means that the data itself is prioritized, with as few advance categories imposed on it as possible. This is not attainable in an absolute sense, because data collection decisions already influence and limit the kinds of questions that can be asked as well as analyses that can be run. Those decisions in turn have been informed by a theoretical understanding of language, and the value attached to types of data. In the present case, as already seen in Section 6, authenticity of the data was held in high esteem, which then led to avoiding elicited material, and situations where English is used for the purpose of learning it (as in ELT classes) or where all participants have the same L1. Metadata gathered about research material also enables certain ways of looking at it – if participants' social status, age group, gender and language background are put on record, this directs the questions that may be put to the data. Corpus tagging is also an important data-compilers' choice: ELFA is tagged among other things for non-English items by a <FOREIGN> tag, which already suggests what might be worth noticing. The parameters for selecting event types have similar effects: disciplinary domain and the self-labelling of events in the academic community open and close analytical possibilities.

The analyses in this study are also context-driven, because external sampling criteria for the data give prominence to social context. Context-driven considerations can be seen from an ELF perspective for instance by taking note of how speakers bring into play shared cultural resources from a wider selection – say, European rather than national, and shared expectations of ELF communication, such as that it may be difficult to achieve communicative success, or that it may be harder or slower for interlocutors to retrieve target items from memory than if it was their L1. These affect the ways in which interaction can be expected to move on, and how discourse tactics may be seen to take shape in response to such circumstances, for instance by enhancing cooperativeness.

The analyses focused on three questions: how languages other than English were negotiated in the lingua franca context, how English was negotiated and how English was manipulated to meet the speakers' needs for communicative progress (see § 2 above).

Analyses for answering the first question, how other languages were negotiated, manifest the context-driven nature of the approach. Other languages in a situation where one language is adopted for use means essentially code-switching or language-crossing. There are a number of classifications of the functions and types of code-switching, notably by Gumperz (1982) and Appel and Muysken (1995), and they have even been applied specifically to ELF (Cogo 2007, 2012; Klimpfinger 2009; Turunen 2012). I nevertheless did not start from those here, but from the instances I found in the data, which reflected the contexts that they were used in. Broadly speaking, the present approach fits into the line of thinking in Gumperz and Cook-Gumperz (2005), who look at code-switching as communicative practice. Expressions in other languages than English ranged in length from pragmatic particles to short dialogical exchanges; unlike Turunen (2012), I also included individual lexical words in the analysis, or what Myers-Scotton (1997) labels 'lexical borrowing'. I do not see lexical switches as distinct from those involving for instance particles, gambits or longer sequences.

A sample of ELF polylogues was selected to get a handle on how other languages than the matrix language appear at the surface and also to allow a look into how English is brought into the interaction. The sample was selected from among events with more than ten non-English items. Of these, ten polyadic events were selected at random, after excluding one outlier; in practice, they were discussion sections from graduate seminars and conferences, 17 h of recordings in all.

The second question, how English was negotiated, was then tackled by using the same sample. The ways in which participants talked about English were first found by looking for mentions of *English* in all the texts. In this case, the process also involved a corpus-based overview by running a search on the whole ELFA corpus for the word *English*, to recover metalingual comments on a larger scale. The numbers were compared to those in the sample, and since the proportions were highly similar, the sample was taken to be a reasonable representation of the whole corpus. The sample thus reflects non-English items and mentions of *English* in roughly similar proportions to the whole corpus, which has just under seven times as many tagged occurrences of foreign elements (1,470 per million words) than there are mentions of *English* (214 per million words).

I started the detailed analysis for the first two questions by a scrutiny of two long seminar sessions and developed a tentative classification on that basis. I then took another eight sessions from among those that had the minimum of 10 instances <FOREIGN> tags and tested the pilot analyses with the new data, adjusting the categories as necessary.

Approaching the last question, negotiating language to achieve mutual intelligibility, followed essentially a similar procedure: first, a small sample was analysed in detail, then categories derived from that were tested and refined in subsequent samples, until it seemed that saturation had been reached, and little new was coming into view with new samples (for sample details, see § 6 above).

In all analyses, I prioritized the preceding context in teasing out the functions of the items. What precedes the use of a particular item is the development of the discourse up to the point where speakers and hearers are at any moment, and this is the information they have at their disposal. The information is used largely to do two things: prospect ahead in the discourse and confirm that earlier prospections were correct – and if not, adjusting further prospections accordingly.

8 Negotiating and adapting language for ELF

When speakers carry out their business with each other, their linguistic responses adapt to the wider social context as well as the changing circumstances of the conversation. At the same time, they negotiate the language they use, bringing to bear the resources they have, and those of their interlocutors. In this section, we first look at the ways in which ELF interactions in academic discussion contexts make use of multilingual resources available in the situation, then in the ways English is commented on and regulated, and finally how English is adapted to the circumstances of lingua franca communication.

8.1 *Negotiating languages in ELFA*

The complex linguistic environment where ELF is used tends to put language to the fore, with participants engaging in metalingual comments and language regulation, or drawing on other language resources than those of the matrix language, by code-switching or language crossing. Other languages than English involved in this second-order contact emerge in ongoing discussions as if they were lying just underneath the surface and come into view whenever something is making waves. In itself, there is of course nothing unusual in language-crossing, as evidenced in the vast research literature on the topic, starting from classic authors who saw it as a problem (e.g. Weinreich 1953/1963) to viewing it as a normal part of bilingual behaviour (e.g. Romaine 2000),

Table 11.1 Negotiating languages: Other
language items and mentions of *English*

Other languages	53
Topical relevance	31
Search for English word	8
Social cohesion	7
Cognitive processing (pragmatic L1 items)	5
Situational negotiation	2
English	9
Negotiating English	4
Talking about English	5
Other	13
Total	75

but since language debates commonly posit English, including ELF, as a monolithic alternative to multilingualism, it is perhaps worth delving into the inherent multilinguality of communication in ELF-using contexts. Code-switching is akin to style-shifting within one language, as pointed out by Romaine (2000), and the same perspective can be extended to ELF (see Seidlhofer 2011). Code-switching has been observed in ELF conversations for example by Cogo (2007), Cogo and Dewey (2006) in more spontaneous and informal contexts and in academia by Klimpfinger (2009) and Turunen (2012). Cogo (2012) recently analysed language use in a business context, which showed participants' multilingual practices to be highly situationally responsive.

ELF polylogues were sampled to illuminate how other languages surface into the matrix language, and the material was subsequently used to find out how 'English' itself appeared in metalingual comments, and how these were employed for language regulation.

To begin with, Table 11.1 shows an overview of the distribution of other-language items and appearances of *English* in the data. The categorization resulted from a data-driven analysis. The type 'other' comprised mostly topically relevant local place names and other similar proper names, and will not be discussed further.

We can see here that it is several times more common to insert non-English elements into the conversation than actually talk about English itself.

8.1.1 Negotiating other languages

Many non-English elements were used in ways that bore essentially social and interactive relevance, and others seemed to reflect ongoing cognitive processes.

To start with the social perspective, situational negotiation was carried out occasionally with same-L1 speakers in their first language, as parallel sequences to the main dialogue involving the whole group. In Example 1, where students negotiate chairperson rotation in their group work, S5 and S7 engage in a quick off-record negotiation about it in Finnish. S5 suggests S7 should take it on, but S7 declines on account of having acted as secretary in the previous group meeting. S5 then quickly goes on to propose two others.

(1)

    <S2> who's the chairman </S2>
    <S1> he was now but </S1>
    <S3> who's now </S3>
    <S1> who wants these </S1>
    <S5> *ooks sää parempi tänään* </S5> ["are you better today"]
    <S7> *minä olin viimeeks sihteeri* </S7> ["I was the secretary last time"]
    <S5> <NAME S2> and <NAME S6> here </S5>
    <S3> congratulations </S3>

An important social function of code-switching is affiliative; often this involves humour and brings about social cohesion. It typically took place in the interlocutor's mother tongue (Ex. 2) or related to shared experiences for instance in fieldwork.

(2)

    <S23> and somebody else so it was no new (xx) all names okay who are you and fr- where are you from </S23>
    <S13 > <NAME S13> from switzerland <S23> from </S23> switzerland </S13>
    <S23> switzerland and where in switzerland </S23>
    <S13> from the north </S13>
    <S23> okay *willkommen* </S23> ["welcome"]
    <S13> @thank you@ </S13>
    <S23> @okay@ *deutsch ist meine lieblingssprache* </S23> ["German is my favourite language"]
    <S13> *ach so* [@@] </S13> ["oh is it"]
    <S23> [*ja ja]* *ja* okay, now i would like. . .["yes yes yes"]

In Example 2, we are in a seminar context where a newcomer to the group (S13) is welcomed by the seminar leader (S23). They use the lingua franca to begin with, but after establishing the newcomer is likely to be German-speaking, S23 acknowledges the information (*okay*) and shifts to German for a welcoming greeting (*wilkommen*). S13 thanks her in English, S23 acknowledges the thanks, continues in German to say that German is her favourite language, to which S13 responds in German (*ach so*), followed by S23's confirmation (*ja ja ja*), then a shift back to business and English. Many code-switching scholars seem to classify such instances as 'specifying an addressee', following Gumperz (1982), but in the present context social cohesion appeared clearly primary. It relates to Cogo's (2007) 'signalling of solidarity'. The extract also shows a metalinguistic comment (*deutsch ist meine lieblingssprache*), although these were rarely made about languages other than English.

Items and concepts relevant to the topic at hand were the largest group of non-English usage, as one might perhaps expect in an academic context. The following extract (Example 3) is from a seminar session in tropical forestry, where students give presentations on projects they have carried out in groups. The ongoing discussion follows a presentation on Sudanese land use; S9, one of the presenters, is answering a question from another student. S13 is a senior staff member.

(3)

> <S9> yeah and these er traditional *usufruct* erm lands where they practice these unregistered lands where they have farms they are usually rain fed not irrigated. and then er problems about this mess in land tenure systems er is that if you don't own the land you cannot use the land as collateral and then you [can't] </S9>
> <S13> [everyone] knows what collateral means *lainan vakuus* </S13> ['security']
> <S9> it's the thing with what you can er borrow money from the bank you need to have some kind of thing to </S9>
> <SU> security </SU>
> <S13> mhm </S13>
> <S9> yeah, so they cannot get credit and it's then er pretty hard to raise from the poverty because. . .

Above, S9 is elaborating on her explanation about the differences between irrigated and non-irrigated land in Sudan and starts out by using a relatively infrequent technical term (*usufruct*). Explaining the consequences of this system triggers a potential problem with English that a senior staff member (S13) takes up, translating it into Finnish (*lainan vakuus*), which probably helps those in the group who know Finnish (a third of the participants). S9, whose L1 is Finnish, does not seem to think the translation sufficient for clarifying the matter and starts to explain it in English (*it's the thing with what you can er borrow money. . .*), until another student provides the English equivalent (*security*), S13 signals his acceptance (*mhm*), upon which S9 continues her analysis.

Local references were not unusual, although many of the topically relevant non-English items were not from the L1 of any of the participants, as the previous example showed. The topically relevant non-English items were not typically from the speaker's L1, or the L1 of any of those present, as the previous case already indicated. Commonly, though, the non-English elements were simply local, as in (4) where an ENL speaker uses the Finnish term (*eduskunta*) when referring to the parliament in Finland.

(4)

> <NS8> . . . i i was thinking about that how you take these these people that have their own thing and want them to embrace this you know the *eduskunta* ["parliament"] the or whatever the government <S1> mhm </S1> and to to symbolise this whole thing that that has nothing to do with. . .

Example 5, from a conference discussion, is less straightforward. Most participants are senior academics with Finnish or Swedish as their L1, one with English. Finns understand Swedish. The speaker (S5, L1 Swedish) inserts a French word (*mentalité*).

(5)

> that's a cultural thing if that m- *mentalité* if that s- social fabric surrounding it doesn't work, then we will have problems.

No signs of misunderstanding arose in the discussion, where the speaker paraphrased the term immediately (*that social fabric surrounding it*), but the choice of French seems to have no immediately obvious motivation. French was not otherwise used in the situation, nor were any equivalents of *mentalité*, which has cognates in Swedish (*mentalitet*), Finnish (*mentaliteetti*) and English (*mentality*). However, it exists as a technical term in the field, and if we move slightly backwards in the context, to S5's presentation preceding this discussion, the choice becomes more comprehensible. S5 used many non-English elements in his talk, nearly all Swedish, with one exception: *mentalité*, which he used once and immediately followed by saying he had come to prefer *social fabric* as a synonymous term.

Example 5 thus cannot be explained on linguistic grounds or on the basis of general concepts like 'creating a discourse persona' (Myers-Scotton 1997). Even if we should extend this to cover a 'professional persona', it would hardly capture the current social import, because the speaker distances himself from this term. It is the social context of the academic conference, shared professional knowledge and the preceding co-text where the speaker presents conceptualizations of issues central to his topic that renders it comprehensible and meaningful. None of these situational factors can be taken for granted, as the paraphrasing indicates, but their combined import is likely to override the heterogeneities of professional, linguistic, and cultural elements in the context.

Sometimes a cognitive interpretation seemed more plausible than a social one. Example 6 illustrates seemingly unmotivated surfacing of another language. The instances (a and b) are not in the speaker's L1, but in German, which she elsewhere reported as her stronger (and favourite, see Ex. 2) foreign language. It would seem that items from other non-L1 repertoires can surface involuntarily, rendered particularly salient by a context of second language use.

(6)

    a. <S23> . . . and here *belgien* is one very very interesting example . . .

    b. <S23> but in *dänemark* there are trains or s- some cabins in trains and they are
       wonderful </S23>
    <SS> @@ </SS>

Cognitive processing slips seem also implicated in using L1 pragmatic particles where
cognitive load tends to be particularly high, like utterance beginnings or other junctures,
and they are often accompanied by hesitation markers. Such cases are nevertheless rare,
and most slips of the tongue were observed to take place in the matrix language.

    It would seem that searching for an expression has an interactional dimension to it,
and while searching, speakers also appeal to their interlocutors for help. In the present
contexts of polylogic multilingual discussions, this is a reasonable strategy, because
all participants are at least bilingual in a second-order language contact. Cases like (7)
were common.

(7)

    <S10> i don't know but then again there there are sort of new new more more subtle
    ways of of controlling schools er i mean *arviointi* [what is it] <S1> [evaluation]
    </S1> evaluation more more subtle ways of instead of sort of like like
    this <S1> mhm </S1> yes </S10> ['evaluation']

Here the speaker flags his uncertainty about an item by hesitation (*er I mean*) and then
makes an explicit appeal for help – interestingly – in English rather than in the language
of the troublesome item. Interactively, returning to English signals to all those present
that he was short of a word. It is nevertheless not uncommon in the ELFA data to ask
for help in the language switched to (Turunen 2012).

    It is also common for an interlocutor to offer an equivalent without explicit prompting
from the speaker (Ex. 8); the word search was inferrable from flagging by repeats of
who and laughter accompanying the switched item (*@asua@*). Such cases suggest
that ELF contexts render some quite ordinary processes particularly salient and
normal, like speakers searching for expressions or hesitating with others coming in
with suggestions. This may also help explain why it is usual for researchers to find ELF
interactions unusually cooperative.

(8)

    they also use charcoal and wood but maybe more strictly these settled farmers who
    who who who *@asua@* <SU-11> *dwell* </SU-11> dwell who dwell in the er in the
    rural areas and then nomadic people of course

As these examples show, code-switching serves important functions in academic ELF
discussions: conceptual (for instance bringing up terms for discussion), linguistic (for

instance sharing linguistic repertoires) and interactional (for instance boosting social cohesion). The present broad categories do not contradict earlier, more generic code-switching findings, but importantly, they arise from the particular contexts under scrutiny here and can thus be seen as context-driven. The academic nature of the situation seems to be a heavily dominant contextual element with its goals of getting conceptually oriented business effectively done, in rendering 'topical relevance' the largest category. Social cohesion and word search are clearly smaller categories but of roughly equal size, which further calls into question deficiency models of code-switching: other languages are mostly not used in desperation when matrix language competence fails, and it is not the speaker's L1 that is mostly resorted to.

8.1.2 Negotiating English

English is a fairly noticeable topic in ELF discussions, judging from its 214 hits per million words in the whole ELFA. The most common uses of *English* are concerned with problems of expression, framed as either generic (*you can't describe it in English*) or personal (*I can't spell it in English*). But above all, speakers used it in eliciting desired expressions from their interlocutors. As we see from the concordance lines in (9), each of which represents a separate example, the single most used five-word unit was *what is X in English*:

(9)

- what are those i don't know *what is it in english* er [the the (pulp)] [yes

- H and and oxygen er er *what is H in english* H two O is er H hydrogen

- take this erm this erm er er *what is it in english* shaver it's not a shaver

- inheriting) theory for this, *what is it in english* pedigree pedigree yeah

- book which is really actually *what is in in english* but it's a, i say it this

- at the hallintotiede *what is it in english* management organisations

- not so much those er *what is* valjaat *in english* [er] [lifts] those lifting

- identification what is *what is this word in english*, and then er maybe

- not blink but er to, *what is it called in english* i'm not a native speaker

- called i don't know *what this is in english* so i think, and it means

It would seem that speakers wanted to pool the contextually available resources in this way. Typically such instances were seen as participants were clarifying the meanings of terms or concepts, as might be expected in academic contexts. While terminology might perhaps be seen as the legitimate domain of academic professionals, a more unexpected observation is that academic expertise seems to extend beyond field-specific idiom in language matters. Below, a student presentation is interrupted by the seminar leader (S13), who points out that the student (S5) is using a word that is not acceptable English. Neither are ENL speakers.

(10)

> <S5> . . . and then <SIGH> again some benefits and disbenefits it's very rapid growth and very adaptable to er different climates [as well] </S5>
>
> <S13> [er*disbenefit*] *is not an english word* so try to find something else </S13>
>
> <S14> which one </S14>
>
> <S13> er disbenefit so it's [er problems] <SU-3> [detriments] </SU-3> or detriments or whatever but <S14> oh yeah </S14> yeah </S13>
>
> <S5> okay [i i didn't] <SU> [@(xx)@] </SU> come up that @one myself@ [but (xx)] </S5>
>
> <S13> [*it's good to develop the english language*] *you can always do it* </S13>
>
> <S5> yeah of course i can </S5>
>
> <SS> @@ </SS>
>
> <S5> er yeah and there's a lots of discussion about the positive and negative effects. . .

After he has suggested alternative expressions for replacing 'disbenefit', the seminar leader mitigates the face threat by a jocular remark (*it's good to develop the English language you can always do it*), which the students take up as a joke, and which also makes light of narrowly conceived linguistic correctness. Despite this, when S5 continues, she uses neither her own earlier attempt (*disbenefit*) nor any of S13's suggestions, but an alternative expression (*positive and negative effects*). This appears to be a safe option for avoiding the problem source altogether. Some of the students in this seminar group were ENL speakers, but they did not participate in this (or other) language regulation discussions, nor were they consulted in language matters.

This compares interestingly to findings from similar academic contexts. Hynninen (2013) found that senior academics assumed the role of a language expert in ELF events despite the presence of ENL students in the situations. Students also turned to the academic experts for help with language problems during seminars. Where ENL speakers were appealed to was in student groups. In these, ENL students were for instance asked to proofread the group's presentation slides.

What these findings seem to suggest is that in a university context, academic expertise overrides linguistic expertise. When academic expertise was equal (and relatively low), as among students, native speakers were appealed to for their assumed expertise in the language. In contrast, where academic expertise was unequally distributed, those high in expertise hierarchy, that is, the senior academics leading seminars, took on the language expert roles as well.

8.3 Adapting: What do speakers do to enhance mutual intelligibility in ELF?

Lingua franca contexts induce language practices that also have consequences for the actual linguistic shape of the matrix language. Speakers engage in discourse practices that eventually drive preferences, expressions and structures. ELF situations seem to alert participants to the possibility that their interlocutors do not share their own linguistic profile, and communicative success depends on proactive strategies for pre-empting potential miscommunication (cf. Mauranen 2006a; Kaur 2009). It would seem useful, therefore, to inspect these briefly in the present context, too. I take a brief glance towards answering the third question of this study in this section: how English is adapted to the circumstances of lingua franca communication.

We already saw above how speakers draw on interactive collaboration, for example collaborative sharing of lexical resources (examples 3, 7, 8), and the simple tactics of asking what something is in English (Ex. 9). However, the forms or senses of individual items are not on their own sufficient to secure successful inferences and a smooth flow of interaction. Speakers make use of two more specifically linguistic processes: prospection and explicitation.

When speakers make sense of each other's contributions and construct their own, they draw on the preceding language, the unfolding co-text that changes with every increment speakers make. In local co-text, multi-word units of meaning, which embody wholes with given senses and functions, play a central role. As larger wholes than words, such units can accommodate more fuzziness than single words, making the speaker's task lighter. The whole also assists the hearer even if the forms are approximate, that is, contain some anomalies (*put an end to X* vs. *put **the** end **on** X*; *it stands to reason* vs. *it stands **for** reason*). The whole thus functions as protective co-textual schema, where it ensures that meanings get across, allowing structural elements to vary within it without disrupting communication.

Perhaps the most notable discourse strategy is enhanced explicitness. The principal means are rephrasing (*because of **the poor nutrition level** this poor diet the whole standard of living was poor*), metadiscourse (*well I have another **point** or or **observation** rather that **i think** could be **mentioned***) and syntactic means of dealing with the topic: headers and tails (e.g. Carter and McCarthy 2006), or more conventionally, left (10) and right (11) dislocation. Both help interlocutors achieve a shared understanding of the discourse topic by making the referential nouns prominent, despite pronominal reference to the same entities in the clauses.

(10)

. . . *wealthy people they* are opposed to this monopoly insurance system

(11)

. . . he says *this* is our greatest problem the *the regional tensions*

Headers (Example 10) front the topic before moving on to the clause, and tails (Example 11) add a referential insurance of a kind, in the wake of the clause.

Accommodation strategies have been observed as crucial to communicative success in lingua franca contexts since Jenkins's landmark study (2000). An illustrative case of accommodation in action is in a doctoral defence in ELFA; after some fluctuation in *description logic(s)* in both the defendant's and the examiner's early turns, the defendant uses the singular *description logic* consistently in three turns (five instances in all), but the examiner uses the plural form *description logics* all through (six turns, 13 instances). Later in the defence, as the defendant talks about it for the fourth time, he switches to the plural (Example 12):

(12)

> <S1> but i still fail to see i mean i i agree completely of this er these semantical
> questions "cause those are the ones that i"m er truly interested in myself but
> in er in connection of er graphical representation of *description logics* is it really
> relevant </S1>

After this point, he maintains the plural form consistently. The defendant's accommodation to the examiner's use seems to reflect the contextual academic hierarchy. It is in accordance with another case in the same data (*register* vs. *registrate*, see Mauranen 2012), where the senior academic's (nonstandard) use overrides a junior's standard form.

9 Conclusion

Two powerful contextual parameters have been simultaneously at play in the situations analysed in this paper. One is English used as a lingua franca, a site of complex language contact, and the other is the academic context, with its institutional traditions, expectations and social hierarchies. ELF implies that any context where it is used is inherently multilingual; it takes place in multiplex language contact and constitutes a second-order contact between similects. Similects are lects of English spoken by those who share a particular first language but do not form a language community based on the use of ELF as a shared language. Apart from the inherent multilingualism of a lingua franca, the languages underlying the surface of a common lingua franca manifest themselves in important cognitive and interactive functions in lingua franca conversations.

From a cognitive viewpoint, what look like indicators of processing difficulty, such as involuntary slips into a different language, seem to serve the useful function of allowing the discourse to proceed rather than halting it. Some of these pragmatic markers are like hesitations and act in similar roles of allowing extra processing time for speakers and hearers alike. In addition, they are interwoven with interactional functions, serving as flags for something like a problematic term or concept, which prepares interlocutors for giving assistance if needed.

In terms of social interaction, code-switching seems to foster social cohesion and also help discussions progress at the conceptual level, by bringing in issues whose interpretation or unscrambling in English – possibly with the help of further languages – takes forward matters that are central to these communities of practice.

Code-switching is also used in asking for linguistic help in searches for English expressions. Assistance is typically provided, which may well account for the often-reported enhanced collaboration in ELF speech situations. One reason for engaging in collaborative behaviour, which largely accounts for the relative absence of miscommunication in ELF, is speakers' reliance on the commonsense assumption that speaking a language that is not participants' mother tongue must be particularly prone to misunderstanding and therefore calls for cooperation from everyone to succeed. More generally, sharing linguistic resources among interlocutors is obviously a useful practice for facilitating communication and helping participants to co-construct meaningful discourse.

ELF contexts thus seem to render some ordinary conversational processes particularly salient and make their frequent occurrence normal. This is also true of explicitation strategies in syntax, such as rephrasing, metadiscourse, and headers or tails: all of these are used in ENL conversation, even if less prominently.

For smaller-scale elements, the cognitive perspective is relevant: the co-text is one kind of context, which among other things makes use of multi-word units of meaning, which tolerate some approximation within the whole. Unfolding co-text provides scaffolding for prospection and successful prediction, which reduces risk of misunderstanding.

The other contextual parameter in addition to ELF is the academic setting, which provides the institutional frame for all the languaging that takes place there. The most interesting thing with respect to that was its apparent power over linguistic concerns: academic expertise seemed to take priority even in matters of language. Professional linguistic expertise was not involved in the situations, but native speakers were, and academic hierarchy seemed to override the potential language expert status that is often bestowed on native speakers in language professions, as for instance shown in Jenkins (2007).

It seems that the academic ELF context prioritizes academic concerns. The community manages in English by pooling its language resources in a collaborative effort, bringing them to bear on the academic targets that the community was set up to achieve in the first place.

References

Anderson, B. (1991), *Imagined Communities*. London: Verso.

Appel, R. and Muysken, P. (2004), *Language Contact and Bilingualism*. London: Arnold.

Carter, R. and McCarthy, M. (2004), *Cambridge Grammar of English*. Cambridge: Cambridge University Press.

Cogo, A. (2007), 'Intercultural Communication in English as a Lingua Franca: A Case Study'. Unpublished Ph.D. thesis. London: King's College.

—(2012), 'ELF and super-diversity: a case study of ELF multilingual practices from a business context'. *Journal of English as a Lingua Franca*, 1(2): 287–314.

Firth, A. (1996), 'The discursive accomplishment of normality: On "lingua franca" English and conversation analysis'. *Journal of Pragmatics*, 26, 237–59.

—(2009), 'The Lingua Franca factor'. *Intercultural Pragmatics*, 6(2), 147–70.

Firth, J. R. (1968), 'A synopsis of linguistic theory, 1930–55', in F. Palmer (ed.), *Selected papers of J. R. Firth*. London: Longman, pp. 168–205.

Granger, S. (ed.) (1998), *Learner English on Computer*. London: Longman.

Granovetter, M. (1973), 'The Strength of Weak Ties'. *American Journal of Sociology*, 78(6), 1360–80.

Gumperz, J. (1982), *Discourse Strategies*. Cambridge: Cambridge University Press.

Gumperz, J. and Cook-Gumperz, J. (2005), 'Making space for bilingual communicative practice'. *Intercultural Pragmatics*, 2(1), 1–23.

House, J. (1999), 'Misunderstanding in intercultural communication: Interactions in English as a lingua franca and the myth of mutual intelligibility', in C. Gnutzmann (ed.), *Teaching and Learning English as a Global Language: Native and Non-native Perspectives*. Tübingen: Stauffenburg, pp. 73–89.

—(2002), 'Communicating in English as a Lingua Franca', in S. Foster-Cohen, T. Ruthenberg and M. L. Poschen (eds), *EUROSLA Yearbook 2*. Amsterdam: John Benjamins, pp. 243–61.

—(2003), 'English as a lingua franca: A threat to multilingualism?' *Journal of Sociolinguistics*, 7(4), 556–78.

Hymes, D. (1972), 'Models of the interaction of language and social life', in J. Gumperz and D. Hymes (eds), *Directions in Sociolinguistics*. New York: Holt, Rinehart and Winston, pp. 35–71.

Hynninen, N. (2011), 'The practice of "mediation" in English as a lingua franca interaction'. *Journal of Pragmatics*, 43(4), 965–77.

—(2013), *Language Regulation in English as a Lingua Franca. Exploring Language-Regulatory Practices in Academic Spoken Discourse*. Unpublished Ph.D. thesis, University of Helsinki.

Jarvis, S. and Pavlenko, A. (2007), *Crosslinguistic Influence in Language and Cognition*. London: Routledge.

Jenkins, J. (2000), *The Phonology of English as an International Language*. Oxford: Oxford University Press.

—(2007), *English as a Lingua Franca: Attitude and Identity*. Oxford: Oxford University Press.

Lave, J. and Wenger, E. (1991), *Situated Learning. Legitimate Peripheral Participation*. Cambridge: Cambridge University Press.

Kaur, J. (2009), 'Pre-empting problems of understanding in English as a lingua franca', in A. Mauranen and E. Ranta (eds), *English as a Lingua Franca: Studies and findings*. Newcastle: Cambridge Scholars Publishing, pp. 107–25.

Klimpfinger, T. (2009), '"She's mixing the two languages together" – Forms and Functions of Code-switching in English as a Lingua Franca', in A. Mauranen and E. Ranta (eds), *English as a Lingua Franca: Studies and findings*. Newcastle: Cambridge Scholars Publishing, pp. 342–70.

Mauranen, A. (2006), 'Signalling and preventing misunderstanding in English as lingua franca communication'. *International Journal of the Sociology of Language*, 177, 123–50.

—(2012), *Exploring ELF: Academic English Shaped by Non-native Speakers*. Cambridge: Cambridge University Press.

—(2013), 'Hybridism, edutainment, and doubt: science blogging finding its feet'. *Nordic Journal of English Studies*, 7–36.

Mauranen, A., Hynninen, N. and Ranta, E. (2010), 'English as an academic lingua franca: the ELFA project.' *English for Specific Purposes*, 29(3), 183–90.

Milroy, L. (2002), 'Social Networks', in J. K. Chambers, P. Trudgill and N. Schilling-Estes (eds), *The Handbook of Language Variation and Change*. Oxford: Blackwell, pp. 549–72.

Milroy, J. and Milroy, L. (1985), 'Linguistic change, social network and speaker innovation'. *Journal of Linguistics*, 21, 339–84.

Mortensen, J. (2013), 'Notes on English used as a lingua franca as an object of study'. *Journal of English as a Lingua Franca*, 2(1), 25–46.

Myers-Scotton, C. (1997), 'Code-switching', in F. Coulmas (ed.), *The Handbook of Sociolinguistics*. Oxford: Blackwell, pp. 217–37.

Ringbom, H. (1992), 'On L1 transfer, L2 comprehension and L2 production'. *Language Learning*, 42(1), 85–112.

Romaine, S. (2000), *Language in Society: An Introduction to Sociolinguistics*. 2nd edn. Oxford: Oxford University Press.

Seidlhofer, B. (2006), 'English as a Lingua Franca and Communities of Practice', in S. Volk-Birke and J. Lippert (eds), *Anglistentag 2006 Halle Proceedings*. Trier: Wissenschaftlige Verlag Trier, pp. 307–18.

Seidlhofer, B. (2011), *Understanding English as a Lingua Franca*. Oxford: Oxford University Press.

Trudgill, P. (1986), *Dialects in contact*. Oxford: Blackwell.

—(2011), *Sociolinguistic Typology. Social Determinants in Linguistic Complexity*. Oxford: Oxford University Press.

Turunen, K. (2012), '<FOREIGN> A study on code-switching in the ELFA corpus'. Unpublished MA thesis, University of Helsinki, Department of Modern languages.

Weinreich, U. (1953/1963), *Languages in Contact: Findings and Problems*. New York: Linguistic Circle 1953. Reprinted: The Hague: Mouton, 1963.

12

A multimodal approach to discourse, context and culture

Kay L. O'Halloran, Sabine Tan and Marissa K. L. E

"Originally, the context meant the accompanying text, the wording that came before and after whatever was under attention. In the nineteenth century it was extended to things other than language, both concrete and abstract: the context of the building, the moral context of the day; but if you were talking about language, then it still referred to the surrounding words, and it was only in modern linguistics that it came to refer to the non-verbal environment in which language was used".

HALLIDAY (2007 [1991]: 271)

1 Introduction

This chapter explores how our understanding of context moves beyond 'the non-verbal environment in which language [is] used' (Halliday 2007 [1991]: 271) when language is considered as one of many semiotic resources (e.g. visual, audio, embodied action and so forth) which combine to create meaning in discourse. The paradigm, variously called 'multimodal analysis', 'multimodality' and 'multimodal studies' (e.g. Jewitt 2009), shifts the focus from language to the study of the interaction of language with other semiotic choices in multimodal discourse which is embedded in situational and cultural contexts which are themselves multimodal in nature. In this chapter, the implications of the multimodal approach to discourse, context and culture are explored through the investigation of the identities and social relationships constructed in news videos mediated on the internet through the multiplicative interplay of verbiage, graphic imagery, audio and video streams. The multimodal analysis reveals that discourse analysis based on language alone is insufficient for interpreting how meaning is created and negotiated today. As a result, the relationship between discourse, context and culture has to necessarily be redefined in multimodal terms.

2 Goals of the study

Specifically, this study explores the implications of moving beyond language as an isolated semiotic system to language and semiotic resources as sets of interrelated systems which construe discourse, the situational context and culture. The multimodal (or multisemiotic) approach follows Halliday and Hasan's (1985: 4) view of culture 'as a set of semiotic systems, a set of systems of meaning, all of which interrelate'. In this case, a multimodal approach provides a common theoretical platform for analysing discourse in context, in relation to both the 'context of situation' and the 'context of culture' (Halliday 1978). Significantly, the approach also provides a theoretical platform for analysing how discourses are resemioticized over time (e.g. Iedema 2001, 2003) with view to 'tracing how semiotics are translated from one into the other as social processes unfold' and investigating 'why these semiotics (rather than others) are mobilized to do certain things at certain times' (Iedema 2003: 29). Resemioticization leads to the construal of new meanings which may function to reinforce and/or somehow negate earlier discourses, collectively referred to as the 'recontextualization' of meaning (see Iedema 2003). In other words, the multimodal approach is concerned with the dynamics of semiotic interactions and resemioticization and re-contextualization processes over space and time.

The multimodal approach is demonstrated by investigating how business news networks contextualize certain events, social actors and social (inter)actions on the internet and television. In consideration of the inherently multimodal nature of the data, we use specialist multimodal analysis software which allows for the array of system choices in both the linguistic and visual semiotic to be displayed, transcribed and analysed simultaneously. The study discusses the assumptions and implications of the ways in which business news networks represent certain events, and how they position themselves, their sources and target audiences within the overall context of hyper-mediated business news discourse. In this way, we explore the relationship between multimodal discourse, the situational context and culture within the realm of business news.

3 The multimodal approach to discourse analysis

The multimodal approach to discourse analysis that informs this study is by design interdisciplinary (e.g. see Fairclough 2001; see also Meyer 2001; van Dijk 2001,

2011), drawing upon theoretical perspectives which include social semiotics, (critical) multimodal discourse analysis and conversation analysis to analyse how business news networks represent certain events, social actors and social (inter)actions on the internet and television. Specifically, the analysis draws upon social semiotic theory (e.g. Halliday 1978; Halliday and Matthiessen 2004; Martin 1992), adaptations of Clayman and Heritage's (2002) formulations of the personal and social roles constructed for participants in television news interviews, Montgomery's (2007) model for the institutionalized discourse roles and participation frameworks for news affiliates, Scollon's (1998) social interaction model for mediated news discourse and van Leeuwen's (1995, 1996, 2008) frameworks for the representation of social actors and social action in discourse.

As LeVine and Scollon (2004: 1–5) claim, new media technologies have opened up areas of research which extend beyond 'talk-centred' genres, particularly as ongoing innovations give rise to new and different forms of meaning-making processes which allow for a multiplicity of semiotic choices to be accessed and displayed simultaneously on-screen. The affordances of new media technology demand the application of integrated, interdisciplinary approaches and methodologies that allow for multiple perspectives on complex data sets, which in turn provide feedback for the development of theoretical approaches to discourse, context and culture, as illustrated in this study.

4 Discourse, context and culture as multimodal semiosis

Discourse is formulated as multimodal semiosis in this study; that is, as sets of interrelated semiotic systems from which choices are made, resulting in discourse as a multimodal process and/or product. Discourse is spatially and temporally embedded in contexts which are themselves multimodal in nature; that is, the context is also a multimodal semiotic process and/or product. From this perspective, context is not external to discourse; on the contrary, the semiotic selections in discourse interact with each other and the semiotic selections in the context to construe meaning in social practices. For example, online business news broadcasts are multimodal in nature, involving language, images, mathematical symbolism, audio effects and other resources such as camera movement, zooming and film editing. The business news broadcasts are embedded within websites which are also multimodal in nature. In this way, online business news broadcasts make meaning in relation to the website which is accessed by users across space and time, which in turn forms the multimodal situational context. From this perspective, discourse and context are interrelated complex semiotic phenomena.

Discourse and context are parts of a much larger semiotic space, however, where semiotic systems interact to form 'multimodal constellations' of meaning at the level of culture, in what Lotman (2005 [1984]) calls the 'semiosphere' (see also Lotman and Uspensky 1978). In this way, discourse, context and culture impact and govern each other as dynamic semiotic phenomena. This view accords with other models of context, such as van Dijk's (1993) cognitive context models in discourse, for example, which propose that context is made up of cognitive structures that control and govern communicative interactions, and which in turn may affect the structure of context models (see van Dijk 1997: 198).

Researchers and theorists studying context acknowledge the need for holistic, flexible and dynamic frameworks and theories that are capable of accounting for the complex interaction of signs and systems within discourses and the contexts they operate in. As Duranti and Goodwin (1992) comment, analysts need to consider 'how participants attend to, construct, and manipulate aspects of contexts as a constitutive feature of the activities they are engaged in. Context is thus analysed as an interactively constituted mode of praxis' (Duranti and Goodwin 1992: 9).

The multimodal approach adopted in this study provides a common theoretical platform for conceptualizing how semiotic choices from different modalities interact and impact on each other at the levels of discourse, context and culture. The approach is demonstrated through a study situated within the cultural context of business news, in this case televised business news discourse which is mediated on the internet by 24-hour business news networks, such as Bloomberg, CNBC and FBN (Fox Business Network). The discourses which are analysed are news videos from the 24-hour business news networks, as displayed in Figure 12.1, where discourse, context and culture are seen as interacting configurations of system choices.

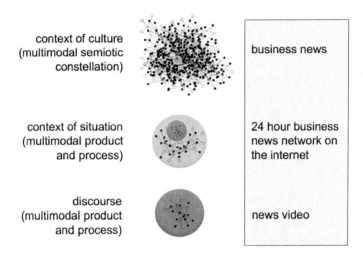

FIGURE 12.1 *Discourse, context and culture as interlocking system choices.*

5 The context of the study: Business news networks

Changes in the financial landscape in the late 1980s and 1990s, with an increasing diversity in the demographic of market participants, led to the emergence of continuous business news networks (e.g. see Leyshon et al. 1998; Pixley 2002; Schuster 2006; Shiller 2005). In addition, advances in technology led to a shortening of news cycles, with a demand for up-to-date financial information transmitted minute-by-minute.

As a specialized discourse field or genre, business news networks differentiate themselves in terms of their history and the different demographics which they target. Bloomberg's history as a financial information service provider to professionals in the field of business and finance is reflected in its more formalistic discourse styles which may appeal to a high net-worth, financially literate audience (Pew Research Center 2007, 2010), whereas CNBC's and FBN's roots in mainstream network television explain the networks' proclivity for more informal, personalized representational styles which may appeal to a wider circle of general audiences.

This study investigates how business news networks such as Bloomberg, CNBC and FBN contextualize certain news events on the internet. While the primary focus of business news networks is stories and events that are of particular interest to the business community, they also feature stories that have implications beyond the sphere of business and finance. One such event involves financier Bernard L. Madoff and his elaborate Ponzi scheme that is considered to be one of the largest instances of financial fraud in the history of the United States. The unfolding series of news stories reported in the space of 50 hours on Wednesday, 21 January 2009 to Friday, 23 January 2009 by Bloomberg, CNBC and FBN was not a 'breaking news' story, but an ongoing event. Bernard Madoff had been arrested on 11 December 2008, and – at the time of data collection – placed under house arrest. Nonetheless, the event continued to attract substantial attention in the finance media as well as in the mainstream press for several months (cf. Pew Research Center 2009).

The study is concerned with the ways in which the event is construed and re-contextualized in the news videos, which themselves consist of different discourse types and genres (that is, different types of multimodal interactions with different generic structures), such as news reports, interviews with financial experts and interviews with Madoff's victims (private individuals and corporate institutions who were defrauded by the Ponzi scheme).

The social actors that feature in news discourse in this study include not only human participants but also abstract entities and concepts (cf. Latour 2004, 2005). The represented social actors are grouped into three broad categories: (a) 'Newsmakers', that is, elite social actors who feature as the primary topic of interest in the verbiage or imagery of a news story or video clip; (b) 'Ancillary News Actors', that is, participants that are featured in a subsidiary role or position in the verbiage or imagery of a news story or video clip; and (c) 'Discourse Participants' who are involved in mediating the event or story.

In the context of this paper, the term 'Newsmaker' refers to ex-financier Bernard Madoff. Ancillary News Actors include not only 'Social Individuals', that is, ordinary people without corporate affiliation, but also 'Corporate Elites' (e.g. top executives of large corporations and business conglomerates) 'Corporate Collectives' (e.g. large corporations or conglomerates) and 'Corporate Objects' (e.g. financial documents). Discourse Participants include 'News Affiliates' such as 'Anchors/Presenters' and 'Affiliated Experts' (e.g. reporters, correspondents, news editors) and their 'Interviewees'.

6 Data collection

The data analysed in this study is from a larger corpus of hyper-mediated business news discourse (Tan 2012) which formed part of a research project at the Multimodal Analysis Lab at the National University of Singapore.[1] In what follows, we present the methodology that was applied to collect the entire corpus of business news discourse and the criteria for selecting a representative sample of business news events.

The vast quantity of data released by news networks on a single day, coupled with the dynamic and ephemeral character of the internet, poses considerable methodological challenges (see Kautsky and Widholm 2008; see also Mautner 2005). As a result, the analysis of hyper-mediated business news discourse provides a condensed 'snapshot' of how a certain event is represented on a given day at the time of data collection. As pointed out by Kautsky and Widholm (2008: 82), collecting a corpus of online news following methods for traditional news media is impractical and 'unsatisfactory'. In order to preserve the 'versionality' of continuously updated stories, Kautsky and Widholm (2008) propose the *Regular Interval Content Capture* method as a technique for collecting a time-series of online news. This approach is deemed compatible for recording a continuous stream of hyper-mediated business news events.

Consequently, a digital record of the networks' web pages was obtained with the aid of *AppleScript*, Apple's native scripting technology for Mac OS X, which allowed the recording process to be automated. The command script instructed the native browser software (*Safari*) to sequentially capture the networks' web pages of initial interest (listed in Table 12.1) in ten-minute intervals, saving each individual web page in the form of (a) a web archive, (b) a PDF-file and (c) a PNG file. The process was repeated continuously for the duration of fifty hours.

In total, 1,995 time-stamped records (644 web archive files, 681 PDF-files and 670 PNG files) were obtained from the designated web pages of the four news networks listed in Table 12.1. In addition, continuous, live-streamed video footage on Bloomberg TV and CNBC TV was recorded over the same 50-hour period with the aid of *WM Recorder* and *WM Capture*, a commercial software toolkit for downloading

Table 12.1 Corpus collection – web pages of initial interest

Web page	URL
Bloomberg.com homepage	www.bloomberg.com
Bloomberg.com More Breaking News	www.bloomberg.com/news/breakingnews/
Bloomberg.com Editors' Video Picks	www.bloomberg.com/news/av/
Bloomberg.com US TV Clips	www.bloomberg.com/tvradio/tv/tvtoday.html
CNBC.com homepage	www.cnbc.com/
CNBC.com Video Gallery, All Video sub-section	www.cnbc.com/id/15839263/?tabid=15839796 &tabheader=false
Foxbusiness.com homepage	www.foxbusiness.com/
Foxbusiness.com video page, Latest Video sub-section	www.foxbusiness.com/video/index.html
Reuters.com homepage	www.reuters.com
Reuters.com Business & Finance page	www.reuters.com/finance
Reuters.com video page, Business sub-section	www.reuters.com/news/video

and capturing streamed internet video. The live-streamed video footage was recorded principally for the purpose of control and comparison and did not form part of the subsequent analysis.

All hyperlinks in the designated areas of interest on these archived web pages were followed to the respective story or event and video pages. Story pages were captured manually as complete web archive files. Flash video clips on the networks' video pages, as well as those embedded within event pages, were recorded with *WM Recorder* and *WM Capture* to facilitate future transcription and analysis.

On account of the transient quality of data derived from internet sources, a 'frozen', deconstructed record of the corpus was also compiled (e.g. see Mautner 2005: 818), by embedding thumbnail images, together with headlines and lead paragraphs, associated URLs, and temporal information, in a *Microsoft Word* document.

The original corpus of business news events collected from the four networks in the space of 50 hours from Wednesday, 21 January 2009 to Friday, 23 January 2009, comprises 1,038 individual story pages and 852 video clips, or approximately 70 hours of video footage. Business news networks, of course, do not report only business or financial news (although they certainly form the majority of content released on the internet). Accordingly, as the research focus of this project is exclusively on events concerning the sphere of business and finance, 163 stories of overt political or contemporary nature were eliminated from the corpus. For example, the reportage relating to President Barack Obama's inauguration, which took place on 20 January

2009, that is, the day prior to corpus collection, was not analysed. In addition, as the present study focuses only on multimodal contextualizations of business events in news videos, stories hyper-mediated in the form of text only were excluded from the streamlined corpus analysed in this paper. The criteria for including an event in the sample required that an event had to be reported more than twice and had to be covered by at least two business news networks.

According to Shiller (2002a: 18), '[a] well-written story can have a powerful impact on public thinking; indeed it can become a news event itself'. Shiller (2002a: 18) further claims that once a well-written story succeeds in capturing the public's attention, it will most likely be followed by 'a long sequence of follow-up stories in competing media outlets', which have the potential for 'setting in motion a *sequence of public attentions*' (Shiller 2005: 91, emphasis in original). In effect, Shiller (2002a–b: 2005) sees the news media as precipitators of 'attention cascades':

> as one focus of attention in public thinking leads to a related but slightly different focus, which leads, in turn, to yet another focus of attention. Thus, shifts in public attention to economic issues are rather like the shifts in topics of conversation at a dinner party. During a party, the focus of attention meanders and jumps as one person after another is reminded of a related interesting story, and there is no telling where the conversation will be in another 10 minutes.
>
> (Shiller 2002a: 18–19)

From Shiller's (2005: 105) point of view, the news media are a vital force in shaping 'public attention and categories of thought, and they create the environment within which the speculative market events we see are played out'. By setting in motion a chain of events, the news media is instrumental in creating public attention that may eventually lead even professional investors to 'take seriously news that would normally be considered nonsense and irrelevant' (Shiller 2005: 93). '[O]perating by word of mouth and facilitated by media transmission of ideas', the news media 'can generate attention focuses that spread rapidly across much of the world' (Shiller 2005: 171). In consequence, news events that are transmitted by way of informal conversation, such as in interviews, debates and multiparty panel discussions, are also more apt to contribute to the 'contagion of ideas' (Shiller 2005: 168). As Shiller explains, it is precisely for this reason 'that television is such a powerful medium, in that it mimics much of the appearance of direct interpersonal conversation' (Shiller 2005: 162).

The unfolding of events meditated on the internet by business news networks are conceptualized in terms of 'information cascades' described by Shiller (2002a–b, 2005). These cascades 'visually' capture an event as an unfolding process of instances over time, which reflect the dynamic and fluid nature of news events which are resemioticized and re-contextualized over time (see Figure 12.2 for illustration). These information or 'event cascades' (which is the term used in this chapter) were used to select a representative sample for multimodal semiotic analysis.

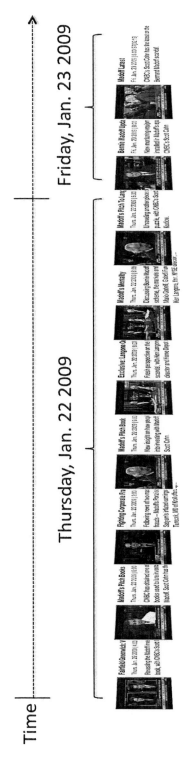

FIGURE 12.2 *Cascade of Bernie Madoff Event on CNBC.*

Table 12.2 Event cascade relating to Bernard Madoff and his Ponzi scheme

Business news network	Story pages	Video clips
Bloomberg	6	1
CNBC	2	9
FBN	1	2
Reuters[2]	3	–

As the primary research goal of this study is to demonstrate how a multimodal approach can be used to investigate how business news events are construed and contextualized on the internet by popular business news networks, or more specifically, how identities and social relationships are constructed and represented in different modes and media by these networks, the criteria for information cascades to be included are driven largely by theoretical and analytical motivations, such as the types of social actors or Newsmakers that feature as the primary topic of interest in the headline or lead paragraph of a news story or video clip.

The entire sample selected for multimodal analysis consists of ten discrete event cascades, comprising 158 individual story pages and 201 video clips. From these, a single event cascade relating to Bernard Madoff and his Ponzi scheme was selected for analysis for this study. The Madoff event cascade comprises 12 story pages and 12 video clips (see Table 12.2). Due to space constraints, only video clips will be discussed in this chapter.

7 Data analysis

The multimodal analysis of the news videos was undertaken using *Multimodal Analysis Video* software[3] (see a description of the prototype software in O'Halloran et al. 2012) which has facilities for entering system networks for language, image and video systems, viewing the video, transcribing the spoken and written discourse, and inserting annotations for different semiotic choices which are stored as time-stamped data (see Figure 12.3a). The system networks contain descriptions of the available semantic options (see Halliday and Matthiessen 2004; Martin 1992), in this case for different linguistic, visual and audio systems. The software permits the multimodal analyst to explore how meanings are construed individually and multiplicatively by annotating semiotic choices as they combine in 'real-time' and become resemiotized across time.

In the graphical user interface (GUI) displayed in Figure 12.3a, vertically ordered annotation 'strips' [1]–[3] represent the respective semiotic resources that are used in the representation of the news event, while colour-coded temporal nodes [a]–[d]

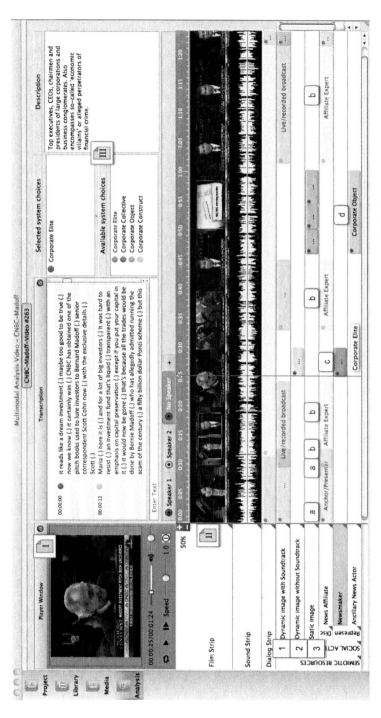

FIGURE 12.3a *Screenshot of Multimodal Analysis Video GUI: movie player window [I], film strip display [II], system panels [III], annotation strips for semiotic resources [1]–[3] and temporal nodes with system choices [a]–[d].*

on the horizontal axis denote the types and categories of social actors (see § 5) that are represented at different points of time in the news video. For example, it can be observed that the filmstrip [II] – which can be viewed synchronously as a video unfolding in real-time with the soundtrack in the movie player window [I] – depicts an Anchor/Presenter[4] [a]. This is followed by a split-frame representation where the visual space is shared by both Anchor/Presenter [a] and Affiliate Expert [b], in this case, a Senior CNBC Correspondent. The shot then cuts to a medium close-up of the affiliate expert [b] (not displayed in the film strip because of the way the video is rendered in the software). In the subsequent shots, the visual locus of attention shifts to a videographic display (without the soundtrack of the Newsmaker in question) of a Corporate Elite [c], returns to the Affiliate Expert [b], followed by a static photographic image of an Ancillary News Actor in the form of a Corporate Object [d], before returning to the Affiliate Expert [b] (see discussion of these categorizations in § 8).

As displayed in Figure 12.3a, these observations have been annotated in the corresponding semiotic resource strips [1]–[3] by assigning a type/category in the temporal nodes [a]–[d] in correlation with the visual display in the filmstrip and the movie time displayed in the movie viewer. The annotations are performed manually by selecting the respective choice from pre-defined inventories of socio-semantic categories of social actors [III], as listed in Section 5. The same steps are repeated for representations in each semiotic resource and resource to capture the multimodal interplay of:

a   static and dynamic moving images in live and embedded videographic footage;

b   visio-textual displays of on-screen captions in the main visual frame and lower-third, studio backdrops, props and settings; and

c   dialogic representations through instances of self-identification, delegated naming, third-party reference and reporting.

The result is a time-stamped video annotation for a range of multimodal semiotic choices, which are stored in the underlying database of the *Multimodal Analysis Video* software.

The multimodal analysis affords a two-dimensional view of the semiotic choices which are selected at different points of time in the news video. However, the emergent patterns of how multiple semiotic choices are co-deployed across different time-spaces are not always easily detected within the annotation interface – especially for large data sets – nor are they readily comparable with the choices made in other news videos.

For these reasons, the study explores how low-level graphic representations (obtained through the annotation interface and word-frequency-based tag clouds) can be correlated with visualization techniques such as network graphs or state-transition diagrams, where combinations of semiotic choices are conceptualized as a series of 'states' which unfold in the video (see Podlasov et al. 2012). The choices assigned to the vertically ordered annotation strips in the annotation interface – which define the various material and embodied semiotic resources that are drawn upon in the representation of social actors and events – together with the time-aligned nodes along the horizontal axis form the basis for generating spring-directed network graphs, rendered with the open-source graph visualization tool *Graphviz*.[5] In the resulting network diagram (Figure 12.3b; read together with Figure 12.3a), the combinations of choices are rendered as differently shaped nodes in various shades of colours, on the basis of a pre-defined notational scheme, whereby the nodes represent 'states' and the graph's 'edges' (that is, the directional numbered vectors) represent 'transitions' between choices. The directionality of the vectors represents changes in 'state'. The percentages displayed in the coloured nodes indicate the total amount of time that is allocated to a particular state in the unfolding chain of multimodal selections in the news video. For example, Figure 12.3(b) displays the choices for the Newsmakers and Discourse Participants (i.e. Newsmakers, News Affiliates and Ancillary News Actors) in one CNBC video, the relative amount of time which they appear on-screen and the accompanying dynamic transitions between their on-screen appearance.

Network diagrams thus afford an alternative perspective on the analysis performed in the annotation user interface, revealing trends and patterns in representational choices that are adopted by different business news networks. In addition, network diagrams highlight the existence of 'outliers', that is, unusual patterns in the representation of certain

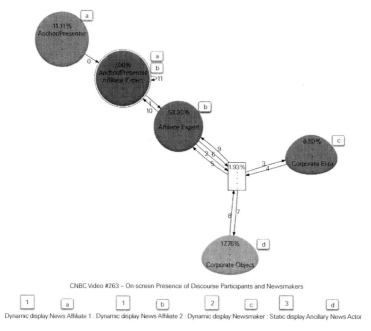

CNBC Video #263 – On-screen Presence of Discourse Participants and Newsmakers

Dynamic display:News Affiliate 1 : Dynamic display:News Affiliate 2 : Dynamic display:Newsmaker : Static display:Ancillary News Actor

FIGURE 12.3b *State-transition diagram: visualization of information in annotation strips for semiotic resources [1]–[3] and temporal nodes [a]–[d].*

events and 'non-present' choices, which are difficult to detect through conventional analytical methods. Network diagrams are also a valuable resource in exploring how much temporal coverage is allocated in varying degrees to representations of social actors and events by different news agencies, which can be indicative of the relative degree of power and authority bestowed upon these social actors by certain news organizations.

8 Findings

While it seems that the primary focus of broadcast news is on actions and events, as Scollon (1998: 216) points out, viewers often see very little of the actual event. Even in cases where (hyper-mediated) news stories are accompanied by, or mediated exclusively through visual images, Knox (2009b) explains that the majority of these images 'do not tell *what happened*; nor do they tell *where, when, why,* or *how* it happened' (Knox 2009b: 153; original emphasis). Rather, the central focus of most images in the news 'is on a social actor in the story, on *who*' (Knox 2009b: 153). This is also the case in the analysed sample of business news 'videobites'. The term 'videobite' follows Knox (2007, 2009a), who identifies two emergent micro-genres on the home pages of online newspapers: (1) 'newsbits' (headline-only hyperlinks to story pages) and (2) 'newsbites' (visual-verbal combinations of abridged news stories, consisting minimally of a headline, a lead paragraph, a thumbnail image and a hyperlink). Business news videos mediated on the internet are similarly complex hybrid genres that draw upon a variety of semiotic resources from both hyptertextual and televisual media. As a meditational means, the videobite deploys both verbal/linguistic semiotic resources in the form of a thumbnail image, a headline and a summary/lead for representing social actors and events.

The videobite represents the entry-point for the viewer (and the analyst) to the embedded news video, and in addition, videobite summary/leads often constitute the only means for identifying represented social actors and social interactants featured in the embedded video clip. Moreover, videobite elements tend to remain visible as part of the surrounding hypertextual display as the videotext unfolds in the websites' media player. The videobite thus forms an integral part of televisual news discourse mediated on the internet.

Videobite thumbnails may depict the following social actors:

a   Newsmakers, that is, elite social actors (categorized in this study as Corporate Elites) who feature as the primary topic of interest in a news story or video clip;

b   Ancillary News Actors, that is ordinary people (categorized as Social Individuals) who are featured in a subsidiary role or positioned as the victims of corporate or financial crime in the analysed data sample; and c   Discourse Participants, that is social interactants involved in mediating the event or story, such as the professional newsworkers or News Affiliates (participants affiliated with, or representing the news organization in the capacity of Anchors/ Presenters or Affiliate Experts), and a select group of Interviewees from the corporate world who are ratified to speak or comment on an event or story on grounds of their expertise or involvement as 'Certified Experts'.

The analysed data sample shows that different business news networks exhibit considerable diversity in terms of the news values that are accorded to different types of social actors represented in the videobite. This diversity is also observed for reports of other events, not just the Bernard Madoff event analysed in this paper. Table 12.3 provides an overview of the types of social actors that are represented in the videobites on different news networks.

As Table 12.3 illustrates, Bernard Madoff, the primary Newsmaker in question, is featured in only three of the thumbnail images (all on CNBC, Rows 2–10). FBN, in contrast, focuses on Ancillary News Actors, for example, Madoff's victims, and other

Table 12.3 Representations of social actors in videobites

Videobite thumbnail/ video no.	Social actor in videobite thumbnail	Videobite headline	Discourse type/genre in embedded video clip
1 Bloomberg Video #50	Certified Expert	Savoldelli Offers Advice on Avoiding Madoff-Type Fraud	Background/ Informational Interview with certified experts
2 CNBC Video #281	Anchor/ PresenterAffiliate Expert	Fairfield Greenwich: Victim?	Affiliated (live-two way) interview, with mixed audio-visual news report (studio location)
3 CNBC Video #263	Affiliate Expert	Madoff's Pitch Books	Affiliated (live-two way) interview, with mixed audio-visual news report (studio location)
4 CNBC Video #231	Certified Expert	Fighting Corporate Fraud	Background/ Informational Interview with certified expert

(*Continued*)

Table 12.3 (Continued) Representations of social actors in videobites

Videobite thumbnail/ video no.	Social actor in videobite thumbnail	Videobite headline	Discourse type/genre in embedded video clip
5 CNBC Video #225	Corporate Elite	Madoff's Pitch Book	Affiliated (live-two way) interview, with mixed audio-visual news report (studio location)
6 CNBC Video #223	Anchor/Presenter Participant-observer/ Certified Expert	Exclusive: Langone on Madoff	Expert Experiential Interview
7 CNBC Video #219	Anchor/Presenter Participant-observer/ Certified Experts	Madoff's Mentality	Expert Experiential Interview
8 CNBC Video #217	Corporate Elite	Madoff's Pitch To Langone	Affiliated (live-two way) interview, with mixed audio-visual news report (studio location)
9 CNBC Video #101	Affiliate Expert	Bernie Madoff Update	Mixed audio-visual news presentation/ Affiliated News Subsidiary
10 CNBC Video #29	Corporate Elite	Madoff Latest	Affiliated News Interview
11 FBN Madoff #53	Social Individual (Madoff victim)	What Can Madoff Victims Do?	Affiliated (live-two way) interview, with expanded news report from the field
12 FBN Madoff #66	Corporate Elite;Social Group	Exclusive Madoff CFO Under Fire	News Presentation with expanded audio-visual news report

social actors who play a subsidiary role in the event (Rows 11–12). The focus of interest in the remaining videobite thumbnails is participants who are involved in mediating the event in the embedded news video. Thus, Newsmakers tend to be excluded or backgrounded in the videobite thumbnails.

CNBC in particular differentiates itself from other business news networks by visually foregrounding the figure of its Anchors/Presenters and Affiliate Experts, who are portrayed smiling affably at the camera, and by extension the potential audience. That News Affiliates should be accorded such prominence is not surprising, however. Anchors/ Presenters and Affiliate Experts are located at the top of the institutional hierarchy and thus represent the 'public face' of the news network (see also Budd et al. 1999: 124).

Newsmakers and Ancillary News Actors are denied direct audience address in the thumbnail images. They are captured at an oblique angle, shown to avert their eyes or turn their back to the audience. This turns them into objects to be looked upon by potential audiences. In some instances, the represented Newsmakers are also divested of their status as human beings in the videobite headline, where they are re-contextualized as a communicative event instead (e.g. as in 'Bernie Madoff Update', 'Madoff Latest'). In this way, Newsmakers generally tend to be 'impersonalized' and 'objectivated' in the videobite.

The way social actors are represented in the videobite is consistently re-contextualized in the embedded news video. For example, Bloomberg's contextualization of the event in the videobite foregrounds the interviewee's perspective on the subject matter ('Savoldelli Offers Advice on Avoiding Madoff-Type Fraud') and features the interviewee in the videobite thumbnail. The Newsmaker, Bernard Madoff, is backgrounded in the videobite headline and summary/lead ('Fabio Savoldelli, chief global strategist at Optima Fund Management LLC, talks with Bloomberg's Eric Schatzker about Bernard Madoff's alleged $50 billion Ponzi scheme and its impact on investors'). In the embedded news video, the discursive contextualizations of the event similarly draw upon the opinion and advice offered by the Certified Expert, Fabio Salvoldelli, who is accorded a considerable amount of on-screen time (70.56 per cent) in comparison with embedded videographic footage featuring Bernard Madoff (3.41 per cent) in indirect audience address (see Figure 12.4a, marked [A] and [B] respectively).

Other involved corporate actors such as large corporations or financial institutions, referred to as 'Madoff's investors' in Bloomberg's coverage of the event, are abstracted and contextualized as Corporate Collectives by means of 'aggregation' (Figure 12.4a, marked [C]; see Section 7, Figure 12.3b, for interpretation of the state transition diagram), whereby their potential losses are quantified and treated as impersonal 'statistics' (e.g. see van Leeuwen 2008: 35–8). Only corporate actors are referred to as 'investors' in Bloomberg's coverage of the event. Non-corporate actors, in turn, are excluded from videographic representations. In the dialogue, they are 'genericized' and referred to collectively as 'people', as illustrated in the word-frequency-based tag cloud (Figure 12.4b), which offers an alternative view of observable trends and patterns in spoken discourse.

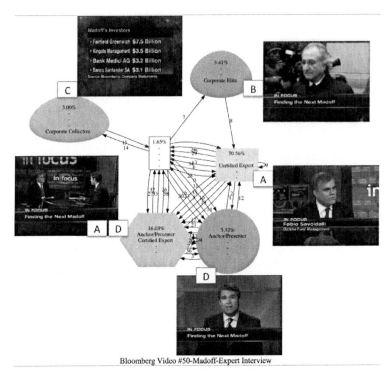

Bloomberg Video #50-Madoff-Expert Interview

FIGURE 12.4a *Patterns in videographic representations of Certified Expert [A], Newsmaker Bernard Madoff [B], Madoff's corporate investors [C], Anchor/Presenter [D], and Anchor/ Presenter and Interviewee in interaction [A, D] on Bloomberg.*

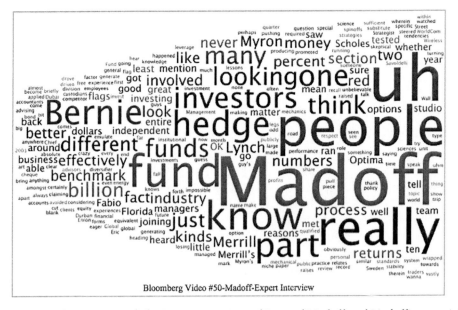

Bloomberg Video #50-Madoff-Expert Interview

FIGURE 12.4b *Patterns in dialogic representations of Bernard Madoff, and Madoff's potential victims ('people') on Bloomberg.*

Contextualizations of the Madoff event on Bloomberg are focused primarily on informing and perhaps shaping investor sentiment and behaviour, involving in-depth discussion and analysis, and advice offered by disinterested Certified Experts. In contrast, contextualizations of the event on CNBC and FNB have a tendency to be dramatized to some extent, with a greater focus on the social actors involved in the event, and their actions and reactions.

The findings of this study seem to confirm Doyle's (2006) observation that stories intended to appeal to general audiences often lean in the direction of 'infotainment'. These stories are expected first and foremost to entertain and to capture and sustain the attention of a non-specialist audience (Doyle 2006: 436–8). This may perhaps explain why the primary Newsmaker, Bernard Madoff, is visually foregrounded in FBN's mediation of this event by being represented multiple times in the news video, utilizing a variety of different semiotic resources. For example, Madoff is depicted leaving an undisclosed location surrounded by security agents, mediated by way of actuality footage without soundtrack, and he is shown being chased by reporters shouting his name 'Bernie, Bernie'[6] in unmediated archival video footage with soundtrack (see Figure 12.5a, marked [A] and [B] respectively). His image is also featured in static photographic images (Figure 12.5a, marked [C]). Visio-verbally, Madoff is resemiotized as the 'Goal' (the target of an action) in a material action process in the story's meta-theme ('Chasing Bernie Madoff'), which is similarly mediated multiple times in the form of on-screen captions as well as dynamically unfolding animated graphic sequences (Figure 12.5a, marked [D] and [E] respectively). These multiple characterizations exude theatricality and emotion, and function to capture the audience's attention.

FIGURE 12.5a *Multiple representations of Bernard Madoff on FBN in terms of actuality footage without soundtrack [A], unmediated video footage with soundtrack [B], static photographic image [C], on-screen captions [D] and animated graphic sequences [E].*

Even the story's secondary Newsmaker, Frank DiPascali, Bernard Madoff's Chief Financial Officer, is re-contextualized several times in videographic display. Interestingly, DiPascali is stripped of his corporate title, affiliation and formal business attire (being depicted casually dressed in a social setting), and referred to cryptically as 'Madoff's Money Man' in verbal spoken discourse and on-screen captions (Figure 12.5b, top).

There appears to be a significant departure in FBN's representations of the event concerning the inclusion of ordinary people (categorized as Social Individuals in this study) affected by the event under discussion. In FBN's representations of this event, the 'Madoff victim' is not only explicitly identified as such visio-verbally in the on-screen

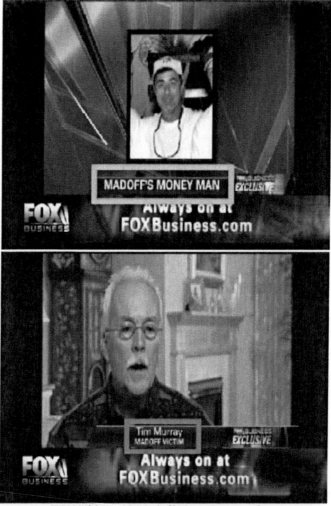

FBN Video #66-Madoff-News Presentation

FIGURE 12.5b *Representations of Madoff's associate Frank DiPascali – 'Madoff's Money Man' (top), and 'Madoff victim' (bottom).*

captions (e.g. 'Tim Murray, Madoff Victim', see Figure 12.5b, bottom), but also in terms of physical appearance and casual attire which forms a distinctive contrast to the otherwise formally attired social actors in the world of business and finance (e.g. see Tan and Owyong 2009). The fact that Tim Murray is filmed in a private setting, presumably his home, also sets him apart from the depicted corporate actors. It is noteworthy that on FBN the social 'Madoff victim' is granted substantial on-screen presence. Moreover, he is granted the right to speak in embedded actuality footage with soundtrack and is referred to as 'victim' repeatedly by the News Affiliate in dialogue.

Although CNBC similarly defers to the experiential 'eyewitness' account of a specific social actor who had dealings with Bernard Madoff, he is appraised verbally as 'Wall Street Titan Ken Langone' and identified both visio-verbally and dialogically as a 'financier', 'former director of the New York Exchange' and 'co-founder of Home Depot' (a US conglomerate), and filmed in a distinctive corporate studio setting (see Figure 12.6a).

Other corporate Madoff victims have their status questioned in the accompanying videobite (e.g. 'Fairfield Greenwich: Victim?', see Table 12.3, Row 2, CNBC Video #281). They are videographically 'impersonalized' and 'objectivated', and re-contextualized entirely in the form of material Corporate Objects, such as financial documents (Figure 12.6b).

In summary, this study suggests that particular ways events and social actors are re-contextualized in the videobites and the embedded news videos reflect the distinctive communicative practices preferred by different news networks which in turn are reflective of their respective institutional norms and tacit beliefs that news networks hold about their target audiences. Consequently, Bloomberg's preference for the conventional, formal news interview and the opinion of certified experts may

CNBC Video #223-Madoff-Experiential Interview

FIGURE 12.6a *Representation of 'corporate' Madoff victim on CNBC.*

CNBC Video #281-Fairfield Greenwich: Victim?

FIGURE 12.6b *Representation of 'impersonalized', 'objectivated' Madoff victim contextualized in the form of Corporate Objects on CNBC.*

be geared towards the specific informational needs of its specialist target audience in the fields of business and finance. In the same way, the fact that CNBC and FBN have their historic roots in mainstream network television may perhaps explain the networks' preference for personalized contextualizations of the event which appeal to a more general audience.

FBN further differentiates itself from Bloomberg and CNBC in its contextualizations of this event by focusing consistently on the social individual, namely the Madoff victim. The inclusion of the ordinary citizen in the portrayal of the event suggests the ideological position of the network in aligning itself – at least videographically – with the concerns of a wider, more general audience. Rupert Murdoch's motivation for founding FBN, for example, was to set itself apart from other financial networks. Murdoch is reported to have said 'CNBC is a financial channel for Wall Street. We're for Main Street. We're looking for different things, different initiatives, and a different look' (Pew Research Centre 2007; see also Businessweek 2007; Li 2007).

9 Discussion and conclusion

As this study has shown, discourse and context are constructed via dynamic interrelated and interactive configurations of multimodal semiotic resources which unfold temporally and spatially. Analysing and modelling such complex relationships requires the development and application of interdisciplinary methodologies and computational techniques to capture the discourse patterns which encode social structures and ideologies that constitute and re-constitute the context in which they function. The analysis of our data was performed using a digital interface, which together with visualizations in the form of state transition diagrams has allowed us to analyse the context structures that govern the multiple interactions which construe an ongoing event.

We have also demonstrated how a multimodal social semiotic approach can inform and complement abstract context models by providing examples of how semiotic resources are utilized to reflect certain social constructs (in this case, visual-verbal representations of corporate villains and their victims) that are present in their associated context (in this case, business news videos mediated on the internet). In this way, context can be modelled as a network of semiotic choices which interact with multimodal discourse choices according to multimodal constellations, in this case business news.

Van Dijk (1997) suggests that context models are complex representations of social meanings and relations, each consisting of its own internal schematic structures. In the social semiotic approach, context models are conceptualized as the organization of semiotic resources in interaction with multimodal discourse systems. Using business news discourse as an example, we have shown how the micro-structures of multimodal discourse reflect the underlying context models that organize and shape social relations and identities that are constructed by and for participants in a particular context. The social roles assigned to participants and Newsmakers are not fixed, but re-contextualized depending on the context of situation of each particular news video. In other words, context models have multiple communicative functions that both reflect, impact and interact with the semiotic structures of discourse. In addition, as Duranti and Goodwin (1992: 6) observe, discourse participants have the capacity to actively 'shape context in ways that further their own interests'. Thus, business news networks via the expertise of their production teams, in tandem with established institutional practices, act strategically to position themselves, their discourse participants, as well as primary and ancillary Newsmakers who feature as topics of interest.

The study also found that the distinctive roles constructed interactively for social actors in discourse are dependent upon the underlying discourse types and genres. These discourse types and genres, in turn, interact with the ideological agenda of individual business news networks, revealing, for example, the dichotomy between a focus on the opinions or expressed views of expert sources from the world of business and finance, or the informal experience of ordinary members of the public. This finding can be further explored with regard to the notions of 'giving the facts straight' or 'dramatizing' the news to enhance excitement and audience appeal.

In this way, the multimodal approach to discourse, context and culture, aided by interactive digital software and visualization techniques, permits the complexity and multi-dimensionality of our social world to be explored as a 'unified conception' (Halliday 1978: 12) in order to understand the patterns and trends which govern our existence. It is evident that discourse, context and culture are multimodal in nature, and they should be modelled as such.

Acknowledgements

The data presented in this article is from *Multimodal Approaches to Business News Discourse Mediated on the Internet and Television* (Tan 2012) which was undertaken as part of the *Events in the World* project at the Multimodal Analysis Lab, Interactive Digital Media Institute at the National University of Singapore. The research was supported by Interactive Digital Media Program Office (IDMPO) in Singapore under the National Research Foundation's (NRF) Grant Number: NRF2007IDM-IDM002-066, Principal Investigator: Kay O'Halloran.

Notes

1 See: http://multimodal-analysis-lab.org/
2 Data from Reuters in not included in this study, as the Bernard Madoff event was not contextualized in the form of a video clip on this news network.
3 See: http://multimodal-analysis.com/
4 The assignment of categorical choices of who or what is depicted in the visual frame is, of course, not self-evident, but dependent upon the unfolding (inter)action in the soundtrack, identification of the social actor in surrounding co-text (e.g. in the videobite or through visio-textual displays in the form of on-screen captions, etc.).
5 http://www.graphviz.org/.
6 It must be noted in this context that in business news discourse personalized social actors and discourse participants are frequently nominated by way of familiar hypocorisms, such as 'Bernie' instead of 'Bernard'.

References

Budd, M., Craig, S. and Steinman, C. (1999), *Consuming Environments: Television and Commercial Culture*. New Brunswick, NJ: Rutgers University Press.
Businessweek, 8 October 2007. "Fox vs. CNBC: Countdown To War." Accessed 29 October 2010. http://www.businessweek.com/magazine/content/07_41/b4053089.htm
Clayman, S. and Heritage, J. (2002), *The News Interview: Journalists and Public Figures on the Air*. New York: Cambridge University Press.
Doyle, G. (2006), 'Financial News Journalism: A Post-Enron Analysis of Approaches towards Economic and Financial News Production in the UK.' *Journalism*, 7(4), 433–52.
Duranti, A. and Goodwin, C. (1992), *Rethinking Context: Language as an Interactive Phenomenon*. Cambridge: Cambridge University Press.
Fairclough, N. (2001), 'Critical Discourse Analysis as a Method in Social Scientific Research,' in R. Wodak and M. Meyer (eds), *Methods of Critical Discourse Analysis*. London: Sage Publications Ltd, pp. 121–38.
'Fox vs. CNBC: Countdown To War.' *Businessweek*, 8 October 2007. Accessed 29 October 2010. http://www.businessweek.com/magazine/content/07_41/b4053089.htm

Halliday, M. A. K. (1978), *Language as Social Semiotic: The Social Interpretation of Language and Meaning*. London: Edward Arnold.

—(2007 [1991]), 'The Notion of "Context" in Language Education', in Jonathan J. Webster (ed.), *Language and Education: Volume 9 in the Collected Works of M. A. K. Halliday*. London: Continuum, pp. 269–90.

Halliday, M. A. K. and Hasan, R. (1985), *Language, Context, and Text: Aspects of Language in a Social-Semiotic Perspective*. Geelong, VC: Deakin University Press [Republished by Oxford University Press 1989].

Halliday, M. A. K. and Matthiessen, C. M. I. M. (2004), *An Introduction to Functional Grammar* (3rd edn, revised by C. Matthiessen). London: Arnold (1st edition 1985).

Iedema, R. (2001), 'Resemiotization'. *Semiotica*, 137(1/4), 23–39.

—(2003), 'Multimodality, Resemiotization: Extending the analysis of discourse as a multisemiotic practice'. *Visual Communication*, 2(1), 29–57.

Jewitt, C. (2009), *Handbook of Multimodal Analysis* (1st edn). London: Routledge.

Kautsky, R. and Widholm, A. (2008), 'Online Methodology: Analysing News Flows of Online Journalism.' *Westminster Papers in Communication and Culture*, 5(2), 81–97.

Knox, J. S. (2007), 'Visual-Verbal Communication on Online Newspaper Home Pages.' *Visual Communication*, 6(1), 19–53.

—(2009a), 'Multimodal Discourse on Online Newspaper Home Pages: A Social-semiotic Perspective.' Unpublished Ph.D. thesis, Department of Linguistics, University of Sydney.

—(2009b), 'Punctuating the Home Page: Image as Language in an Online Newspaper.' *Discourse & Communication*, 3(2), 145–72.

Latour, B. (2004), *Politics of Nature: How to Bring the Sciences into Democracy*, trans. Catherine Porter. Cambridge, MA: Harvard University Press.

—(2005), *Reassembling the Social: An Introduction to Actor-Network Theory*. Oxford, UK: Oxford University Press.

LeVine, P. and Scollon, R. (2004), *Discourse and Technology: Multimodal Discourse Analysis*. Washington, DC: Georgetown University Press.

Leyshon, A., Thrift, N. and Pratt, J. (1998), 'Reading Financial Services: Texts, Consumers, and Financial Literacy.' *Environment and Planning D; Society and Space*, 16, 29–55.

Li, K. (2007), 'Fox Business Network Aims for Mass Appeal.' *Reuters*, 11 October. Accessed 29 October 2010. http://www.reuters.com/article/2007/10/11/television-foxbusiness-dc-idUSN1042863620071011

Lotman, Y. N. (2005 [1984]), 'On the Semiosphere.' Translated by W. Clark. *Sign System Studies*, 33(1), 205–29.

Lotman, Y. N. and Uspensky, B. A. (1978), 'On the Semiotic Mechanism of Culture.' *New Literary History*, 9(2), 211–32.

Martin, J. R. (1992), *English Text: System and Structure*. Amsterdam/Philadelphia: John Benjamins Publishing Company.

Mautner, G. (2005), 'Time to Get Wired: Using Web-Based Corpora in Critical Discourse Analysis.' *Discourse & Society*, 16(6), 809–25.

Meyer, M. (2001), 'Between Theory, Method, and Politics: Positioning of the Approaches to CDA,' in R. Wodak and M. Meyer (eds), *Methods of Critical Discourse Analysis*. London: Sage Publications Ltd, pp. 14–31.

Montgomery, M. (2007), *The Discourse of Broadcast News: A Linguistic Approach*. New York: Routledge.

O'Halloran, K. L., Podlasov, A., Chua, A., and E. M. K. L. (2012), 'Interactive Software for Multimodal Analysis', in Jana Holsanova (ed.), *Special Issue: Methodologies for Multimodal Research, Visual Communication*, 11(3), 352–70.

Pew Research Center (2007), 'Fox News – Ready For Business.' *Pew Project For Excellence In Journalism*. Accessed 29 October 2010. http://www.journalism.org/node/7968

—(2009), 'PEJ News Coverage Index, 9–15 March 2009: Media Focus on Economic Villains: Bonuses, Bernie and Blather.' *Pew Project For Excellence In Journalism*. Accessed 29 October 2010. http://www.journalism.org/index_report/news_coverage_index_march_9_15_2009

—(2010), 'The State of the News Media 2010: An Annual Report on American Journalism.' *Pew Project For Excellence In Journalism*. Accessed 28 October 2011. http://www.stateofthemedia.org/2010/index.php

Pixley, J. (2002), 'Finance Organizations, Decisions and Emotions.' *British Journal of Sociology*, 53(1), 41–65.

Podlasov, A., Tan, S., and O'Halloran, K. L. (2012), 'Interactive State-Transition Diagrams for Visualization of Multimodal Annotation.' *Intelligent Data Analysis*, 16(4), 683–702.

Schuster, T. (2006), *The Markets and the Media: Business News and Stock Market Movements*. Lanham, MD: Lexington Books.

Scollon, R. J. (1998), *Mediated Discourse As Social Interaction: A Study Of News Discourse*. London; New York: Longman.

Shiller, R. J. (2002a), 'Bubbles, Human Judgement, and Expert Opinion.' *Financial Analysts Journal*, 58(3), 18–26.

—(2002b), 'Irrational Exuberance in the Media,' in *The Right To Tell: The Role of Mass Media in Economic Development*. Washington, DC: The World Bank, pp. 84–94.

—(2005), *Irrational Exuberance*. Princeton, NJ: Princeton University Press.

Tan, S. (2012), 'Multimodal Approaches to Business News Discourse Mediated on the Internet and Television.' Unpublished Ph.D. thesis, National University of Singapore.

Tan, S. and Owyong, M. Y. S. (2009), 'The Semiotic Function of Clothing and Gender Roles on Broadcast Business News.' *Business Communication Quarterly*, 72(3), 368–72.

Van Dijk, T. A. (1993), *Elite Discourse and Racism*. Newbury Park, CA: Sage Publications.

—(1997), 'Cognitive Context Models and Discourse', in M. Stamenov (ed.), *Language Structure, Discourse, and the Access to Consciousness*. Amsterdam: John Benjamins, pp. 189–226.

—(2001), 'Multidisciplinary CDA: A Plea for Diversity,' in R. Wodak and M. Meyer (eds), *Methods of Critical Discourse Analysis*. London: Sage Publications Ltd, pp. 95–120.

—(2011), *Discourse Studies: A Multidisciplinary Introduction*. London: Sage.

Van Leeuwen, T. (1995), 'Representing Social Action.' *Discourse & Society*, 6(1), 81–106.

—(1996), 'The Representation of Social Actors,' in C. Rosa Caldas-Coulthard and M. Coulthard (eds), *Texts and Practices – Readings in Critical Discourse Analysis*. London; New York: Routledge, pp. 32–70.

—(2008), *Discourse and Practice: New Tools for Critical Discourse Analysis*. New York: Oxford University Press.

13

Intervening in contexts of schooling

David Rose and J. R. Martin

1 Introduction

Building on Halliday's view of linguistics as an ideologically committed form of social action, a major goal of language research in the Sydney School (Hyon 1996; Johns 2002; Martin 2000; Rose 2008, 2011; Rose and Martin 2012) has been to analyse and redesign the pedagogic contexts through which school knowledge is acquired and evaluated. The research has drawn on two complex theories of social context, including the model of text-in-context developed within systemic functional linguistic theory (SFL) and the model of pedagogic contexts developed in the sociological theory of Basil Bernstein (1975, 1990, 2000). On the one hand, the Sydney School research has applied the model of text-in-context to describe the systems of 'knowledge genres' that students are expected to read and write in school. On the other, it has adapted Bernstein's theory of pedagogic discourse to describe the 'curriculum genres' (Christie 2002) through which control of the written genres of schooling are acquired and evaluated.

The study reported here applied these theories in a large-scale educational intervention in Australian primary and secondary schools. The goal of the study was to measure the effectiveness of genre-based literacy pedagogy developed in the Sydney School research. Approximately 400 teachers were trained in the pedagogy over the course of the 2010 school year, in western NSW. Teachers implemented the pedagogy and measured their students' literacy growth by analysing their writing at the beginning and end of the training programme. The chapter begins by outlining the Sydney School model of text-in-context, Bernstein's theory of pedagogic contexts and the context of the study. The model of text-in-context is then applied to analysing students' writing growth, and the overall findings of the educational intervention are presented and discussed.

2 The Sydney school model of text-in-context

Halliday (2013: 215) rehearses the question 'Can we actually model and represent and interpret context within the framework of what is generally involved as a theory of language?', noting that his teacher Firth thought you could and that he thinks so too, 'if only because it's the best chance you've got'. His remarks reflect the long-standing concern in Firthian and neo-Firthian linguistics with modelling context as a level of meaning (Monaghan 1979). As Firth comments (1957/1968: 200–1), 'The meaning of texts is dealt with by a dispersal of analysis at mutually congruent series of levels, beginning with contexts of situation and proceeding through collocation, syntax (including colligation) to phonology and phonetics . . .'. Halliday, more influenced by Hjelmslev (1961) and W. S. Allen than Firth in this regard, had modelled this dispersal as a realization hierarchy such as that outlined in Figure 13.1, with phonology realizing lexicogrammar, lexicogrammar realizing semantics, and semantics realizing context. This privileges context as a stratum of meaning in Halliday's model (akin to Hjelmslev's connotative semiotics), realized through patterns of language choice (e.g. Halliday 2005).

Halliday's linguistic perspective on context, in which language construes, is construed by and over time reconstrues and is reconstrued by context, can be termed supervenient. It contrasts with the circumvenient perspective whereby language is

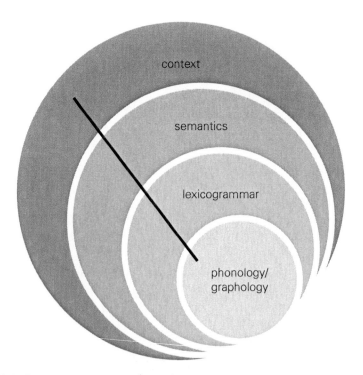

FIGURE 13.1 *Context as a stratum of meaning.*

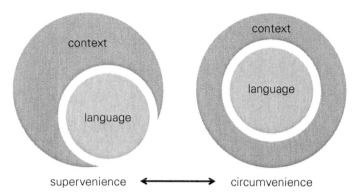

supervenience ←——————→ circumvenience

FIGURE 13.2 *Supervenience and circumvenience.*

conceived as embedded in context, where context is treated as extra-linguistic and not itself modelled in linguistic terms as a system of meaning. The two perspectives are outlined in Figure 13.2, using co-tangential circles for the supervenient perspective and concentric circles for the circumvenient one.[1]

Martin (e.g. 1985, 1992) further develops the supervenient perspective, suggesting that Halliday's stratum of context needs itself to be stratified into two levels which he calls register and genre (Figure 13.3).[2] In doing so, Martin is proposing a model in which context can be mapped as a system of genres (Christie and Martin 1997; Martin and Rose 2008), realizing through field, tenor and mode systems (collectively referred to as register). One of his reasons for stratifying context as genre and register is to foster Halliday's proposals (e.g. 1978) for using intrinsic functionality (ideational, interpersonal and textual meaning within language) to map extrinsic functionality (field, tenor and mode respectively) as dimensions of context (Martin 2001), without having to incorporate considerations of genre that muddy the waters (for argumentation see Martin 1999, 2001). Also significant is Martin's recontextualization of Halliday's semantics (cf. Figure 13.1) as discourse semantics (e.g. Martin 1992; Martin and Rose 2003), by way of emphasizing that register and genre are realized through meaning relations in text which regularly extend beyond the clause. Context is not in other words a pattern of lexicogrammatical patterns, but a pattern of a pattern of lexicogrammatical patterns – the basic unit of analysis in contextual linguistics has to be text, not clause.

One strategy for mapping the genres of a culture is to group them according to their broad social goals and distinguish them by their local organization (Martin and Rose 2008). Figure 13.4 presents such a map of genres that students are expected to read and write in school, identified in Sydney School research, that we have referred to as 'knowledge genres'. They are classified first in terms of three broad social goals: engaging readers, informing them and evaluating texts or points of view. Of course any text has multiple purposes; it is its primary social goal that generates the recognizable staging of the genre, the stages that participants expect to go through to achieve the goal.

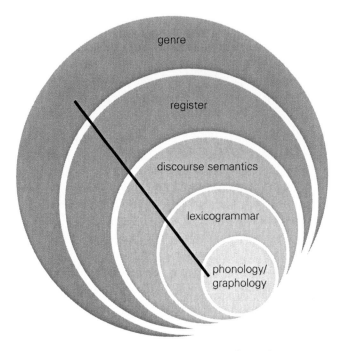

FIGURE 13.3 *Martin's supervenient model of language and social context.*

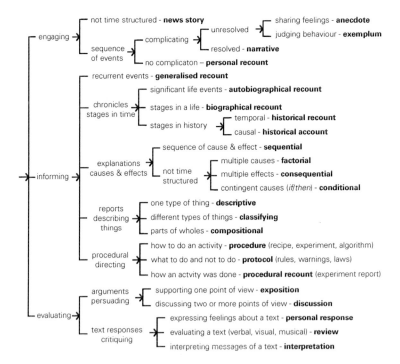

FIGURE 13.4 *Knowledge genres in the school.*

3 Bernstein's theory of pedagogic contexts

Bernstein (1975, 1990, 2000) provides two complementary perspectives on pedagogic contexts, as institutional structures, and as rules governing institutional practices. From the structural perspective, he describes education systems as a 'pedagogic device' operating at three levels: (1) fields of production of knowledge, primarily in the upper echelons of academe; (2) recontextualizing fields, where this knowledge is transformed for pedagogic purposes, for example, teacher training or textbook publishing; and (3) fields of reproduction, where recontextualized knowledge is transmitted and acquired by learners. From the perspective of sociological rules, Bernstein distinguishes (1) distributive rules regulating the distribution of resources to social groups, including discursive resources distributed by education; (2) recontextualizing rules regulating the transformation of knowledge into pedagogic discourse; and (3) evaluative rules regulating transmission and acquisition of knowledge.

These three levels of rules are interrelated. Evaluation regulates the distribution of different types and levels of education to different groups of students through their school years, and hence to professional, vocational or manual levels of occupations. Distributive rules in turn shape the forms in which knowledge is recontextualized for different groups of students, according to their evaluations, for example, as detailed scientific knowledge for students destined for science-based occupations or as simple hands-on science activities for less successful students.

All these dimensions of the pedagogic device are realized in the school as what Bernstein terms pedagogic discourse, in which he distinguishes two aspects: an instructional discourse 'which creates specialised skills and their relationship to each other', and a regulative discourse 'which creates order, relations and identity' (2000: 46). Bernstein emphasizes that the instructional is embedded in and dominated by the regulative, that the acquisition of knowledge is regulated by the social order and relations underpinning pedagogic discourse.

From the standpoint of genre and register theory outlined above, Bernstein's use of the term discourse refers to fields of social activity, coloured by tenor.[3] Thus, pedagogic discourse can be interpreted in terms of pedagogic register, including sequences of learning activities (field), pedagogic relations between learners and teachers (tenor), and modalities of learning – spoken, written, visual and manual (mode). These three dimensions are summarized in Figure 13.5. In this perspective, it is the social relations enacted over time in pedagogic activities that create 'order, relations and identity'.

The instructional discourse thus includes the fields of knowledge (or skills) acquired through these pedagogic activities, relations and modalities. In social semiotic terms, knowledge is projected by the pedagogic register, as the act of saying projects a locution, or thinking projects ideas (in Halliday's 1994/2004 terms). On this model, knowledge is projected by activities of teaching and

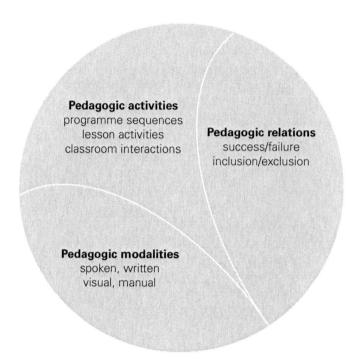

FIGURE 13.5 *Pedagogic register.*

learning. There are thus two fields involved in Bernstein's 'instructional discourse': the field of pedagogic activity and the field of knowledge projected by it. The entire configuration of pedagogic activities, relations, modalities and projected knowledge constitutes a genre that Christie (2002) has termed 'curriculum genre', illustrated in Figure 13.6.

As Figure 13.6 suggests, it is not only knowledge that learners acquire through pedagogic activities, relations and modalities, but identities as learners that are more or less successful, and more or less included in the community of learning in the school. Differentiation in learner identities is a product of (1) continual evaluation, which positions them on a hierarchy of success and failure, (2) varying degrees of engagement in lesson activities and classroom interactions, and (3) varying control over modalities of learning, particularly reading and writing. By these means, pedagogic discourse creates an unequal social order and asymmetric social relations. The creation of differential learner identities internalizes and thus naturalizes the social order produced by the pedagogic device, as Bernstein (2000:5) points out, 'How do schools individualize failure and legitimize inequalities? The answer is clear: failure is attributed to inborn facilities (cognitive, affective) or to the cultural deficits relayed by the family which come to have the force of inborn facilities'.

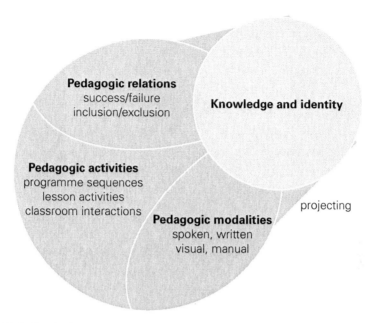

FIGURE 13.6 *Curriculum genres.*

4 The context of the study: A genre-based literacy intervention

The aim of the intervention reported on here was to subvert the hierarchy of success and failure and creation of differential learner identities, by equipping teachers with tools to enable all their students to succeed with the same levels of reading and writing tasks. The genre-based methodology employed to do so is known as Reading to Learn (or R2L), which provides three levels of guidance for reading and writing tasks. In the first level, teachers prepare students to comprehend challenging texts, by giving an oral summary of the field as it unfolds through the genre, in terms that all students can understand. At this level, students are also guided to write successful texts, by jointly deconstructing the stages and phases of model texts in target genres, and jointly constructing new texts organized with the same stages and phases (for stages and phases of knowledge genres see Martin and Rose 2008; Rose 2005). In the second level, teachers guide students to read passages of text in detail, by preparing them to recognize groups of words in each sentence, and elaborating on their meanings as students identify each word group. At this level, students are also guided to use what they have learnt from reading, by jointly rewriting the text passage that has been read in detail, using the same grammatical patterns for literary or persuasive texts, or the same field for factual texts. In the third and most intensive level, teachers guide students to manually manipulate wordings, by cutting up sentences they have been reading, and rearranging them. At this level, they also practise spelling the words they have cut up, and rewrite the sentences they have been manipulating. The Reading to Learn programme thus includes nine designed curriculum genres, as follows.

	Reading	Writing	
1st level	Preparing for Reading	Joint Construction	Individual Construction
2nd level	Detailed Reading	Joint Rewriting	Individual Rewriting
3rd level	Sentence Making	Spelling	Sentence Writing

In Individual Construction, students practise writing new texts with the same stages and phases that have been guided in Joint Construction, before attempting a completely independent writing task. Similarly in Individual Rewriting, students practise the same task that has been guided in Joint Rewriting.

These curriculum genres are practised in daily and weekly programmes, with the goal of students independently writing a new genre each month or so. The programme as a whole constitutes a curriculum macro-genre, with variable pathways through sub-genres depending on need, schematized in Figure 13.7. The teacher training programme is designed for teachers to learn and practise each curriculum genre in manageable

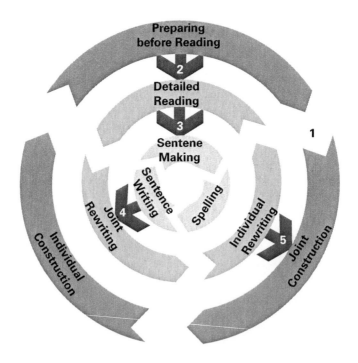

FIGURE 13.7 *Sequencing options for R2L curriculum genres.*

steps. Face-to-face training workshops provide the knowledge about pedagogy and knowledge about language needed to select and analyse texts, plan and implement lessons, and evaluate students' reading and writing.

5 Data analysis

Students' growth is assessed by teachers in the Reading to Learn programme, through formative testing of reading comprehension in each lesson unit and through summative testing of writing towards the end of each 10 week school term. The writing assessment developed in the programme is designed to accurately reveal the language resources that each student brings to the writing task. Teachers identify these language resources in students' writing, using 14 criteria. The criteria are derived from the SFL model of text-in-context outlined above, recontextualized to facilitate a simple, practicable text analysis for each piece of writing.

At the level of genre, evaluation focuses on the social purpose, stages and phases of the text. At the level of register, it focuses on the text's field, tenor and mode. At the level of discourse semantics, lexical, appraisal (evaluative), conjunction and reference resources are identified. At the level of grammar, the variety and accuracy of grammatical resources are evaluated, and at the level of graphic features, spelling, punctuation and graphic presentation are marked. The sequence of analysis is thus from the 'top-down', from genre to register, to discourse semantic resources that realize field, tenor and mode, to grammatical patterns that realize discourse semantics, to graphological features that express these patterns in writing. Questions are used to interrogate each of these criteria, summarized in Table 13.1.

Students' writing samples are compared with analysed writing exemplars at each school year level, and each criterion is given a score from 0–3 against the standard in the exemplar. Teachers are asked to assess the writing of students from low-, middle- and high-achieving groups, in order to compare the growth of each group in the class. Samples of these students' independent writing are assessed each term (four times a year), using the 14 criteria on a score sheet, exemplified in Figure 13.8. The totals at the bottom of the score sheet give a clear indication of each student's progress through the year. They also clearly show the rate of progress of the whole class and of the low-, middle- and high-achieving groups in the class.

By way of illustration, Texts 1–2 illustrate growth for one low achieving student in Year 7/8. The pre-intervention Text 1 is a very brief personal response to a book. The post-intervention Text 2 is the type of text response known as interpretation, in which the novel is appreciated and its themes are interpreted.

We'll deploy the model of language in context to analyse the improvement exemplified in Texts 1–2. Text 1 is the genre known as a personal response (see Figure 13.4 above). This is a typical response produced by weaker students when asked to evaluate a text (Rothery and Macken-Horarik 1991; Martin and Rose 2008). In terms of appraisal, it is characterized by expressions of personal feelings and reactions to the text (Martin and Rose 2007; Martin and White 2005). Appraisals are marked in bold in Text.

Table 13.1 Writing assessment criteria

CONTEXT	[Quick judgements are made about these context criteria.]
Purpose	*How appropriate and well-developed is the genre for the writing purpose?*
Staging	*Does it go through appropriate stages, and how well is each stage developed?*
Phases	*How well organized is the sequence of phases in the text?*
Field	*How well does the writer understand and explain the field in factual texts, construct the plot, settings and characters in stories, or describe the issues in arguments?*
Tenor	*How well does the writer engage the reader in stories, persuade in arguments, or objectively inform in factual texts?*
Mode	*How highly written is the language for the school stage? Is it too spoken?*
DISCOURSE	[Discourse criteria are marked in the text, to give an accurate measure.]
Ideation	*What are the writer's lexical resources? How well is lexis used to construct the field?*
Appraisal	*What are the writer's appraisal resources? How well is appraisal used to engage, persuade, evaluate?*
Conjunction	*Is there a clear logical relation between all sentences?*
Identification	*Is it clear who or what is referred to in each sentence?*
GRAMMAR and GRAPHIC FEATURES [Grammar features are judged overall rather than one-by-one.]	
Grammar	*Is there an appropriate variety of sentence and word group structures for the school stage? Are the grammatical conventions of written English used accurately?*
Spelling	*How accurately spelt are core words and non-core words?*
Punctuation	*How appropriately and accurately is punctuation used?*
Presentation	*Are paragraphs used? How legible is the writing? Is the layout clear.? Are illustrations/diagrams used appropriately?*

Text 1: Pre R2L personal response

> In this book **I like that I could connect with it** as **it's suitable for my age**. By the end **it dragged on a bit to much for my liking**.

Of the three evaluations here, two are reactions to the text – positively appreciating the text's appeal to the reader *I like that I could connect with it* (reaction: impact), but negatively appreciating its emotional effect *it dragged on a bit to much for my liking*

Student names	Jayden				Ada				Corrine				Dean				Robin				Vivian			
	Pre writing	Term 2	Term 3	Term 4	Pre writing	Term 2	Term 3	Term 4	Pre writing	Term 2	Term 3	Term 4	Pre writing	Term 2	Term 3	Term 4	Pre writing	Term 2	Term 3	Term 4	Pre writing	Term 2	Term 3	Term 4
PURPOSE	0	1	1	2	0	1	2	2	2	2	2	2	1	2	2	2	2	2	3	3	2	3	3	3
STAGING	0	1	1	2	0	1	2	2	1	1	2	2	1	2	2	3	2	2	3	3	2	3	3	3
PHASES	0	1	1	2	1	2	2	2	0	0	2	2	1	2	2	2	2	2	2	2	2	2	2	2
FIELD	0	1	1	2	0	2	2	2	1	2	2	1	1	2	3	3	2	2	2	2	2	2	2	3
TENOR	0	1	1	1	0	1	1	2	1	2	2	2	1	2	2	3	2	2	2	2	2	2	2	2
MODE	0	0	1	1	0	0	1	2	1	1	1	2	1	1	2	3	1	1	2	3	2	2	3	3
LEXIS	1	1	2	2	1	2	2	2	1	1	2	2	2	2	2	3	2	2	2	2	2	2	2	3
APPRAISAL	0	0	1	1	1	1	1	2	1	1	2	3	1	2	2	3	2	2	2	2	2	2	2	2
CONJUNCTION	1	2	2	2	1	1	1	2	0	0	0	3	1	0	2	3	0	1	2	3	2	2	3	3
REFERENCE	0	2	2	2	1	2	2	2	1	1	1	2	1	1	2	3	1	2	2	3	2	3	3	3
GRAMMAR	0	2	2	2	1	2	2	2	1	1	2	2	2	2	2	2	2	2	2	2	2	3	3	3
SPELLING	1	1	2	2	2	2	2	2	1	1	1	1	2	2	2	2	2	2	2	3	2	2	3	3
PUNCTUATION	0	1	1	2	1	2	2	2	1	1	1	1	0	1	1	1	1	2	3	3	2	3	3	3
PRESENTATION	0	0	1	2	0	0	1	2	1	1	1	2	0	1	2	3	1	2	2	3	2	2	3	3
TOTAL	3	14	19	25	9	19	24	28	13	15	22	27	15	22	28	35	22	26	31	38	28	33	37	40

FIGURE 13.8 Sample score sheet for writing assessment.

In this book I like that I could connect with it, as it's suitable for my age. By the end it dragged on a bit to much for my liking.

PRE R2L

TEXT 1 *Pre-intervention writing sample by a low-achieving student in Year 7/8.*

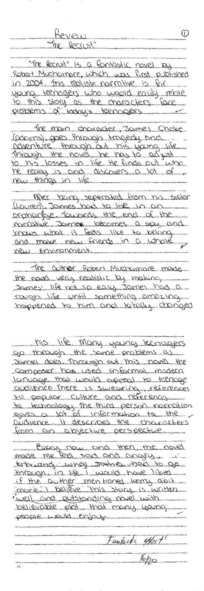

Review ①
"The Recruit"

"The Recruit" is a fantastic novel by Robert Muchamore, which was first published in 2004. This realistic narrative is for young teenagers who would easily relate to this story as the characters face problems of today's teenagers.

The main character, James Choke (adams), goes through tragedy and adventure through out his young life. Through the novel, he has to adjust to his losses in life. He finds out who he really is and discovers a lot of new things in life.

After being seperated from his sister (Lauren), James had to live in an orphange. Towards the end of the narrative James becomes a spy, and knows what it feels like to belong and make new friends in a whole new environment.

The author Robert Muchamore made the novel very realistic by making James' life not so easy. James had a rough life until something amazing happened to him and totally changed

his life. Many young teenagers go through the same problems as James does. Through out this novel, the composer has used informal, modern lanuage that would appeal to teenage audience. There is swearing, references to popular culture and references to technology. The third person narration gives a lot of information to the audience. It describes the characters from an objective perspective.

Every now and then, the novel made me feel sad and angry, knowing why James had to go through in life. I would have liked if the author mentioned kerry abit more. I believe this story is written well and outstanding novel with believable plot, that many young people would enjoy.

Fantastic effort!

Tops

TEXT 2 *Post-intervention writing sample by the same student in Year 7/8.*

(reaction: quality). The third positively appreciates the text's value *it's suitable for my age* (valuation). One evaluation is amplified, *a bit to much* (graduation), and all are sourced explicitly to the writer (engagement). Ideationally, the only lexical items realized here are 'this book' and 'my age'. The lack of any description of the text and its contents is inadequate for a text response. Textually, there are several personal references *I, I, my, my*, and text references *this book, it, it's, the end, it*, which serve to contextualize the response interpersonally (to the writer) and ideationally (to the book).

In terms of tenor variables of status (un/equal) and contact (close/distant), this very personal response implies a familiar peer relationship with the reader; in terms of field, it lacks any description of the book; in terms of mode, it is context-dependent speech written down. As this student is soon to enter secondary school, the tenor would be regarded as too familiar for its academic context, the field as inadequate, the mode as far too spoken and the genre as inappropriate for the task of evaluating a literary text.

Text 2 is an interpretation, which appreciates a novel and interprets its themes. This is the canonical genre of literature studies in the secondary school. Interpretations typically begin with an Evaluation, followed by a Synopsis of elements of the text that carry its themes and conclude with a Reaffirmation of the evaluation. Again, appraisals are in bold.

Text 2: Post R2L review

Evaluation	'The Recruit' is a **fantastic** novel by Robert Muchamore, which was first published in 2004. This **realistic** narrative is for young teenagers who **would easily relate** to this story as the characters **face problems** of today's teenagers.
Synopsis themes	The main character, James Choke (adams), goes through **tragedy and adventure throughout** his young life. Through the novel, he **has to adjust to his losses** in life. He finds out who he **really is** and discovers **a lot of new things** in life.
plot	After being separated from his sister (Lauren), James had to live in an orphanage. Towards the end of the narrative, James becomes a spy and knows what it feels like to belong and make new friends in a whole new environment.
Reaffirmation relevance	The author Robert Muchamore made the novel **very realistic** by making James' life **not so easy**. James had a **rough** life until **something amazing** happened to him and **totally changed** his life. **Many** young teenagers **go through the same problems** as James does.
composition	Throughout this novel, the composer has used informal modern language that **would appeal** to teenage audience. There is swearing references to popular culture and

references to technology. The third person narration gives **a lot of** information to the audience. It describes the characters from an **objective perspective**.

appeal

Every now and then the novel **made me feel sad and angry,** knowing what James had to go through in life. **I would have liked** if the author mentioned Kerry **a bit more. I believe** this story is **written well** and **outstanding** novel with a **believable** plot that **many** young people **would enjoy**.

Within its staging, the Synopsis includes two paragraphs which identify the novel's themes and synopsize its plot. The Reaffirmation evaluates its relevance to teenage readers, its literary composition and its appeal to the writer and potential readers. While genre stages are highly predictable, phases within each stage tend to be more variable, depending on the field and writers' imagination.

Appraisals are concentrated in the Evaluation and Reaffirmation, including a much wider range of text **valuations**: *fantastic novel, realistic narrative, very realistic, a lot of information, objective perspective, written well and outstanding novel, believable plot*; reader **reactions**: *easily relate, would appeal, made me feel sad and angry, I would have liked, many young people would enjoy*; and **judgements** of characters: *not so easy, rough life, something amazing happened to him, totally changed his life, young teenagers go through the same problems*. Resources for **graduation** are also more diverse: *easily relate, throughout, a lot of, whole new, very realistic, not so easy, totally changed, every now and then, a bit more*. **Engagement** is now far more objective, with personal sourcing limited to the final evaluation: *made me feel sad and angry, I would have liked, I believe*, and valuations attributed to potential readers: *young teenagers who would easily relate, young teenagers go through the same problems, many young people would enjoy*.

Ideationally, lexical resources construe the texts' themes and their relevance to readers: *tragedy and adventure throughout his young life, has to adjust to his losses, finds out who he really is, discovers a lot of new things in life, young teenagers, problems of today's teenagers*. They also construe the field of literature: *novel, narrative, story, characters, main character, tragedy and adventure, plot; author, composer, published; informal modern language, swearing, references, popular culture, technology; third person narration, information, objective perspective*. Some of these literary resources have clearly been scaffolded by the teacher, but they are used coherently here by the student writer. Thirdly, the novel's plot is condensed as an activity sequence in just two sentences:

After being separated from his sister (Lauren),
James had to live in an orphanage.
Towards the end of the narrative James becomes a spy
and knows what it feels like to belong
and make new friends in a whole new environment.

Textually, reference to the book now begins by **naming** it '*The Recruit*' and then **presuming** it variously as *a novel, this narrative, this story, the novel*. Characters are also presented by **naming**: *the main character, James Choke,* and then **presumed**: *his young life, he, him, his losses, who he really is, James' life, the same problems as James.* In addition to presenting each phase as separate paragraphs, the shift from phase to phase is also signalled by clause Themes that are made prominent, either by doubling an identity or by starting with a time or place, underlined as follows:

Evaluation	"The Recruit"
Synopsis	
themes	<u>The main character</u>, James Choke
plot	<u>After being separated from his sister (Lauren)</u>, James
Reaffirmation	
relevance	<u>The author</u> Robert Muchamore
composition	<u>Throughout this novel</u> the composer
appeal	<u>Every now and then</u> the novel

Tenor unfolds subtly through the text, beginning with **strong valuation** to engage the reader: *a fantastic novel*, then **amplified judgement** for its themes: *totally changed his life* and **amplified valuation** for its relevance: *very realistic*. While there is little explicit appraisal for its composition, the listing of its qualities serves to amplify its value. While these are all presented objectively, the personalized reactions in the last paragraph enact solidarity with teenage readers. The field here is multi-layered, with one field, the novel's plot, projecting a field of personal growth (its themes), and the field of literary appreciation (Rothery 1997). The mode is now at an appropriate level of written language for the end of primary school, and the genre is masterfully controlled. This student is now well prepared for the writing demands of secondary literature studies.

6 Findings

Table 13.2 illustrates how the writing assessment criteria are applied to Texts 1–2, to produce a numerical score to measure students' progress. Text 1 scored 0 for most contextual and discourse criteria, as its two sentences are so far below the standard expected for junior secondary school, although they meet minimum standards for lower level criteria. In contrast, Text 2 scored 2–3 for all criteria, as it meets a top to average standard for genre, register and discourse criteria. A score of 2 recognizes potential for improvement in a criterion. The total scores show growth from well below the grade standard (less than 15/42), to around a high standard for the grade (around 35/42).

    To measure the overall trends for the whole intervention, teachers' score sheets were collected and the total scores were recorded for analysis. Scores were analysed from approximately 100 randomly selected classes. As students targeted for assessment in

Table 13.2 Assessment of Texts 1–2

	Text 1	Text 2
PURPOSE	0	3
STAGING	0	3
PHASES	0	2
FIELD	0	2
TENOR	0	2
MODE	0	2
LEXIS	0	3
APPRAISAL	0	2
CONJUNCTION	1	3
REFERENCE	1	3
GRAMMAR	2	3
SPELLING	2	2
PUNCTUATION	2	2
PRESENTATION	2	2
Total	10	34

each class were selected from low-, middle- and high-achieving groups, the scores are representative of results for these groups in whole classes, helping to minimize bias. The sample thus represents a large set (~400 classes × 20–30 students per class, or ~8–12,000 students).

Charts 13.1 and 13.2 show the gap between low-, middle- and high-achieving student groups, before and after the intervention. Chart 13.1 shows the pre-intervention scores for each student group and school stage in Term 1. Chart 13.2 shows the post-intervention scores for each student group and school stage, after 3 terms of R2L teaching.

School stages surveyed include kindergarten (K), junior primary (Yr1/2), middle primary (Yr3/4), upper primary (Yr5/6) and junior secondary (Yr7/8). Note that the same students are represented in each cohort in Charts 13.1 and 13.2, for example the K group includes the same students in Charts 13.1 and 13.2, before and after the intervention. Note also that the data do not show longitudinal growth rates from year to year. Rather these are data from the year that teachers were being trained in the R2L programme.

In Chart 13.1, pre-intervention scores at the start of kindergarten show that the gap between low- and high-achieving students is 16 per cent of the total possible score. By the start of Yr1/2, average scores have risen by 25 per cent of the total, but the gap between low and high students has tripled to over 50 per cent of the total – the

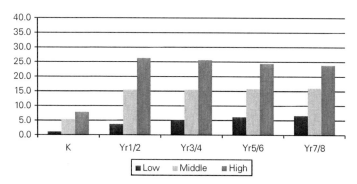

CHART 13.1 *Pre-intervention scores show gap between student groups before R2L teaching.*

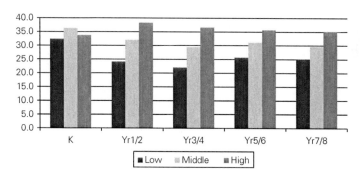

CHART 13.2 *Post-intervention scores show growth and reduction in gap after R2L teaching.*

high group has accelerated but the low group is still near zero. This gap then continues throughout the years, decreasing slowly. The low group improves very slowly from Yr1/2 to Yr7/8, the middle group remains steady and the high group falls slightly.

Comparing results between Chart 13.1 and Chart 13.2, post-intervention scores show average growth in kindergarten is 70 per cent above pre-intervention scores, and the gap between low- and high-achieving groups is halved to 9 per cent. In the other year levels, growth is 30–40 per cent above the pre-intervention scores, and the gap is reduced to 20–30 per cent.

The pre and post-intervention data in Charts 13.1 and 13.2 are combined as trend lines in Chart 13.3 below. The bottom two lines are pre-scores for low and high groups (i.e. without R2L teaching) and the top two lines are the post-scores for low and high groups (after R2L teaching).

Chart 13.3 clearly shows the contrast between outcomes with and without the R2L intervention, for low- and high-achieving student groups. Without R2L, the low group improves slowly each year, but stays within the failing range (~5 points). The high group improves faster in kindergarten and then stays in a high average range (~25 points), falling slightly. In contrast, following the R2L intervention, both low and high groups improve in kindergarten to a high range (~35 points). In other school stages, the low group improves to a high average range (~25 points), and the high group improves to the top range for their schools stages (~35 points).

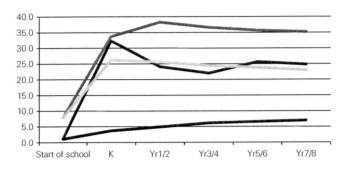

CHART 13.3 *Pre- and Post-data combined.*

TEXT 3–4 *Outcomes of standard and R2L teaching in early years.*

These generalized data are unpacked in more detail for each school stage as follows. Literacy growth of low-achieving groups is illustrated with pre- and post-intervention writing samples. For reasons of space, these samples are limited to kindergarten, middle primary and junior secondary stages.

Texts 3–4 illustrate the contrast between the outcomes of R2L and standard early literacy practices in kindergarten. The left hand Text 3 was written and drawn early in Yr1 (with teacher's translation), after a full year of standard early literacy practice in kindergarten. Text 4 on the right is by the same student 2 months later, after the R2L intervention.

The pre-intervention sample is a typical standard for the low-achieving student group at the start of Yr1/2, as shown in Chart 13.1 above (< 5 points). This student's reading level would be similarly very low. Without the R2L intervention, this student would probably have continued in the failing range throughout primary school, as shown for the low group in Charts 13.1 and 13.3. Within 2 months of R2L teaching, the same student has independently written a detailed, coherent and legible description on a topic the class has studied, has self-corrected while drafting it and has incorporated key elements in the illustration, including the mother seal, the hole in the ice with a line for the direction of her dive, and the storm gathering in the sky above. This text is already well above the average standard for Yr1.

Chart 13.4 restates the growth rates and gap between students in Yr1/2, with and without R2L. The data show little change over two years of junior primary, in the proportions of high-, middle- and low-achieving students (with a slight improvement for the low group). In contrast, after three terms of R2L teaching, the low group are almost at the level that the high group normally achieves. This growth rate is 17 times the normal growth of the low group. For the high-achieving students, the growth rate after R2L teaching is 30 per cent above their normal achievement.

Despite the growth using R2L, the gap between high- and low-achieving students remains at 34 per cent. While this is an improvement on the 49 per cent gap without R2L, it demands further work. The gap for this cohort of students may reduce further in following years, given consistent genre-based teaching.

Chart 13.5 restates the growth rates and gap between students in middle primary, with and without R2L. After 2 years without R2L, there has been a slight improvement in the scores of low-achieving students and a slight decrease in the high group. After 3 terms with R2L, the growth for the low group is 13 times what it was without R2L, and the high group has improved 26 per cent more than without R2L. However, the gap between the high and low groups is still 35 per cent, so further work is still needed to reduce this gap.

Growth for the low-achieving group in Year 3/4 is exemplified with writing samples from one student in Texts 5–6. The pre-intervention Text 5 on the left is an incomplete

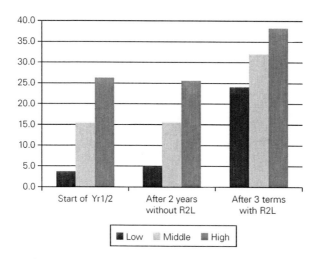

CHART 13.4 *Growth rates in Yr1/2, with and without R2L teaching.*

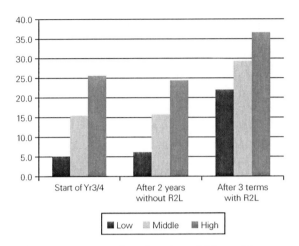

CHART 13.5 *Growth rates in Yr3/4, with and without R2L teaching.*

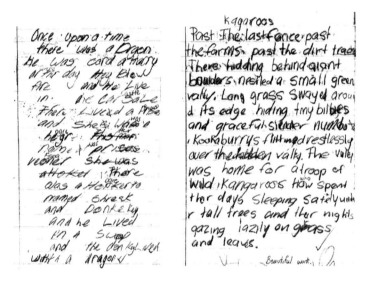

TEXT 5–6 *Outcomes of standard and R2L teaching for a low-achieving students in middle primary.*

recount that borrows elements from the animated movie Shrek. The post-intervention Text 6 on the right is modelled on a literary description studied in detail by the class.

Chart 13.6 restates the growth rates and gap between students in upper primary, with and without R2L. After 2 years without R2L, the growth is very similar to Yr3/4 – there is a slight improvement in the low group and a slight decrease in the high group, so the gap is reduced to 41 per cent. In contrast, after 3 terms with R2L, the low group is now achieving above what the high group achieved without R2L. This improvement for the low group is 49 times what it was without R2L. The high group has improved 28 per cent more than without R2L. The gap between the high and low groups is reduced to just 24 per cent.

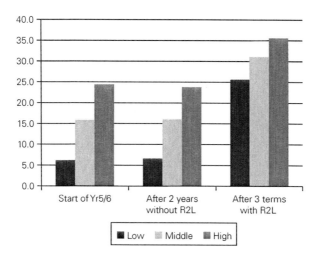

CHART 13.6 *Growth rates in Yr5/6, with and without R2L teaching.*

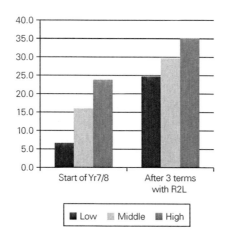

CHART 13.7 *Growth rates in Yr7/8 using R2L.*

Chart 13.7 restates the growth rates and gap between students in junior secondary, using R2L. Chart 13.7 does not compare the growth rates in Yr7/8 with and without R2L teaching, as these data were not available. However, given the consistent trends we have seen without R2L from Yr1/2 to Yr7/8, it may be assumed that a similar trend continues into the secondary school years. That is, the low group remains around 5 points, the middle group around 15 and the high group around 25. Nevertheless, after 3 terms with R2L the low group is now achieving slightly above what the high group achieved at the start of Yr7/8, and the high group has improved 28 per cent. This is a similar pattern to that shown above in Yr5/6. Likewise, the gap between the high and low groups is just 25 per cent.

7 Discussion

These data provide an unusual opportunity to compare the outcomes of different approaches to teaching and learning, from a large set of students, classes and schools. This is not a comparison between teachers, classes or schools, because it is averaged across a large set of schools and classrooms. Rather it is strictly a comparison between teaching approaches. What is compared in Charts 13.1, 13.2 and 13.3 are the outcomes of standard teaching practices in each stage of school, with the outcomes of carefully designed strategies in the R2L intervention. The pre-intervention scores in each stage represent the outcomes of the preceding 1–2 years of standard teaching practices. This data is unusual in that it compares these normal outcomes with those of a large-scale teaching intervention.

As Charts 13.1 and 13.3 show, the gap that begins in kindergarten normally continues throughout the following stages of school, as low-achieving students remain in the failing range, the middle group in the low average range and the high group within the high average range. The maintenance of low-achieving students in the failing range remains an intractable outcome of standard teaching practices in the primary and secondary school, as innumerable international reports attest.

In order for the high-achieving group to maintain its position in the high average range, these students must keep developing their literacy skills at a standard average growth rate. In terms of the R2L assessment, this standard average growth rate is about 7 score points per year or 16.6 per cent of the total possible score. However, for low-achieving students to get out of the failing range, up to a passable average range, they must develop their skills at more than double the rate of the high-achieving students. This rarely happens with standard teaching practices. Nor does it happen with targeted interventions such as phonics programmes, withdrawal reading programmes, levelled readers, levelled reading groups or special education programmes, which may produce incremental but not exponential growth (Hattie 2009).

A key reason that these interventions have little significant long-term effects on the literacy rates of low-achieving students is that they do not work with the curriculum texts that the class is studying. Instead they use low-level texts and activities that are targeted at the assessed 'ability levels' of the low-achieving students, their so-called 'instructional level'. It seems unlikely that students who are learning more slowly, with low-level texts and activities, will ever catch up with their peers who are learning faster with higher-level texts and activities.

A critical difference with R2L is the use of high-level-quality curriculum texts, which teachers select and prepare, and carefully designed strategies that teach every student in the class to read and write them at the same time. These are whole class strategies, in which the teacher is the expert guide. Crucially, the intensive Level 2 and 3 strategies are used with whole classes, as well as with small groups and one-on-one for additional support. But these intensive strategies also use the same high level texts that the whole class is studying. There are no withdrawal sessions for low-achieving students using low-level texts and activities. Independent research has shown that better results are obtained with whole class teaching using R2L than with withdrawal sessions (Culican 2006).

8 Conclusion: Enhancement, inclusion and participation

In our discussion of language/context relations, we focused on the hierarchy of abstraction from language to register to genre. In discussing the genre-based literacy intervention above, we have also incidentally explored a hierarchy of individuation (Martin 2010), from the language community of the school, to groups of high-, middle- and low-achieving students, to individual students. In this regard, we have been concerned with differences between learners in their engagement in curriculum genres, their mastery of knowledge genres and their identities as learners (cf. Maton forthcoming). In Bernstein's terms, this hierarchy of individuation relates the reservoir of meanings in a culture to the repertoire available to a person.

> I shall use the term *repertoire* to refer to the set of strategies and their analogic potential possessed by any one individual and the term *reservoir* to refer to the total of sets and its potential of the community as a whole. Thus the *repertoire* of each member of the community will have both a common nucleus but there will be differences between the *repertoires*. There will be differences between the *repertoires* because of the differences between members arising out of differences in members' context and activities and their associated issues. (2000: 158)

Each person possesses a set of strategies for recognizing contexts and for realizing the texts expected in a context, for which Bernstein uses the terms recognition and realization rules. In terms of genre and register theory, a student may be able to recognize the curriculum genre that their class is engaged in, but may not be able to realize the responses needed to participate successfully. Or they may be able to neither recognize a knowledge genre nor realize it successfully as a written text.

Yet Bernstein also points out that each person possesses an analogic potential, which we understand as the potential for expanding one's repertoire from the known to the new. A central function of the school is to facilitate the expansion of each student's repertoire to incorporate more and more of the culture's reservoir of potential meanings. For some students, the expansion of their repertoire builds steadily, year by year, in sync with the curriculum sequence of the school, while the repertoire of others lags behind, sometimes far behind. These differences in the realization of students' analogic potential are not incidental to the functioning of the school; they are central to the creation and maintenance of social inequalities, not only in the resources that education affords, but also in the personal identities that are shaped by education.

In our view, inequality of outcomes is sustained by failing to explicitly teach all students the skills they need to independently read and write the curriculum at each stage of school. Instead, successful students tacitly acquire skills at each stage that will prepare them for the next stage. The practices for each school stage, outlined above, concretely illustrate this process. Rather than explicitly teaching skills needed in each stage, students are evaluated on skills they may have tacitly acquired in preceding stages, beginning with parent–child reading and associated orientations to meaning in the home (Hasan 2009; Williams 1995, 1999b, 2001). This sequence of tacit preparation and evaluation is diagrammed in Figure 13.9.

Figure 13.9 represents the contexts of schooling diachronically as an ontogenetic pathway, beginning with engagement in reading and talk-around-text that are characteristic modes of curriculum genres in the school. This engagement is a necessary condition for participating actively in classroom learning in the junior primary, and for becoming independent young readers and writers. This active participation and independent literacy skills are in turn the conditions for learning to learn from reading, and for demonstrating what has been learnt by writing in the upper primary, which are in turn necessary for successful independent learning in the secondary school (see Rose 2004, 2007 for further discussion).This 'hidden curriculum' of literacy development has evolved in the school to enable the children of literate middle-class families to progress smoothly towards university matriculation, stage-by-stage, but the practices outlined above at each school stage simultaneously ensure that children from other backgrounds are less likely to progress so smoothly.

The evaluative rules that govern differentiated progression through the school thus realize the distributive rules that govern unequal access to society's resources. Our approach to this contra-democratic system has been to design curriculum genres that

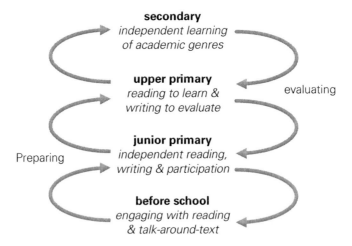

FIGURE 13.9 *Tacit learning sequence in school.*

can provide all students with the skills needed for success and can be integrated with curriculum teaching at all school stages. The intervention reported on here put these designs into practice.

Bernstein (2000: 5) warns that 'Biases in the form, content, access and opportunities of education have consequences not only for the economy; these biases can reach down to drain the very springs of affirmation, motivation and imagination'. To counter these biases, Bernstein (2000: 8) proposes for each student three 'pedagogic democratic rights of "enhancement," "inclusion" and "participation" as the basis for *confidence, communitas* and *political practice'.* 'Enhancement' we interpret as the expansion of each student's repertoire, building confident identities as successful learners as they progress through the school's curriculum sequence. In terms of genre and register, this includes accumulating knowledge of curriculum fields through reading, and control of knowledge genres in writing. 'Inclusion' we interpret as active engagement in the curriculum genres of the school, building identities as authoritative members of a community of learners. This requires enabling all students to participate successfully in curriculum genres, to be continually affirmed, and so benefit equally from pedagogic activities. 'Participation' we will interpret as an outcome of enhancement and inclusion, since both knowledge and belonging are necessary conditions for exercising informed citizenship; they are, as Bernstein says, 'the necessary and effective conditions for democracy'.

For us, the contexts of texts written in the school thus go well beyond their specific settings in field, tenor and mode. Minimally, it is also essential to consider the types of knowledge genres that are realized by configurations of field, tenor and mode. Secondly, we need to examine the curriculum genres through which knowledge genres are acquired in the school. But the purpose of these analyses is not simply to contemplate pedagogic contexts; they are merely a necessary first step towards intervening in them. For this purpose, we need a far broader view of social contexts than linguistics can offer on its own. Bernstein's sociological interpretation provides such a model, with which our linguistic understandings can be articulated. The results of the intervention reported here illustrate the power that can be generated from combining these two formidable theories of language in context.

Notes

1 We are indebted to Chris Cleirigh for this terminology (which he no longer deploys); we are not using the terms in quite the way he originally intended.

2 Genre and register are both dimensions of 'context of culture' in Malinowski's terms, and both are instantiated as text in 'contexts of situation'. Genre and register are related stratally, while 'situations' are instances of 'culture'.

3 The term 'discourse' is also used similarly by critical theorists and discourse analysts such as Gee (e.g. 2005).

References

Bernstein, B. (1975), *Class, Codes and Control 3: Towards a Theory of Educational Transmissions*. London: Routledge & Kegan Paul (Primary Socialisation, Language and Education).

—(1990), *Class, Codes and Control 4: The Structuring of Pedagogic Discourse*. London: Routledge.

—(2000), *Pedagogy, Symbolic Control and Identity: Theory, Research, Critique*. London and Bristol, PA: Taylor and Francis [Revised edition Lanham, Maryland: Rowan and Littlefield, 2000].

Christie, F. (2002), *Classroom Discourse Analysis*. London: Continuum.

Christie, F. and Martin, J. R. (eds) (2007), *Language, Knowledge and Pedagogy: Functional Linguistic and Sociological Perspectives*. London: Continuum.

Culican, S. (2006), *Learning to Read: Reading to Learn, A Middle Years Literacy Intervention Research Project*, Final Report 2003–04. Catholic Education Office: Melbourne, http://www.cecv.melb.catholic.edu.au/Research and Seminar Papers

Dreyfus, S., Hood, S. and Stenglin, M. (eds) (2011), *Semiotic Margins: Reclaiming Meaning*. London: Continuum.

Firth, J. R. (1957/1968), 'A Synopsis of Linguistic Theory, 1930–55', *Studies in Linguistic Analysis* (Special volume of the Philological Society). London: Blackwell, pp. 1–31. [reprinted in F. R. Palmer (ed.) (1968), *Selected Papers of J R Firth, 1952–1959*. London: Longman, pp. 168–205]

Gray, B. (1987), 'How natural is "natural" language teaching: employing wholistic methodology in the classroom'. *Australian Journal of Early Childhood*, 12(4), 3–19.

Halliday, M. A. K. (1978), *Language as a Social Semiotic: The Social Interpretation of Language and Meaning*. London: Edward Arnold.

—(1994), 'On language in relation to the evolution of human consciousness', in S. Allen (ed.), *Of Thoughts and Words*. London: Imperial College Press, pp. 45–84.

—(1994/2004), *An Introduction to Functional Grammar* (2nd edn). London: Edward Arnold. [1st edition 1985, 3rd edition with C. M. I. M. Matthiessen, 2004].

—(2005), 'Computing meanings: some reflections on past experience and present prospects', *Computational and Quantitative Studies*. [Volume 6 in the Collected Works of M. A. K. Halliday, edited by Jonathan Webster]. London: Continuum, pp. 239–67.

—(2013), *Interviewing Michael Halliday: Language Turned Back on Himself*, ed. J. R. Martin. London: Continuum, in press.

Hattie, J. A. C. (2009), *Visible Learning: A Synthesis of Over 800 Meta-analyses Relating to Achievement*. London: Routledge.

Hjelmslev, L. (1961), *Prolegomena to a Theory of Language*. Madison, WI: University of Wisconsin Press.

Hyon, S. (1996), 'Genre in Three Traditions: implications for ESL'. *TESOL Quarterly*, 30(4), 693–722.

Johns, A. M. (ed.) (2002), *Genre in the Classroom: Applying Theory and Research to Practice*. Mahwah, NJ: Lawrence Erlbaum.

Martin, J. R. (1985), *Factual Writing: Exploring and Challenging Social Reality*. Geelong, VC: Deakin University Press [republished London: Oxford University Press, 1989].

—(1991), 'Intrinsic functionality: implications for contextual theory'. *Social Semiotics*, 1(1), 99–162.

—(1992), *English Text: System and Structure*. Amsterdam: Benjamins.

—(1999), 'Modelling context: the crooked path of progress in contextual linguistics (Sydney SFL)', in M. Ghadessy (ed.), *Text and Context in Functional Linguistics*. Amsterdam: Benjamins (CILT Series IV), pp. 25–61.

—(2000), 'Grammar meets genre – reflections on the "Sydney School"'. *Arts: The Journal of the Sydney University Arts Association*, 22, 47–95. [reprinted in *Educational Research on Foreign Languages & Arts*. Sun Yat Sen University, Guangzhou (Special issue on Functional Linguistics & Applied Linguistics) 2, 2006, pp. 28–54].

—(2001), 'A context for genre: modelling social processes in functional linguistics', in J. Devilliers and R. Stainton (eds), *Communication in Linguistics: Papers in Honour of Michael Gregory*. Toronto: GREF (Theoria Series 10), pp. 287–328.

—(2007), 'Metadiscourse: designing interaction in genre-based literacy programs', in R. Whittaker, M. O'Donnell and A. McCabe (eds), *Language and Literacy: Functional Approaches*. London: Continuum, pp. 95–122.

—(2010), 'Semantic variation: modelling system, text and affiliation in social semiosis', in Bednarek and Martin, pp. 1–34.

—(2011), 'Multimodal semiotics: theoretical challenges'. Dreyfus et al., pp. 243–70.

Martin, J. R. and Rose, D. (2003), *Working with Discourse: Meaning Beyond the Clause*. London: Continuum [2nd Revised Edition 2007].

—(2007), 'Interacting with Text: the role of dialogue in learning to read and write'. *Foreign Languages in China*, 4(5), 66–80.

—(2008), *Genre Relations: Mapping Culture*. London: Equinox.

Maton, K. (forthcoming), *Knowledge and Knowers: Towards a Realist Sociology of Education*. London: Routledge.

Monaghan, J. (1979), *The Neo-Firthian Tradition and its Contribution to General Linguistics*. Tubingen: Max Niemeyer.

Rose, D. (2004), 'Sequencing and Pacing of the Hidden Curriculum: how Indigenous children are left out of the chain', in J. Muller, A. Morais and B. Davies (eds), *Reading Bernstein, Researching Bernstein*. London: Routledge Falmer, pp. 91–107.

—(2005), 'Democratising the Classroom: a Literacy Pedagogy for the New Generation'. *Journal of Education*, 37, 127–64, http://dbnweb2.ukzn.ac.za/joe/joe_issues.htm

—(2006), 'Reading genre: a new wave of analysis'. *Linguistics and the Human Sciences*, 2(2), 185–204.

—(2007), 'Towards a reading based theory of teaching'. Plenary paper in L. Barbara and T. Berber Sardinha (eds), *Proceedings of the 33rd International Systemic Functional Congress*. São Paulo: PUCSP, pp. 36–77. ISBN 85-283-0342-X, http://www.pucsp.br/isfc/proceedings/

—(2008), 'Writing as linguistic mastery: the development of genre-based literacy pedagogy', in R. Beard, D. Myhill, J. Riley and M. Nystrand (eds), *Handbook of Writing Development*. London: Sage, pp. 151–66.

—(2010), 'Meaning beyond the margins: learning to interact with books', in S. Dreyfus, S. Hood and M. Stenglin (eds), *Semiotic Margins: Reclaiming Meaning*. London: Continuum, pp. 177–208.

—(2011), 'Genre in the Sydney School', in J. Gee and M. Handford (eds), *The Routledge Handbook of Discourse Analysis*. London: Routledge, pp. 209–25.

Rose, D. and Martin, J. R. (2012), *Learning to Write, Reading to Learn: Genre, knowledge and Pedagogy in the Sydney School*. London: Equinox.

Rose, D., Gray, B. and Cowey, W. (1999), 'Scaffolding Reading and Writing for Indigenous Children in School', in P. Wignell (ed.), *Double Power: English Literacy and Indigenous Education*. Melbourne: National Language & Literacy Institute of Australia (NLLIA), pp. 23–60, http://www.readingtolearn.com.au

Rothery, J. (1994), *Exploring Literacy in School English (Write it Right Resources for Literacy and Learning)*. Sydney: Metropolitan East Disadvantaged Schools Program.
—(1996), 'Making changes: developing an educational linguistics', in R. Hasan and G. Williams (eds), *Literacy in Society*. London: Longman, pp. 86–123.
Rothery, J. and Macken, M. R. (1991), 'Developing critical literacy through Systemic Functional Linguistics: unpacking the "hidden curriculum" for writing in junior secondary English in New South Wales', in *Monograph 1 in Issues in education for the socially and economically disadvantaged*. Metropolitan East Disadvantaged Schools Program.

14

Turn-allocation and context: Broadening participation in the second language classroom

Hansun Zhang Waring

1 Introduction

Seeking the active participation of all learners in the language classroom has remained a constant challenge for language teachers (Allwright 1980; Paoletti and Fele 2004; Mohr and Mohr 2007). Common solutions such as pair or group work to maximize learner participation are useful but not applicable to whole-class interactions. A plaguing question for teachers-in-training, for example, is how to deal with silent students and create a more inclusive classroom. Neither teacher training materials nor scholarly research on classroom turn-taking, however, has been addressed to this particular aspect of pedagogical concern. In this paper, I take a small step towards building a descriptive account of teacher practices designed to widen participation frameworks during whole-class interactions. Aside from describing the discourse of turn-taking in the context of a language classroom, I also consider how the notion of context is understood in my approach to the data.

2 Goal of the study

In line with the theme of this book, the goal of this study is twofold. First, by describing a specific aspect of discourse as produced in the situational context of an adult ESL (English as a Second Language) classroom, I hope to expand the literature on turn-taking (e.g. Sacks, Schegoff, and Jefferson 1974) in the context of the classroom (e.g. McHoul 1978). Second, by articulating how context is construed in my particular approach to data, I also hope to contribute to the ongoing discussion on the methodological issue that revolves around discourse and context (e.g. McHoul, Rapley and Antaki 2008; van Dijk 2009; Waring, Creider, Tarpey and Black 2012).

3 Approach to discourse analysis that informs the study

The approach to discourse analysis that informs this study is conversation analysis (henceforth CA), and it is important to keep in mind that CA is not simply a methodology, but a theory as well (Heritage 2008; Kasper and Wagner 2011). As a theoretical framework, CA is informed by the two giants of American social theory–Harold Garfinkel (1967) and Erving Goffman (1967), and as such, comprises the following set of assumptions that prioritize analytic induction (ten Have 2007) and participant orientations (Schegloff and Sacks 1973): (1) social interaction is orderly at all points, that is, no detail can be dismissed *a priori*; (2) participants orient to that order themselves, that is, order is not a result of the analyst's conceptions or any preformulated theoretical categories; (3) such order can be discovered and described by examining the details of interaction.

Two further observations are in order with regard to CA as a theoretical framework. First, CA aims to discover 'social members' own implicit theory of interaction' (Kasper, personal communication) or their interactional competence (Wong and Waring 2010). By engaging in analytic induction (Pomerantz 1990) or abductive reasoning (Svennevig 2001), CA analysts discover in each case a theory that undergirds and specifies the practices of social interaction. After all, '[th]ere is a delicate form of the empirical which identifies itself so intimately with its object that it thereby becomes theory' (Johann Wolfgan von Goethe 1829 in Schegloff 2007a). Second, CA offers a range of theoretical tools for analysing social interaction. Concepts such as turn-constructional unit (TCU), transition-relevance place (TRP), adjacency pair (AP) and preference constitute a lens through which social interaction may be viewed and understood. Notably, such theoretical tools are not conceptualized by the researcher in the abstract but grounded in meticulous empirical work. As Clayman and Gill (2004) aptly write, as 'a predominantly data-driven or inductive enterprise', CA is 'guided by a well-developed conceptual foundation grounded in empirical findings from past research' (p. 590).

With a commitment to 'naturalistic inquiry' (Schegloff 1997: 501), CA insists on using data collected from naturally occurring interaction as opposed to interviews, field notes, native intuitions and experimental methodologies (Heritage 1984: 236). Analysts work with audio or video recordings along with the transcripts of these recordings, using transcription notations originally developed by Gail Jefferson. A CA transcript captures a full range of interactional details such as volume, pitch, pace, intonation, overlap, inbreath, smiley voice, the length of silence as well as nonverbal conduct (see Appendix). It is in these minute details that evidence is located for how social actions such as requesting or complaining are accomplished.

The advantage of uncovering the methods of social interaction in this particular way is that we get a sense of how a particular practice is produced and treated by the participants themselves in real time. While sharing the ethnographic tradition of naturalistic observation, CA is distinct in its insistence on directing its observation towards 'conduct as it has been preserved in audio and video recordings' (Clayman and Gill 2004: 590). It is worthy of note that CA's interest in uncovering participant orientations may be misunderstood by scholars from different paradigms. One might wonder, for example, 'if you want participant orientations, wouldn't the best way be to ask them?' The trouble is that the participants don't always know the answers. Methods of social interaction are often part of members' tacit knowledge, thereby not subject to explicit articulation even for native speakers. Koshik (2005), for example, shows that an alternative question is often used in such a way that the first alternative identifies the problem/error and the second the solution/correction (e.g. *Is it simple present or present progressive?*). I have used Koshik's paper on numerous occasions for my classes, and this finding never fails to astound. I have yet to hear a native speaker or anyone say, 'Oh I knew that'.

Analysts may approach the data with or without any specific focus in mind. Regarding the CA principle of 'unmotivated looking', Psathas (1990) writes that it is 'a contradiction or paradox since looking is motivated or there would be no looking being done in the first place' (p. 24). The key is to refrain from searching for instances with a preformulated notion of what specific practices should look like or how they should work. In my study on the discourse marker 'now' (Waring 2012a), I began with a hunch that there is something inexplicable in the use of 'now' based on my own exposure to the English language. With that hunch, I started to search for instances of 'now' in all my existing data sets. In other words, the analysis began with a targeted interest on my part. My 'looking' was 'motivated' by an initial noticing that is free of any preconceptions of how 'now' might work systematically in interaction. Such guided search is not foreign to foundational CA practice. During the Conversation Analysis Advanced Studies Institute (CA-ASI) at UCLA led by Manny Schegloff and Gene Lerner, for instance, we would be working on gathering instances and developing analyses of 'answer turns' in a given set of data. Put simply, beginning a research journey with some sort of focus in mind is not forbidden fruit in the CA kingdom. On the other hand, in my work on classroom discourse, I always begin with a line-by-line analysis of the data I have, with no specific focus whatsoever. From such analyses, various themes of interest begin to emerge (e.g. teacher question, learner initiatives, playful language), one of which is the topic of this current paper: turn-taking. I then start to build collections of cases for each theme. Over the years, I have found this approach to be the most fruitful; it leads me to discoveries that would never have occurred to me otherwise.

Most CA studies are such collection-based studies (see Schegloff 1997 for a lucid description of how collections are assembled), the aim of which is to identify practices of social interactions (e.g. understanding-check questions in Waring 2012b). Not all CA studies are collection-based, however. Some are single-case studies, where the existing findings of CA are employed to illuminate the nature of a specific case of interaction within a specific setting (e.g. Schegloff 1987a; Waring 2009).

4 How context is understood in the study

For the purpose of this project, I understand context to be both sequential and institutional. Crucial to CA analysis is the sequential context of particular practices– their positioning within a sequence or a larger course of action (Schegloff 2007a). This sequential aspect of context is succinctly articulated in Heritage's (1984) words that any communicative action is both 'context-shaped' and 'context-renewing' (p. 242). Put otherwise, the interpretation of what X is doing is deeply entwined with what comes before and after X in a sequence of talk. Every current action is shaped by the context set up by the preceding action, and every current action renews the context for its next action. For a brief illustration, let me use a transcript from my daughter Zoe's (4-years-old) preschool meeting, where Zoe is showing her finger puppets:

```
01   Zoe:        I'm ready to take questions.
02   Isa: →      What is that little orange thing?
03   Zoe: →      The little orange thing, which animal do you think it is?
04   Isa:        A lion.
```

Our understanding of Isa's question in line 02 is in part constrained by Zoe's prior turn in line 01. Isa is not simply directing a question to Zoe; she is specifically raising a question in response to Zoe's invitation. In other words, by asking a question, she is responding to Zoe's invitation. Isa's question itself then sets up the context for Zoe's next turn, where an answer to the question is expected. Against that expectation, in line 03, we specifically hear an absence of answer from Zoe. In other words, our hearing of Zoe's turn as a non-answer is shaped by the context set up by Isa's previous turn. By producing what is now hearable as a counter-question (Markee 1995) given the prior turn, Zoe also renews the context for the next turn, which is to be heard as a response to that question.

Institutionally, classroom interaction exhibits a clear departure from ordinary conversation, which may be captured in a set of three features (Drew and Heritage 1992). First, it is goal-oriented. Teachers and students come to the classroom with the expectation that some sort of learning will occur. To promote such learning, teachers may have specific interactional goals such as maximizing participation (Young and Miller 2004). Second, special constraints exist upon what is allowable contribution to the business at hand. The democratic machinery that drives turn-taking in ordinary conversation (Sacks, Schegloff and Jefferson 1974), for example, is suspended in the classroom, where turn-allocation is to a large extent orchestrated by the teacher (Mehan 1979). Finally, inferential frameworks and procedures particular to the classroom context may be in place. For example, while silence in ordinary conversation typically embodies trouble, in the classroom, silence after a teacher's understanding-check question is often treated as *no-problem* (Waring 2012b). (For further discussion on the classroom context with specific reference to turn-taking, see 'The Context of the Study' section below.)

Importantly, this institutional context, from a CA perspective, does not determine the conduct of the participants as captured in the 'bucket theory' of context. Instead, in what Heritage and Clayman (2010) call the 'Yellow Brick Road' (see Beatle's *Yellow Submarine* movie) view of context, participants continuously maintain, create and alter the context through their actions (p. 22). As such, the institutional context of a classroom is talked into being. That means one need not be physically sitting in a classroom to do classroom talk. In the example above, Zoe and Isa are most likely to be introduced as 4-year-old preschoolers in the first instance, but the specific identity categories they orient to within the exchange appear to be teacher-student (or presenter-audience). This is evidenced in the specifics of turn-taking and the nature of the sequence inside the data (which I will not detail here). In other words, in conducting the interaction in a particular way, Zoe and Isa are performing the category-bound activities of teacher-student (Schegloff 2007b) and thereby invoking the institutional context of a classroom, and herein lies the central mandate of the CA approach to institutional context: one would have to show that this institutional context is being oriented to by the participants themselves as 'demonstrably relevant' and 'procedurally consequential' in Schegloff 1987b).

It is worth emphasizing that the commonly referred to CA insistence on not going outside the data is sometimes subject to a rather dogmatic and unproductive reading, instantiated in misleading remarks such as any consideration outside the immediate data extract is forbidden. In CA data sessions, for instance, each new data is introduced with who the participants are, what the specific setting is, etc. Such information is part and parcel of grasping what is going on. As Maynard (2003) writes, ethnography complements conversation analysis in describing settings and identities, clarifying unfamiliar references or courses of action, and explaining 'curious' patterns revealed by the sequential analysis (p. 73). In the 'Zoe and Isa' example above, one would have to draw upon knowledge about routine classroom conduct (e.g. teachers ask display questions) *outside* the immediate data extract to establish the claim that these preschoolers are doing being teacher and student, but the connection is made with careful grounding in the sequential details *inside* the data. On the other hand, insofar as such 'external' knowledge is well-established by prior analyses of classroom data, we are not going outside the data after all in the broader sense of 'data'.

Insofar as the focus of my current analysis is on the teachers' practices of broadening participation, not on how such practices maintain, create or alter the classroom context, I will not be devoting any energy to detailing how the institutional context is made demonstrably relevant or procedurally consequential in the interaction data by highlighting observations such as the classroom context becomes procedurally consequential as the teacher regulates who speaks next. I will, however, draw upon the institutional context of the classroom to illuminate or shed further light on the teachers' practices of broadening participation in the 'Discussion and Conclusion' section (also see Waring and Hruska 2011, 2012). The analysis of the practices themselves, on the other hand, will be entirely grounded in their sequential contexts.

Finally, there is yet another sense of context that can be articulated in questions such as: Does the teacher routinely ignore incorrect student contributions so that such ignoring can be understood as negative evaluation? When does each teacher call on specific students and when does he allow any student to respond? Do they ever direct a follow-up question to a first respondent? These are indeed important questions for understanding the interactional dynamics of a particular classroom. They are less relevant, however, to uncovering the specific practices of broadening participation (i.e. the focus of this paper) – as practices that any other teacher can potentially employ. CA's interest is in uncovering the methods of social interaction rather than documenting who does what with what frequency. Knowing whether the teacher ever directs a follow-up question to a first respondent, for example, will not change how directing a follow-up question away from the first respondent serves to broaden participation frameworks (see analysis below).

5 The context of the study

In the case of the current study, the classroom context provides a baseline understanding of the practices and issues related to turn-taking, which have received a substantial amount of scholarly attention. Some have produced meticulous descriptions of the relatively constrained nature of classroom turn-taking compared to that in ordinary conversation (McHoul 1978; Mehan 1979; van Lier 1988). Mehan (1979) describes three ways in which the teacher can select a student respondent: invitation to reply, invitation to bid and individual nomination. Xie (2011) shows that the teachers' turn-allocation practices can affect opportunities of learning in various ways. Others have further specified how current-selects-next or self-selection is accomplished in classroom talk (e.g. Lerner 1993; Mortensen 2008; Sahlstrom 2002). Still others have delved into the cross-cultural difference in turn-taking by way of illuminating uneven participation in the classroom (e.g. Philips 1972; Schultz, Florio and Erickson 1982; McCollum 1989; Poole 2005). Particularly notable for the purpose of the current paper are various observations of the problematic nature of the classroom turn-taking system. Paoletti and Fele (2004) remark on the tension between maintaining control and inviting participation (p. 78). According to McHoul (1978), asking a question without inserting a student's name can create 'chaos' (p. 199), and practices such as the raising of hands (as in invitation to bid), pre-allocation or pre-selection have been provided as recommendations for avoiding overlapping turns (Paolette and Fele 2004: 72). With regard to securing an even distribution of participation, Allwright (1980) writes, 'some learners will negotiate for more than their "fair" share, others for "less"' (p. 166). The existing knowledge of the institutional context with regard to turn-taking in the classroom then constitutes an important backdrop against which my analysis of teacher practices to widen participation frameworks may be understood and appreciated.

With regard to its specific situational context, this study was conducted at a Community English Programme (CEP) in a major city on the east coast of the United States. As a lab school for an MA TESOL programme within a major graduate school of education, CEP serves the adult immigrant and international population in the neighbourhood surrounding the university by offering three levels of ESL classes: beginning, intermediate and advanced. The two classes (Class 1 and Class 2), drawn from a larger collection of videotaped interactions at the CEP, are both at the advanced level and taught by two native-speakers of English with over 10 and 14 years of teaching experiences, respectively. The classes met regularly three days per week with a 2-hour session on each day. A total of 20 students from a wide variety of first language backgrounds, including Chinese, Danish, French, Georgian, Italian, Japanese, Korean, Persian, Polish, Portuguese, Russian, Serbian-Croatian and Spanish were enrolled.

6 Data

The data for Class 1 were collected in Fall 2005 and those for Class 2 in Spring 2009. For Class 1, I conducted the videotaping by placing a camera (Canon ZR 100) at a position that maximized the view of the classroom. At the same time, I adjusted the tripod handle and sometimes moved the entire tripod to capture different frames of interaction. Because I was not focusing on any particular practice at the time of the videotaping, my camera angle was essentially guided by my intuitive behaviour as an observer in the classroom. In other words, my 'electronic' eye very much replicated my naked eye. This means that I was not able to gather consistent data on gaze, gesture or bodily stance, which certainly constitutes a limitation to my analysis. A research assistant then transferred the video cassette tapes into Quicktime files using iMovie. For Class 2, a flip video camera was set up by the teacher himself at the beginning of each class in various locations depending on the room situation of the day. No additional camera person was present throughout the data collection. The digital video clips from each class session were then transferred into the computer instantly as Quicktime files for subsequent transcription and analysis. In the end, the baseline data set for this study includes a total of 6 hours of videotaped classroom interaction with 1 session from Class 1 and two sessions from Class 2. The videos were fully transcribed using a modified version of the system developed by Gail Jefferson (see Appendix). The modifications are made to accommodate the specific features of the classroom (e.g. 'BB' for 'board') and to specify the co-occurrence of verbal and nonverbal conduct (Waring 2008). All the names in the extracts below are pseudonyms.

7 Analysis

As will be shown in the ensuing analysis, two specific practices constitute useful resources for broadening the participation frameworks during whole-class interactions:

(1) bypass the first respondent and (2) select an alternative category. In the extracts below, the original line numbers from the full transcripts are maintained.

Bypass the first respondent

I use 'bypass' to capture the teacher's conduct of not selecting the first respondent as the next speaker. In most cases, this involves directing the follow-up question to parties other than the first respondent while offering the latter minimal or no acknowledgement. The responses that are bypassed manifest various degrees of adequacy, and the teacher may ask the follow-up question to simply seek further information, pursue extension to an insufficient response or challenge a prior answer. In the following segment, the teacher is leading a discussion on why a particular joke is funny. In line 57, he initiates a question that introduces the word 'incongruity' (lines 57–8):

(1) Class 1 incongruity

```
57   T:           Okay:, (0.6) So:, how- how is this an example o:f
58                incongruity.-((to class))
59                (0.8)
60   T:           According to- (.) >according to what we heard in
61                the introduction [(there's) incongruity.     ]
62   Stacy:                        [Very unexpected ending.]
63                (0.6)-((T looks to Stacy))
64   T:      →    ((points to Stacy but looks toward rest of class)) so
65                what's the expected ending.
67   Stacy:       That- (0.2)
68   Angie:       °It was silly ending. Yeah. ((T gestures 'come here'
69                motion with hand)) It was unusual.°
```

After a (0.8) second gap where no one responds, the teacher offers a clue by directing the learners' attention to the introduction to the joke in the textbook. Stacy's delayed response 'very unexpected ending' in line 62 is produced interruptively. Although the teacher immediately turns to Stacy upon his turn completion, his follow-up question is notably directly away from Stacy to the class. By pointing his finger at Stacy at the same time, however, he acknowledges the relevance of the latter's contribution. In line 67, Stacy starts but stops, and soon thereafter, we hear Angie's attempt (line 68–9). In this case, the teacher implicitly acknowledges and accepts the first respondent Stacy's contribution by building his next question as seeking a specification of that contribution. Meanwhile, by not yielding the floor to the first respondent but seeking the follow-up specification from the class, he is able to keep the opportunity space open for others to join in, and as can be seen, Angie does indeed.

In the next segment, the teacher also seeks specification of the initial response, but in this case, treats that response as somewhat insufficient. The class is engaging in a discussion on the pros and cons of visiting New York City. In lines 507–8, the teacher checks the class' understanding of 'pros' and 'cons'. The yes-no question is structured in such a way that elicits claims, but not necessarily displays, of understanding:

(2) Class 2 pros and cons

```
507   T:              ((lines omitted)) {(4.6)-((writes "Pros"' and
508                   'Cons' on BB))} Does everyone know what the:se are.
509   Sato:           {°Yeah.°-((T looks to Sato and away))} and ((T scans
510                   class))
511   T:        →     Pro:::s, and cons. What's a pro?
512   LL:             [(((many LL say words at once))]
513   Rodrigo:        [        Advantage.              ]
514   T:              Advantage, o:::r, ((writes "P__/" before "Pros")) what's
515                   another wo:rd with a P-((to class))
```

What Sato offers in *sotto voce* in line 509 is precisely such a claim. Meanwhile, note that the teacher briefly looks to Sato's direction but immediately shifts his gaze to the rest of the class, thereby in part treating one person's response to his understanding-check question as insufficient. He then repeats 'pros and cons' and proceeds to seek a *display* of understanding with regard to 'pro', not from Sato, but from the rest of the class, after which multiple voices arise in lines 511–12. Thus, by seeking a follow-up display of understanding not from the first respondent, but from the class, the teacher is able to keep the participation framework open to a wider range of potential respondents.

Observe another case where the teacher does *bypassing* not once, but twice, to keep the participation framework open. In this case, the teacher's follow-up question constitutes an implicit challenge to the prior answer. The task for the class is to make sentences with the 'not as . . . as . . .' structure using ten adjectives (e.g. 'various', 'spicy'). In lines 62–3, the teacher asks if everyone agrees with Cindy's statement 'English food is not as various as Italian food':

(3) Class 2 English food

```
60    Cindy:          u::h (.) English food is not as various as Italian food.
61                    (0.2)
62    T:              ((lifts head up once and looks back at BB)) >does
63                    everyone agr↑ee.<
64                    (0.2)
65    Sato:           yeah.
66    L:              °mm hm°
67    T         →     >has anyone< ha:d English food. ((raises right hand))
68    Miyako:         ((raises hand))
69                    (0.5)-((both T and M with raised hand and T sees M))
70    T:        →     what is [tr a d i t i o n a l] (.) English]-
```

71	Miyako:	[((*withdraws hand*))]
72	Yoshi:	[what is it.] huh huh huh]
73	T:	>G↑ood.< Good question. What is English food.
74	Miyako:	fish and chips.
75	T:	y(hh)es. Y(h)es.-((*nods*))
76	L:	( )
77	T:	*pu*dding.
78	Robin:	Steaks.
79	T:	St(h)eaks. Y(h)es. Yes. okay? Okay?
80		>so yeh< ((*continues*))

In response to the teacher's solicitation, Sato utters a 'yeah' after a (0.2) second gap, which is followed by another learner's 'mm hm' rather than any uptake from the teacher. In line 67, without acknowledging either response, the teacher proceeds to address his next question to the class with an invitation to bid (see raised hand) (Mehan 1979), essentially querying whether there is sufficient experiential basis among the learners for making the relevant judgement about English food. In so doing, he implicitly treats either 'yeah' or 'mm hm' as potentially problematic. More specifically, by placing the stress on 'had', he appears to be calling into question the students' ability to make a judgement about 'English food'. In line 68, Miyako promptly responds with a raised hand, thus indicating a 'yes' response that claims epistemic access to the subject at hand. Despite the fact that the two establish eye contact, the teacher in line 70 offers no acknowledgement but continues to address the class with yet another question, and this time a *wh-* one which specifies the general category 'English food' into 'traditional English food'. Thus, the teacher bypasses two opportunities to acknowledge the earlier respondents and close the sequence, first in line 66 and then in line 69. In both cases, rather than shifting his attention towards the individual who has or claims to have the answer, he preserves the participation framework in which the entire class remains the addressed recipient of his subsequent questions, and in so doing, widens the potentials for possible self-selectors. As can be seen, others join in the discussion (lines 75 and 77) after Miyako, who would not have gotten a chance to speak had the teacher accepted Sato's answer in line 66 and closed the sequence.

So far, we have considered cases where the teacher directs follow-up questions away from the first respondents to the rest of the class, where the first response may be minimally registered with nonverbal conduct or not at all, and in so doing, maintains an open participation framework. The endeavour does not always succeed, however. In the segment below, the teacher initiates the topic on possessives, asking the class whether this is a new item for them (lines 05–08). As it becomes clearer later, he seems to think that possessives are too easy to be included as advanced-level materials:

(4) Class 1 possessive

| 05 | T: | >IF YOU LOOK at page one-hundred forty ni:ne< |
| 06 | | we see that there is possessive "s." |

```
07                  (0.4)
08    T:            Have you: studied this before,=
09    Stacy:        =Yes.
10    L1:           [°(Yeah)°   ]
11    L2:           [°Mhm°      ]
12    T:      →     [How lo:ng] ago.-((to class))
13                  (0.5)
13    Stacy:        °not-°-((looks down to book))=
14    T:      →     =((shifts gaze to Stacy and back to class))
15                  ((to class))- <or wh- when was the first time that you
16                  sa:w a possessive "s."
17                  (0.6)
18    T:            In a- in an English class.
19    Stacy:        In seventh gra:de.
20    T:            (So) seventh grade,
21    Stacy:        °(Yes.)°
22    T:            Angie has it been a while?
```

'Have you studied this before' (line 08) is a yes-no question designed to seek a 'yes' response, which Stacy offers without a hitch in line 09 followed by similar responses by two other students in *sotto voce*. Note that the teacher offers no acknowledgement of these responses either verbally or nonverbally (no gesture or gaze as observed in the prior two extracts). Instead, he implicitly accepts these responses by addressing the entire class, not these particular students, with the follow-up question 'How long ago?' (line 12). After a brief gap, there is a brief but aborted response from Stacy that briefly draws the teacher's gaze, which is immediately shifted back to the class. In line 15, the teacher rushes to launch his reformulated question that seeks specification of the original 'how long', again addressing the question to the class. By twice not yielding to Stacy the first respondent then, the teacher keeps the participation framework open to the entire class with his continuing questioning. Still, no one volunteers, and Stacy speaks again in line 19. As shown, just because the teacher strives for a broader participation framework does not mean he always succeeds in doing so.

The final case for this section is slightly different from those considered so far on two accounts. First, the initial response is not simply insufficient, but clearly incorrect. Second, bypassing is not done via directing a follow-up question elsewhere. Rather, the teacher simply waits to select a different student to answer the same question. In lines 663–5, the teacher solicits the class' input on why the sentence in line 666 may sound wrong:

(5) Class 2 adjective instead of noun

```
663    T:            Mm, >it doesn't sound right. What-< what sounds
664                  wrong.
```

665			(0.4)-((*scans class*))
666			New York has <u>so</u> amazing <u>a</u>rchitecture tha::t,
667			(0.6)
668	Sato:		So <u>ma</u>ny.
669			(7.0)-((*T not looking to Sato but continues to scan class;*
670			*several students talking quietly, hard to hear*))
671	T:	→	Ah, <u>Miya</u>ko just came <u>u</u>p with something. Go ahead
672			Miyako.
673	Miyako:		After the (.) <u>so</u>, (you)/(we) should put the: (.)
674			adjective, instead of noun.
675	T:		Aa:h. {((*writes "so+<u>adj</u>" on BB*))- So (.) plus (0.4)}
676			<u>a</u>djective o:nly. {((*writes "+that"*))- Plus (.) th<u>a</u>t.}
677			But <u>Miya</u>:yo, how do I <u>u::s</u>e this. So whaddu I d<u>o</u>.
678	Miyako:		Umm, (6.0) umm, (0.4) So: architectu:re,

In line 668, after a very brief gap, Sato offers 'So many' as a candidate replacement for 'so amazing'. The correction is a problematic one given the combination of 'many' with the uncountable noun 'architecture'. Rather than working on this formulation, however, the teacher offers no acknowledgement either verbally or nonverbally despite the fact that Sato is clearly within his view. A long (7.0) second gap follows as the teacher continues to scan the class. In line 671, he does a noticing that leads to the selection of Miyako as the next speaker, who offers a correction (lines 673–4), which is then partially accepted by the teacher with a slight, but important, modification, adding 'only' with emphasis. He then explicitly solicits advice from Miyako on how this general principle may be applied to the specific case of 'architecture' (line 677). In this extract, the teacher withholds offering any uptake of the first respondent's undesirable contribution, lets pass a long 'wait time', and selects another learner to respond to his original question.

In sum, the teacher may bypass the first response by directing a follow-up question away from the first respondent. He may also do so by selecting someone else after some wait time. By not yielding the floor to the first or earlier respondents as such, the teacher manages, not always successfully, to maintain a broad participation framework.

Select an alternative category

Another practice for broadening participation involves selecting a category of speakers that excludes those who have spoken so far. In my data, such categories may be cultural or spatial. Unlike *bypass the first respondent*, which is deployed *within* a sequence that typically involves a post-expansion (Schegloff 2007a) beyond the base adjacency pair in the form of a follow-up question, *select an alternative category* is typically done at the beginning of a new sequence. In the following segment, the class is discussing the culturally specific nature of humour. In response to the teacher's elicitation in lines

11–12, Stacy self-selects to assert the differences between American and Danish humour (lines 16–17), which leads to a long sequence on the topic (not shown here):

(6) Class 1 Japanese humour

11	T:	Can you- Can you feel any big differences betwee:n
12		(.) say- (.) Am- American humour or English
13		humour?- ((*to class*))
14	Stacy:	Yeah.
15	Daisy:	Mhm.
16	Stacy:	Well not- (0.2) I- I can feel it from Danish humour
17		°to° (.) to American.
18	T:	Yeah?
((*lines omitted*))		
19	Stacy:	I think that's (0.2) you have to be careful with.
20		°with that.°
21	T:	Okay. A'right, (0.2) ((*to Naomi and Mo*))-
22	→	Wha- What about- What about Japanese
23		humour.=Uh (.) Can y- Can you say anything about
24		(0.2) differences between a (0.4)}
25	Mo:	I don't know the difference.=But (0.2) ↑there is a
26		cartoon <South (.) Park,>
27	T:	[Uh huh.]
28	L:	[(Mhm.)]
29	Mo:	I think <u>that's</u> (0.2) >American Joke in there< (0.2)
30		<u>that</u>'s not (.) um fo:r (.) someone li- (.) Japanese.
31	T:	Rea:lly.
32	Mo:	Yea:h. >Because it's< too black.

In line 21, the teacher receipts Stacy's talk so far with a minimal acknowledgement and addresses his next question to Japanese humour, and in so doing, implicitly specifies the eligibility for potential next speakers (Lerner 2003) that effectively excludes Stacy who has been occupying the floor so far. More specifically, the selection targets an alternative category of respondents *vis-à-vis* the ones that have spoken so far, thereby widening the participation framework.

In the next segment, the teacher initiates a discussion on why English is difficult. The adverbial 'to everyone' specifies the entire class as the addressee, and both Kara (Polish and German speaker) and Cindy (Georgian and Russian speaker) volunteered their thoughts, and in particular, Kara in her account invokes the notion of English being an Indo-European language (not shown here):

(7) Class 2 why is English difficult

| 01 | T: | Okay question number one to everyone. |
| 02 | | Question number one. ↑Why is English difficult? |

```
((lines omitted))
20    Kara:              [So::, (0.5)
21                       I need to adjust (.) different for uh: feel this
22                       language.
23    T:     →           .hhhh Okay now what about people who do not
24                       have Indo European backgrounds. Especially the
25                       Asian students >and some of the other students
26                       here.< ↑How is it for English.=why is English
27                       difficult for you.
28                       (0.7)
29    L3:               (    and grammar is different?      )
30    T:                mm hm?-((nods)) mm hm okay.
31    L3:               (                              )
32    T:                Okay, okay. Very true, very true, very true,
33                      ((gestures go-ahead to L in the back))
```

In line 23, the teacher begins with a big inbreath that foreshadows a multi-unit turn, where he initiates a sequence that potentially selects students with non-Indo-European (non-IE) language backgrounds as the next speakers. He then further specifies that category by singling out 'Asian students' although the rushed addition 'some of the other students here' subsequently relaxes the criterion for eligible next speakers. Two more students responded, presumably of Asian backgrounds. What the teacher does in lines 23–5 then is engaging in a current-selects-next technique that targets an alternative category *vis-à-vis* those who have spoken so far, and in so doing, widens the possibilities for potential next speakers.

Finally, the alternative category need not be ethnicity-based. In the next segment, in keeping with the 'why English is so difficult' theme, the class has been working on a task that involves figuring out the pronunciation and vocabulary in a list of five sentences, an example of which is 'The bandage is wound around the wound'. As the segment begins, the class has just finished discussing the third sentence (lines 1–3):

(8) Class 2 this side over here

```
01    T:                So, the farm was used (.) to: produ:ce (0.2) produce.
02                      (1.0)
03                      {((to Sato))-°or fruits.°} Ok↑ay.
04                      (0.5)
05    T:     →          >Let's get someone< fro:m (0.5)
06                      ((gestures to left))-°this side over here. =to do
07                      number three.°
08                      (0.8)-((T mild sweeping gesture))
09                      Who's brave.=over here to do number three.
10                      Robin, you wanna try?
```

```
11   LL:        heh heh [heh
12   Robin:           [well-
13   T:               [Go ahea[d.]
14   Robin:               [can] I- can I do the number four?
15   LL:          [heh hhe heh heh hahahahhahahhaha hahh]
16   T:           [You wanna do number four? hahhahahha   ]
17                I'll let you do number four then.=
18                okay, [okay.]
19   Robin:             [thank] you.
```

After a brief gap, the teacher in line 05 turns to treat those on his left side as potential next speakers. The criterion for selection appears to be geography here (i.e. 'this side' vs. 'that side') as the teacher selects a side of the room alternative to the side that has been heard so far. Without securing any volunteers in lines 08–09, where he does a nonverbal 'this side' gesture as well as an invitation for the 'brave' one, the teacher proceeds to select Robin as the next speaker. In line 12, Robin responds to the invitation with a disaffiliative 'well' and requests a different item. Thus, in this extract, using 'geography' as a resource, the teacher widens the participation framework by selecting those from a different side of the room as potential next speakers.

Thus, the teacher may broaden participation by selecting a category of speakers whose voices have not yet been heard. One might argue that the action of broadening participation is accomplished in part by what is referred to in membership categorization analysis as 'going categorical' (Stokoe 2012). In the above cases, this is done after a brief 'okay' acknowledgement of the talk produced by those who have spoken so far, and the selection is implemented at the beginning of a new sequence either implicitly (e.g. 'Japanese humor') or explicitly ('Let's hear someone from X'.).

8 Findings

In this paper, I have shown how two teachers manage to broaden learner participation by (1) bypassing the first respondent or by (2) selecting an alternative category of speakers. In the first case, the teachers refrain from yielding to the first respondent, whose response may be subsequently treated as warranting further specifications or somehow less than desirable. The bypassing is done by directing follow-up questions to parties other than the first respondents or waiting to select a different learner after a period of silence. Importantly, rather than offering an explicit acknowledgement of the first response and potentially yielding the floor to that person, the teacher continues to treat the entire class as the addressed recipient (Goffman 1981), and in so doing, preserves the relevance of a yet-to-be-produced answer – from others in the room. In the meantime, it is important to note that the first or earlier self-selector does sometimes receive implicit acknowledgement via gaze or gestures or by virtue of the fact that teacher's next question is built upon his/her response. The particular teacher conduct of bypassing the first respondent resonates with Sahlstrom's (2002) finding that '"first" hand-raises in relation to teacher questions do not get allocated public turns at talk, . . . By selecting "lasts" as next speakers, the teacher can reward late hand-raisers with turns – and thus increase participation from the students' (p. 54). In the second case, the teachers implicitly or explicitly select an alternative category of speakers *vis-à-vis* those who have spoken so far. Such categories in my data have been cultural or spatial although it is conceivable that other 'alternative' categories would work in very similar ways. We might recall explicit remarks from our own experiences such as 'Let's hear from those who haven't spoken yet', where 'those who haven't spoken' is a category in itself. While *bypass the first respondent* is deployed typically as post-expansions within an ongoing sequence, *select an alternative category* finds its sequential position in the beginning of a new sequence. In both cases, the practices involve moving away from particular individuals or groups who have been speaking so far. So in a sense, these practices are in part mechanisms for curtailing the participation of those who are negotiating more than a fair share of the floor.

9 Discussion and conclusion

By detailing how the teachers manage the selection of the next speakers in question-answer sequences, findings of this study contribute to our growing understanding of classroom as an institutional context. While Mehan's (1979) useful framework (i.e. invitation to reply, invitation to bid, and individual nomination) focuses on the *how* of current-select-next in classroom turn-allocation, the practices identified in the study bring into sharp relief the issue of *who (not) to select* as a poignant interactional and pedagogical issue for the teacher at any given moment. Insofar as the choice of 'who' directly impacts the participation structure (and by extension, learning opportunities) in the classroom, it should constitute a critical element in teachers' pedagogical decisions. What the above analysis shows is precisely how the problem of who to select can be interactionally managed in such a way that inclusiveness is achieved or at least attempted. Since securing even participation is a vital part of teachers' practical concerns, findings of this study provide some much needed specifications of how such problems have been and can be managed, which also form an empirical basis for exploring alternatives and devising innovative solutions.

While the sequential context for each utterance constitutes a decisive resource that helps me arrive at the above findings, the institutional context of a classroom makes it possible for such findings to be understood and appreciated with greater depth. Without the knowledge that achieving even participation or maximizing participation is a coveted goal in communicative language teaching, the teachers' conduct to bypass a first self-selector may seem peculiar or even callous. Moreover, recognizing the ingenuity of such conduct is also contingent upon the contextual knowledge that managing students who dominate the floor is a practical concern for classroom teachers. The reader may have noticed that the extracts presented above frequently involve Stacy in one class and Sato in another. Both are the 'talkative' participants in their respective classes. In other words, by widening the participation framework, the teachers are also doing the job of managing the dominant students. Put otherwise, because of the shared history with these students, the teachers may be (un)wittingly directing their attention to those students who don't participate. Alternatively, one may observe that part of the teachers' practices involves allowing the more talkative students to respond first. Finally, the very fact that I as the analyst associate the practices of *bypass the first self-selector* and *select an alternative category* to issues of participation is inextricably linked to my familiarity with the classroom context as a language teacher and an applied linguist.

Acknowledgements

I would like to thank John Flowerdew for inviting me to contribute to this important volume on discourse and context. I am also grateful to the two anonymous reviewers for their insights and suggestions. Finally, thank you to Di Yu for helping me shape this manuscript into its required format promptly and meticulously.

Appendix: CA transcription notations

(.)	untimed perceptible pause within a turn
underline	stress
CAPS	very emphatic stress
↑	high pitch on word
.	sentence-final falling intonation
?	yes/no question rising intonation
,	phrase-final intonation (more to come)
-	a glottal stop, or abrupt cutting off of sound
:	lengthened vowel sound (extra colons indicate greater lengthening)
=	latch
→	highlights point of analysis
[]	overlapped talk
°soft°	spoken softly/decreased volume
> <	increased speed
(words)	uncertain transcription
(syl syl)	number of syllables in uncertain transcription
.hhh	inbreath
Hhh	outbreath

$words$	spoken in a smiley voice
((*words*))	comments on background, skipped talk or nonverbal behaviour
{((*words*))-words}	dash to indicate co-occurrence of nonverbal behaviour and verbal elements; curly brackets to mark the beginning and ending of such co-occurrence if necessary.
BB	board
T	teacher
L	unidentified learner
LL	learners

References

Allwright, T. (1980), 'Turns, topics, and tasks: Patterns of participation in language learning and teaching', in D. Larsen-Freeman (ed.), *Discourse analysis in second language research*. Rowley, MA: Newbury House Publishers, Inc, pp. 165–87.

Clayman, S. E. and Gill, V. T. (2004), 'Conversation Analysis', in A. Bryman and M. Hardy (eds), *Handbook of data analysis*. London: Sage Publications, pp. 589–606.

Drew, P. and Heritage, J. (1992), 'Analyzing talk at work: an introduction', in P. Drew and J. Heritage (eds), *Talk at work: Interaction in institutional settings*. Cambridge: Cambridge University Press, pp. 3–65.

Garfinkel, H. (1967), *Studies in Ethnomethodology*. Englewood Cliffs, NJ: Prentice-Hall.

Goffman, E. (1967), *Interactional Ritual*. New York: Anchor Books.

—(1981), *Forms of Talk*. Philadelphia: University of Pennsylvania Press.

Heritage, J. (1984), *Garfinkel and Ethnomethodology*. Oxford: Basil Blackwell.

—(2008), 'Conversation analysis as social theory', in B. Turner (ed.), *The new Blackwell companion to social theory*. Oxford: Blackwell, pp. 300–20.

Heritage, J. and Clayman, S. (2010), *Talk in Action: Interactions, Identities, and Institutions*. Malden, MA: Wiley-Blackwell.

Kasper, G. and Wagner, J. (2011), 'A conversation analytic approach to second language acquisition', in D. Atkinson (eds), *Alternative approaches to second language acquisition*. New York: Routledge, pp. 117–42.

Koshik, I. (2005), 'Alternative questions used in conversational repair'. *Discourse Studies*, 7(2), 193–211.

Lerner, G. H. (1993), 'Collectivities in action: Establishing the relevance of conjoined participation in conversation'. *Text*, 13(2), 213–45.

McCollum, P. (1989), 'Turn-allocation in lessons with north American and Puerto Rican students: a comparative study'. *Anthropology & Education Quarterly*, 20(2), 133–56.

McHoul, A. W. (1978), 'The organization of turns at formal talk in the classroom'. *Language in Society*, 7, 183–213.

McHoul, A., Rapley, M., and Antaki, C. (2008), 'You gotta light? On the luxury of context for understanding talk in interaction'. *Journal of Pragmatics*, 40, 827–39.

Markee, N. (1995), 'Teachers' answers to students' questions: Problematizing the issue of making meaning'. *Issues in Applied Linguistics*, 6(2), 63–92.

Maynard, D. W. (2003), *Bad News, Good News: Conversational Order in Everyday Talk and Clinical Settings*. Chicago: University of Chicago Press.

Mehan, H. (1979), *Learning Lessons: Social Organization in the Classroom*. Cambridge, MA: Harvard University Press.

Mohr, K. A. J. and Mohr, E. S. (2007), 'Extending English language learners' classroom interactions using the response protocol'. *The Reading Teacher*, 60(5), 440–50.

Mortensen, K. (2008), 'Selecting next-speaker in the second language classroom: How to find a willing next-speaker in planned activities', *Journal of Applied Linguistics*, 5(1), 55–79.

Paoletti, I., and Fele, G. (2004), 'Order and disorder in the classroom'. *Journal of Pragmatics*, 14(1), 69–85.

Philips, S. U. (1972), 'Participant structures and communicative competence: Warm Springs children in community and classroom', in C. B. Cazden et al. (eds), *Functions of language in the classroom*. New York: Teachers College Press, pp. 370–94.

Pomerantz, A. (1990), 'On the validity and generalizability of conversation analytic methods: Conversation analytic claims'. *Communication Monographs*, 57(3), 231–5.

Poole, T. (2005), 'Cross-cultural variation in classroom turn taking practices', in P. Bruthiaux (ed.), *Directions in applied linguistics*. Clevedon, UK: Multilingual Matters, pp. 201–19.

Psathas, G. (1990), 'Introduction: methodological issues and recent developments in the study of naturally occurring interaction', in G. Psathas (ed.), *Interaction Competence*. Washington, DC: University Press of America, pp. 1–29.

Sacks, H., Schegloff, E. A., and Jefferson, G. (1974), 'A simplest systematics for the organization of turn-taking for conversation'. *Language*, 50(4), 696–735.

Sahlstrom, J. F. (2002), 'The interactional organization of hand raising in classroom interaction'. *Journal of Classroom Interaction*, 37(2), 47–57.

Schegloff, E. A. (1987a), 'Analyzing single episodes of interaction: An exercise in conversation analysis'. *Social Psychology Quarterly*, 50(2), 101–14.

—(1987b), 'Between macro and micro: Contexts and other connections', in J. Alexander, B. Giessen, R. Munch, and N. Smelser (eds), *The macro-micro link*. Berkeley and Los Angeles: University of California Press, pp. 207–34.

—(1997), 'Practices and actions: Boundary cases of other-initiated repair'. *Discourse Processes*, 23, 499–545.

—(2007a), *Sequence Organization in Interaction*. Cambridge: Cambridge University Press.

—(2007b), 'A tutorial on membership categorization'. *Journal of Pragmatics*, 39, 462–82.

Schegloff, E. A. and Sacks, H. (1973), 'Opening up closings'. *Semiotica*, 7, 289–327.

Schultz, J., Florio, S., and Erickson, F. (1982), 'Where's the floor?: Aspects of the cultural organization of social relationships in communication at home and at school', in Gilmore and Glatlhorn (eds), *Ethnography and education: Children in and out of school*. Washington, DC: Center for Applied Linguistics, pp. 88–123.

Stokoe, E. (2012), 'Moving forward with membership categorization analysis: Methods for systematic analysis'. *Discourse Studies*, 14(3), 277–303.

Svennevig, J. (2001), 'Abduction as a methodological approach to the study of spoken interaction'. *Norskrift*, 103, 1–22.

ten Have, P. (2007), *Doing Conversation Analysis* (2nd edn). Thousand Oaks, CA: Sage Publications.

Van Dijk, T. A. (2009), *Society and Discourse: How Context Controls Text and Talk*. Cambridge: Cambridge University Press.

Van Lier, L. (1988), *The Classroom and the Language Learner*. London: Longman.

Waring, H. Z. (2008), 'Using explicit positive assessment in the language classroom: IRF, feedback, and learning opportunities'. *The Modern Language Journal*, 92(4), 577–94.

—(2009), 'Moving out of IRF: A single case analysis'. *Language Learning*, 59(4), 796–824.

—(2012a), 'Doing disaffiliation with now-prefaced utterances'. *Language and Communication*, 32(3), 265–75.

—(2012b), '"Any questions?:" Investigating understanding-checks in the language classroom'. *TESOL Quarterly*, 46(4), 722–52.

Waring, H. Z., Creider, S., Tarpey, T., and Black, R. (2012), 'Understanding the specificity of CA and context'. *Discourse Studies*, 14(4), 477–92.

Waring, H. Z. and Hruska, B. (2011), 'Getting and keeping Nora on board: A novice elementary ESOL student teacher's practices for lesson engagement'. *Linguistics and Education*, 22, 441–55.

—(2012), 'Problematic directives in pedagogical interaction'. *Linguistics and Education*, 23, 289–300.

Wong, J. and Waring, H. Z. (2010), *Conversation Analysis and Second Language Pedagogy: A Guide for ESL/EFL Teachers*. New York: Routledge.

Xie, X. (2011), 'Turn allocation patterns and learning opportunities'. *The ELT Journal*, 65(3), 240–50.

Young, R. F. and Miller, E. R. (2004), 'Learning as changing participation: Discourse roles in ESL writing conferences'. *The Modern Language Journal*, 88(4), 519–35.

15

Political discourse analysis – Distinguishing frontstage and backstage contexts. A discourse-historical approach

Ruth Wodak

"[the utterance itself] becomes only intelligible when it is placed within its context of situation . . . which indicates on the one hand that the concept of context has to be broadened and on the other that the situation in which words are uttered can never be passed over as irrelevant to the linguistic expression. . . . ".

(MALINOWSKI 1923: 206)

"Verbal communication can never be understood and explained outside of . . . connection with a concrete situation. . . . Language acquires life and historically evolves . . . in concrete verbal communication and not in abstract linguistic system of language forms, nor in the individual psyche of speakers".

(VOLOSINOV 1973: 95)

1 Introduction: Discourse and/about politics

The philosophical approaches of Aristotle and Machiavelli can be regarded as the two main roots for the meanings of *politics* used in the domain of 'language and politics' (see Holly 1990, 2008; Chilton 2004; Wodak 2011a): emphasizing ethics and morals, on the one hand; or violence, power and hegemony, on the other. The Aristotelian goal to discover the best form of government is thus linked to values for a given society: what is believed to be 'good' or 'bad'. The definition of values always depends on the *specific sociopolitical and historical context* and the political system of governance: for example, what might have been 'good' for a totalitarian state like Nazi Germany was certainly experienced as 'bad' for democratic systems. On the other hand, we encounter the second ideological position endorsing 'the dark view of political power'. All politics is necessarily driven by a quest for power, but the exertion of power is inherently unpredictable, irresponsible, irrational and pervasive. This view has been articulated most prominently by Michel Foucault (Foucault and Rabinow 1984), but traces and roots can be detected in many authors from Niccolò Machiavelli (Zorn 1972) to Antonio Gramsci (1977) (for more details, see Charteris-Black 2011).

In this chapter, I will mostly explore some aspects of political communication in context and more specifically of *doing politics in context*. I present and extend selected results from my research on politics on frontstage and backstage while drawing on extensive fieldwork conducted in European Union (EU) organizations in recent years (1996, 2002/3 and 2008/9) (see Muntigl et al. 2000; Krzyżanowski and Oberhuber 2007; Wodak 2011a; Wodak et al. 2012 for more details). Before first summarizing recent directions of research into political communication, I briefly point to salient issues which currently determine the field of 'language and/in politics' and which have also influenced my research (Wodak 2011b). Of course, I have to limit myself to just a few relevant aspects in this chapter, due to space restrictions.

a How broadly or narrowly should 'political action' (or 'political language behavior') be defined? Do we restrict ourselves to the study of the traditional political genres (like speeches, slogans, debates) or are all everyday actions in some way 'political'?

b What is the role of the political elites? Who determines political issues? What is the role of grass-root movements?

c How do ideologies and belief systems manifest themselves in various genres of political discourse? What is the relationship between media and politics?

d What are the main roles and functions of political discourses? How do power structures relate to decision-making strategies?

e Finally, what are the main settings where political practices take place (*doing politics*)? How do the structures of various organizations and institutions influence political discourses?

There are certainly many more and related questions, like the influence of globalizing processes or the change of political rhetoric and its functions over time (Chilton et al.

2010) or the rise of rightwing and leftwing populist movements in times of crisis (Triandafyllidou et al. 2009; Wodak et al. 2013). When confronting all these questions, it is necessary to contextualize the research, both from a macro-structural point of view and from a micro perspective; that is, when analysing language use in a detailed and systematic way – which is what both Malinowski and Volosinov (and many others) (see quotes above) have already pointed to many decades or even centuries ago. In the following, I briefly summarize some important strands in the study of political communication (see also Hansson 2013).

Language and politics have been studied from the perspectives of a number of disciplines, including political science, journalism and communication studies, sociology, law, economics/management, linguistics, psychology, philosophy, anthropology, and education. Each of these fields and approaches tends to presuppose certain sets of theoretical and methodological points of departure which may not always be compatible or easily comparable with others. However, there seems to be a consensus among most scholars that research on political communication generally requires some kind of inter- or transdisciplinary approach. Some approaches to political communication can thus be labelled *source-centred* (if they focus on politicians' strategic actions as information sources), *message-centred* (if the focus is on language use in the manifold genres of political text, talk and images), *media-centred* (if mainly interested in the practices of media professionals as transmitters of political information) or *audience/citizen-centred* (focusing on how citizens participate in political communication) (see Hansson 2013 for an extensive overview and discussion). Scholars who adopt a source-centred approach focus on the communicative behaviour of powerful groups and individuals in society: the rulers, the political elites. For example, McNair (2003) emphasises his interest in how the actions of politicians and journalists influence media content and focuses "on the nature of the interface between politicians and the media, the extent of their interaction, and the dialectic of their relationship." (p. xv).

Many studies illustrate how politicians use numerous strategies and techniques to get public attention, present themselves in a positive light and their adversaries in a negative light, convince audiences to support certain policy programmes and so forth. These activities are labelled in manifold ways, such as political public relations, strategic communication, political propaganda, political media management, political marketing (Henneberg et al. 2009), political (or party) branding, 'spin' or 'spin doctoring' (Hood 2011), image-making and mass self-communication (Castells 2009) and so forth. Moreover, we observe an increase in the 'mediatisation of politics' – a process by which politics (and society in general) becomes more and more dependent on the media (Strömbäck 2008) which contributes to the increasing professionalization of political communication. Importantly, as Hansson (2013: 4) claims, public officeholders' communication is influenced by their preoccupation with individual blame avoidance (Hood 2011), the perceived risk of mediated scandal (Allern and Pollak 2012) and constant concern with their organizational reputation (Carpenter and Krause 2012).

Reisigl (2008a, b) proposes a transdisciplinary, so-called *politolinguistic approach* that combines rhetoric, political science and discourse analysis; he suggests differentiating between a variety of 'fields of political action' (e.g. the lawmaking procedure, the organization of international relations, and political advertising) and subgenres (e.g. parliamentary debate speech, inaugural address, and election speech) (Jarren et al. 1998). Many scholars working within critical discourse studies have developed essential tools for the systematic and detailed analysis of political text and talk. For example, they have investigated how racism, antisemitism, ethnicism and right-wing populism are reflected in text, talk and visuals (Reisigl and Wodak 2001; Krzyżanowski and Wodak 2009; Wodak and Richardson 2013; Wodak et al. 2013) and have traced the discursive construction of history and national identity (Flowerdew 2012; Heer et al. 2008; De Cillia and Wodak 2009). This discourse-centred research also includes the following:

- Studies of political metaphor and discursive framing in persuasive political text and talk (Charteris-Black 2011; Lakoff 2008);

- Cognitive and evolutionary linguistic analyses of political discourse with a focus on expressions of spatial, temporal and modal dimensions (Okulska and Cap 2010; Chilton 2004; Cap and Okulska 2013)

- Corpus-assisted and qualitative research of a political party and/or politician (Fairclough 2000; Flowerdew 2012).

- Studies of argumentation in parliamentary debates and government reports (Fairclough and Fairclough 2010; Ilie 2010; Wodak and van Dijk 2000).

2 Goals of the study

In this chapter, it is, of course, impossible to answer all questions and challenges mentioned above. I will thus mainly explore two particular dimensions of political discursive practices in more detail: *politics as usual* on the *backstage* – this implies investigating the daily work of politicians in their respective workplace, that is, national and transnational political institutions, as such accounts are difficult to access and thus rarely documented and analysed; I then juxtapose this analysis briefly with some examples from *frontstage* which has been documented much more thoroughly as political speeches, TV interviews, policy documents and parliamentary debates (to name just a few genres) are widely available and thus usually form the backbone of research into political discourse and communication. This is why I elaborate on some dimensions of our fieldwork in the European Parliament and ethnography of communication below (§ 3). Due to space restrictions, I focus only on some brief vignettes – the time when the agenda for the entire day are negotiated and prepared by Members of the European Parliament (MEPs), together with their assistants, and on some conversations on the corridor (the politics *de couloir*) as well as on extracts from a committee meeting as example from the *frontstage*. At this point, it is important to emphasize that these data have been extensively analysed in Wodak (2011a) – but without elaborating on the impact of the manifold contextual factors and without applying the *Four-Level Model of Context* systematically (see below). The data from the morning provide relevant insight into the logistics and strategies of politicians (MEPS) throughout the particular day as these depend largely on adequate briefing and preparation in the early morning, before the hectic sequence of meetings which characterize the daily agenda in the European Parliament. Hence, many relevant aspects of organizational discourse studies also have to be considered. My main questions are as follows: What do politicians actually *do*? How is the profession of politics organized, apart from scarce impressions which are sometimes accessible to laypeople? And what is the role of the complex and multi-layered structural and situational contexts when *doing politics*? The opacity of *politics as usual* has severe consequences, as Hay (2007) has rightly claimed: disinformation and non-information about the work of politicians might be some of many factors leading to disillusionment and depoliticization – or to what in the European Union is labelled as 'democratic deficit' (see also Abélès 1992; Koller and Wodak 2008; Wodak 2010a, b, 2011a, c).

3 Politics on 'frontstage' and 'backstage': An interdisciplinary, discourse-historical approach to political communication

In this study, I integrate various social theories with critical discourse studies, specifically with the discourse-historical approach (DHA) (Weiss and Wodak 2003a, b). I make use of symbolic interactionism and Goffman's concepts of frontstage and backstage (1959); Bourdieu's theory of *habitus*, social fields and capitals (1991); Lave and Wenger's notion of *community of practice* (1991); various approaches to the construction of individual and collective identities (Wodak et al. 2009 [1999]); and Weber's approach to *legitimacy* and *authority* (2003). These approaches conceptualize different aspects of politicians' everyday performances and activities, and allow analysing their socialization into the rules and conventions of the field of politics and thus the dynamics of acquiring the habitus of a politician.

Developed in the field of *Discourses Studies*, the DHA provides a vehicle for looking at latent power dynamics and the range of potentials in agents, because it integrates and triangulates knowledge about historical, intertextual sources and the background of the social and political fields within which discursive events are embedded (see *Four-Level Context Model* below). Moreover, the DHA distinguishes between three dimensions which constitute textual meanings and structures: the topics which are spoken/written about; the discursive strategies employed; and the linguistic means that are drawn upon to realize both topics and strategies (e.g. argumentative moves, *topoi*, presuppositions [see Wodak 2011a, b; Reisigl 2008 a, b; Reisigl and Wodak 2009 for an extensive discussion]).

Furthermore, two concepts are salient for analysing political events: *Intertextuality* refers to the linkage of all texts to other texts, both in the past and in the present. Such links can be established in different ways: through continued reference to a topic or to its main actors; through reference to the same events as the other texts; or through the reappearance of a texts' main arguments in another text as well as certain syntactic (grammatical) and also rhetorical parallelisms and other tropes. The second important process is labelled *recontextualization*. By taking an argument, a topic, a genre or a discursive practice out of context and restating/realizing it in a new context, we first observe the process of de-contextualization and then, when the respective element is implemented in a new context, of recontextualization. The element then acquires a new meaning, because, as Wittgenstein (1967) has rightly claimed, meanings are formed in use.

Moreover, when analysing political communication, the *performance* (the staging) of the respective event has to be carefully deconstructed and contextualized. Goffman distinguishes between *frontstage* and *backstage*. Frontstage is where the performance takes place and the performers and the audience are present (Goffman 1959: 17). Backstage is where performers are present but the audience is not, and the performers can step out of character without fear of disrupting the performance (Goffman 1959: 112). It is where facts suppressed in the front stage or various kinds of informal actions may appear which are not accessible to outsiders. No members of the audience can or should appear in the backstage; thus, access is controlled by gate keepers. It is, of course, much more difficult to perform once a member of the audience is in the backstage; politicians would not want the audience to see when she or he is practicing a speech or being briefed by an advisor (see Wodak 2011a: 7–11 for an extensive overview of Goffman's approach).

As MEPs, for example, move in, and transgress various collectives during their entire day, the concept of *community of practice* seems adequate to grasp the conventions, rules, traditions, jargon and functions of each group. Specific committees meet on a regular basis and are staffed with a stable number of MEPs. Hence, these committee members create and establish their own history, their intertextual references and their common-ground and knowledge. Each MEP belongs to several such committees, apart from the political party and their group meetings, and possibly also nationally organized meetings. MEPs shift and accommodate their behaviour quite automatically when moving between these various communities of practice (as MEPs have been socialized into these communities of practice by experience). Thus, as will be elaborated below, the European Parliament (EP) cannot be regarded as one big community of practice; rather, this huge organization consists of many communities of practice which all have their own dynamic.

Figure 15.1 (below) provides a heuristic (and thus necessarily crude) summary of the theoretical cornerstones of *Politics as Usual* (adapted from Wodak 2011a: 192).

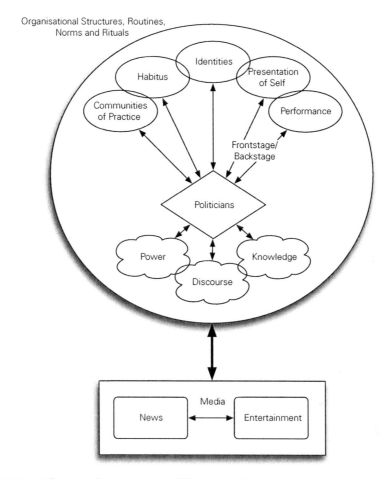

FIGURE 15.1 *Theoretical cornerstones of 'Politics as Usual'.*

4 The salience of context

In this chapter, I focus on the *Four-Level Context Model* of the DHA which has made the systematic analysis of context and its dialectical relationships to meaning-making to one of its priorities.

The DHA enables analysis of the historical (i.e. *intertextual*) dimension of discursive practices by exploring the ways in which particular genres of discourse are subject to change through time, and also by integrating social theories to explain context. Following Foucault (1972), 'historical context' can also mean the history and sub-system of meetings and narratives in an organization or any other institutional or everyday event. Consequently, 'history' can involve studying how language use changes over shorter timescales, for example, during one meeting (over a certain amount of time) or over several meetings, as part of latent and manifest rules and norms that serve to rationalize, explain and make sense of organizational events. Or history can indicate how perceptions of particular events have changed over time due to conflicting narratives and accounts of a specific experience – a phenomenon which can be frequently observed in the discursive construction of national or transnational identities (Heer et al. 2008; Wodak et al. 2009; see also Flowerdew 2012).

Conceptually, the empirical event under investigation is viewed as a phenomenon that has discursive manifestations across four heuristic *levels of context* (Wodak 2011a):

i　the immediate text of the communicative event in question (e.g. a particular detailed transcript of talk);

ii　the intertextual and interdiscursive relationship between utterances, texts, genres and discourses (e.g. other conversations with the same participants in different settings);

iii　the extralinguistic social (e.g. physical gestures, facial expressions, postures, etc.) and environmental (e.g. room size and layout) variables and institutional frames (e.g. latent or formal hierarchical structure, informal power relations in a friendship, cultural constraints and conventions, etc.) of a specific 'context of situation' (derived, for example, from observer notes and reflections on direct observations of the communicative event); and

iv　the broader sociopolitical and historical context which discursive practices are embedded in and related to (e.g. knowledge derived from ethnographic study of the relationships, aspects of the broader social and cultural macro-environment that influence the talk and conversations).

Researching instances on backstage usually requires a different theoretical and methodological approach than frontstage phenomena. In this chapter, I primarily view ethnography as an intricate and complex process that guides research across the four different levels of context presented above. Thus, the definition of ethnography goes beyond its common definition as 'fieldwork' or as just a 'method' or 'data-collection technique' (Hammersley 1992). Instead, the approach taken by Brewer (2000: 11) makes sense, in arguing that 'ethnography is not one particular method of data collection but a style of research that is distinguished by its objectives, which are to understand the social *meaning* and activities of people in a given "field" or setting' (emphasis in the original). Hence, ethnography should be understood as a complex and ordered, though not necessarily linear, research process which informs research. Ethnography is thus analytically mobilized in this research as an overall framework which allows triangulating between a set of stages of analytical research and between different sets of data (genres, publics).

Both the Four-Level Context Model and the *ethnography of communication* imply an abductive and recursive approach in the analysis, proceeding from text and co-text to structure and sociopolitical context. Obviously, the ethnography in organizations draws on the vast experiences of sociolinguistic ethnography of communication. However, research in the tradition of ethnography of communication as developed by Dell Hymes and John Gumperz focused primarily on rigidly stratified speech communities where roles were strictly compartmentalized and associated varieties of language clearly differentiated (Saville-Troike 1982: 87). Of course, organizational contexts are much less distinct and rigid; they are dynamic, role definitions are sometimes blurred and boundaries tend to be frequently redefined. In this way, the tradition and the immediate context of the European Parliament have to be traced systematically and in much detail as well as the space and setting of the specific instances of political communication on frontstage and backstage analysed below. I will come back to these stages in sections 5 and 6 below.

5 'Politics as usual' in the context of the European Parliament (EP)

The *European Parliament* (Europarl or EP) is the only directly elected parliamentary institution of the EU (Ginsberg 2007: 192–9). Together with the Council of the EU, it forms the bicameral legislative branch of the Union's institutions and has been described as one of the most powerful legislatures in the world. The EP and Council form the highest legislative body within the Union. The EP is composed of 785 MEPs, who serve the second largest democratic electorate in the world (after India) and the largest trans-national democratic electorate in the world (375 million eligible voters in 2009) (*structural context*).

Below, I analyse the beginning of a typical day in the life of one MEP who I call Hans. Hans wore a tiny microphone attached to his jacket and a tape recorder in his pocket. He invited us to follow him to meetings inside and outside of the European Parliament, and to sit and observe when he spent time in his tiny office cubicle, preparing, phoning or talking to his personal assistant M or to other visitors and colleagues (*immediate situational context*).

Moreover, he frequently commented on the encounters and explained his behaviour towards other MEPs or elaborated on the statements he had made during a committee meeting. In this way, we gained access to the many latent norms, functions and rules in the various communities of practice, to coded and shared knowledge, and to the otherwise inaccessible subtext of many conversations. To take a typical example, on 20th May 2008, 17 different items, from 6 standing committees (including the Committee on the Environment, Committee on Transport and Tourism, Committee on legal Affairs, and the Committee on Employment and Social Affairs[1]) were discussed and put to motion in the plenary, starting at 9 a.m. and scheduled to end at midnight (*intertextual and interdiscursive context*).

Of course, most MEPs do not primarily spend their days attending plenary debates; they only participate if their own agenda from the committees to which they belong are to be discussed. Otherwise, they have their own schedules which may periodically overlap with the official agenda or run parallel.

The fieldwork was conducted during the enormously hectic and conflictive negotiations about EU-enlargement; that is the access of countries from the former Eastern Bloc in 2004. This *sociopolitical context* is, of course, most influential for the analysis on the micro-level as the struggle for access to the EU and the positioning against such access determines the entire work of MEPs in that period. There were many relevant discussions which also interpenetrated the debates which I briefly illustrate below. Some MEPs were very worried about the conditions for access of the former Communist countries such as the standards of welfare, the creation of trade unions and standardization of working conditions, the freedom of press and the implementation of the Human Rights Charta, and so forth. Most importantly, Social-Democratic and Green MEPs were concerned about the possible costs of EU accession: how much money would have to be spent on raising the economies and the living standards in Eastern Europe in order to reach similar conditions like in the Western countries. In contrast, some national politicians and bureaucrats employed in the Commission defended the opinion that no additional costs would be necessary; these debates were highly political and politicized and manifested quite opposing ideologies and positions (*sociopolitical context, interdiscursive and intertextual relationships*).

6 Data

6.1 *Triangulating data: Interviews, shadowing and participant observation, tape-recording and field notes*

In studying the *performance of politicians*, many MEPs were interviewed about their socialization into the EP, their motives, their daily work routines and their visions for the European Union. Moreover, I shadowed some MEPs throughout their daily life, from morning to evening and tape recorded all instances of talk which occurred.

Hence, we first conducted *28 interviews* with 14 MEPs, all members of the Committee on Employment and Social Affairs, and 10 Commission officials (see Wodak 2011a, for more details of the fieldwork; Gilbert Weiss, Caroline Straehle and Peter Muntigl were part of the team and assisted in the fieldwork and interviewing).

The interviews focused on four general topic areas: although certain topic-related questions were generally included in all interviews, they were structured loosely enough so that interviewees had considerable freedom in developing the topics and steering the conversation as they wished. The main topic groups in the interview protocol, each with several subcategories of possible questions, comprised (1) unemployment, including reasons for, possible solutions to, and perspectives on current employment-related policy making; (2) the role of the EU organization in which the interviewee works, including relationships with other EU bodies, the interviewee´s own role within the organization, and his or her 'access points', or contact with 'ordinary' EU citizens; (3) day-to-day working life, including multicultural issues and the development of documents such as reports, opinions, etc.; and (4) the interviewee's personal history, for example, career development, and definition of *being European*. In this way, it was possible to gather information about the perspectives, ideologies, opinions and the daily experiences of the interviewees.

A further aspect of this study which I primarily focused on examined the rules, norms, routines and constraints that structure MEPs' daily working environment and thus shape the *social order* of the European Parliament. In other words, I investigated the order behind the apparent chaos of the backstage by combining my ethnography of MEPs' daily lives with the analysis of interviews with MEPs and other written and spoken genres.

Of course, for all its valuable insights, it would be wrong to suggest that ethnography (i.e. observation) is *the* methodological path to some kind of 'truth' about the object of analysis, or a window on the 'entire empirical world'. Quite the contrary, as Danermark et al. (2002: 57) rightly argue,

> it is not sufficient to make empirical observations; these very rarely succeed in capturing the underlying mechanisms producing phenomena. . . . Power and other mechanisms may be present and working without us being able to immediately perceive any connection between them and the effects they produce.

When asking Hans if he would mind being shadowed by two researchers, he immediately gave his consent. In this way, Hans was shadowed for several consecutive days, from 8 a.m. till late at night, until the official and semi-official parts of work were over. We wrote extensive field notes in the evening and later explained the daily events of *politics as usual* to the entire team. Systematic, critical ethnography transcends the anecdotal and leads from the particular to the general (see above; Krzyżanowski and Oberhuber 2007; Wodak et al. 2012).

6.2 *Main assumptions and categories of analysis*

Before embarking on the qualitative analysis below, I briefly summarize the main theoretical assumptions which guided the analysis and thus also the selection of pragmatic, discursive and linguistic indicators (although I necessarily have to restrict myself to the analysis of four extracts of data in the following section):

- First, I assumed that *there is order in the apparent disorder of the everyday life*, in the backstage and frontstage activities, and also in the transitional phases between modes of performance. This order follows a *strongly context-dependent logic*, alongside the rules of the political game. These activities encompass a range of genres and modes, from brief encounters to narratives and argumentative speeches as well as descriptive reports (see also Scollon 2008). Thus, in contrast to other approaches (e.g. Fairclough and Fairclough 2010), I claim (and also provide the evidence) that the work of politicians and 'doing politics' does not only consist of well-planned persuasive argumentative forms of text and talk. Quite the contrary is the case! Such a view would imply reducing political communication mainly to the frontstage and to publicly (easily) available data (such as newspapers reports, debates in parliament or in the media, and public speeches).

- Secondly, the *ordering principle is constructed through specific agenda and forms of expert knowledge*, tied to the presuppositions governing actions and decision-making procedures. This knowledge is only accessible *via the ethnography of backstage* activities while also confronting this available knowledge with information from interviews and other documents.

- Thirdly, *managing and organizing knowledge implies different forms of constructing, employing, negotiating, and distributing power,* as well as the struggle for hegemony related to particular ideological agenda. Here, I assumed that *small-scale policy entrepreneurs* do much work in the politics *de couloir* and employ diverse tactics and strategies which are realized linguistically in various forms and genres throughout the day, on frontstage and backstage.

In the concrete analysis below, I focus on presuppositions, insinuations and implicatures and ways of constructing intertextuality which indicate shared knowledge and communities of practice and which shape the inclusion and exclusion of various topics, interest groups or strategic alignments. Strategies of positive self and negative other presentation realize group identity constructions and might also scapegoat 'others'. Moreover, conversational styles manifest types of public or semi-public performance and the respective situational role (as political colleague, as expert, as friend, etc.) which Hans adopts in specific contexts as well as the choice of genres or genre mixing. Linked to role performance is also the use of pronouns and of professional language. When a politician is promoting a specific agenda, s/he will use persuasive rhetoric including argumentation, *topoi* and fallacies as well as other rhetorical tropes (metonymies, metaphors, personifications, etc.). Finally, in debates and discussions, important turn-taking procedures occur as do – typically – interruptions, ad hoc interventions and comments. Many linguistic-pragmatic devices are, of course, inherently and necessarily related to particular genres and contexts.

7 Analysis: Beginning the working day in the life of a MEP

In what follows, I analyse three brief episodes which occurred during one day in the life of Hans, a member of the Social-Democratic Party and an expert on matters related to trade unions and social affairs, to illustrate backstage activities of politicians (e.g. Wodak 2011a: 120ff. for the detailed analysis of an entire day at the EP). Hans' assistant comes from Carinthia, a Slovenian Austrian; I call him M in this chapter. The entire day evolves across the controversy about possible costs of EU accession (see above). Hans is convinced that achieving similar welfare-, human rights- and working conditions as in the Western countries would imply much financial investment and would take much time. He uses all opportunities during this day to repeat his 'message' and hopes to convince both other MEPs and members of the Commission of his standpoint.

7.1 Episode: Starting the day

At 8 a.m., MEPs usually start their official day. Hans meets M in his small office (a cubicle with a desk of ca. 8–10 square metres, a computer, a few book shelves and a telephone) for a quick briefing and organization of upcoming events. M has prepared all the relevant documents for the day and organized them neatly into specific folders. Hans mainly poses quick questions; the dialogue takes on a staccato form; quick, often elliptic and abrupt – thus rapid question and answer sequences conveying urgency and pressure. If we regard the whole day as an entire communicative activity and unit of analysis, consisting of several 'language games' (Wittgenstein 1967) which are realized in different genres and modes, then this *orientation* in the morning would serve as introduction and overall structuring device and frame for all upcoming events:

Text 1.

    H: hey social security systems are included
    M: I have already contacted (xxx)
    H: We haven't received any answer yet (huh)?
    M: no obviously I'm glad I sent that off
    H: on Friday?
    M: no no I sent it off last week – no Sunday I sent it
    H: Sunday
    M: yes
    H: they're coming
    M: Sunday the 14th of November
    H: in fact they're coming again with the social security systems we would have needed that for today
    M: no we don't have that

Text 1 offers an insight into the sort of rapid-fire exchange, relying on shared language and organizational knowledge, which is typical for a MEP and his or her personal assistant, impatiently chasing up on the whereabouts of some document or letter urgently needed for a committee meeting. In this exchange, both M and Hans have obviously forgotten on which day Hans' letter was actually sent off, and the inferred argument consists of the following sequence:

If the letter had already been sent off the previous week, then it is reasonable to expect that they should have had a response by now. If, however, the letter hadn't been sent until Sunday or Monday, then they can't really expect an answer yet (thus, implying a counterfactual presupposition). Hans' questions also imply an indirect speech act of accusation: that M might have sent the letter too late. In any case, it seems obvious that the response to this letter is crucial for a meeting on insurance and social security systems for which Hans is now preparing – indirectly referring to events from previous days; hence, a typical example of context-dependent intertextuality. Hans emphasizes quite clearly that he needed this response to his letter, which – by analysing the various existential and counter-factual presuppositions – we can infer must have contained some salient information. Already in this brief sequence, we thus encounter the reliance on shared and presupposed organizational, intertextual knowledge and the overall responsibility of the personal assistant who has to take the blame if something doesn't go according to plan.

In Text 2, the quick dialogue continues with a frame-shift: the search for the document ends because – as M reveals – he has found the relevant document. Hans and M then quickly start discussing and preparing the statement for the committee later on that day (a persuasive genre, a brief speech), and switch to a dense strategy and tactics debate about the wording of this statement: what to change, to amend, to include or delete, and so forth. At the same time, we encounter another frame shift and change of footing: the collegial, friendly relationship on quasi-equal terms where Hans asks M to give him a cigarette (6). M complies but in a humorous way (7), with a joke. This brief interlude eases the tension by re/producing the good interpersonal relationship and by shifting, in line 10, to a discussion of content after the frantic search for the missing document.

Text 2.

1	H:	that (would be) bad
2		uh
3	M:	I have (xxxx^2) our paper there
4	H:	oh you have (xxxx) our paper there too?
5	M:	yes
6	H:	(c'mon gimme one)
7	M:	alright fine (because it's you)
8	H:	do you have a (xxxxx)
9	M:	no (a German)
10	H:	what does a sixteen mean
11	M:	for the ÖGB
12	H:	okay
13	M:	also, in the mean time I'm supposed to put his ethical work with your

14	H:	yes
15	M:	next to your hundredth
16	H:	social clause on the WTO last paragraph
17	M:	WTO social clause is in there?
18	H:	yes (xxx social clause xxxxxxxx)
19	M:	where where in here?
20	H:	of course last paragraph
21	M:	which last paragraph?
22	H:	WTO social clause (xxxx) that belongs
23	M:	where where?
24	H:	yes
25	M:	no not there in that paper there
26	H:	in that (xx) paper
27	H:	yes
28	M:	in that one there?
29	H:	yes
30		linguistic confusion
31	M:	WTO social clause
32	H:	yes there there WTO social clause
33		(can you remember)
34	M:	yes oh yes yes yes yes yes yes
35	H:	that's currently the established discussion
36	M:	sub subsume
37	H:	yes yes nobody understands it like this
38		if we don't add the social clause
39		ah, and the other part is naturally an awful exaggeration
40	M:	a terrible one, as usual
41	H:	but seriously
42		we can't do something like that I think we can't do that
43		this is really in ( ) width
44		It's like this so that I
45		(xxxxxxxx give me)
46	M:	hehehe
47	H:	(I've) noted that there
48		but that's always the same
49	H:	there's nothing useful there

This hectic and elliptical discussion continues for more than 20 minutes. Hans and M read through the draft statement together and stop at various points while questioning specific formulations which Hans eventually labels as 'linguistic confusions' and could be interpreted as typical organizational ambiguities (30, 38, 42). They support and acknowledge each other's suggestions and comments through brief interjections and supportive comments (backchannels), or laughter (34, 47). The quick turn-taking illustrates the shared routines of their team work, and they do not interrupt each other but automatically sense when transition-relevant points occur or when support is needed to reassure the other. The interaction also builds solidarity between the two, notably through jokes, allusions to shared experiences, elliptical comments and more generally through evaluative language. On the one hand, the document is defined as 'useless' (49), the ongoing discussion about social benefits and the WTO are believed to be totally 'exaggerated' (39) or even 'terrible' (40). The meta-comments and assessments oscillate between evaluating the committee, the ongoing debates and particular parts, sentences or even words in the draft document. In line 32, Hans briefly checks if M still remembers the genesis of the discussion; after M asserts (33) that he indeed does share the same memories, their rapid exchange continues with highly truncated utterances that presuppose much expert knowledge (existential presuppositions).

Finally, this part of the day comes to an end: the first appointment is scheduled for 9.15 a.m. M also informs Hans of a photo appointment at 12.45 p.m. which becomes a prominent feature of this particular day because it has to be rescheduled several times, requiring the afternoon's schedule to be repeatedly renegotiated. This final intimate exchange involving the banter over the cigarette is interpersonal talk that serves primarily as a transition and frame shift from the formal discussion of the draft document, onto the time and organizational talk (another typical genre for *politics as usual* which I call *walk and talk* (see Wodak 2010a, b) that they launch into while walking to their first official appointment).

Next, I present a brief segment of the statement in the *Employment and Social Affairs Committee* which had to prepare a resolution and is currently discussing a document proposed by a group of political scientists and other experts, on the possible implications and consequences of enlargement. The resolution proposes that the Commission and the EU member states offer greater and more effective support to the candidate countries particularly in their social policies. Hans is very concerned that the enlargement countries are not helped enough when creating and protecting their social institutions. Furthermore, Hans rejects 'myths' that enlargement can take place at no additional cost to the union; on the contrary, he argues, the cost of enlargement for core member states is likely to be very high, since they will have to offer financial support to the new countries to allow them to reach similar social and economic standards.

Hans speaks German as German is one of the three official working languages adopted for committee internal use. German is translated for other members of the committee, into English and French; this necessarily implies that MEPs who have a different native language might be discriminated against when having to speak in a foreign language.

Text 3.

uhm I am very thankful for this working paper of the (xxx) science directorate
we probably could have used that much earlier, for example when we began the

Eastern enlargement discussions on a parliamentary level . . .
in reality we would have had better management at the European level
then we could have like at the time of the single market
when we began with the single market concept (xxx)
[and] thoroughly discussed what the possibilities [and] chances are
then we could have (xxxxxxxxx) very very differently in terms of Eastern enlargement

Here, Hans presupposes that everybody knows and has read the document he is referring to; he also presupposes that every committee member is well informed about the problems related to enlargement and about the many debates and decisions which have already taken place (*intertextual context*). He employs the discursive strategy of painting an 'unreal scenario' – 'what would have happened if' – in order to highlight how much better it would have been had the debate management of the enlargement issue begun much earlier. He also refers intertextually to past debates on the Single Market, where he claims better procedures had been used. By drawing on this as a *shared* past experience ('when *we* began with . . . and thoroughly discussed') as a model of how things should have been done in relation to enlargement, he is assuming not only that this event is shared knowledge but also that everybody agrees with his evaluation of it. The macro argumentative strategy consists of a justification for missed opportunities and obviously wrong decisions and policies, in Hans' view. He shifts the blame to the Commission (a typical fallacy) which serves to unite the committee members and also relieves them of responsibility, thus creating a common identity via a bonding strategy. In this way, the introduction sets the ground for more detailed criticism and some constructive proposals. Already this brief extract illustrates the different genre and register employed by Hans. He has obviously quickly adapted to a different, official context and to the persuasive argumentative genre which is expected in the debate. This statement, which is analysed in much detail elsewhere in respect to its argumentative structure (Wodak 2011a), illustrates well the difference between the official performance on frontstage and the hectic backstage preparation before the meeting.

After the meeting, Hans stays outside of the meeting room, in the corridor, for another five minutes and chats with a German MEP, M and another assistant (see Text 4 below). Such informal conversations are invaluable data as they offer an insight into the reflective mode of politicians – in contrast to their official roles and performance on frontstage, they use this opportunity to make comments they might have strategically withheld in the more official setting. In this conversation, the MEPs also make sense of what happened in the meeting and analyse the dynamics of the debate; that is, they co-construct what I label as '*post-hoc coherence*'. In doing so, numerous moves, statements and interventions suddenly become understandable for them (and the researcher) because they are related to particular experiences with certain MEPs, with policies, with the genesis of discussions and debates, and with the norms and conventions of this committee (and in this way, the four context levels are integrated (see Wodak 2011a for the entire extract)).

Text 4. Politics *de couloir*

Speaking: Hans
Others present: M (personal assistant) and two colleagues (one of whom is German)

 1 H: the Swedes already have a different opinion
 2   and when one then talks with the unions and organizations themselves about
 3   deregulatory pressure in general (xxxxx)
 4   Eastern Enlargement (xxx) can
 5   then suddenly then suddenly
        then suddenly it becomes a European question then the Netherlands is more at the core and more in the core that is completely
 6   unaffected by it
 7   but rather indirectly affected later
 8   then there is an economic uh discussion about winners and losers
 9   . . . that's the way it is
10   because otherwise no one realizes what is at stake

The post-hoc interpretation of political positions and oppositions constructs, via referential strategies, several distinct generic groups defined by their nationality, positions or by their professional expertise: the Swedes who are said to have a different opinion, the Dutch who believe themselves to be largely unaffected by enlargement, given their geographical position at the 'core', the countries which border on the enlargement countries, the enlargement countries themselves, and finally, the economists in the Economic Council. Hans' meta-analysis existentially presupposes that the economists are making mistakes and that the MEPs who align with Hans' position are right. Moreover, Hans emphatically repeats that the social agenda must be integrated with the economic agenda and proudly refers to the fact that he has been able to amend the document accordingly, thus employing multiple discursive strategies of positive self-presentation. The German MEP nods, Hans has convinced him. This brief exchange functions as a transition to the next appointment, it constructs a reflective space for afterthoughts, and it also serves as an opportunity for Hans to restate his opinions once more, presumably in the hope of lending them greater credence through repetition; repetition can thus certainly be interpreted as a salient strategy of persuasion in pushing one's agenda. Hans and M then hurry to the next appointment. Text 4 is thus an example of politics *de couloir*, of the transition between frontstage and backstage, of salient conversation which make sense of the preceding debates.

8 Discussion

While following Hans throughout his entire day, it became apparent that he constructs his multiple identities in ever new ways, *depending on the specific context*. Hans shifted frames quite automatically from friendly and collegial exchanges to pushing and setting agenda determinedly and even aggressively; to advising newcomers in an authoritative manner; to presenting an ideological party programme in an analytic and thoughtful lecture. In other words, Hans smoothly switched between different frames and contexts, each time selecting and employing the appropriate genre, politeness markers, professional jargon, salient *topoi,* and argumentative moves. Of course, in this chapter, I was only able to provide one example in a more explicit and retroductable way; I have to refer readers to Wodak (2011a, b, c) for more details of this extensive research.

Moreover, it became apparent while shadowing Hans that he has set himself a very concise political agenda which he recontextualizes (and repeats) whenever possible, in his attempt to lobby for support. One could even speculate as to whether this agenda might serve as one of many organizing principles throughout the daily chaos, something to hold on to because one is completely convinced of its importance. By repeating the arguments for enlargement and against the Commission's policies over and over again – explicitly or via insinuations or implicatures, Hans seems to manoeuvre himself from one meeting to the next, leaving (intertextual and interdiscursive) oral and written traces of his agenda, before abruptly departing for the next appointment.

It also becomes apparent how important it is to know the routines and rules of various communities of practice which are situated and active in the EP: in a given day, an MEP (or any politician) ventures into several different communities to which s/he belongs and which s/he is expected to know well. In our case, Hans oscillates between his *micro community* (the team consisting of himself and his assistant M) and various more or less formalized and ritualized meetings and groups, with long histories and traditions. First he joins the Committee of Employment and Social Affairs where Hans reads out a prepared statement (and few would guess that Hans and M had finished formulating this statement just minutes before), then he briefly rejoins M on their way to lunch where Hans recontextualizes his official statement for newcomers to the EU (Slovenian trade union delegates). Finally, he delivers a lecture in the evening, where the complex problem of enlargement is elaborated in greater detail, and in more analytic and programmatic terms, and translated into socialist concepts for party colleagues and comrades, thus into a rhetoric integrating strategies, analysis, arguments, evidence and proposals. In between, Hans rushes through the corridor, squeezing in smaller meetings (politics *de couloir*), as well as informal chats after meetings that provide space for reflection and comment – and which, from an ethnographic point of view – provide most valuable evidence for any valid interpretation which draws on the analysis of the previous interactions.

Although I have only documented here some snippets of the daily life of one single MEP, many features and characteristics of this single day and the behaviour of the actors involved could be generalized to other politicians and their professional lives. Indeed, the salience of rituals is obvious, as are the many varieties of performance, on frontstage (in the committee and at the lecture), and on backstage, with his assistant, his politics *de couloir* and at lunch. The importance of the distinct levels of context becomes apparent: Hans' knowledge of the details of accession politics combined with his political stance and experience of the range of immediate situational contexts and expectations, coupled with genre and language proficiency.

Hence, I conclude that politicians do not merely perform on the publicly visible frontstage represented through the media; but rather they *always* perform, more or less automatically and intentionally, with mask or without mask. Their professional habitus is embodied and thoroughly integrated in their everyday activities. Thus, rather than drawing a strict separation between the frontstage performance captured in the media and online genres, and the backstage realm of *real politics*, I argue it makes more sense to distinguish between *ritualized performances* with a public audience, and between less formal performances with insiders as audience, defined through distinct functions and settings, according to the specific rules of the game. Hence, the specific context and context models are decisive and salient for the respective meanings of the interaction.

Moreover, *organizational, expert and political knowledge* is linked in many intricate ways to enhance these performances. Thus, political power-knowledge is also distributed according to politicians' capacity to promote their own agenda more frequently and more effectively than others, which in turn involves managing knowledge via presuppositions (and many other pragmatic devices) in clever ways. It makes sense to point to Chilton's justified claim at this point: '[P]resupposition can be seen as a way of strategically 'packaging' information' (Chilton 2004: 64).

Apart from many subtle – and frequently surprising – details, this case study has helped shed light on the phenomenon of *depoliticization*, making it easier to understand. Since most of us only acquire our knowledge about politics and politicians' activities from the media (which commonly represent ritualized frontstage performances), people are suspicious and sceptical about what goes on 'behind the scenes'; about decision-making procedures, the distribution of power and the actual processes of political representation. Not only are we situated far away from the European stage, there is also no easy entry to the backstage – to the daily life where politics in action becomes visible and, therefore, open to challenge, criticism and participation. Shut out from the backstage, we are left only with many unsubstantiated rumours, gossip, anecdotes and stories.

9 Politics as usual: Perspectives and limitations

Common sense presupposes that politicians are very well organized in spite of the many urgent and important events they must deal with which have an impact on all our lives. Moreover, most people (including scholars) only have access to (or only focus on) frontstage activities of politicians. We all have cognitive models (*event models, experience models, context models*; van Dijk 2005) which quickly and automatically update, perceive, comprehend and store such frontstage events – and usually most people wrongly assume that the frontstage performances are *the* salient contexts where major decisions are taken. My research however illustrates and provides much evidence that backstage activities are frequently much more important than or at least just as important as the frontstage performances. Usually, decisions are taken prior to meetings or debates; decision making, as many studies prove, is usually staged to get participants 'on board' (Wodak 2000; Wodak et al. 2011).

Thus, a *multi-level approach to context*, and a *triangulation of methodologies and data samples while including a longitudinal dimension* allow for a much more precise understanding and explanation of a specific phenomenon under investigation. Many of Hans' or any MEP's activities would remain incomprehensible without the knowledge gained via a multi-level context approach as provided by the DHA. Intertextual references would remain undetected; presuppositions and implicatures which are salient for the interpretation of linguistic and discursive practices would not be analysed in any adequate way; and thus, it would be difficult if not impossible to *make sense* of politicians' work and the impact on political decision making.

Shadowing one MEP, Hans, through his entire day provides some important answers to the questions posed above which, again, could be generalized to other political realms. Hans employs both strategic and tactical knowledge when trying to convince various audiences in different contexts of his political agenda. These discursive strategies and tactics also structure his day which might otherwise, from the outside, seem totally chaotic, or very ritualized and bureaucratic, oriented, for example, solely towards the drafting and redrafting of documents. Hans knows the 'rules of the game', he oscillates between a range of communities of practice in very well planned and strategic ways, and he employs a wide range of genres suited to the immediate context, to push his agenda (see also Scollon 2008: 128–37, for the range of multimodal modes employed in bureaucracies and political institutions).

In Hans' case, different genres are used to convince members of various committees, other MEPs of various political parties, visitors and diverse audiences outside of the institution and 'at home' of his mission: in this particular case, to enable EU enlargement in a rational way, to be honest about the likely costs however politically unpopular and to support the social agenda and the trade unions in the accession countries. Hans' entire day (and, of course, many following months) is dedicated to this mission which he pursues in statements, written resolutions, speeches, conversations at lunch, lectures and in the politics *de couloir* as well as *at home* (in his local community), when trying to convince his electorate and national political party (e.g. Wodak 2011 a, b for more details). In this way, Hans is an example of a *small-scale policy entrepreneur*, one of many MEPs all of whom are striving to push their various and very diverse agenda with varying degrees of success.

In this chapter, I was only able to provide a small example of how I assume that *politics works*, due to reasons of space. Most importantly, I believe to have substantiated the salience of theorizing context and including multiple layers of context into the analysis of political communication. Hans, as a small-scale policy entrepreneur, does political work, all the time, everywhere, in many different modes and genres; however – as citizens are excluded from the backstage and the many communities of practice where Hans implements his strategies and pushes his agenda – these activities and practices usually remain invisible. Of course, this is not only the case for one MEP; this is generally true for the field of politics as a whole. To challenge the *democratic deficit*, at the very least, information about daily political work would need to be made more publicly accessible to a certain degree.

Notes

1 see http://www.europarl.europa.eu/sides/getDoc.do?pubRef=-//EP//TEXT+AGENDA+20080521+SIT+DOC+XML+V0//EN&language=EN [downloaded 1 May 2008])

2 (xxx) in the transcription signifies non-understandable noise/words.

References

Abélès, M. (1992), *La Vie Quotidienne au Parlement Européen*. Paris: Hachette.

Allern, S. and Pollak, E. (2012), 'Mediated scandals', in S. Allern and E. Pollak (eds), *Scandalous! the Mediated Construction of Political Scandals in Four Nordic Countries*. Göteborg: Nordicom, pp. 9–28.

Aristotle (1999), *The Politics and The Constitution of Athens*, trans. S. Everson. Cambridge: Cambridge University Press.

Bourdieu, P. (1991), *Language and Symbolic Power*. Cambridge: Polity Press.

Brewer, J. D. (2000), *Ethnography*. Buckingham: Open University Press.

Cap, P. and Okulska, U. (eds) (2013), *Genres in Political Discourse* Amsterdam: Benjamins.

Carpenter, D. P. and Krause, G. A. (2012), 'Reputation and public administration'. *Public Administration Review*, 72(1), 26–32.

Castells, M. (2009), *Communication Power*. Oxford: Oxford University Press.

Charteris-Black, J. (2011), *Politicians and Rhetoric: The Persuasive Power of Metaphor* (2nd edn). Basingstoke: Palgrave.

Chilton, P. (2004), *Analysing Political Discourse. Theory and Practice*. London: Routledge.

Chilton, P., Tian, H., and Wodak, R. (2010), 'Reflections on Discourse and Critique in China and the West'. *Journal of Language and Politics* (Special Issue) 9(4), 489-507.

Danermark, B., Ekstrom, M., Jakobsen, L., and Karlsson, J. C. (2002), *Explaining Society*. London: Routledge.

De Cillia, R. and Wodak, R. (eds) (2009), *Gedenken im Gedankenjahr*. Innsbruck: Studienverlag.

Fairclough, N. (2000), *New Labour, New Language?* London: Routledge.

Fairclough, N. and Fairclough, I. (2010), 'Argumentation Analysis in CDA', in R. De Cillia, H. Gruber, M. Krzyżanowski and F. Menz (eds), *Diskurs, Politik, Identität*. Tübingen: Stauffenburg, pp. 59–71.

Flowerdew, J. (2012), *Critical Discourse Analysis in Historiography. The Case of Hong Kong's Evolving Political Identity*. Basingstoke: Palgrave.

Foucault, M. (1972), *The Archeology of Knowledge*. London: Routledge.

Foucault, M. and Rabinow, P. (1984), *The Foucault Reader*. New York: Pantheon Books.

Ginsberg, R. H. (2007), *Demystifying the European Union. The Enduring Logic of Regional Integration*. New York: Rowman & Littlefield.

Goffman, E. (1959), *The Presentation of SELF in Everyday Life*. Garden City, NY: Doubleday, Anchor Books.

Gramsci, A. (1977 [1921–26]), *Selections from the Political Writings*, ed. Qu. Hoare. London: Lawrence & Wishart.

Hammersely, M. (1992), *What's Wrong with Ethnography? Methodological Explorations.* London: Routledge.

Hansson, S. (2013), *Blame Avoidance in Coalition Government Politics.* Unpublished Ph.D. thesis, Lancaster University (forthcoming).

Hay, C. (2007), *Why We Hate Politics* (Polity Short Introductions). Cambridge: Polity Press.

Heer, H., Manoschek, W., Pollak, A., and Wodak, R. (eds) (2008), *The Discursive Construction of History. Remembering the German Wehrmacht's War of Annilihation.* Basingstoke: Palgrave.

Henneberg, S. C., Scammell, M., and O'Shaughnessy, N. J. (2009), 'Political marketing management and theories of democracy'. *Marketing Theory*, 9(2), 165–88.

Holly, W. (1990), *Politikersprache. Inszenierungen und Rollenkonflikte im informellen Sprachhandeln eines Bundestagsabgeordneten.* Berlin: De Gruyter.

—(2008), 'Tabloidization of political communication in the public sphere', in R. Wodak and V. Koller (eds), *Communication in the Public Sphere. Handbook of Applied Linguistics,* vol. IV. Berlin: De Gruyter, pp. 317–42.

Hood, C. (2011), *The Blame Game: Spin, Bureaucracy and Self-preservation in Government.* Princeton, NJ: Princeton University Press.

Hood, C. and D. Heald (eds) (2006), *Transparency: The Key to Better Governance?* Oxford: Oxford University Press.

Jarren, O., Sarcinelli, U. and Saxer, U. (eds) (1998), *Politische Kommunikation in der demokratischen Gesellschaft: Ein Handbuch.* Opladen: Westdeutscher Verlag.

Ilie, C. (ed.) (2010), *European Parliaments under Scrutiny.* Amsterdam: Benjamins.

Koller, V. and Wodak, R. (2008), 'Introduction: Shifting Boundaries and Emergent Public Spheres', in R. Wodak and V. Koller (eds), *Communication in the Public Sphere.* Berlin: De Gruyter, pp. 1–21.

Krzyżanowski, M. and Oberhuber, F. (2007), *(Un) Doing Europe. Discourses and Practices of Negotiating the EU Constitution.* Bern: Peter Lang.

Krzyżanowski, M. and Wodak, R. (2009), *The Politics of Exclusion: Debating Migration in Austria.* New Brunswick, NJ: Transaction.

Lakoff, G. (2008), *The Political Mind: Why You Can't Understand 21st-century American Politics with an 18th-century Brain.* New York: Penguin.

Lave, J. and Wenger, E. (1991), *Situated Learning: Legitimate Peripheral Participation.* Cambridge: Cambridge University Press.

Machiavelli, N. (2004 [1532]), *The Prince.* New York: Simon and Schuster.

Malinowski, B. (1923), 'The problem of meaning in primitive languages', in C. K. Ogden and I. A. Richards (eds), *The Meaning of Meaning.* New York: Harcourt, pp. 146–52.

McNair, B. (2003), *An Introduction to Political Communication* (3rd edn). London: Routledge.

Muntigl, P., Weiss, G., and Wodak, R. (2000), *European Union Discourses on Un/ Employment. An Interdisciplinary Approach to Employment Policy-Making and Organisational Change.* Amsterdam: Benjamins.

Okulska, U. and Cap, P. (eds) (2010), *Political Discourse: New Perspectives.* Amsterdam: Benjamins.

Reisigl, M. (2008a), 'Analyzing Political Rhetoric', in R. Wodak and M. Krzyżanowski (eds), *Qualitative Discourse Analysis in the Social Sciences.* Basingstoke: Palgrave, pp. 96–120.

—(2008b), 'Rhetoric of Political Speeches', in R. Wodak and V. Koller (eds), *Communication in the Public Sphere. Handbook of Applied Linguistics,* vol. IV. Berlin: De Gruyter, pp. 243–71.

Reisigl, M. and Wodak, R. (2001), *Discourse and Discrimination. Rhetorics of Racism and Antisemitism*. London: Routledge.

—(2009), 'The Discourse-Historical Approach in CDA', in R. Wodak and M. Meyer (eds), *Methods of Critical Discourse Analysis* (2nd rev. edn). London: Sage, pp. 87–121.

Saville-Troike, M. (1982), *The Ethnography of Communication*. Oxford: Oxford University Press.

Scollon, R. (2008), *Analyzing Public Discourse*. London: Routledge.

Strömbäck, J. (2008), 'Four phases of mediatization: An analysis of the mediatization of Politics'. *The International Journal of Press/Politics*, 13(3), 228–46.

Triandafyllidou, A., Wodak, R., and Krzyżanowski, M. (eds) (2009), *European Media and the European Public Sphere*. Basingstoke: Palgrave.

Van Dijk, T. A. (2005), 'Contextual Knowledge Management in Discourse Production', in R. Wodak and P. Chilton (eds), *A New Agenda in (Critical) Discourse Analysis. Theory, Methodology and Interdisciplinarity*. Amsterdam: Benjamins, pp. 71–100.

Volosinov, V. I. (1973), *Marxism and the Philosophy of Language*. London: Seminar Press. (Original work published 1928).

Weber, M. (2003), *Political Writings* (3rd edn). Cambridge: Cambridge University Press.

Weiss, G. and Wodak, R. (eds) (2003a), *Critical Discourse Analysis. Theory and Interdisciplinarity*. Basingstoke: Palgrave.

—(2003b), 'Theory and Interdisciplinarity in Critical Discourse Analysis. An Introduction', in G. Weiss and R. Wodak (eds), *Theory and Interdisciplinarity in Critical Discourse Analysis*. Basingstoke: Palgrave, pp. 1–34.

Wenger, E., McDermott, R., and Snyder, W. (2002), *Cultivating Communities of Practice*. Boston: Harvard Business School Press.

Wittgenstein, L. (1967), *Philosophische Untersuchungen*. Frankfurt: Suhrkamp.

Wodak, R. (2000), 'From Conflict to Consensus? The co-construction of a policy paper', in P. Muntigl, G. Weiss and R. Wodak (eds), *European Union Discourses on Unemployment*. Amsterdam: Benjamins, pp. 73–114.

—(2010a), 'Staging Politics in Television: Fiction and/or Reality?', in S. Habscheid and C. Knobloch (eds), *Discourses of Unity. Creating Scenarios of Consensus in Public and Corporate Communication*. Berlin: De Gruyter, pp. 33–58.

—(2010b), 'The glocalization of politics in television: Fiction or reality?' *European Journal of Cultural Studies*, 13(1), 43–62.

—(2011a), *The Discourse of Politics in Action: Politics as Usual* (2nd rev. edn). Basingstoke: Palgrave.

—(2011b), 'Politics as usual. Investigating political discourse in action', in J. P. Gee and M. Handford (eds), *The Routledge Handbook of Discourse Analysis*. London: Routledge, pp. 525–41.

—(2011c), 'Disenchantment with Politics and the Use of Images', in M. Stocchetti and K. Kukkonen (eds), *Images In Use: Towards the Critical Analysis of Visual Communication*. Amsterdam: Benjamins, pp. 69–88.

Wodak, R. and Meyer, M. (2009), 'Critical Discourse Analysis: History, Agenda, Theory, and Methodology', in R. Wodak and M. Meyer (eds), *Methods of CDA* (2nd rev. edn). London: Sage, pp. 1–33.

Wodak, R., de Cillia, R., Reisigl, M., and Liebhart, K. (2009 [1999]), *The Discursive Construction of National Identity*. Edinburgh: Edinburgh University Press.

Wodak, R., Kwon, W., and Clarke, I. (2011), '"Getting people on board": Discursive leadership for consensus building in team meetings'. *Discourse & Society*, 22(5), 592–644.

Wodak, R., Krzyżanowski, M., and Forchtner, B. (2012), 'The interplay of language ideologies and contextual cues in multilingual interactions: Language choice and code-switching in European Union institutions'. *Language in Society*, 41(2), 157–86.

Wodak, R., KhosraviNik, M., and Mral, B. (eds) (2013), *Rightwing Populism across Europe. Politics and Discourse*. London: Bloomsbury.

Wodak, R. and Richardson, J. E. (eds) (2013), *Analyzing Fascist Discourse: European Fascism in Talk and Text*. London: Routledge.

Wodak, R. and Van Dijk, T. A. (eds) (2000), *Racism at the Top*. Klagenfurt: Drava.

Zorn, R. (ed.) (1972), *Machiavelli, Nicolo: Der Fürst. "Il Principe".* Stuttgart: Klett.

Index